Game Development with GameMaker

A Primer on Game Development and Design

Second Edition

Sebastiano M. Cossu

Apress®

Game Development with GameMaker: A Primer on Game Development and Design, Second Edition

Sebastiano M. Cossu
LONDON, UK

ISBN-13 (pbk): 979-8-8688-0878-4
https://doi.org/10.1007/979-8-8688-0879-1

ISBN-13 (electronic): 979-8-8688-0879-1

Copyright © 2024 by Sebastiano M. Cossu

This work is subject to copyright. All rights are reserved by the Publisher, whether the whole or part of the material is concerned, specifically the rights of translation, reprinting, reuse of illustrations, recitation, broadcasting, reproduction on microfilms or in any other physical way, and transmission or information storage and retrieval, electronic adaptation, computer software, or by similar or dissimilar methodology now known or hereafter developed.

Trademarked names, logos, and images may appear in this book. Rather than use a trademark symbol with every occurrence of a trademarked name, logo, or image we use the names, logos, and images only in an editorial fashion and to the benefit of the trademark owner, with no intention of infringement of the trademark.

The use in this publication of trade names, trademarks, service marks, and similar terms, even if they are not identified as such, is not to be taken as an expression of opinion as to whether or not they are subject to proprietary rights.

While the advice and information in this book are believed to be true and accurate at the date of publication, neither the authors nor the editors nor the publisher can accept any legal responsibility for any errors or omissions that may be made. The publisher makes no warranty, express or implied, with respect to the material contained herein.

    Managing Director, Apress Media LLC: Welmoed Spahr
    Acquisitions Editor: Spandana Chatterjee
    Development Editor: James Markham
    Coordinating Editor: Kripa Joseph
    Technical review: Alynne Keith

Cover designed by eStudioCalamar

Distributed to the book trade worldwide by Apress Media, LLC, 1 New York Plaza, New York, NY 10004, U.S.A. Phone 1-800-SPRINGER, fax (201) 348-4505, e-mail orders-ny@springer-sbm.com, or visit www.springeronline.com. Apress Media, LLC is a California LLC and the sole member (owner) is Springer Science + Business Media Finance Inc (SSBM Finance Inc). SSBM Finance Inc is a **Delaware** corporation.

For information on translations, please e-mail booktranslations@springernature.com; for reprint, paperback, or audio rights, please e-mail bookpermissions@springernature.com.

Apress titles may be purchased in bulk for academic, corporate, or promotional use. eBook versions and licenses are also available for most titles. For more information, reference our Print and eBook Bulk Sales web page at http://www.apress.com/bulk-sales.

Any source code or other supplementary material referenced by the author in this book is available to readers on GitHub (https://github.com/Apress). For more detailed information, please visit https://www.apress.com/gp/services/source-code.

If disposing of this product, please recycle the paper

To the dreamers and hard workers.

Table of Contents

About the Author xv

Acknowledgments xvii

Introduction xix

Chapter 1: Overview 1

    The Right Tool for the Job 2

    What Is GameMaker? 3

    About Game Design 4

    About Coding 5

    How to Use This Book 5

    Additional Content 9

    Pricing 9

    Installing GameMaker 10

        Windows 11

        Mac 14

        Installing from Steam 15

Chapter 2: Hello, World! 17

    UI Overview 19

    Sprites 23

    Objects 25

        Events 27

        Code 29

TABLE OF CONTENTS

- Tile Sets 30
- Fonts 30
- Rooms 31
- Hello, GML! 32
  - Create Event 33
  - Left Pressed (Mouse) Event 38
  - Draw 39

Chapter 3: Card Game (Part 1) 45

- The Design 45
  - A Game Design Document Primer 46
  - Memory GDD 47
  - Assets 50
- From GDD to Development 52
- Cards 52
  - Implementation 54
- Deck 62
  - Array 63
  - Stack 65
  - Queue 66
  - List 68
  - Map 68
  - Priority Queue 69
  - Grids 70
- Designing Decks 71
  - Code Loops 73
- Making Decks 76
  - Every Day I'm Shuffling 79

Chapter 4: Card Game (Part 2) 87
- Finite-State Machines (FSMs) 87
- From State Machine to Code 93
    - A Matter of Time 102
    - Play to Win! 109

Chapter 5: Fixed Shooter 117
- History of the Genre 117
- Space Gala (GDD) 119
    - Story and Setting 120
    - Gameplay 120
    - Victory Conditions 120
    - Controls 120
    - Menu 121
    - Pacing 121
    - Enemies 121
    - Game Modes 122
    - Level 1 122
    - Similar Games and Influences 122
    - Target Audience 122
- From GDD to the Game 123
    - Assets 123
    - Making Features, Not Objects 130
    - Shooting 138
    - Designing rm_level_1 149
    - Game States 150
    - Making HUDs 159
    - What About Victory? 162
    - Menu 163

TABLE OF CONTENTS

Chapter 6: Shoot 'Em Up! 173
    Fixed vs. Scrolling Shoot 'Em Up! 174
    Space Gala v.2.0 (GDD).. 175
        Story and Setting.. 175
        Gameplay.. 175
        Victory Conditions... 176
        Controls 177
        Menu... 177
        Pacing... 177
        Enemies.. 178
        Game Modes.. 179
        Level 1 179
        Level 2 179
        Similar Games and Influences 179
        Target Audience 180
        Assets... 180
        Cameras and Viewports... 186
    Designing Color-Switching... 197
    Inheritance 201
    Color Shooting... 206
    More Enemies 209
        Ain't Nothing but the Blues... 210
        Walkers on Paths... 212
        Unidentified Flying…Instance!.. 216
    Super-Attack 219
    How to Design a Good Shmup Level 225
    Boss Fighting 226
    Conclusion 231

TABLE OF CONTENTS

Chapter 7: Designing Bosses 235
Teaching and Experimenting..237
Motivation! 238
How Can We Use This?..240

Chapter 8: Single-Screen Platformer.....................................243
Cherry Caves...246
    Story and Setting..246
    Gameplay...247
    Victory Condition 247
    Controls 248
    Enemies..248
Assets 249
    Sprites 249
    Fonts..253
    Sounds...253
How to Create a Hero 253
Setting the Boundaries 257
Everything That Goes Up Comes Down 262
Get a Jump on Gravity!..265
Climbing the Ladder...266
Controlling the Game Flow...272
    HUD...282
How to Die..285
Cherry-Picking 288
Through Cherries, to the Star...289

ix

TABLE OF CONTENTS

Level Design: The Art of Creating Worlds 292
    Designing Caves 293
    Level 2! 294

Chapter 9: Scrolling Platformer 301

Story and Setting 302
Gameplay 302
Victory Condition 303
Items 303
Controls 304
Enemies 305
    Attack 305
Miscellaneous 306
Similar Games 307
Assets 307
    spr_land 307
    spr_skybg 308
    spr_platform_falling 309
    spr_platform_trampoline 309
    spr_platform_moving 309
    spr_octopus_green 310
    spr_octopus_purple 310
    spr_titlescreen 311
    spr_coin 311
    spr_terrain 312
Fonts 312
    fnt_title 312
Sounds 312

The More You Do It 313

Title Screen 314

Tiles and Level Design 323

Scrolling Camera 333

Fixing and Re-adapting 337

Different Ways to Move 345

Gotta Squash 'Em All! 354

Items and Power-Ups 361

    Coins 361

    Cherries 363

Creating the First Level 366

Chapter 10: Designing Platformers 375

Controls Are Key 375

It's My Fault! 377

Keep It Simple! 379

Power-Ups, Items, and Gear 381

Interesting Collections 381

World Makers 384

Conclusion 388

Chapter 11: Metroidvania (Part 1) 389

History 390

Isolation (Game Design Document) 391

    Story and Setting 392

    Gameplay 392

    Victory Condition 392

    Controls 392

TABLE OF CONTENTS

- Enemies ... 394
- Attack ... 394
- Skills ... 394
- Maps ... 395
- Inventory ... 395
- Similar Games ... 396
- Assets ... 396
  - spr_player_idle ... 396
  - spr_player_walk ... 397
  - spr_player_jump ... 397
  - spr_player_jump_fall/spr_player_dash ... 397
  - spr_player_wallslide ... 398
  - spr_heart ... 398
  - spr_warp ... 399
  - spr_marker ... 399
  - spr_upgrade ... 400
  - spr_cure ... 400
  - spr_octopus_green ... 400
  - spr_ground_brown ... 401
  - spr_checkpoint_inactive ... 401
  - spr_checkpoint_active ... 402
  - spr_bullet_heavy ... 402
  - spr_bullet_light ... 402
  - Fonts ... 403
  - Sounds ... 403
- Creating the Platforming Base ... 404
  - Gamepad Support! ... 409

Gravity, No Escaping!	412
Making the Leap	414
Another Kick in the Wall	416
Moving Forward with a Dash	423
The Game Flow	430
Warped!	439
Conclusion	444

Chapter 12: Metroidvania (Part 2) 447

About Maps	448
Map Makers, Grids, and Semaphores	449
Items and Inventory	469
Creating the Combat System	485
Old Enemies	490
Saving Maria	496
file_text_open_read(fname)	498
file_text_open_write(fname)	498
file_text_open_append(fname)	498
file_text_write_string(file_id, my_string)	499
file_text_close(file_id)	499
Conclusion	508

Chapter 13: Extra: Artificial Intelligence 511

Isolation: CR – Artificial Intelligence	515
Change Request Document	515
Description of Change	516
Justification	517
Impact Analysis	518
Raycasting-Based Detection	519

TABLE OF CONTENTS

Octopus, Behave! 523
Patrol 525
Chase 527
Conclusion 530

Chapter 14: Designing Fun Games 533

Document Your Design! 533
Respect Your Game 534
Keep Your Players Immersed 535
    Autonomy 536
    Competence 537
    Relatedness 538
Having Fun Means Learning 539
Conclusion 541

Chapter 15: What's Next? 543

Itch.io 543
GOG 547
Humble Store 549
Steam 550
End Game 552

Index 553

About the Author

Sebastiano M. Cossu is a software engineer and game developer, currently employed in Electronic Arts. Video games have always been his greatest passion, and he began studying game development at an early age. Sebastiano started working with GameMaker in 2002 and has worked with every version of the software since then.

He is the author of *Game Development with GameMaker Studio 2* and *Beginning Game AI with Unity*, both published by Apress.

Acknowledgments

I would like to express my deepest gratitude to my family, whose unwavering support has fueled my lifelong passion for video games. Your encouragement and belief in me have been the cornerstone of my journey.

To my closest friends, thank you for sharing this passion with me and for your continuous support. Our shared love for video games has been a constant source of inspiration and motivation.

To everyone who purchased the first edition of this book, thank you. I hope it was helpful in achieving your goals, and your feedback has been invaluable in shaping this second edition.

Lastly, to all the dreamers aspiring to be the game developers of tomorrow, this book is for you. May your journey be as rewarding and fulfilling as mine has been. Keep dreaming, keep creating, and never stop playing.

Introduction

When I was a kid, the game industry was rapidly growing, becoming bigger and more advanced. There was little room for homemade games or one-person companies, like those that had initially expanded the industry. Creating games was turning into an elite activity, with most gamers drawn to big AAA productions, complex worlds, cutting-edge graphics, and intricate mechanics.

This was when I discovered GameMaker, a very accessible game engine that allowed anyone to create simple 2D games without a programming or software engineering background, thanks to its visual programming and easy-to-learn scripting language. GameMaker was surrounded by a prolific and inclusive community, where amateurs and passionate gamers met in virtual chat rooms (mostly IRC) to exchange knowledge, provide feedback, and help each other create their own video games. It was an environment of passion and creativity, where everyone could turn their dream of making their own video games into reality. Many kids who grew up in this environment have become today's professional game developers in both the indie and AAA industries.

In recent years, game engines for beginners and amateurs have become much more powerful, and the gaming industry has shifted its focus from huge AAA productions to indie and smaller products. GameMaker itself has grown and evolved, playing a significant role in today's indie games landscape. Consider titles like Undertale, Hotline Miami, Spelunky, Risk of Rain, Hyper Light Drifter, Gods Will Be Watching, and Katana Zero, all created with GameMaker by small teams or even solo developers.

INTRODUCTION

This book will guide you through learning the basics of GameMaker and designing and developing your first video games. We will embark on a journey to understand the fundamentals of game development, analyzing successful games to learn valuable lessons for creating fun and engaging experiences. We will explore various game genres, designing and developing them while understanding and internalizing the principles of game design and development, using the power and accessibility of GameMaker. Buckle up and prepare to embark on an exciting journey into game development, where you'll dive deep into the essential skills and creative processes needed to craft your own games.

CHAPTER 1

Overview

"How can I make video games?" This is a question I asked many times to a lot of people (and mostly to Google) when I was a kid. The desire to create games is something that nearly every gamer happens to have at a certain point. It's something that is common between all media consumers, from books to movies to video games: we try to create the things that make us feel good. We dedicate a lot of time to video games, and they give us strong emotions and wonderful stories in return. Sometimes they help us in hard times – like if a piece of software can understand us better than a person – and sometimes they just entertain us when we are bored or when we just need some fun. We give them time, and they give us emotions and wellness in return.

Driven by their fascination with the power of video games, many gamers become game developers. These developers are often among the most passionate you'll find. Their mission goes beyond just creating software—they aim to share emotions and build entire worlds.

In this chapter, you will be introduced to the tools and topics that we are going to cover in this book. You will also learn how to install GameMaker on your PC or Mac, the first necessary step to start making great games!

CHAPTER 1 OVERVIEW

The Right Tool for the Job

Video games are a very special kind of medium. They can be just fun pastimes or very intense experiences. They can teach us concepts, they can train us on specific activities, they can stimulate our creativity and problem-solving, and entertain us with great stories. These special software use graphics, music, gameplay, and technology to do all this and much more!

There was a time when the requirement to make even very simple text-based applications was to learn some very complex CPU-specific programming language called Assembly. Some of the simplest old games you can think of, like *Rogue*, *Pitfall*, *Super Mario Bros. (SMB)*, or *Wolfenstein 3D*, are made fully or partly in Assembly.

Fortunately, we live in a time in which game development is way more accessible, to the point in which sometimes coding is not even strictly required. Today, to make games, we have at our disposal a number of software specialized in making games, called game engines.

Game engines offer a number of features that simplify the process of making games, like the possibility to show an image, play a sound, get keyboard input, and so on.

In this book, we will explore *GameMaker*, a professional yet easy-to-use game engine which offers two ways of making games: a proprietary scripting language and a no-coding drag-and-drop system. We will opt for the proprietary scripting language GML (*GameMaker Language*) to reach the full potential of the engine and to have maximum flexibility. But don't worry, this is not a programming manual, but a game development manual. Our focus is not only on how to code our games, but also on game design good practices and how to deliver fun gaming experiences. You will learn how games are made using real-world video games as study cases.

CHAPTER 1   OVERVIEW

What Is GameMaker?

GameMaker (*GM*) is a game engine that's perfect for both beginners and professionals. It supports 2D and 3D game development and allows you to create games with either a visual programming approach called *Drag and Drop* (DnD) or with a proprietary scripting language called GameMaker Language (*GML*). Let's take a closer look at those options.

DnD is a system that allows you to create game logic by combining blocks representing objects and functionalities. The specific order of those blocks defines an algorithm. DnD is the right choice for everyone that wants to explore game development and game design, but has no interest in learning how to code.

In Figure 1-1, you can see an example of DnD programming in GameMaker. From left to right, we have the object's properties, the list of the object's events, possible parent or children classes (more on that later), the DnD code blocks related to the selected event, possible comments related to the code blocks, and finally the list of possible code blocks that we can drag and drop into the event.

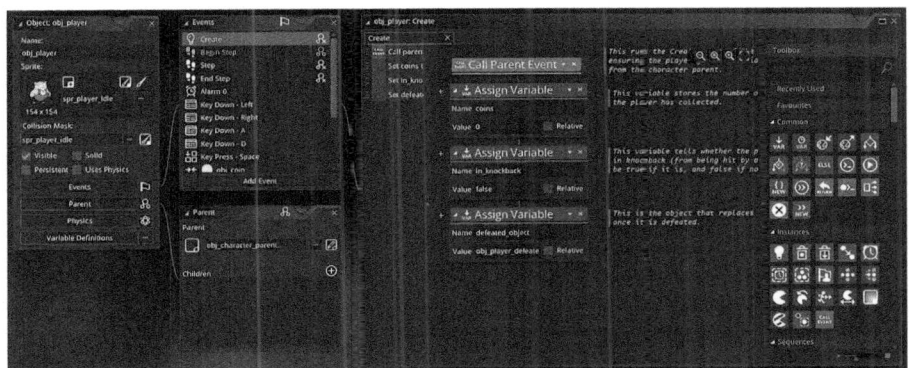

Figure 1-1. *An example of DnD programming with GameMaker*

3

CHAPTER 1   OVERVIEW

GML (*GameMaker Language*) is GameMaker's own scripting language. It's a highly specialized scripting language, which means that it's very easy to use, but it's also quite powerful. It's the best choice if you want maximum control on the features of your game and their implementation.

Many indie developers choose GameMaker for its ease of use and completeness of features. Some examples of great indie games made with GM are *Undertale, Hyper Light Drifter, Spelunky, Hotline Miami, Katana Zero, Forager, Nuclear Throne, Gunpoint, Nidhogg 2, Risk of Rain,* and so on.

GameMaker offers an *IDE* (Integrated Development Environment) containing all the tools you need to develop your game. The IDE includes a file browser to manage resources, a text editor to write GML code, a visual programming interface to create functionalities with DnD, a 2D graphic editor to create and edit images, an animation editor to make flipbook and skeletal animations, a compiler (YoYo Compiler, aka YYC) to export your games to many platforms in machine code, an interpreter to run and debug your games using the GameMaker virtual machine, and everything else you may need to create your game.

About Game Design

Gaming is something that I always did with an inquisitive mind. I always played games (and I still do it now) asking myself questions like *"How is this made?"*, *"How does it work?"*, *"Is this fun? Why?"*, *"Why is it not fun?"*, and most importantly *"How can this be more fun?"* Only much later I realized that what I was doing all my life was (to some degree) **Game Design**.

Game Design is the process of imagining games, planning and defining all their main features. Game designers can focus on a single aspect of a video game, or they can direct or supervise the whole game by making sure that there is coherence and consistency between the various components of the game and that the overall experience is at least honoring the user's expectations.

To be a game designer, most of the time it means to be able to ask the right questions and come up with the right answers. It's a constant learning process made of testing, experimenting, fine-tuning and even questioning ideas, mechanics, and every component of a game.

About Coding

Coding could be described as the act of writing a list of commands in a specific computer language, to instruct a machine on how to respond to some specific input provided by the user. This list of commands (or instructions) is translated by a software called *compiler* into *machine code*, which is the "native" language of a computer. The result of this translation is a binary file (a file made of ones and zeroes), which can be executed. The binary file is the software itself – the game, in our case. On Windows systems, binary (executable) files are called *EXE* files.

The projects in this book are created with GML. You can find a detailed reference manual about GML and everything concerning GameMaker in GameMaker's online documentation at manual.gamemaker.io.

How to Use This Book

This book is designed to guide beginners into the world of game development one project at a time, exploring development techniques and GameMaker's features little by little. So if you're a beginner, the advice is to read the book cover to cover.

However, if you already have game development foundations or you're not new to GameMaker, feel free to use this book as a collection of game projects that can be explored in any order you prefer.

CHAPTER 1   OVERVIEW

Here is an overview on the chapters and the topics they will cover:

1. **Overview**: The chapter that you're reading! An introduction to game development and to the topics covered in the book.

2. **Hello, World!**: In this chapter, you will create your first simple project with GameMaker learning some basics about the software.

3. **Card Game (Part 1)**: In this chapter, we will design and develop the first version of a memory card game – a game about pairing matching cards. Card games are a good starting point to create some solid game development foundations.

4. **Card Game (Part 2)**: This chapter will conclude the development of Memory, the card game about pairing matching cards started in Chapter 3. At the end of this chapter, you will have completed your first game!

5. **Fixed Shooter**: This chapter will be dedicated to the creation of a fixed shooter game inspired by classics like Space Invaders and Galaga. Enemies and bullet system are only two of the many topics that this project will cover.

6. **Shoot Em Up!**: In this chapter, we will extend the work done in Chapter 5 introducing new features inspired by classics like Ikaruga, R-Type, and Tyrian. This is also the chapter in which we will develop our first boss fight.

CHAPTER 1   OVERVIEW

7. **Designing Bosses**: This chapter covers some interesting in-depth analysis of boss fights design taking as examples real-world video games that created memorable boss fights.

8. **Single-Screen Platformer**: In this chapter, we will explore the design and implementation of platformer games by creating a single-screen platformer game. You will learn how to create a platforming system from scratch and to design levels and enemies.

9. **Scrolling Platformer**: In this chapter, we will build on the ideas introduced in Chapter 8 and develop a scrolling platformer, one of the most famous and long-lasting game genres. Topics covered include gameplay features like power-ups, different kinds of enemies, a simple combat system, and different types of platforms that will allow us to get creative designing levels.

10. **Designing Platformers**: In this chapter, we analyze the history of platformers and how they evolved in the years. Considerations about how to make a platformer fun and challenging are the main topic of the chapter. There is an in-depth analysis of masterpieces of the genre like Super Mario games that will help us understand the golden rules for a good platformer.

11. **Metroidvania (Part 1)**: In this chapter, we cover the design and implementation of the first part of a *metroidvania* game system. Main features of this genre are exploration, platforming, and combat.

7

CHAPTER 1   OVERVIEW

We will start creating this project by using the concepts studied in the previous chapters and introducing new concepts like exploration skills (dash and wall jump).

12. **Metroidvania (Part 2)**: This chapter concludes the metroidvania project. You will learn how to implement all the defining features of a metroidvania including on-screen maps, a checkpoint system, a shooting system, and an inventory and equipment system.

13. **Game AI**: This chapter introduces the concept of AI in video games and teaches one very effective (and still very used) game AI technique: FSM-based AI.

14. **Designing Good Games**: This chapter concludes our game design exploration introducing some principles and techniques that can help you on your journey to make great games. We will analyze famous and successful games to understand what they did good, why they are considered masterpieces, and how we can use this knowledge to design good games.

15. **What's Next?**: Our journey ends with a little guide on how to go forward in your game development career. We will explore the available options to sell or distribute your game as an indie developer on the most popular digital games stores.

Additional Content

This book is heavily based on the use of GameMaker and revolves around the projects proposed in every chapter. So, if you're having some problem following the instructions or you just want to see the working project before you start, you can take a look at the source code on GitHub (via the book's product page located at https://github.com/Apress/Game-Development-with-GameMaker-2nd-Edition for more detailed information, please visit https://www.apress.com/gp/services/source-code).

Pricing

GameMaker comes in different flavors (see Table 1-1) depending on your needs and if you are a professional or amateur developer. Below, you can find a useful table that can help you out making your decision based on your own needs.

My suggestion is to go with the free version while you are learning or developing your game and only switch to the professional or enterprise version if you are ready to sell your game.

Table 1-1. *GameMaker comes in different flavors. This table shows a list of all the possible licenses that GameMaker offers*

License	Price	GX.games Export	Desktop Export	Web Export	Mobile Export	Console Export
Free (Non-commercial)	X	✓	✓	✓	✓	X
Professional	$99.99	✓	✓	✓	✓	X
Enterprise	$79.99 monthly - $799.99 yearly	✓	✓	✓	✓	✓

CHAPTER 1   OVERVIEW

Installing GameMaker

Installing GameMaker is as easy as going to the official website (https://gamemaker.io/en/download) and pressing the download button (Figure 1-2).

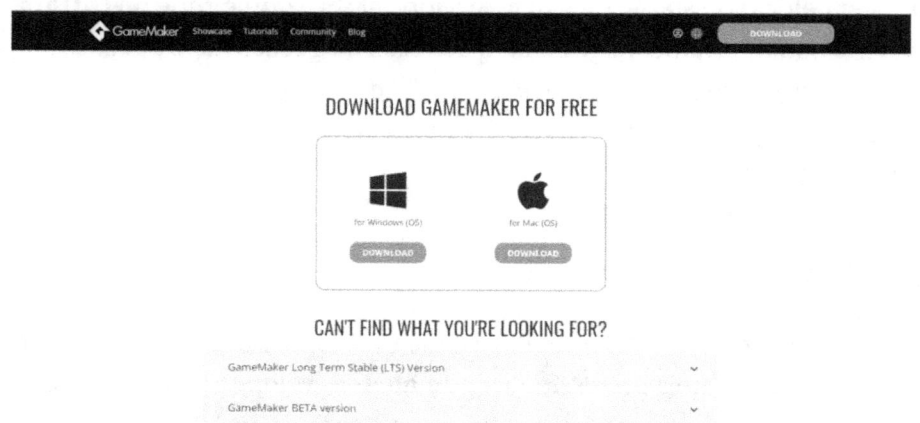

Figure 1-2. *GameMaker: Studio 2 download page*

To be able to use GameMaker, you will have to create an Opera account in which you will have to log in when running GameMaker.

Other than the Opera account, here are some system requirements that you need to meet to be able to run GameMaker:

Minimum Spec:

- Windows 7 with SP1 or Mac OS Big Sur
- Dual Core CPU
- 2GB RAM
- OpenGL 4-compliant onboard graphics
- HDD (at least 3GB free disk space)

Recommended Spec:

- Windows 10/11 or macOS Monterey
- Quad Core CPU
- 8GB RAM
- Dedicated graphics card
- SSD (at least 3GB free disk space)

Windows

When you execute the installer client, you will be prompted to a license agreement (Figure 1-3) that you need to accept to use the software. Note that if you're updating to a new version, you will be asked if you want to delete the previous version before continuing the installation process.

Figure 1-3. *Windows installer's License screen*

CHAPTER 1   OVERVIEW

After that, you will be taken to the Choose Components screen (Figure 1-4) where you can check the additional components to install and some other options like creating Start Menu shortcuts, Desktop shortcuts, or choose to associate YYP and GML files with GameMaker. If you're in doubt, the default choice is the safe one. Don't overthink this step, as you will be able to install the missing package or set any of those options even after the software is installed.

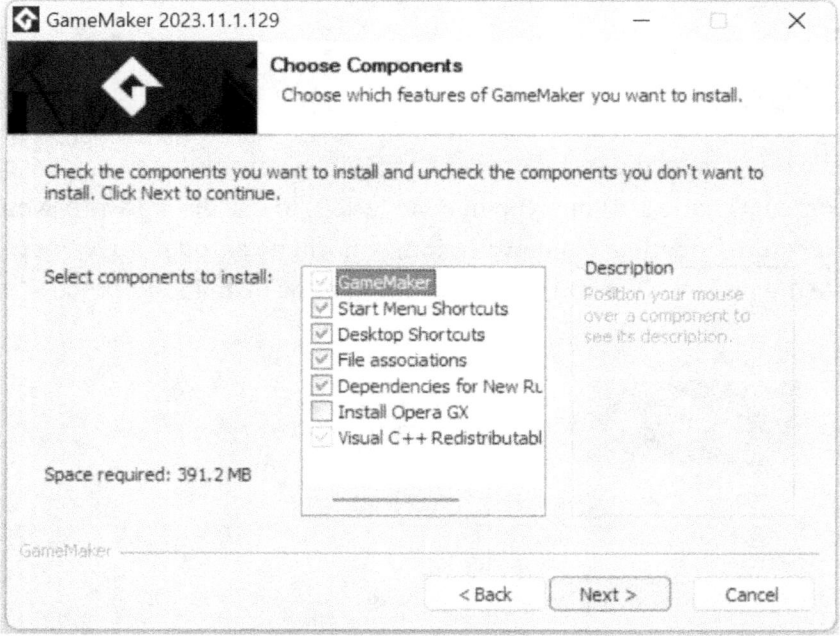

Figure 1-4. *Windows installer's Choose Components screen*

Clicking Next, you will be asked to choose the destination of the installation (Figure 1-5). If you don't know what to do, just stick with the default choice. It will install GameMaker in your main disk.

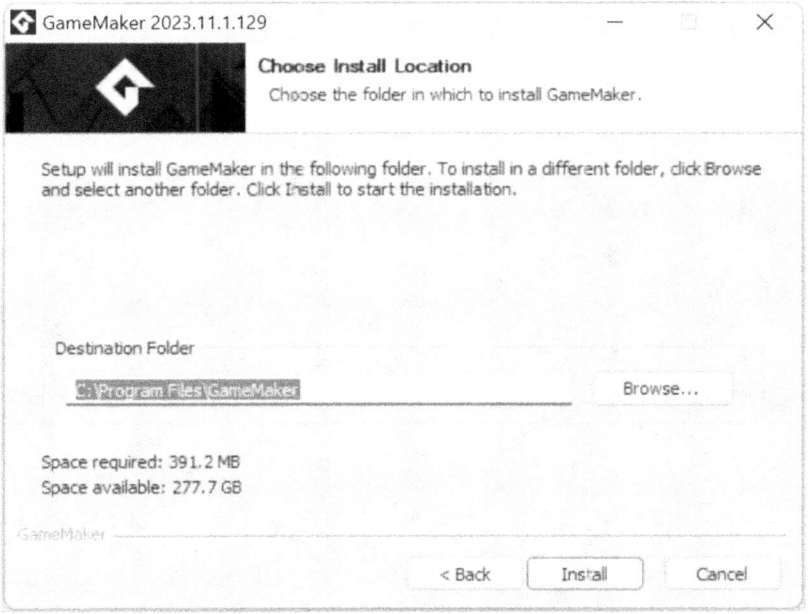

Figure 1-5. *Windows installer's Choose Install Location screen*

Note that even if you specify a destination folder, some components will be installed in the *%programdata%*, *%Localappdata%*, and *%appdata%* folders. You can change this after the installation heading to *GM*'s menu bar and selecting *File* ➤ *Preferences*.

Clicking the *Install* button will start the installation process, at the end of which you will be able to click the *Finish* button to close the installer and start *GameMaker*. *Note that if you decided to install additional optional modules, the installation process might take more time, and the installer might start additional installers before you can get to the Finish button.*

Additional updates may be needed by *GameMaker* to properly work, but they will be managed by the IDE. In fact, every time you start up the software, if you are logged into your Opera account, GameMaker will check for updates and automatically install them.

CHAPTER 1   OVERVIEW

Mac

Choosing the Mac version, you will download a *PKG* file that you can double-click to start the installation (Figure 1-5).

Figure 1-6. *GameMaker's Mac installer*

Clicking Continue on the Introduction screen, you will be prompted to accept the license agreement and then asked where you want to install GameMaker (Figure 1-6). A main difference from Windows is that you can't decide the folder, but only the disk you wish to use. Sticking with the default choice is the right decision if you're in doubt.

CHAPTER 1 OVERVIEW

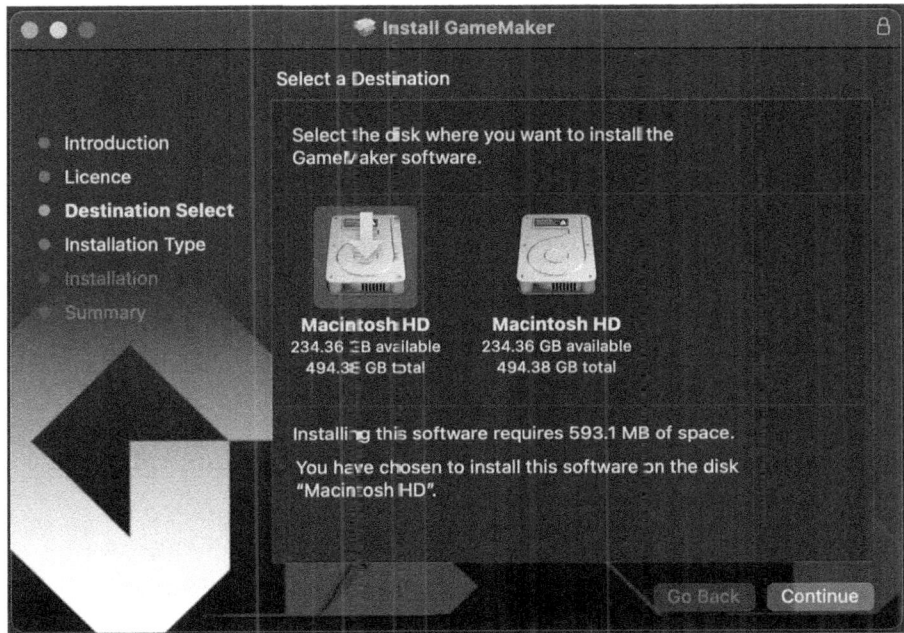

Figure 1-7. *Mac installer's Select a Destination screen*

Just go ahead and click Continue to choose the default setup until you reach the Summary. Then click Close to finish the installation process. You will be asked if you want to move the installer to the trash folder.

You will find GameMaker in your Application folder, as it's the standard on Mac OS.

Installing from Steam

It's also possible to install GameMaker using Steam. Just open your Steam client, and search for "GameMaker" in the search bar as shown in Figure 1-7.

CHAPTER 1   OVERVIEW

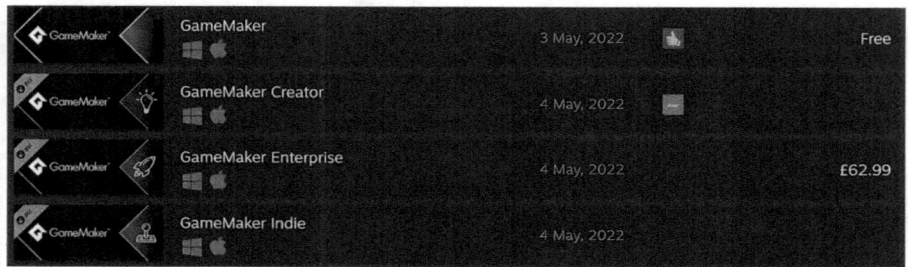

Figure 1-8. *Searching for GameMaker on Steam's search bar will prompt you all the different versions of the software*

Now you just need to choose your GameMaker version (use the table in the "Pricing" section as a reference) and purchase/download it as any other software on Steam.

The IDE will be installed in the Steam folder as any other game, and you may access it from the Steam library or double-clicking the executable file.

Note that you will still need an Opera account to use the software, just as if you downloaded it from the official website.

If you purchased GameMaker from the official website and you want to link it to your Steam client, just go to your Opera account's Overview, scroll a bit, and you will see an option to link the account to your Steam account. Click the *Link* button and log into your Steam account to approve the link request.

You are now all set up, and we can finally start this magic journey into the world of game development!

CHAPTER 2

Hello, World!

Welcome, fellow developers! This is the very beginning of our journey into game development!

There is a tradition, in developers' culture. Every time you're going to learn a new language, framework, or library, you start with a program that just displays the message "Hello, World!"

This tradition started in the 1960s, during the writing of the manual of BCPL programming language by Prof. Brian Kernighan who wrote a program that displayed the string "hello, world" to show how I/O (input and output) worked in BCPL. This example program was later used by Kernighan in his own tutorial to the C programming language (1972) and in *The C Programming Language* book by Brian Kernighan and Dennis Ritchie (often referred as K&R), and then it was used again as the first test program for the C++ compiler by Bjarne Stroustrup (the creator of the C++ programming language).

The Hello World test program became the standard to teach and test new programming languages and technologies, and we will keep the tradition alive by building our own Hello World program with GameMaker.

In this chapter, we will explore the elements that compose GameMaker, and we will end up writing our first program in GML.

Let's start by opening GameMaker (Figure 2-1)!

CHAPTER 2   HELLO, WORLD!

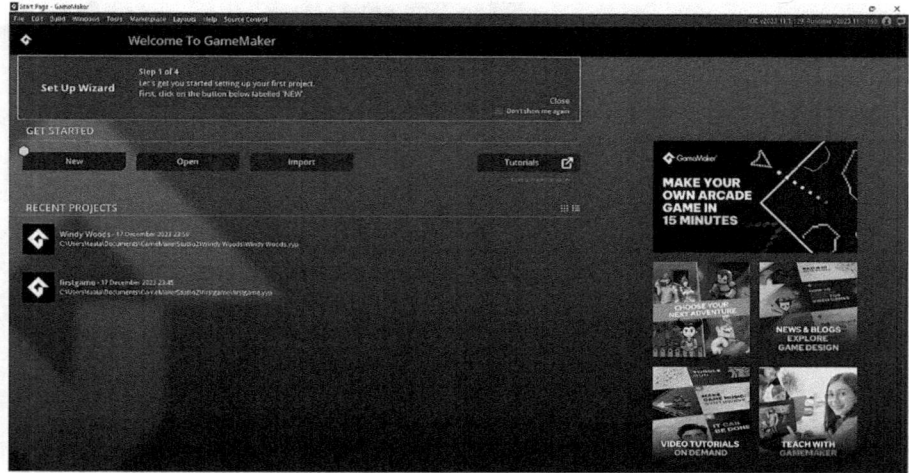

Figure 2-1. *GameMaker's Start Page*

At the very top, right under the *title bar*, there is the *menu bar*, full of functionalities and settings that at this stage are grayed out. The only ones we can access at this stage are in the *Help* menu, where we can access GameMaker's documentation; and in the *File* menu, where we can start a new project, open a new IDE, load an existing project, or check the settings.

Under the *menu bar*, we can see a little tutorial to help you get started, and right under it, a set of buttons:

- **New**: Creates a new project
- **Open**: Opens an existing project
- **Import**: Imports a packaged project in the supported extensions (*GMX*, *GMZ*, *YYZ*)
- **Tutorials:** Opens the tutorials portal on GameMaker's website in your default browser

Finally, under those buttons, there are the recently opened projects, if you opened any so far.

CHAPTER 2   HELLO, WORLD!

When selecting *New*, a subsection will open allowing you to choose if you want to create a Game, a Live Wallpaper, or a Game Strip. The last two are features of the Opera GX browser.

In this book, we will cover only the process of developing a game, so that's going to be our selection. When selecting a game, we can decide to either create a new game from scratch or to start from a template. Templates are a great starting point to study the implementation of a specific type of video game! I encourage you to try and open up some of those, after completing this book. For now, select *Blank Game* and choose a title for your first project, for example, *MyFirstGame*, as shown in Figure 2-2.

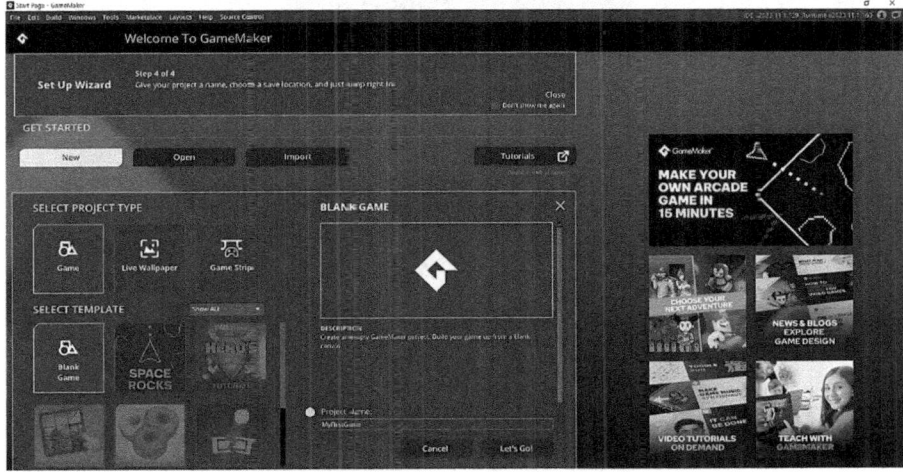

Figure 2-2. *Creating a new blank game in GameMaker*

UI Overview

Creating a new project, the interface will change into the main GameMaker user interface (UI).

CHAPTER 2　HELLO, WORLD!

On the right-hand side of the UI, there is the *Assets Browser* (Figure 2-3) that will allow you to see, create, and access all the assets composing your project.

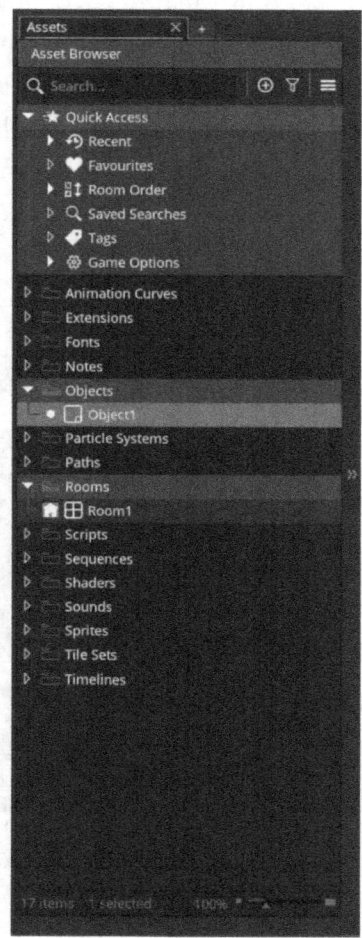

Figure 2-3. *Asset Browser*

CHAPTER 2 HELLO, WORLD!

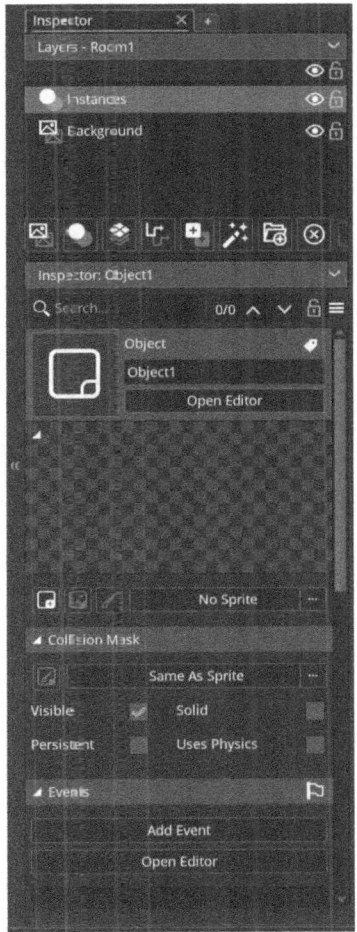

Figure 2-4. *Inspector*

Clicking on any of the game assets in the *Assets Browser* will open it up in the middle area, in a tab, where it can be modified (Figure 2-5). Multiple tabs can be created to organize work.

On the left-hand side of the UI, there is the *Inspector* (Figure 2-4), where settings and details regarding the selected asset can be found. Here you can modify any asset's configuration or setting.

CHAPTER 2   HELLO, WORLD!

Figure 2-5. *GameMaker's workspaces*

On top of the *Assets Browser*, you can find the build settings (Figure 2-6), where you can select

- **Platform** (depending on your GM version): GX.games, Windows, MacOS, Ubuntu, HTML5, Android, iOS, tvOS, Playstation 4, Playstation 5, Xbox One and Series X/S, Switch

- **Output**: Either GameMaker Virtual Machine (GMS2 VM) or YoYo Compiler (GMS2 YYC)

- **Device**: Where you can configure different devices for the target platforms that you wish to compile and test on (note that the platforms available will depend on the license that you have, and not all of them may be visible).

CHAPTER 2 HELLO, WORLD!

- **Config**: GM allows you to create different configurations that allow you to quickly switch between different splash screens, icons, and included files and test or export only those that are relevant to the target platform or client at any time, all from the same base code.

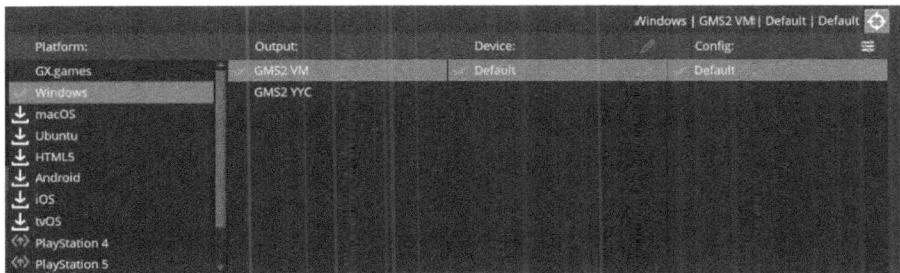

Figure 2-6. GameMaker's build settings

Finally, on the left-hand side, on top of the Inspector and Workspace tabs, you can find the *Quick Buttons* (Figure 2-7), which are a series of buttons that represent the most useful functions (like creating, saving or opening a project, running and compiling, etc.).

Figure 2-7. GameMaker's quick buttons

Sprites

A GameMaker project can have many types of asset; one of the most important ones is the *sprite* asset type.

A *sprite* is an image that can represent anything in your game from UI elements to any character in a game.

CHAPTER 2   HELLO, WORLD!

To create a new sprite, right-click the Sprites category in the Asset Browser and select *Create* ➤ *Sprite*.

Creating a new sprite, you will be displayed a new window in the Workspace tab (Figure 2-8). This new sprite window will show every property about that particular sprite. In this window, you can edit everything about a sprite from its name to its size and even its appearance. Note that you can access and modify all those information also in the Inspector, after selecting the sprite in the Asset Browser.

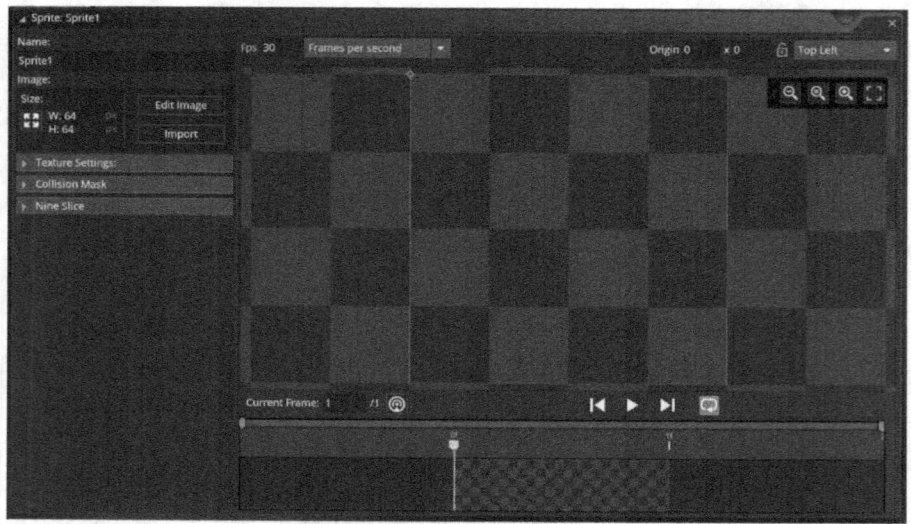

Figure 2-8. *This is the sprite creation window, which can be used to easily create and edit sprites*

The sprite window is also the place where you can define if that sprite represents an animation concatenating multiple images, how the game should consider this sprite for collisions with other sprites, and where the pivot point in this sprite is.

Sprites can be made in any graphics software, like Gimp, Photoshop, and even MS Paint. To make the development process faster, GameMaker includes a basic sprite editor. By clicking the Edit Image button in the sprite window, you can edit the currently selected image or create a new one from scratch.

A sprite, in GameMaker, can be made of more than just one image. To add a new image to the sprite, click the *Edit Image* button to open the Sprite Editor. Here, on the top bar, you will see a collection of frames that compose the sprite; just click the button with a circled plus (Figure 2-9), and a new frame (image) will be created. You can add as many images as you like.

Figure 2-9. *GameMaker's Sprite Editor*

Objects

Objects in GameMaker represent concepts and contain the logic of the game. They can be programmed to respond to certain events with predefined actions.

CHAPTER 2   HELLO, WORLD!

You can create a new object by right-clicking the *Objects* category in the *Assets Browser* and selecting *Create* ➤ *Object* in the pop-up menu that follows.

Creating a new object, just like creating a new sprite, will display the object window (Figure 2-10) that will allow you to define the object's properties and to program it to respond with predefined actions to certain events. A subset of those properties can be found in the Inspector after selecting the object in the Asset Browser.

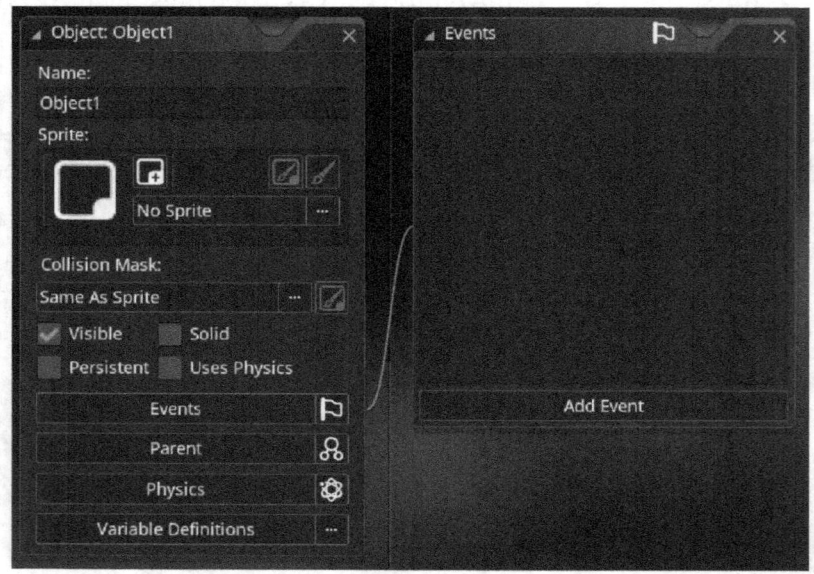

Figure 2-10. *The Object Editor allows for the creation and edit of objects. It is also the place where you can program the behavior of the object*

Objects can have a sprite associated, so that they are visible on screen when placed in a room. You can also define a collision mask to determine what area of the sprite will count in collision detection.

CHAPTER 2 HELLO, WORLD!

The object window is also the place where you can adjust physics options for the selected object and define inheritance (e.g., if the object derives from another parent object), and most importantly, it's the place where you can define how the object will interact with specific events.

The objects you define in this way can be used in the game, for example, they can be put in a *room*. When you run the game, GameMaker uses the object you just defined to create a sort of copy of it, called *instance*. You can make many instances of the same objects, and they will all be independent from each other, following the rules defined in the object from which they generate.

Think of an object in GameMaker as a blueprint of a house. From that blueprint, you can create two identical houses (instances). Then you can put different people and furniture in them, and you can paint them differently and demolish one of them (or both). Whatever thing you do to the houses created from the blueprint, it's not going to affect the blueprint itself, which can still create more houses.

Events

When you run a game, it will listen to events that may occur and react to those. An event can be anything from the press of a button, to a timer going off or two sprites overlapping. This repetition of checks and actions is called **game loop**.

For example, a clicker game constantly checks if the player is clicking the left mouse button and acts accordingly.

You can direct the logic of a game, by controlling the game loop, and you do that by programming events.

An event is a discreet moment inside the game loop.

CHAPTER 2   HELLO, WORLD!

GameMaker offers a set of predefined events that can be used in your objects to program behaviors. Some of the most important are

- **Create**: It occurs when the object's instance is created inside the game.

- **Destroy**: It occurs just before the object's instance is destroyed.

- **Clean Up**: It occurs when the object's instance is destroyed, the room changes, or the game is closed.

- **Step**: It occurs every frame, so its rate of recurrence depends on the number of frame per second (FPS) your game runs.

- **Alarm**: It occurs every time a certain timer runs out. In GameMaker, you can set up timers (called alarms) to count down from a certain value to zero. When a timer finishes counting, it triggers the Alarm event.

- **Draw**: This event runs once per frame per view and is the one that governs what you see on the screen when you run your game and is split into various separate "sub-events" that allow you to better organize the drawing of the graphical elements on the game screen.

- **Draw GUI**: This event runs once per frame and is specialized in managing Heads-Up Display (HUD) drawing. When you're drawing in this event, keep in mind that coordinates won't change: 0,0 will always refer to the top-right corner of the screen, not the room.

- **Mouse**: This allows you to wait for a mouse-related event (right/left clicking, hovering, etc.) and execute actions when that event occurs.

- **Mouse Global:** This occurs every time a mouse event is triggered, regardless of the instance. For example, if you want to execute an action when you click, regardless of where the mouse pointer is positioned, you should use Mouse Global, instead of Mouse.

- **Key Down:** This event triggers for all the time the defined key is held down.

- **Key Pressed:** This event triggers every time the key is pressed.

- **Key Up:** This event triggers every time the key is released.

- **Gesture:** This event allows you to specify a gesture that you want to use as a trigger.

- **Collision:** This event occurs when an instance collides with another instance.

- **Other:** This allows you to specify other events related to GameMaker features like starting/ending the game, entering/exiting rooms, and so on.

- **Asynchronous:** This allows you to select an asynchronous function as a trigger, like HTTP requests, In-App purchases, and so on.

For more advanced or customized events, you will want to use a combination of events and actions.

Code

When you create a new event in a GML project, the IDE will open a window related to that event where you can write your GML code (Figure 2-11).

CHAPTER 2   HELLO, WORLD!

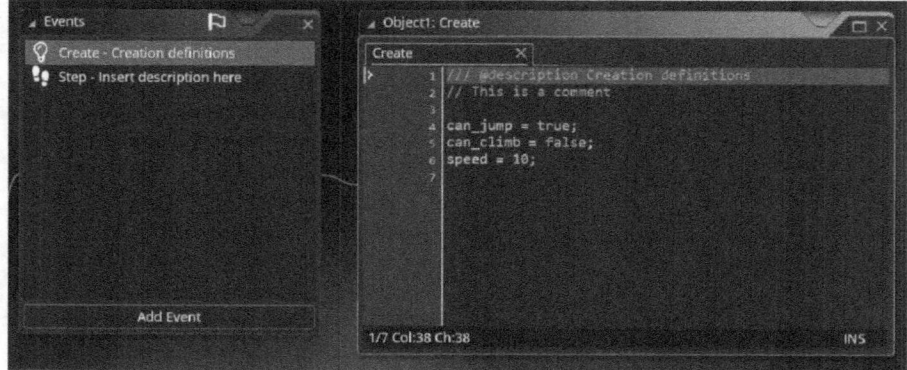

Figure 2-11. *An example of GML code associated to a Create event*

Think about GML code as a list of instructions or actions that you want your game to execute when that specific event triggers.

If you are confused about what to write and how, don't worry! We will cover this exhaustively in this book!

Tile Sets

A tile set is an image that represents a collection of smaller images (tiles) with which you can build up your level. Tiles are just squares of fixed size that represent the fundamental graphical element of a level, just like real tiles on a real floor.

To create a tile set, just right-click the *Tile Set* category in the Asset Browser and select *Create* ➤ *Tile Set*.

Fonts

Fonts are exactly the same kind of asset you are used to work with in word processing software like Microsoft Word or similar. They are used to create texts with customizable aesthetics. You can use the ones installed into your

CHAPTER 2 HELLO, WORLD!

system, or you can download new ones from the Internet and import them into your project.

To create a font, right-click the *Font* category of the Asset Browser and select *Create ➤ Font*.

Rooms

A game in GameMaker is organized in rooms. Rooms are levels and screens for your games. They can be anything from title screens to menus to playable levels. You start your game in the first room listed in the Asset Browser. All the rooms should be connected so that you can pass from one to another.

To create a room, right-click the *Room* category of the Asset Browser and select *Create ➤ Room*.

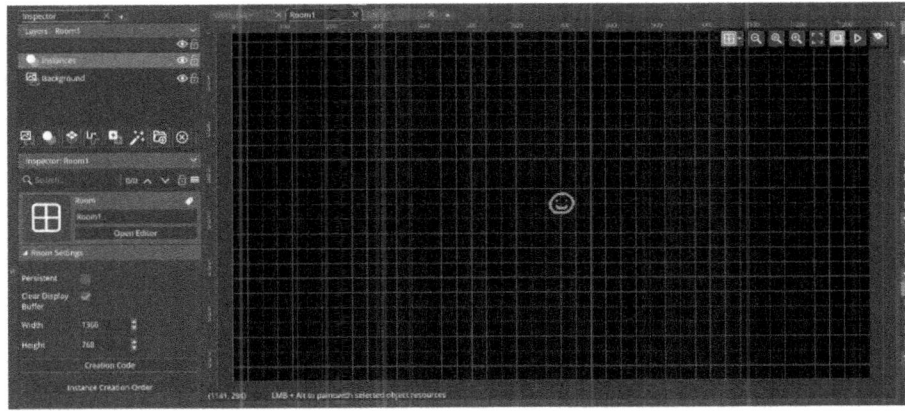

Figure 2-12. *An example of a generic game room in a test game*

Opening or creating a new room will show its details in the Inspector (Figure 2-12), where you can check/edit things like

CHAPTER 2   HELLO, WORLD!

- **Layers**: They allow you to manage objects' drawing order, in the room.
- **Room Settings**: Properties of the room, like size and resolution.
- **Viewport and Cameras**: Useful to manage how the game is viewed by the player (window size and others).
- **Room Physics**: Allows you to set up some settings for the physics engine.

The room in Figure 2-12 shows an empty room with a sprite inside. You can reshape a room dragging and dropping objects into it and editing its appearance with tile sets.

Remember that the first room in the Rooms list is always the first to be shown when the game starts.

Hello, GML!

Now that we have our empty project and we saw a bit of the interface, we can finally work on creating our Hello World program!

First of all, we need to create a new sprite. To do it, right-click the Sprites category, in the right sidebar, and select *Create* ▶ *Sprite*.

You can either create the image for the sprite from scratch clicking the *Edit Image* button or import an already existing image by clicking the *Import* button. Alternatively, if you want to use my same image, you can find any resource used in this book on the book's GitHub page.

Give the sprite a name that makes sense, like `spr_funnyguy`.

It is important to stick with a naming convention in your project. It's very common in GameMaker to use as a prefix for any resource two or three letters that represent the type of that resource. In this case, "spr" stands for sprite.

CHAPTER 2 HELLO, WORLD!

Now we need an object that will make use of that sprite! Right-click the Objects category in the Asset Browser, and create a new object (*Create ➤ Object*). Let's call it something similar to the sprite, in my case obj_funnyguy.

We want to associate the sprite we created to our new object, so that it can be visible when we put the object in a room. Click the "No Sprite" text right into the object's properties section, and select the sprite you just created (in my case spr_funnyguy).

Let's stick with the default collision mask (same as sprite) and move right to event programming.

We want this object to display a text on a random position inside the game room every time you click on it.

For this purpose, we need to use the *Create* event to set up some initializations and the *Mouse (Left Pressed)* event to change the text's coordinates every time the user clicks on the object. We will also use the *Draw* event to draw the text on screen.

Create Event

With obj_funnyguy selected, click the *Events* button on the object's window, and a little Events window will appear. There, click the *Add Event* button and select the **Create** event. This will add the Create event to your Events window's list, and it will open another window on the side where you can write your GML code to program what behavior this object will have when the Create event occurs.

We want to randomize the horizontal and vertical position of the text that we will display. To do that, first we need to create two containers for those two values.

CHAPTER 2   HELLO, WORLD!

Introducing Variables

Variables are containers that we use to store values that we need for calculations or other actions in our games.

You probably already met something like variables in your life. Do you remember when you were solving mathematical problems in school and you were asked to find the value of x for a certain function? In that problem, x was a variable that had a value associated to the function. The value of x was sometimes one; sometimes it was a range of possible values. That's exactly what a variable is: a label that can assume different values according to some rules and a context. The value of a variable in GML can be changed as many times as you like, and it can be associated either with a simple constant value or with an expression involving functions and other variables (just like in math).

Variables in GML can contain different types of values. The most common are undefined, strings, numbers, and Booleans.

Undefined is a special data type that means *no-data*. In other programming languages, it's called NULL or nil, and it represents the concept of void. You can check whether a variable contains the type undefined by using the built-in function *is_undefined*. Check the official documentation for more information.

Strings are simple text expressed between quotation marks. They are mostly used to compose messages to show on screen or to write on a file. Strings can be manipulated using some specific built-in functions and can be concatenated by using the plus sign (+). Check the official documentation for more information. You can declare a string in GML like this:

```
my_string = "Hello, World!";
```

Numbers are just real numbers stored as 32-bit floating point. You can operate on numbers using the most common mathematical operators: plus to add (+), minus to subtract (-), slash to divide (/), and asterisk to multiply (*). There are also some more advanced functions offered by GameMaker. We will check some of them further on. You can assign a number to a variable like this:

```
my_number = 24.4;
```

Booleans are a special type of data that can either be true (associated with 1) or false (associated with 0). You can operate on Booleans using logical operators like *AND*, *OR*, and *NOT*. The result of operations on Boolean values is another Boolean value. The combination of multiple Boolean values concatenated by logical operators is called Boolean expression.

AND is a binary operator expressed in GML with the keywords *and* or &&. It can be used to compare two Boolean values and returns true when the two values are both true; otherwise, it returns false.

For example:

```
my_true = true;
my_false = false;
result = my_true and my_false; // FALSE
result = my_true and my_true; // TRUE
result = my_false and my_false; // FALSE
```

Note that the // prefix tells GameMaker that everything that follows until the end of line is a comment, so it shouldn't be treated as an instruction (or action).

OR is a binary operator expressed in GML with the keywords *or* or ||. It can be used to compare two Boolean values and returns true when at least one of the two values is true; otherwise, it returns false.

For example:

```
my_true = true;
my_false = false;
result = my_true or my_false; // TRUE
```

```
result = my_true or my_true; // TRUE
result = my_false or my_false; // FALSE
```

NOT is a unary operator expressed in GML with the keywords *not* or *!*.

It can be used to negate the value of a Boolean: if the original value is true, it returns false; if the original value is false, it returns true.

For example:

```
my_true = true;
my_false = false;
result = not my_true; // FALSE
result = not my_false; // TRUE
```

In GML, we can declare a variable in many ways, depending on how long we want it to live on. In fact, variables have an area of reach, which is where they operate and can be accessed. This is called **scope**. Scope determines the lifespan of a variable and defines if a variable is local, global, or instance related.

In GML, variables can be as follows:

- **Instance Related**: The most common variables. They live inside the instance for all its life cycle. They are destroyed when the instance is. Instance variables can be accessed by other instances using the dot notation (instance.variable).

- **Local**: Local variables are declared using the **var** keyword. They live only in the block of code in which they are declared, and they're destroyed when the game exits that code block. It's good practice to use an underscore as a prefix name for local variables.

CHAPTER 2 HELLO, WORLD!

- **Global**: They live on for all the duration of the game. They belong to the game itself and not to an instance. You must declare them using the **global** keyword. Global variables can be accessed by all the instances in the game.
- **Built-In**: Those are variables built-in in some elements of GameMaker (like objects, rooms, etc.). You can access them by using the dot notation (object.variable). Note that built-in variables are never local, but they can be instance related or global.

The way to define those three kinds of variables is shown in the following code:

```
1   foo = 10; // this is an instance variable
2   var _bar = 100; // this is a local variable
3   global.foobar = 1000; // this is a global variable
```

The var keyword is used to tell GameMaker that we are going to define a local variable, while we don't need any special prefix to define an instance variable. The var keyword is followed by the variable name and the value we want to assign to it.

To define a global variable, you need to use this syntax (as also shown earlier):

```
global.<variable_name> = value;
```

The semicolon, in GML (and many other languages), indicates the end of the instruction. You must terminate every instruction with a semicolon (with some exception that we will explain later).

37

CHAPTER 2   HELLO, WORLD!

Now that we know what a variable is, we can declare a couple of them to store X- and Y-coordinates for the text to be displayed. So just put those lines inside the **Create** event code:

```
1    txt_x = 0;
2    txt_y = 0;
```

Here we are just creating two instance variables called txt_x and txt_y to which we are associating a value of 0.

Left Pressed (Mouse) Event

Now that we have our variables set up, we need to randomize them based on the room dimensions.

We will use an 800 × 600 room, so our text's X- and Y-coordinates shall not grow bigger than those values.

To do that, we will generate the value of `txt_x` in a 0–800 range and the value of `txt_y` in a 0–600 range.

So create a new event and choose the *Mouse* option. You will see a number of different events related to the mouse device. Just click the *Left Pressed* event.

Now a Left Pressed event tab will be displayed into the *Events* window so that we can start writing the code.

When the Left Pressed event occurs, we want to generate a couple of random numbers and assign them to our txt_x and txt_y variables.

To do that, we will have to call some built-in functions. A **function** is a piece of code that contains a list of instructions to execute.

Simply put, a function is a piece of code that given an input (that can be empty) executes some actions and returns an output (that can be empty too).

Now that we know what a function is, let's add those lines to the Left Pressed event:

```
1   randomize();
2   txt_x = random(800);
3   txt_y = random(600);
```

randomize() (or randomise()) calls the randomize built-in function, which is a function defined by GameMaker that sets the RNG (Random Number Generator) seed to a random number.

randomize() takes no input (actually an empty input), executes the action of randomizing the RNG seed that will provide us the random numbers; it returns no output (an empty output).

The random(max) function does take an input (max – that must be a number) and returns a random number between 0 and max-1 as a result of its actions.

So, in this code, we first generate a random number between 0 and 800, and we assign it to txt_x, then we generate a number between 0 and 600, and we assign it to txt_y.

Note that if you want to define the minimum value of the random range, you just need to add that value to the result of the random function like this:

```
var adult = 18 + random(100);
```

Or you can use random_range(min, max), where *min* is your minimum number and *max* is the maximum. This function will return a number between *min* and *max-1*. Here's an example of how to use it:

```
var teenager = random_range(13, 19);
```

Draw

Now we just need to display the message at the randomized coordinates. But before we do this, we have to create a new font to use!

CHAPTER 2 HELLO, WORLD!

Right-click the Fonts section in the right sidebar, and select *Create ▶ Font*.

A new font will be created and displayed with a dedicated window in the Workspace. There is really nothing much to say at this stage about fonts, since we are going to use a standard one.

Click Select Font and choose Arial. Now give this font a reasonable name like fnt_arial. That's it!

Go back to our obj_funnyguy and create a new Draw event.

The Draw event is triggered every time the room is drawn on screen, which means that this event is triggered every frame. The frequency depends on the frame-rate at which the game is running.

The first thing to do in a Draw event is to draw the object itself using the **draw_self()** function, or its sprite won't be shown during the room drawing.

Note that you don't need to do it if you're not using the Draw event. This is because the room will use a default Draw event containing the **draw_self()** action for every object that doesn't specify a custom Draw event. When you specify your own Draw event, you are overriding the default one, which means that you are responsible of executing the actions that the default implementation would execute.

We also have to set the font we just created to be active, set its color, and then define the text to show.

To do that, we will use **draw_set_font, draw_set_color,** and **draw_text** functions.

Let's write some code to better understand.

Create a Draw event into the obj_funnyguy object and put inside this code:

```
1   draw_self();
2   draw_set_font(fnt_arial);
3   draw_set_color(c_black);
4   draw_text(txt_x, txt_y, "Hello, World!");
```

CHAPTER 2 HELLO, WORLD!

Line 1: The draw_self() function draws the object's own sprite on screen.

Line 2: The draw_set_font(fnt) function defines fnt as the font that is going to be used to display the text (in this case fnt_arial).

Line 3: The draw_set_color(col) function defines col as the color that is going to be used to display the text (c_white corresponds to the white color).

Line 4: The draw_text(x, y, msg) function displays the message msg (can be a string or a variable name) at the coordinates x and y, inside the current room.

That's it. Now click the Run button in the toolbar or press F5 to compile and start your first GameMaker project!

If you followed all the steps, the room will be displayed along with our funny guy and the "Hello, World!" message in the top-left corner of the room (Figure 2-13). Every time you will click the funny guy, the message will change its position to a random one inside the room.

41

CHAPTER 2 HELLO, WORLD!

Figure 2-13. *The final result of our Hello World project*

Congratulations! You made the first step toward video games development! Cheers to that!

In the next chapter, we will go further, starting to design and create real video games. You will learn how to create a Memory card game with GML and GameMaker.

TEST YOUR KNOWLEDGE!

1. How can you access the assets of your game in GameMaker?
2. What is a sprite?
3. Can you create the image of a sprite inside GameMaker?

4. What is an object?
5. What's the difference between objects and instances?
6. What is the game loop?
7. What is an event?
8. Can you give an example of an event to control mouse input?
9. Can you give an example of an event that occurs when an instance is destroyed?
10. What is GML?
11. What is a tile set?
12. How can you create customizable texts inside your game in GameMaker?
13. What is a room?
14. What is a variable?
15. What is the scope of a variable?
16. How many different variable scopes exist in GM?
17. What is a global variable?
18. How can you randomize a value?
19. How can you draw a text in your game?
20. Can you modify the Hello World project to show the text only in one half of the window?

CHAPTER 3

Card Game (Part 1)

Card games are one of the best starting points to learn game development because they contain the main components of a generic game application, like data structures, manipulation of data, mouse/keyboard interactions, graphics, victory conditions, etc.

In this chapter, we are going to develop a **Memory** card game (also known as Concentration or Pairs). This is a game that will help you familiarize with some important concepts of game development and design.

The Design

The rules of Memory are pretty straightforward: A deck of cards made of pairs is shuffled, and the cards are placed facedown; each turn, the player picks two cards, and if they match, the player wins the two cards; otherwise, the cards should be put back in their place facedown.

Now that the rules of the game are defined, we need to formalize them in what is called a game design document (GDD). This document is the reference and point of contact for all the parties involved in the development process. The GDD represents a sort of blueprint of the video game, but differently from the blueprint of a building, this one evolves and changes during the development, reflecting the creative process and the decisions made by the designers and the other stakeholders.

CHAPTER 3   CARD GAME (PART 1)

A Game Design Document Primer

A game design document (GDD) is a design specification of a video game. It describes the game rules, its goals and mechanics, the ways the game can be played, and everything else concerning the way it should work. In cases of games with a story, the GDD also includes story background, character descriptions, and so on.

The GDD is a vital piece of documentation for your project, even if you are a solo developer or a total beginner. It's very important that you write your GDD with a simple language making it easy to read, since you and anyone involved will probably need to consult it and modify it multiple times. You should also keep in mind that a GDD is a living document. Things will change during development, and new ideas may be considered valid, while old ones may be archived.

To help you keep the GDD simple, you may (and should) use images, graphs, and any graphical elements you like to better give the idea of what you mean. Mockups and concept art as well as external references are very welcome and help a lot with the general comprehension of the project and its goal both from a technical and a narrative point of view.

It's time to write our very first GDD. Just be aware that our first GDD will be littered with comments and explanations of what we are doing (things that you don't want to keep on a GDD, but are crucial in this book for you to understand).

Note   Writing a design document is crucial to better understand how to develop your project!

A common mistake is to think that a project is too simple to have a design document and that making one would be a waste of time. Keep in mind that a design document is never a waste of time! It's the opposite: A design document is going to save you a lot of time, because it lets you face development difficulties and implications before they happen. This allows you to better organize your work and do a brilliant job!

Memory GDD

Memory is a single-player card game using a deck of pairs of cards in which the player has to flip matching cards from a set of covered cards. To add some challenge, the game will be time-based.

Rules

- The game is time-based (the player has to reach the goal before the time expires).
- The player can flip only two cards per turn.
- The cards match if they have the same face.
- The player can reset the game anytime losing their progress and resetting the timer.
- **Victory**: If the player finds all the matching pairs, they win the game.
- **Game Over**: If the time runs out, the game is lost.

Tip   Rules are one of the most important aspects of the GDD. They define the laws that your game should never break, and they strongly impact on the game's **fun factor**. Never forget: your game should always be fun. Writing good rules for your game is half the work done!

CHAPTER 3   CARD GAME (PART 1)

Game Flow

When the game starts, the player is taken to the game screen so that they can immediately start to play.

The gameplay follows the rules we just defined in the previous section, as you can see in the flow chart in Figure 3-1.

> **Note** In this case, it is very convenient to use a flow chart as it makes very easy to see and understand the game loop and the flow that the whole application should follow.

> **Tip** Having a good understanding of how your game should act allows you to better understand how to implement it. That is why a design document is extremely useful in software development.

Similar Games

There is a huge quantity of Memory card games for PC. Probably one of the most relevant is Mickey's Memory Challenge (1990) by Walt Disney Computer Software (now Disney Interactive).

Game Modes

Time-based mode is the only mode we want to support. We want to keep the project simple, since it's our first project.

CHAPTER 3 CARD GAME (PART 1)

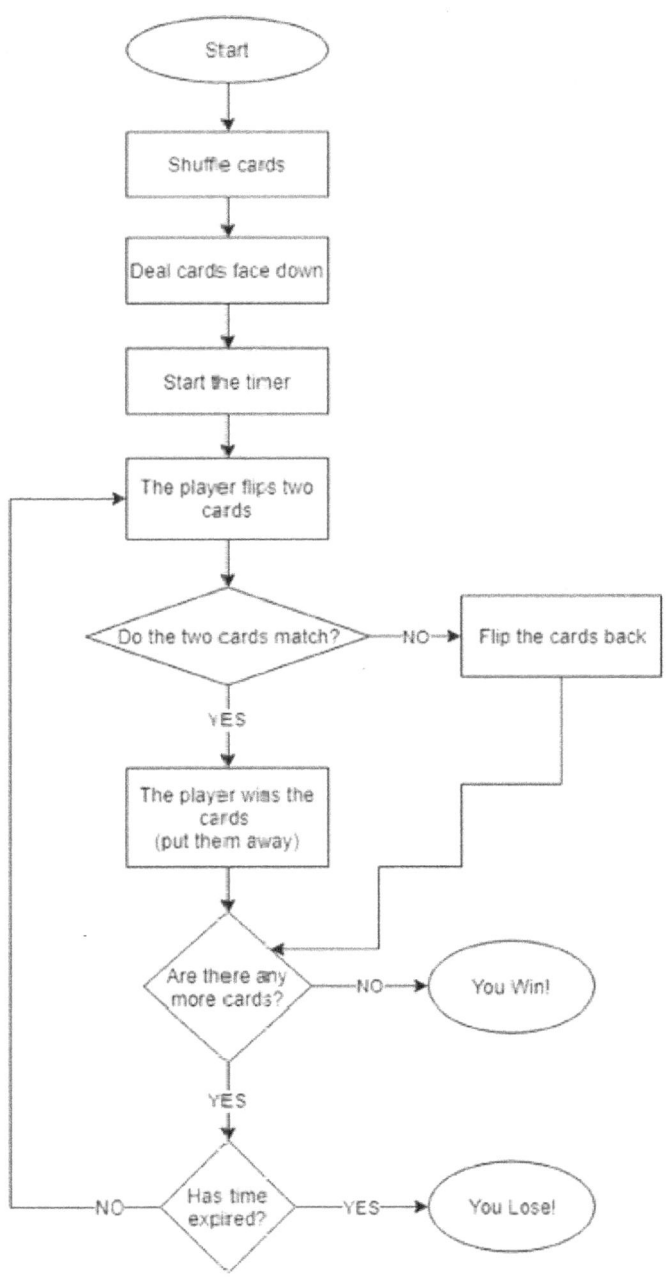

Figure 3-1. *Memory card game logic flow*

CHAPTER 3　CARD GAME (PART 1)

> **Note** In the future, you may want to extend the game with some more modes, for example, a free mode, in which you can play without worrying about the time, or a 3D mode like Mahjong, in which you can only pick cards that are on the top.
>
> Keep in mind that one of the best things about Game Design is that it gives you endless possibilities to improve the fun in a game. Even if you have to deal with classics, like we are doing, you can experiment and borrow ideas from other games (or other fields) to make it better and funnier. After all, complex games like Total War or Pokémon game series are just evolutions of Rock-Paper-Scissors.

Target Audience

This is a game that suits every age. It will probably attract more a casual audience that is looking for a quick and simple gaming experience.

Target System

The game is designed to be playable on a PC using a mouse.

Assets

For this game, you will need a set of ten sprites for the cards: nine sprites for the different types of cards and one sprite for the back of the cards.

You can take inspiration from any kind of existing cards. In the following, there is an example of what those sprites may look like.

spr_cardback

Pivot Point: Middle-center
Size: 100 × 150

spr_rain

Pivot Point: Middle-center
Size: 100 × 150

CHAPTER 3   CARD GAME (PART 1)

From GDD to Development

The GDD so far is pretty basic, but it has anything we need to start creating our game.

From the rules of the game and the game flow, we know that we will need to implement some concepts:

- **Card**: The basic element of the game. A card can be flipped and has two faces, a type and a unique ID.
- **Deck**: A collection of cards. It can be shuffled and dealt.
- **Timer**: Counts the time passed. It can be reset to the initial state anytime with the enter key.
- **Game Controller**: An object that setups the game and checks on rules and victory conditions.

Those four concepts are all we need for our Memory game.

In the next sections, we will cover the complete design and implementation of the first half of the game, and we will complete it in the next chapter. Let's start from the cards!

Cards

The card object is the basic brick to build and play our game. We need to design it thinking about what properties we want it to have and what actions we want to use it for.

For our cards to be flippable, they need to have two faces (back and front, as shown in the assets section above). To be recognizable, they need a graphic art on their front, which represents their type. We also need an index that we can use to know their position inside the deck; this is essential to implement some functionality in the future.

Summarizing what we just said, our cards should have those properties:

- **Type**: The figure drawn on the card
- **Face**: Tells us if the card is facing down or up
- **Index**: Unique index that represents the position of the card in the deck

The next question is: *How do we want to use our cards in the game?*

From the rules, we know that the player should be able to flip two cards to see their type and then check if they match. So, we need an action to change the face of a card from front to back (and vice versa) and another action to store in memory the type of a card to do a later check. We can call those actions flip and select:

- **Flip**: Changes the visible face of the card. If the card is faced up, it turns it facedown and vice versa.
- **Select**: Stores the current card in memory for a future check.

GameMaker is built around the **event-driven programming** paradigm. So, to implement the Flip and Select actions, we need to understand which event should trigger them.

Since we are playing on a PC, we want to use the click of the left mouse button to select and flip our cards. So, when the player clicks on a card, the card is flipped and then stored in memory to be checked with a second card. The selected card will remain selected and faceup until a second card is clicked. When two cards are selected, we need to check if they match and then clear the selection.

CHAPTER 3 CARD GAME (PART 1)

Translating all that we just said about the card object in GML concepts, we need to create an **obj_card** game object and set those two events:

- **Create**: This will include the initialization of the card's properties (type, face, index).
- **Left Mouse Button Pressed**: This will contain the Flip and Select actions code.

We defined everything we need for the card object design. We can go ahead and implement it in GameMaker.

Implementation

First of all, we need to create a number of sprites for our different cards, plus one for the back of the cards. Let's say eight different designs for the front and one for the back (total: nine sprites). Feel free to use my cards; you can find them in the official GitHub repository of this book.

To represent the different kinds of cards in the code, we will use a variable to point to a number (from 0 to 7) that represents the sprite we want to assign to that card.

The Card Object

Let's create a new object called **obj_card**. This will describe the behavior and characteristics of every card in the deck.

In the **obj_card** object, make a new **Create** event. This will be the place in which we are going to define the card's properties. To recap, we want our card to have a variable that determines if the card is showing the front or back. We also want a variable that tells us the type of the card and its place in the deck.

We will use a number (from 0 to 7, since we have eight different sprites for our cards) to indicate the type of the card. This number will be stored in a variable called *type* and will be used to access the right sprite in the array **cardtype** that contains all the cards' sprites.

CHAPTER 3 CARD GAME (PART 1)

We will initialize the value of the variable *type* for now to 0 for testing purposes, but normally we would want to initialize it to a default value of *noone*, which is a keyword of GML to indicate an invalid value.

```
1   // Initializing the main properties for a card object
2   index = noone; // the position of the card in the deck
3   type = 0; // associates the card with its sprite
4   face = 1; // (0 = back, 1 = front)
```

In the code above, we are initializing the card properties (lines 2–4). The index of the card is the position of the card in the deck, the type of the card is used to associate a card with a sprite, and the face variable tells us if the card is showing the back or the front.

Now we need to write the code to tell the card to flip when the player clicks on it with the mouse. This is very simple: we only have to tell the game that whenever the player clicks with the mouse on the card, we should change the variable **face** from 1 (front) to 0 (back) or vice versa.

To be able to do that, we need a piece of programming knowledge: we have to understand how to decide things if GML.

In programming, you can check for certain conditions and act accordingly using conditional statements like if-then-else and switch.

If-Then-Else

If-then-else is a conditional statement that allows you to check for a condition and execute a block of code if that condition is verified. You can also execute a specific block of code in case that condition is not satisfied.

If-then-else logic is very simple: if this condition is true, then do this; or else do that.

For example:

```
if a == b
{
    // do this
```

55

```
}
else
{
    // do that
}
```

You can specify multiple options by concatenating if and else like this:

```
if a == b
{
    // do this
}
else if a < b
{
    // do that
}
else
{
    // do other things
}
```

Switch

Switch works similarly to if-then-else, but it's specialized in checking which value a variable is assuming parsing a list of possible values.

For example:

```
switch ( a )
{
    case 0:
        // code for the case that a == 0
        break;
```

```
   case 1:
      // code for the case that a == 1
      break;
   default:
      // code for all the other cases where a is neither
         equal to 0 or 1
      break;
}
```

The keyword *case* is used to ask GameMaker to check if the variable we are testing is equal to a specific value. The code to execute if that condition is true is included between case and break.

The *default* case holds the code to execute when none of the previous cases occurred.

Let's immediately use those new tools! Create a new event in the **obj_card** object **Mouse⊙Left Pressed** and write the following code inside of it:

```
1  if (face == 0)
2  {
3      face = 1;
4  }
5  else
6  {
7      face = 0;
8  }
```

The code above states that every time we left-click on the **obj_card** object, if the card is showing its back (**face** is equal to 0), we flip it changing the value of **face** from 0 to 1 and vice versa.

> **Caution** The *double equal sign* (==) is not to be confused with the *single equal sign* (=)!
>
> The former is used to compare two expressions, while the latter is used to assign the rightmost value to the leftmost variable.

> **Note** You can compare numbers using comparison operators, which are <, <=, ==, !=, >, and >=. They are binary operators that allow you to compare two expressions or variables returning a Boolean value (true or false) as the result of the comparison.
>
> a == b returns true if a and b are equal; otherwise, it returns false.
>
> a != b returns true if a and b are different; otherwise, it returns false.
>
> a > b returns true if a is greater than b and false otherwise.
>
> a >= b returns true if a is greater than or equal to b and false otherwise.
>
> a < b returns true if a is less than b and false otherwise.
>
> a <= b returns true if a is less than or equal to b and false otherwise.

Ok, now we have the functionality to flip the cards, but we won't see anything yet, because we don't have a way to update the visual style of the card when we click. To do this, we need an event that can constantly check if the card is showing the front or the back.

This event in GM is called **Step. This** is an event that is recurring once per frame (so it depends on how many frames per second your game runs). We will use this event to constantly check which face the card is showing, so that the game can draw the right sprite on screen. So let's create a new **Step** event for our **obj_card** and put this code inside:

```
1    /// @description Show the correct sprite
2    if ( face == 0 )
3    {
4        sprite_index = spr_cardback;
5    }
6    else
7    {
8        switch(type)
9        {
10           case 0:
11               sprite_index = spr_fire;
12               break;
13           case 1:
14               sprite_index = spr_mountain;
15               break;
16           case 2:
17               sprite_index = spr_rain;
18               break;
19           case 3:
20               sprite_index = spr_sun;
21               break;
22           case 4:
23               sprite_index = spr_river;
24               break;
25           case 5:
26               sprite_index = spr_moon;
27               break;
28           case 6:
29               sprite_index = spr_morning;
30               break;
```

```
31            case 7:
32                sprite_index = spr_afternoon;
33                break;
34            default:
35                break;
36        }
37    }
```

Lines 1–4: We check if **face** is equal to 0. If it is, it means that we want to show the back of the card. So, we assign the back sprite (spr_cardback) to the property **sprite_index**.

Lines 5–8: When the value of face is 1, we check the type of the card and assign the right sprite to the object. Each sprite represents a type of card.

Caution **sprite_index** is a reserved word. It is a property that any GameMaker object has and represents the sprite that the object is showing. If you change its value, you change the sprite the object shows. Be careful, though, because **sprite_index** only accepts sprites as values or -1 to indicate that there is no sprite.

Now we have everything we need to flip cards. We need to test if we did everything alright! So, let's open the main room (if it doesn't exist, create one) and Drag and Drop the **obj_card** in the middle of it. Since we are here, let's also change the size of the window. You can do that by changing **Width** and **Height** in the room's **Property** tab. Let's make it 600 × 800.

Now run the game, and you will see your card standing there, showing its back. If you click on it, the card will flip, showing the front (Figure 3-2); if you click a second time, the card will flip back.

Good job!

CHAPTER 3   CARD GAME (PART 1)

Figure 3-2.   *Our first flipping card!*

Now that we have our card working and flipping, we can start thinking about the deck and the shuffling feature.

CHAPTER 3 CARD GAME (PART 1)

Deck

Now that we successfully coded the cards mechanics, we need to take care of how to create a deck of cards for our game. To do that, we have to ask ourselves a question: *What is a deck of cards?*

A deck of cards is a collection of cards that can be ordered, shuffled, and accessed (e.g., searching for a single card inside the deck, picking the top card, etc.).

In computer science, there are some concepts that are used to represent different types of collection of items: they are called **data structures**.

A number of operations can be done on data structures:

- **Access**: You can access their elements.
- **Add**: You can add elements to them.
- **Delete**: You can delete their elements.
- **Search**: You can search for a specific element.
- **Sort**: You can sort their elements following a specific criterion.

GameMaker supports some commonly used data structures. The good thing is that the choice you have is wide enough to let you make whatever you need. The bad thing is that GML is not flexible enough to let you create new data structures easily. Anyway, you will hardly need to.

GameMaker offers seven different types of data structures:

- Array
- Stack
- Queue
- List

CHAPTER 3   CARD GAME (PART 1)

- Map
- Priority Queue
- Grid

Array

An array is a collection of elements ordered sequentially (Figure 3-3). The most basic kind of array is the one-dimensional array: a list of elements linked to one another and accessed using a sequential number starting from 0 (that tells us that item's position in the array).

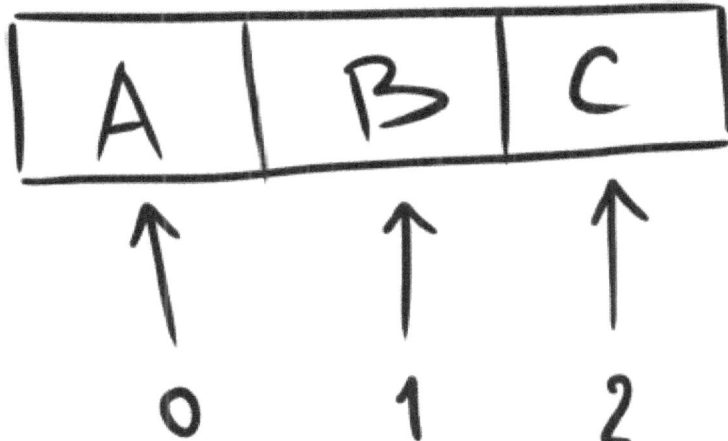

Figure 3-3. *An array made of three elements*

A two-dimensional array is a table (or grid) made of two arrays (Figure 3-4), as if they were the rows of the table. To access the elements in a two-dimensional array, you need two indexes: one to refer to the row and the other to refer to the column.

63

CHAPTER 3 CARD GAME (PART 1)

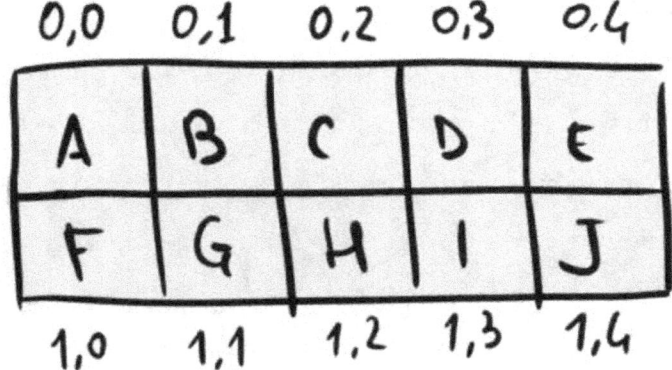

Figure 3-4. *A two-dimensional array*

Arrays are very useful to organize information in a schematic form so that you can easily access them. Here are some real-world applications of arrays in games:

- Menus
- RPG stats
- Inventory
- Game statistics
- Others

To create an array, you just need to initialize it:

my_array = [10, 20, 30];

You can access the single elements by using their index like this:

my_array[0] = 10;

The line above initializes the first element of the array named my_array (element number 0) to a value equal to 10.

CHAPTER 3 CARD GAME (PART 1)

To add more items to the array or change their value, you can do the same thing for every other item:

```
1   my_array[1] = 20;
2   my_array[2] = 30;
```

The code above initializes (if they don't exist) or assigns new values to the second and third elements in the array **my_array**.

To access the value from an item in an array, we just call the array with the right index, like this:

```
var third_element = my_array[2];
```

Note GML's arrays are not fixed in size. You can freely extend or reduce their size after the creation.

Stack

Just like a pile of dishes, a stack is organized as a pile of elements in which the element on the bottom is the oldest, while the one on the top is the most recent. This order is called **Last-In First-Out (LIFO)**. Going ahead with the pile of dishes analogy, stacks offer two main actions: push and pop (Figure 3-5).

Figure 3-5. *A stack is just like a pile of dishes*

65

CHAPTER 3   CARD GAME (PART 1)

If you push an item in a stack, you will place it on the top of it, so that it will become the new first item of the structure, while the pop action deletes the topmost element of the stack.

As you can easily guess, stacks are very good for lists of elements that need to be accessed always from the most recent to the oldest. Indeed, stacks' performance is optimal with push and pop actions and suboptimal if you need to search an item in a specific position. For example, if you need to access the fifth item in the stack, you have to start from the topmost (the first item) and go down through the items one by one until you reach the fifth item.

Better not to use a stack to represent our deck of cards. Why? Well, imagine trying to sort a pile of dishes in chromatic order without making other little piles to help you in the process and without being able to keep the dishes you remove.

In GML, stacks are called **DS Stacks**.

Queue

A queue is very similar to a stack, but it differs in some crucial details. In fact, queues follow a **First-In-First-Out (FIFO)** policy. That means that the oldest element of the queue is always the first to be accessed.

Just think about a queue at a post office (Figure 3-6). The first people to be served are always the ones who are waiting the longest, and every new person who needs to access the post office goes on the end of the queue and waits for their turn.

This is exactly how a queue in coding works. Each new element added to the queue is put in the end of the queue, and the elements of the queue are consumed from the oldest to the newest.

Let's think, for instance, that we need to instruct a robot on how to get from point A to point B in a maze. We will say things like "Go forward for 1 meter," "Turn 90 degrees," "Go forward for half a meter," and so on. We want the robot to follow precisely the instructions we are giving, in exactly

CHAPTER 3   CARD GAME (PART 1)

that order: from the oldest to the newest. We don't want him to follow the instructions randomly or in reverse order. This is a perfect situation in which we can use a queue! We just add each instruction in a queue, then we pass the queue to the robot, and it will follow the instructions in the right order.

Queues are very good to manage cases like that! They're very efficient in queueing and dequeueing elements in a FIFO fashion, but just like stacks, they're not good for random access.

We can't use queues for our deck of cards, since, just like a stack, they are not made to be accessed in other ways than the one they're designed for.

In GML, queues are called **DS Queues**.

Figure 3-6. *A queue is like a bunch of people standing in a line. The head of the line is the first item of the queue, while the last one is called tail*

67

List

A list is a data structure that organizes elements sequentially. In a list, each element is associated to an integer value called index, so that you can immediately access an element in any position of the list.

A list can be sorted in ascending or descending order or shuffled (randomized). They are very flexible and can be modified in length with ease (unlike arrays).

Lists are very good to represent collections of items that can vary in size, that need to be sorted, and that require quick random access (accessing elements in any position). That sounds like a very good candidate for our deck of cards! Let's remember that!

In GML, lists are called **DS Lists**.

Map

A map is a data structure that stores key and value pairs (Figure 3-7). Both key and value can be of any type. You can quickly insert a new pair in a map or pick an existing value if you know the associated key. Beware, though, that maps are not sorted; so, if you don't know the key associated to a specific value, you will have to iterate through all the existing pairs, before you find the right one; and that's very slow! Be aware that you can't assign more than one value to a key and that keys are unique (you cannot have doubles).

Maps are very useful in all those situations in which you need to assign a value to a concept. For instance, let's think about an RPG: your character will likely have an inventory containing all their items. They may have two health potions, an apple, and three keys. You can easily represent the inventory with a map associating to each item, the value representing its quantity:

CHAPTER 3   CARD GAME (PART 1)

- Health Potion, 2
- Apple, 1
- Keys, 3

That's it! Whenever your character uses an item, you just have to access it searching for the right key (e.g., "Keys") and modify its quantity, if needed.

Even if we could represent a deck of cards with a map, it's very inconvenient, since as we just said, it's an unsorted data structure and being unsorted also means to be non-randomizable (so we won't be able to shuffle a deck made with a map data structure).

In GML, maps are called **DS Maps**.

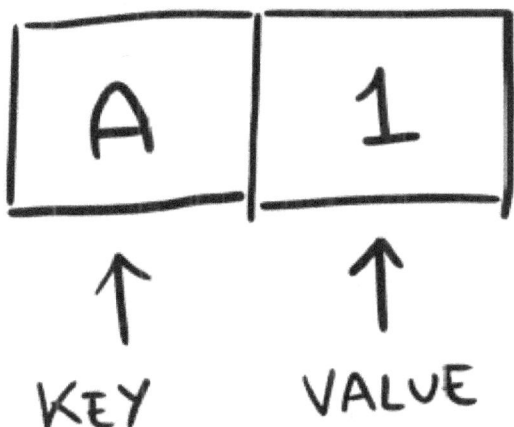

Figure 3-7. *In a map, each element is a couple made of a key and a value*

Priority Queue

A priority queue is very similar to a queue, with the only difference that it's ordered by a priority value.

Let's make an example to better understand the principle. Think, for instance, about the queue in an emergency room. People don't just queue in the order they arrive. There is a priority value that is the actual gravity of the injury. The more the injury is serious, the more the patient is high in the queue.

A priority queue has a numeric (real) value – called weight – that expresses the order in the queue for every element.

Priority queues are very useful in situations in which you need a data structure that should be sorted all the time. For example, if you need to make a leaderboard, you don't want to sort it every time you add an item to the queue; it would be very time consuming! In this and many other cases, a priority queue is just what you need to get the job done!

Another interesting and common usage for priority queue is the management of processes to execute in an operating system. In fact, some operating systems use process scheduling algorithms based on priority queues. They just give ratings to tasks based on how critical they are for the system and the user experience and then put the tasks into the queue to be executed.

For our case of building a deck of card, we don't need a priority queue, since we do want the deck to be randomly sorted and it wouldn't be possible using a data structure that remains ordered all the time based on a specific rating.

In GML, priority queues are called **DS Priority Queues**.

Grids

Grids are basically two-dimensional arrays. Just think about a table: you define the number of rows and columns, and then you can access items with *x,y* pairs.

A very common application for grids is representing maps and playgrounds. For instance, think about *Battleship* (or *Sea Battle*): you have a map in which you can place your ships, and to identify a single spot on the map, you call a number that represents the row and a letter that represents the column. Grids are based on the same principle. You have a grid, and you can access every item by using the number of the row and the number of the column.

We can totally represent a deck using a grid, but it is effective only if you're designing a game with a deck of cards made of more than one card suit. Since we don't have card suits, it would be overkill. Also, we need the deck to be ordered randomly, and it would be difficult using a grid (it could increase time complexity). So, we are not using grids.

In GML, grids are called **DS Grids**.

Designing Decks

All in all, our best option to design a deck of cards for our Memory card game is a **DS List**. In fact, as we already saw, DS Lists are very flexible: they can be used to represent data that need to be sorted (or randomized), and they also feature good random access time performances. That's exactly what we need!

A DS List is a bit different to use than an array. To create a DS List, you need to call a special function called *constructor*. We will explain later in more detail what a function is, but for now just think that a function is an action and a constructor is an action that serves to the goal of constructing an object.

You can create a list and associate it to a variable name like this:

```
var _mylist = ds_list_create();
```

To add an item to a DS List

```
ds_list_add(_mylist, 10);
```

The previous code creates a new element in the list **_mylist** with the value 10. The new element is positioned in the last position.

CHAPTER 3 CARD GAME (PART 1)

To access the value of an item at position _i, you can either do this

```
var _item_i = ds_list_find_value(_mylist, _i);
```

or use this equivalent notation:

```
var _item_i = mylist[| _i];
```

Note Following the GML coding convention, every local variable declared using the keyword *var* should have an underscore (_) prefix. This helps to quickly identify local variables from variables that reside in other objects, since specifying a namespace is not mandatory in GML. As an additional good practice rule, it's a good habit to always explicitly specify the namespace of an external variable.

There are other interesting and useful functions that you can use with your DS Lists. Feel free to check them out in the official GML documentation.

Since the deck is only a collection of cards represented by a DS List, we don't need to create an object for it. So, we will include the code for the deck into another object: the **game controller**.

The game controller is the object that rules upon our game, checking that the game is working properly and managing every object involved.

Because of its role, the game controller is perfect to take care of the creation and management of our deck.

Note To merge and combine two concepts is a common thing in software design. As designers, we have to understand when it's convenient to keep two concepts separated or when it's better to merge them into one. In this case, since we don't need a deck object, it's better to simplify our project avoiding it and delegating the creation and management of the deck of cards to the game controller.

CHAPTER 3   CARD GAME (PART 1)

Create a new object called **obj_controller**. This will be the object that will rule upon our game checking that everything is working properly.

First of all, we need a *Create* event in which we will create the deck and fill it with 16 cards, each of which should be initialized properly. We definitely don't want to initialize the deck one card at a time, as it would be extremely dull. We need a tool that allows us to repeat an action for a set amount of times. This concept in programming is called **loop**.

Code Loops

A **loop** is a flow control statement that allows a block of code to be repeated until a certain condition is met.

There are four loop control statements in GML:

- Repeat
- While
- Do
- For

Let's see how and when to use them.

Repeat

Repeat has the form

```
repeat(<expression>)
{
    <statement>
}
```

Repeat will execute `<statement>` a number of times according to the result of `<expression>`, which is always a number.

Repeat is very useful when you have to execute some actions a specific number of times.

73

CHAPTER 3   CARD GAME (PART 1)

While

While has the form

```
While(<expression>)
{
        <statement>
}
```

While doesn't just repeat <statement> a number of times expressed by <expression>. In fact, here, <expression> is not just a number, but a Boolean expression. This means that **while** will evaluate <expression> at every loop, and if the result is **true**, the code inside the curly brackets (<statement> in this case) will be executed.

While is very useful if you have to repeat some action as long as a certain condition is met, but it's very inefficient if you already know the exact number of iterations that you want to execute (in which case, **repeat** is the best choice).

Do-Until

Do has the form

```
do
{
        <statement>
}
until(<expression>)
```

Do is a bit different from the other loops. It executes the code inside the curly brackets at least once and then starts to evaluate <expression> for all the next iterations. **Do** executes <statement> the first time, and then it keeps executing it until <expression> is **true**.

Do is very useful if you need to execute the actions inside your loop at least once.

For

For has the form

```
for(<initialization>; <expression>; <post-loop-actions>)
{
      <loop-actions>
}
```

The for loop executes <loop-actions> as long as <expression> is **true**, just like the **while loop**. The difference is that the **for** loop allows you to execute some actions at the beginning of the loop and after each iteration. In the example above, <initialization> is executed before the first iteration of the loop and never again. After this, <expression> is evaluated, and if it returns true, <loop-actions> are executed and then <post-loop-actions> are executed. The loop keeps checking <expression> and executing <loop-actions> and <post-loop-actions> until <expression> turns out to be false.

The for loop is used to count up (or down) to a certain value. Let's say that you want to calculate the factorial of 10. You need a counter variable that starts counting from 1 to 10 multiplying all the numbers by one another.

You can do something like that using the **for loop**:

```
1   var _result = 1;
2
3   for(var _i = 1; _i <= 10; _i += 1)
4   {
5       _result *= _i;
6   }
```

At line 3, inside the brackets, we are declaring the **i** variable and assigning a starting value of 1 (`_i = 1`).

For every iteration of the **for** loop, we are checking if `_i` is less than 10 (`_i< 10`). If it is, we multiply **result** by the value of `_i` (`_result *= _i`). After this, we increase the value of **i** by 1 (`_i+= 1`) so that we can pass to the next number.

The For loop is very useful when you have to repeat a piece of code until a condition is met, and that condition is being ruled by the value of a counter variable.

Caution Loops are a very powerful programming concept that can be the cause of bugs or bad performance in your code, if not used properly.

Make sure that the conditions of your loops can be met, or you will experience endless loops that will continue to run until your game crashes or your memory runs out.

Making Decks

Let's get back to our deck! We now know how to repeat a set of instructions for a number of times or until a condition is met. We can use this concept to automate our deck creation and the setup of our cards.

Let's make a **Create** event for our new **obj_controller** and add this code to it:

```
1   /// @description Set up deck
2   cards_number = 8;
3   deck = ds_list_create();
4   var _deck_size = cards_number * 2;
5
```

```
6   for(var _i = 0; _i < _deck_size; _i+=1)
7   {
8   ds_list_add(deck, instance_create_layer(0, 0, "Instances",
    obj_card));
9   }
10
11  // assign card types to card objects and set up cards
12  for(var _i = 0; _i < _deck_size; _i+=1)
13  {
14  deck[| _i].type = _i % cards_number;
15  deck[| _i].face = 0;
16  deck[| _i].index = _i;
17  deck[| _i].visible = false;
18  }
19
20  // shuffle cards
```

Lines 2-4: We define variables to keep track of the number of available cards, the deck's size, and the number of different cards that we have (the deck will be of size *cards_number* * 2).

Lines 6-9: We fill the DS List with 16 cards (as we already said, *deck_size = cards_number * 2 = 16*).

Lines 12-18: We assign a *type*, *face*, and *index* to every card in the deck. We need eight couples of cards. Each couple is made of two copies of the same card.

To access card properties like type, face, and index, we are using the **dot notation**. Dot notation allows us to access variables declared inside objects.

At line 14, we are using the modulo operator "%" which returns the remainder of a division operation. For example, 7 % 3 would yield 1 because when 7 is divided by 3, the remainder is 1. In our case, we are using it because we want to have only *cards_number* types of different

CHAPTER 3 CARD GAME (PART 1)

cards, but we are making a deck of *cards_number*2* cards, so we want 2 cards for each type. The modulo operator helps us in this process, because it will always make sure that the value of type will always be between 0 and *cards_number*.

We are also turning off the visible property for our cards (line 17), so that the game will not show them (the sprite won't be drawn on the screen).

The visible property is present in every object in GameMaker and tells the game if an object should be drawn or not to the screen. We are turning this off because we want to show the cards only after we shuffled them. We will turn this back on right after the shuffling and dealing of our deck of cards. Speaking of shuffling, how can we do it?

Note To create a new object in GML, you can use the instance_create_layer function that allows you to create a new object into a specific layer of the room.

For example:

`instance_create_layer(0, 0, "Instances", obj_card);`

This will create a new instance of obj_card in the Instances layer (the default one) at position 0,0 in the current room.

Warning! The **dot notation** is very useful to access object's variables, but you can't access local variables declared with the keyword **var** using the dot notation. Variables declared with the **var** keyword are bond to the scope in which they are declared and they are not exposed outside.

CHAPTER 3   CARD GAME (PART 1)

Every Day I'm Shuffling

Shuffling is a very important feature in our game, and we need to repeat this action more than once. More precisely, we need to shuffle cards when the player

- Starts the game
- Presses the **enter** key
- Restarts the game (e.g., after a game over)

These are three different moments in our games that reside in three different areas of our code. Our first instinct might be to write the instructions to shuffle the cards in those three parts of the code by repeating the same instructions three times. That would just work fine, until we need to change something in the algorithm! That will cause us to keep doing any modifications to that behavior three times, and we will have to keep remembering all the places that we have to touch in our code to avoid problems and bugs. For this reason, repeating code is a terrible practice (and a horrible sin) in software engineering! Code duplication increases the probability of introducing bugs and makes the code unstable and more difficult to maintain, especially if you are working with other people.

Anyway, we do need to execute this code three times! So how can we do that? Well, there's another tool we can add to our game developers' belt: **functions**!

How Do Functions Function?

Functions are blocks of code associated to a label. You can call a function from anywhere in your code.

When you call a function, you can pass it some parameters that can alter its behavior.

CHAPTER 3   CARD GAME (PART 1)

A function can return a value – called output – that often represents the result of an evaluation or the outcome of the function (e.g., if everything's gone well or not). When a function accepts input parameters and returns an output as a result, we can say that the output is dependent on the input.

In nearly every programming language, functions are called like this:

`my_output = my_function(my_input)`

Functions are a mathematical concept defined as a relationship between variables of different domains or sets, where each input variable is associated with exactly one output variable. In other words, a function f associates the input variable x that exists in the domain set X to the output variable y that exists in the codomain set Y. The following notation represents this concept in math:

$$y = f(x)$$

Mathematical functions are very important and are widely used for a plethora of evaluations. Just think about trigonometry. In trigonometry, you use sin and cos functions to get the value associated (in the range [0,1]) to a given angle expressed in degrees or radians. And you do it this way:

$$y = sin(x)$$

That means y is the value associated to the sin function applied to the angle x.

You already used some functions in GML, like **ds_list_create()** to create a new DS List or **ds_list_add(deck, instance_create_layer(0, 0, "Instances", obj_card))** to add a card to the deck (a ds_list).

In both cases, you got a result: **array_length_1d** returned a result in function of the input: a number representing the length of the array passed as input; **ds_list_create** created and returned a DS List structure without the need of an input (formally, we would say that it was in function of a void input).

GML Functions

A function in GML can be created with this syntax:

```
function my_func(argument0)
{
    // your code goes here
}
```

where

- **function** is a keyword of the language to indicate the creation of a function.
- **my_func** is the name of the function.
- **argument0** (always between parenthesis) is the name of the argument (the x input variable, in our previous explanation) – it can be a list of arguments, rather than just one: in that case it will be, for example, *my_func(arg1, arg2, arg3)*, for a function with 3 arguments.
- The curly brackets that contain the set of instructions that compose the code of the function.

To make things tidier, we want to put this function in a separate file, so let's create a new *script* by right-clicking **Scripts** in the **Resources** tab and name it **shuffle_cards**.

Scripts in GameMaker have evolved significantly since version 2.3.0. Previously, scripts were essentially containers for single functions that were executed when called. Now, they function as modules loaded at the start of the game. These scripts can define multiple functions, all of which gain global scope. Additionally, any code defined outside of function definitions within a script is executed during the game's startup.

So, now that you created the script, define the skeleton of our function inside it:

```
1  function shuffle_cards(gamedeck)
2  {
3  }
```

To shuffle a deck of cards, we need to get access to the deck we want to shuffle; that's why we added the *gamedeck* argument to the *shuffle_cards* function.

Let's implement our "shuffle_cards" function! We need to randomize our deck of cards. To shuffle a DS List in GameMaker, we can use the "ds_list_shuffle" function. Remember, as we discussed in the previous chapter, to randomize the random number generator (RNG), we must call the "randomize" function first. So, let's add those two lines to our function:

```
1  randomize();
2  ds_list_shuffle(deck);
```

Shuffle Cards Code

Now that we faced every concept, we needed to shuffle our cards, we can rewrite our **shuffle_cards** function, so that we can include the ability to visualize our cards.

```
1   function shuffle_cards(gamedeck)
2   {
3       var _deck_size = ds_list_size(gamedeck);
4       var _cards_x = 130;
5       var _cards_y = 160;
6
7       randomize();
8       ds_list_shuffle(gamedeck);
9
10      // position cards on the table
```

CHAPTER 3   CARD GAME (PART 1)

```
11      var _cards = 1;
12      for(var _i = 0; _i < _deck_size; _i-=1)
13      {
14          obj_controller.deck[| _i].x = _cards_x;
15          obj_controller.deck[| _i].y = _cards_y;
16          obj_controller.deck[| _i].index = _i;
17          obj_controller.deck[| _i].visible = true;
18          if(_cards % 4 == 0)
19          {
20              _cards_x = 130;
21              _cards_y += 160;
22          }
23          else
24          {
25              _cards_x += 110;
26          }
27          _cards += 1;
28      }
29  }
```

Woah! That's some long piece of code! Let's break it and analyze it!

Lines 3-8: As we did before, we're importing the deck and shuffling it. The only new thing is that we now have two variables representing the proportions of the cards:

- **cards_x**: The horizontal starting position of the cards (the x value of the first card that we will place in the room)

- **cards_y**: The vertical starting position of the cards (the y value of the first card that we will place in the room)

Those two variables will help us positioning the cards in the room.

Line 11: Here we are declaring a new variable called **cards**. This variable will keep track of how many cards we have placed in the room.

83

Line 12: We start a *for* loop that will iterate for every card, counting from 0 to **deck_size**.

Lines 14–17: We set the coordinates of the i-th card and its index value, and we make it visible, so that it can be drawn in the room.

Lines 18–28: We want to place our cards in a 4 × 4 grid (since they are 16), so every time we place a card, we do a right shift on the X-axis to place the next one. When we place four cards in a row, we reset our X-coordinate to the starting value and increase the Y-coordinate so that we can start a new row.

To properly count how many cards we are placing in a row, we are using a mathematical function called *modulo*. The modulo function, in GML, is represented with the percent operator (%) and tells you what the remainder of the division between two numbers is. If the remainder of a division between A and B is 0, it means that you can divide an A number of elements in a number of groups of exactly B elements. So, we can know if we have placed four cards in a row with the following line of code:

```
(cards % 4) == 0
```

That way we can decide to start over from a new row. In fact, cards % 4 equals 0 only when **cards** is equal to a multiple of 4 (4, 8, 12, 16, etc.). This means that line 20 will be true only in that case.

Line 30: At the end of the loop, we increase the value of the **cards** variable to keep track of the number of cards we placed.

This is all we need to shuffle our cards and place them in the right position.

As we stated before, we want to be able to shuffle cards every time we press the enter key, so that we can reset the game. Let's do this right now!

Create a new **Key Press⊙Enter** event in *obj_controller* and add this single line in it:

```
1    shuffle_cards(deck);
```

Now, every time we press the enter key, the deck is going to be shuffled!

CHAPTER 3 CARD GAME (PART 1)

We are now ready to test what we did so far! Let's open the main room of our game, and let's get rid of the **obj_card** we put in there last time. Now Drag and Drop an instance of **obj_controller** in the room. Save and run (Figure 3-8)!

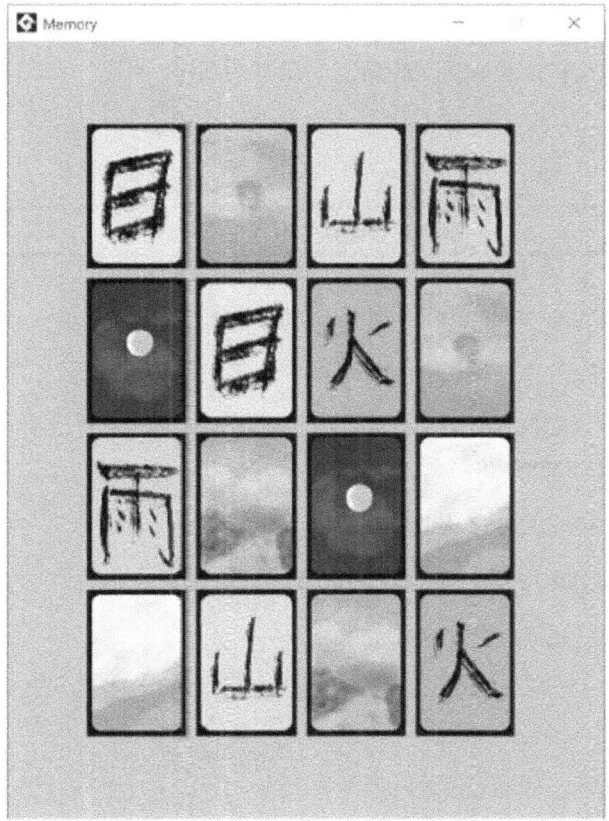

Figure 3-8. *The first version of the game allows for card shuffling and flipping*

Running the game, you will see a grid of cards showing their back. If you click them, they will flip. Cards are shuffled every time you run the game, and you can also shuffle them by pressing the enter key (Figure 3-8).

That's great! We are half the way to complete our Memory card game!

CHAPTER 3   CARD GAME (PART 1)

In the next chapter, we will complete our Memory card game, and we will see how to make it enjoyable by adding some new and fun features like the following:

- The constraint to flip no more than two cards per turn
- Some checks to see if the cards flipped are matching
- Victory checks to actually win the game
- A timer (when the time runs out, we lose the game)

TEST YOUR KNOWLEDGE!

1. What is a game design document (GDD)?
2. What are the most important characteristics of a GDD?
3. Why is it important to prepare a design of your game before you start coding?
4. What is an array? Why is it useful?
5. How can you access an element of an array?
6. What is a conditional statement?
7. Which conditional statements can we use in GML? How do they work?
8. What is a data structure?
9. What data structures does GameMaker offer?
10. Can you tell the difference between a stack and a queue?
11. What is a function? How can you make one in GameMaker?
12. What is a loop?
13. What is the difference between a while loop and a do-until loop?
14. Why do we use lists to represent a deck of cards for our game?

CHAPTER 4

Card Game (Part 2)

A game, by definition, needs to be playable, and so far, our card game is not – unless you enjoy flipping things endlessly for no reason.

So, let's add some fun to our Memory game!

In this chapter, we will define the game rules we designed in Memory GDD (in the previous chapter) to make it playable and enjoyable. We will implement the constraint to flip at most two cards per turn, and then we will add the functionality to check whether the cards are matching or not; we will also define some victory conditions and create a countdown to add some time-based gameplay that will make our game more challenging and fun.

So, get ready! We are going to learn new concepts and make our very first video game with GameMaker!

Finite-State Machines (FSMs)

A video game, just like any other software, is an interactive application. It takes inputs from the player and returns outputs generated from an elaboration. To get from inputs to outputs, the game (or the application) passes through a series of states.

Let's make an example: we want to buy a drink from a vending machine. We see from the machine's display that it's ready to take our money, so we insert cash. After receiving our money, the machine's display tells us the total amount we inserted, and it asks us to specify the product we want to buy. If we select a more expensive drink, the machine will just

CHAPTER 4   CARD GAME (PART 2)

say that the drink is too expensive, and it will request a top-up from you; if we choose a drink that costs exactly the amount we inserted or less, the machine will release the drink and store the money. The displayed import will be now the money we inserted minus the price of the drink. During the process of buying a drink, the vending machine passes through a number of states to get from input (money inserted) to the output (drink received).

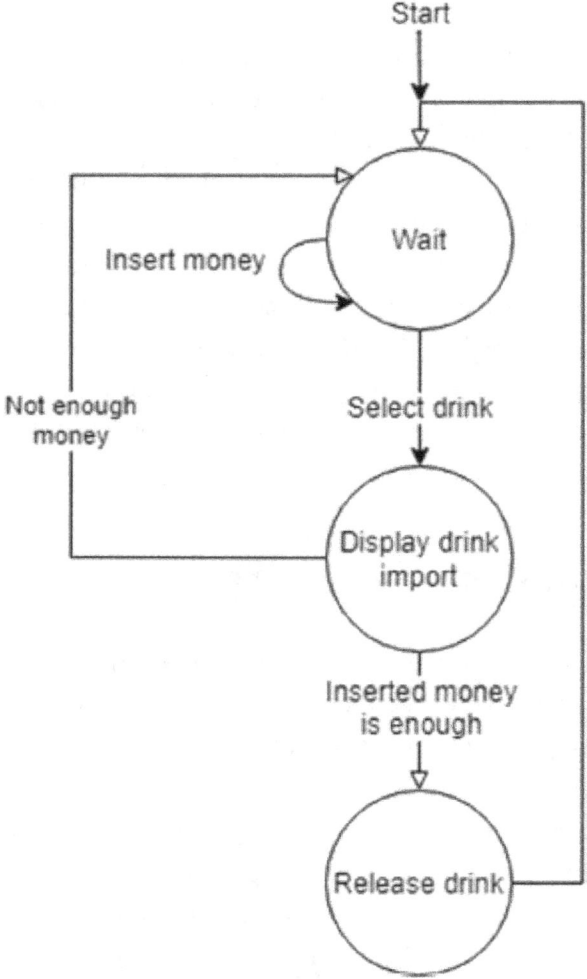

Figure 4-1. *FSM scheme of a vending machine*

Figure 4-1 represents the different states of the process of buying a drink from a vending machine. Black-headed arrows are user inputs, while white-headed arrows are consequences to the machine's elaborations.

When we approach the machine, it is in a waiting state (Wait), and it's ready to get an input. We can interact with the machine only in two ways (if you don't count kicking it when it doesn't work as expected): inserting money and selecting a drink.

If we insert money, the machine displays the import and remains in the Wait state.

If we select a drink, there are two possible cases:

- If we inserted enough money, the machine passes in the Release drink state giving us the drink we paid for (and possibly the change), and then it returns in the Wait state to start over again.

- If we didn't insert enough money, the machine just displays the amount of money needed and goes back to the Wait state waiting for you to insert the right amount of money.

Schematizing the process like we did is useful to have a clear idea of the set of actions and states that need to be implemented. You can get rid of all the technical details in the process (like counting money, recognizing coins, etc.) and focus on the important bits of the flow, like the interactions and the responses of the application (inputs and outputs).

That way of organizing flows is called **finite-state machine** (or just state machine).

A finite-state machine (FSM) is an abstract machine that can be in only one state at any given time. The state of that machine can change according to inputs; that change is called *transition*.

CHAPTER 4   CARD GAME (PART 2)

FSM is a huge topic that we don't need to explore in its entirety here. There are very interesting university courses about it that can give you a deep understanding of the power of this mathematical modeling tool widely used in computer science. Don't worry, I will give you all the information needed to use this tool for the purpose of this book.

An FSM has an entry point, a finite number of states, and a *transition function* that allows us to pass from a state to another.

But enough with that academic gibberish! How can an FSM help us with our game?

FSMs can be useful in design and development of video games because they can effectively represent the flow of a game, and a crucial point for the design and the correct implementation of any software is to be able to clearly represent their flow.

That being said, let's consider the flow that we want to implement in our card game.

First, we need a state where we can play; this will be a state in which the game will be waiting for the user's input. We can call this state **Playing**, as this will be the state where we can actively play. In this state, the input will be activated allowing us to flip cards.

When we flip two cards, we want the game to check if those two cards are the same: if they are, they get removed from the table; otherwise, they get flipped back. This is a phase in which the user input is blocked, and so we can say that the game is in a **Paused** state. In this phase, we will also check if there are any cards left on the table: if that's the case, the game goes back to the ***Playing*** state; otherwise, we check the victory condition, and the game will pass to either a ***Won*** or a ***Lost*** state.

Organizing our game flow like this, we can control our gameplay and our code more clearly, dividing it in separate moments.

So, we know that our game will have four states:

- **PLAYING**: We are playing, and the game is waiting for the player's inputs.

CHAPTER 4   CARD GAME (PART 2)

- **PAUSED**: No inputs permitted. The game checks the consequences of the player's actions and if the victory conditions are met. The player must wait until the end of the elaboration.

- **WON**: No more cards on the table. The player won the game!

- **LOST**: Time's up and there are still cards on the table. The player lost the game.

Now that we decided the states we need for the game, we can draw our FSM scheme connecting those states according to the game flow we just described (Figure 4-2).

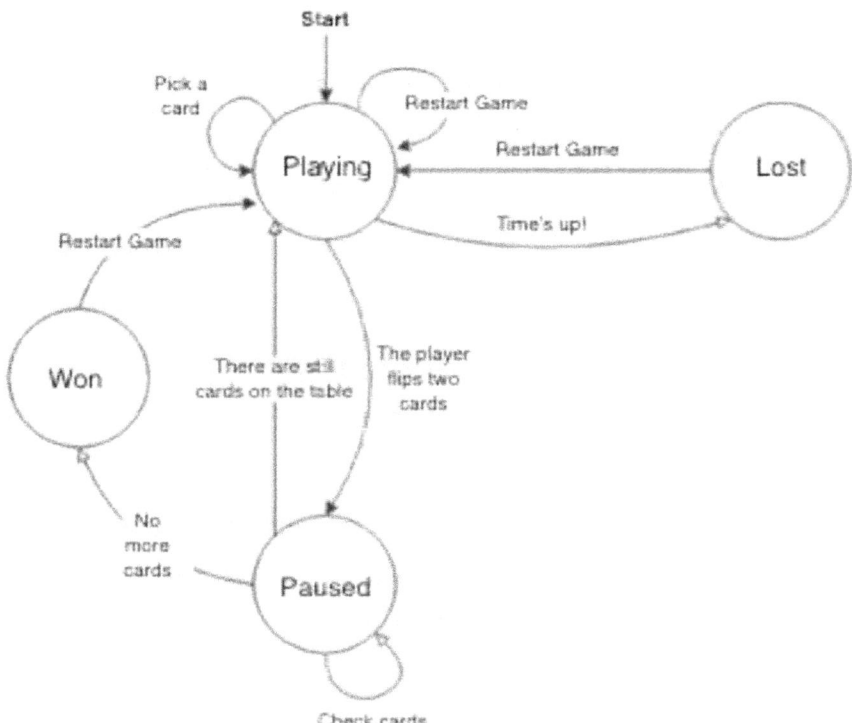

Figure 4-2. *FSM scheme for our Memory card game*

CHAPTER 4   CARD GAME (PART 2)

The FSM scheme makes clear the flow of the game and gives us a clear division between the separated moments of our gameplay and gives us an idea of what we need to develop. Let's make a list of all the features we are missing for each state:

- **Playing**
    - Flip cards: We already have it!
    - Pick cards: We need a system to store in memory the cards that we flipped, so that we can compare them.
    - Constraint of two cards: We need to make sure that the player cannot pick/flip more than two cards.
    - Restart game: We give the player the possibility to restart the game anytime.

- **Paused**
    - Confront cards: We need the game to check if the flipped cards match and then act consequently (take them out or flip them back).
    - Check victory: We want the game to check if we won the game (no more cards to pick) or not and act consequently.

- **Victory**
    - Victory message: We just show a victory message.
    - Restart game: We give the player the possibility to restart the game and play again.

- **Loss**

  - Game over message: We just show a message to tell the player he just lost the game.

  - Restart game: We give the player the possibility to restart the game and play again.

Structuring the tasks like that is very useful to keep the development clear and easy to follow.

This is something I want you to do anytime you have to code: spend time designing! The more time you spend thinking about what you're going to do and organizing it, the less time you spend coding and fixing bugs. Having a well-designed project and a clear set of features to implement, it's priceless and makes the coding way easier and faster.

Now that we have a clear plan, we can finally start coding!

Tip Spending time designing a game covering its flow and features before starting to code is very convenient and allows you to create a project that is not just a good game, but also a good software. This is very important to keep the game easy to modify and update by anyone. This is especially important when you have to work with other people.

Keep your design and your implementation easy to follow and well documented.

From State Machine to Code

We will code our game following the design we just created with our FSM.

CHAPTER 4　CARD GAME (PART 2)

First, we have to decide how to implement the concept of *game state*. The game state can be seen as a checkpoint, an information that tells you where you are in a certain moment of the execution of the game. This means that a game state is no more than a label that we associate to a certain moment of the application. A common way to create those labels is by declaring an **enumerator**. An enumerator (often shortened as enum) is a data type that allows you to create a list of objects with unique IDs associated (generally represented by integers). Using an enumerator, you can create labels with a human-readable name. In this case, we can use an enumerator to label game states.

You can declare an enumerator in GML like this:

```
1  enum MYENUM {
2      ITEM1,
3      ITEM2,
4      ITEM3
5  };
```

It's a GML's good practice to name your enums with all capital letters.

The game state will change according to what the player does, and this will direct the game flow and make things happen in the right moment.

Let's declare the game state enumerator and the current state global variable in obj_controller'sCreate event:

```
1  enum STATES {
2      PAUSED,
3      PLAYING,
4      WON,
5      LOST
6  };
7  global.game_state = STATES.PAUSED;
```

CHAPTER 4   CARD GAME (PART 2)

A couple of things to note:

- In GML, enumerators are implicitly declared as global scope variables, so we can access them from anywhere in the game.

- We need a global variable of type to represent the current state of the game.

The next problem we have to solve is how to pick and remember the cards that the player clicks. The simplest way to do this is to have two variables in the obj_controller object to store the cards selected.

It's a good idea to also add a third variable that will be just a counter of how many cards have been selected. This will help us getting that information with just one check.

Those three variables, I would suggest to have them global, as they need to be accessed by other instances, and we don't want to have more versions of them in other instances. It wouldn't make sense to have more than one counter telling us how many cards we selected, for example; same applies to the two selected cards.

Open up obj_controller's Create event, and add these lines just under the previous lines we added:

```
1   global.cards_picked = 0;
2   global.card_sel_1 = noone;
3   global.card_sel_2 = noone;
```

In the code above, we initialize the counter of the cards picked to 0 and the two global variables representing the two cards that the player can pick to *noone*. *Noone* is a special value that represents the lack of a value. We will use that value to represent the fact that the player has not selected any card.

CHAPTER 4   CARD GAME (PART 2)

Another line that we want to add, right after those, is a call to the function get_game_speed, which will allow us to set the speed of the game that we like. This is something we need to set, so that we can use time-bound features, like alarms. So, let's add this line right under the ones we just added to *obj_controller*'s *Create* event:

game_set_speed(30, gamespeed_fps);

Note **game_set_speed** is a new function that substituted the old way of setting a game speed in GameMaker, which was by defining a room speed in the room editor.

To access this value, for example, when you want to set an alarm, you can use the function **game_get_speed**.

Room speed-based methods are currently deprecated by the GML coding standard.

When the player clicks a card, we want the game to flip that card and check if the player already selected a card before; and if they have, we want the game to check if the two selected cards match. If they do, we put them away; if they don't, we flip them back.

We can use those global variables to store the selected cards as soon as the player selects them. When we see that the player is picking a second card, we can run the checks on the cards to see if it's a pair or not.

To know if the player picked one or two cards, we could rely on the order in which we access the two variables. In fact, if the code is consistent with the data access order and always fills the variables in the same order, we can be sure of those cases:

- If the first variable is empty, then the second will be empty as well, and we will be able to assign the selected card to the first variable.
- If the first variable is not empty, then the second will be empty, and we can assign the selected card to the second variable.

As soon as both the variables are filled with data, we run the checks, and then we set the values of the variables back to *noone*.

Now that we designed it, let's code it! Open up obj_card's Left Pressed event, and replace the existing code with the following:

```
1   if(visible and global.game_state == STATES.PLAYING)
2   {
3       face = 1;
4       global.cards_picked += 1;
5
6       if(global.cards_picked > 1)
7       {
8           global.card_sel_2 = self;
9           global.game_state = STATES.PAUSED;
10
11          if(global.card_sel_1.index == global.card_sel_2.index)
12          {
13              reset_selection(obj_controller.deck);
14              cover_all_cards(obj_controller.deck);
15              global.game_state = STATES.PLAYING;
16          }
17          else
```

```
18              {
19                      // check pair
20              }
21      }
22      else
23      {
24              global.card_sel_1 = self;
25      }
26 }
```

Line 1: Since we are writing the functionality to pick cards and we know that we can allow the player to pick cards only in the PLAYING state, here we check that we are in such a state. We also check that the card is visible because even if not visible, the card would be clickable anyway.

Line 3: This line flips the card by showing its face.

Lines 4: We update the counter of the selected cards. This is useful to trigger the victory checks that we will implement later.

Lines 6–9: We check if we already selected one card before this one; in that case, we assign the current card to global.card_sel_2, and we set the state of the game as PAUSED, so that we can start the checks.

Lines 11–16: Here we check the case in which the player just clicked twice on the same card. In this case, we reset the selection, we cover all the cards, and we set the state of the game back to PLAYING. We will see the implementation of reset_selection in a moment.

Lines 17–20: If the player clicked on two different cards, we need to run the checks to see if the two cards match or not. For now, we just added a placeholder comment because we still have to introduce a concept to be able to write that code. We will take care of this code in a bit.

Lines 22–24: If this is the first card that we select, we assign it to global.card_sel_1.

> **Note** Every instance in GameMaker has the `visible` property. It can be set as `true` or `false`, and it decides whether the instance is visible or not.
>
> When an instance is not visible, its Draw event won't be drawn. All the events that interact with the sprite of a non-visible object will still trigger, but the sprite won't be visible.

In the code we wrote for the Left Pressed event in the obj_card object, we added a placeholder comment for the code that checks the pairs, and we also referenced a function called **reset_selection** and another one called **cover_all_cards**. Let's take care of this code!

Let's start from the reset_selection script. What we want from this script is to reset the card selection in the global variables *card_sel_1* and *card_sel_2*. Let's create a new script by right clicking on the *Scripts* section in the *Assets Browser* and selecting *Create* ➤ *New* ➤ *Script*. Call the script "reset_selection" and add this code to it:

```
1  function reset_selection()
2  {
3      global.cards_picked = 0;
4      global.card_sel_1 = noone;
5      global.card_sel_2 = noone;
6  }
```

This piece of code resets all our global variables related to cards picking, and we can call it every time we need to reset the cards selection.

The second script we need to implement is cover_all_cards, which has the task of resetting the state and appearance of all the cards on the table and show them all covered (face on the table).

CHAPTER 4 CARD GAME (PART 2)

Create a new script called "cover_all_cards" and add this code to it:

```
1   function cover_all_cards(argument0)
2   {
3       var _deck = argument0;
4       if (!ds_list_empty(_deck))
5       {
6           var _deck_size = ds_list_size(_deck);
7
8           for(var _i = 0; _i< _deck_size; _i+=1)
9           {
10              _deck[| _i].face = 0;
11          }
12      }
13      else
14      {
15          show_error("ERROR: argument is not a ds_list!", true);
16      }
17  }
```

Line 3-6: We take the argument passed to the function, and we associate with a variable. Then we check that variable to make sure that it contains a list, and if it does, we pass it to the functionds_list_size, which will return the size of the ds_list that we will use in the following lines to loop in the elements of the ds_list.

Lines 8-11: We loop through the ds_list and set the face value of the cards to 0, so that all the cards will be associated with the spr_cardback sprite, according to the Step event of obj_card.

Lines 13-16: If the argument is not a ds_list, send an error through a the function show_error which will show the message on screen and terminate the game. This would make the function a bit easier to debug.

And that is all we need for those two supporting functions, but we have a bigger topic to go through and a new concept to introduce, to be able to check the pair of cards we selected. The thing is that we cannot let the check happening instantly; otherwise, the player will just see the cards flipping in a split-second on their back and will never be able to figure out which one is the second card that they flipped and caused the check to fail and both cards to be put face down. Because of that reason, we want to introduce a little delay, between the checks and the resulting action. This can be achieved using a software development concept called timer. A timer is a time measurement that happens at a certain point in an algorithm putting the calculations on hold for a specific amount of time, with the only aim of delaying some specific action. This concept is generally used to wait for the availability of a device or a system, or for user experience (UX) reasons, like in this case. In fact, it's not uncommon to have a necessity of just slowing down some actions for the user to be able to witness what is going on and get some kind of visual feedback. This is a very important step, as it allows the user to never lose track of what is going on; therefore, they will stay focused, and they will have a smoother experience.

Another way of achieving this result in software development (way more in use in modern applications, compared to a timer) is through the concepts of events and callback functions. An event is just a specific state of an application (yes, you can think about states in an FSM), and when this state is reached, we say that the event was triggered. When an event is triggered, there is one or more (depending on the programming language) callback functions that get called. An example of events and callback functions is shown by the events system in GameMaker: a click event is triggered, and as a consequence a callback function called "Left Pressed" is triggered.

If you should be using a timer or a combination of events and callback functions, it really depends on if your actions need to happen after a set amount of time or when a specific event is happening.

CHAPTER 4   CARD GAME (PART 2)

A Matter of Time

In GameMaker, we can express the concept of a timer using a feature called alarm. A GameMaker alarm is a combination of the concepts of timers and events and callback functions that we introduced in the previous section.

GameMaker's alarms are a set of callback functions associated with an array of integers. The array of integers, called alarm, has the purpose of holding the delay associated with each one of those callback functions. When you set a value different from zero in any of the elements of the alarm array, the game will start to countdown from that value to zero and then call the function associated with that specific array element. You can have up to 12 alarms per object in GameMaker, and you can define them just like you define any other event. You can define alarms as events because after all, this is a system of events and callback functions; the only difference is that the event that gets triggered is the expiration of the alarm.

In GameMaker, we can express the concept of a timer using a feature called alarm. A GameMaker alarm is a combination of the concepts of timers and events and callback functions that we introduced in the previous section. There's up to 12 alarms that you can set for every object in the game. Every alarm has a number and a function associated: the number represent the delay before the function gets called. So as you can see, it works a bit like a timer and a bit like a callback function.

This all works thanks to an array of integers that holds the delay values. To every one of those array elements, there is an associated callback function.

When the delay value of an alarm is set, the countdown starts, and when it reaches zero, the function gets called.

We need an alarm event and the associated callback function to be able to run the cards checks for our game using a little delay. Let's see how to do that!

CHAPTER 4 CARD GAME (PART 2)

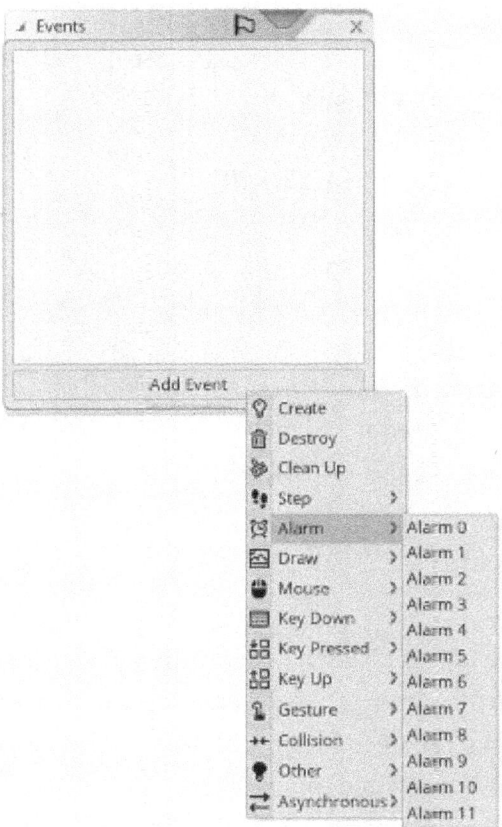

Figure 4-3. *Creating an alarm event*

Create an event for alarm[0] in obj_controller, by selecting Add Event
► Alarm ► Alarm 0 (as in Figure 4-3), and put this code inside:

```
1  /// @description Check pair
2  if(global.card_sel_1.type == global.card_sel_2.type)
3  {
4      var _card1 = global.card_sel_1.index;
5      var _card2 = global.card_sel_2.index;
6  deck[| _card1].visible = false;
```

103

CHAPTER 4   CARD GAME (PART 2)

```
7    deck[| _card2].visible = false;
8
9       if(check_victory(deck))
10      {
11   global.game_state = STATES.WON;
12      }
13   }
14
15   reset_selection();
16   cover_all_cards(deck)
17
18   if(global.game_state == STATES.PAUSED)
19   {
20   global.game_state = STATES.PLAYING;
21   }
```

Lines 2–13: We are checking if the cards have the same value, and in that case, it means that there is a match and we can remove the cards from the table. So, we grab the deck indexes of the selected cards (lines 4–5), and we set them to be invisible (lines 6–7).

Finally, we call a function that we didn't implement yet. This will run a check on the victory conditions, to see if that was the last pair.

Lines 15–21: After making the check on the selected pair, we reset the selection and flip back all the cards, and finally we reset the state to PLAYING (in case we didn't already), so that the player can keep playing.

The auxiliary function that we mentioned in the previous code, it's simple: it just loops through all the cards of the deck and checks if there is at least one card that is visible; if that's the case, it means that the game is not over and there is at least one more pair to match.

Let's create a new script called check_victory, and let's put this code inside:

```
1   function check_victory(argument0)
2   {
3   var _deck = argument0;
4   
5   if (ds_list_empty(_deck))
6   {
7   show_debug_message("ERROR: argument is not a ds_list!");
8   return false;
9   }
10  
11  var _deck_size = ds_list_size(_deck);
12  
13  for(var _i = 0; _i< _deck_size; _i+=1)
14  {
15          // not yet game over
16  if(_deck[| _i].visible == true)
17  {
18  return false;
19  }
20  }
21  
22  return true;
23  }
```

Lines 3-9: First of all, we grab the list from the argument, and we check if it's empty; if it is, we send a warning in form of a debug log to make the function a bit easier to debug. It's not ideal that we return false, in this case, because here false means the player lost the game, which is not technically true, if they never managed to play because the deck is empty.

CHAPTER 4   CARD GAME (PART 2)

Lines 11-22: After we checked that the list is not empty, we take its length and we iterate through all the elements of the list, and we check if there is at least one element that is visible, in which case it means that there is at least one pair of cards that still needs to be selected and matched. Hence, the player lost the game, because they didn't manage to match all the pairs before the time was up, so we return false (line 18); otherwise, if there is no element in the list that has the visibility set to true, it means that all the pairs have been matched and so we can return true (line 22).

We're nearly done! We only need to substitute the comment we put in the *Left Pressed* event in *obj_card* with a reference to the code associated with alarm[0].

So now that code should look like that:

```
1   if(visible and global.game_state == STATES.PLAYING)
2   {
3       face = 1;
4       global.cards_picked += 1;
5
6       if(global.cards_picked > 1)
7       {
8           global.card_sel_2 = self;
9           global.game_state = STATES.PAUSED;
10
11          if(global.card_sel_1.index == global.card_sel_2.index)
12          {
13              reset_selection(obj_controller.deck);
14              cover_all_cards(obj_controller.deck);
15              global.game_state = STATES.PLAYING;
16          }
17          else
```

```
18          {
19  obj_controller.alarm[0] = 1 * game_get_
    speed(gamespeed_fps);
20          }
21      }
22      else
23      {
24          global.card_sel_1 = self;
25      }
26  }
```

I highlighted for you line 19, because it's the only one we changed. Here we set the value of obj_controller's alarm[0] to 1 second, so that the check is done after 1 second from the selection of the second card, which gives the player enough time to see both the cards selected and memorize their position before they get flipped back.

This is the new way of setting the time for alarms in GameMaker. This new function *game_get_speed* returns the value that has been set for the game's speed in terms of frames per second (FPS), and it substitutes the old method of using individual room's speed values. But to be able to use *game_get_speed*, we need to set this game speed, and we are going to do it in obj_controller's Create event. So just add this one line to the code:

```
1   game_set_speed(30, gamespeed_fps);
```

We can finally test what we did! Go ahead and run the game. Now everything works fine (Figure 4-4)!

When you pick two cards, the game shows them to you for half a second and then decides if they match or not. If they do, they disappear; if they don't, they are flipped back. In any moment, when you press the enter key, the cards are reset and shuffled.

Awesome!

CHAPTER 4   CARD GAME (PART 2)

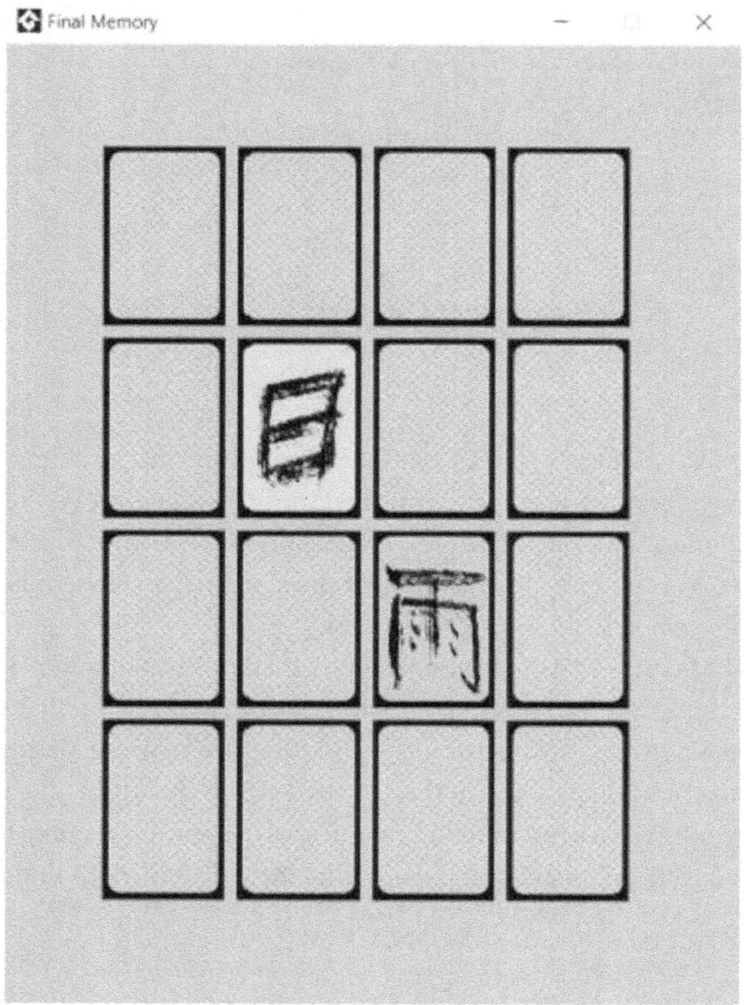

Figure 4-4. *Now we can see both the cards for some seconds before the game decides if they match or not*

We have this smooth gameplay, but we still lack the thrill of winning and losing. It's time for us to implement some fun victory condition!

CHAPTER 4   CARD GAME (PART 2)

Play to Win!

In this game's GDD, we specified that the game will be time-based. Meaning that the game needs to be won before the time's up.

To implement this, in our game, we can use the concept that we just introduced in the previous section: alarms.

We will set the alarm every time we start or restart the game at a fixed value of 60 seconds. When the game starts, the time decreases until it reaches 0. When this happens, we check if the game is lost or won using our function *check_victory*.

To keep track of the time passing, we need a couple of variables: one that represents the total amount of game time we have (we will use it to set and reset the alarm) and one that represents the current time. The current time variable will decrease while we play, and it will be displayed on screen to give the player a measure of the remaining time.

Open obj_controller and add the following lines inside its Create event:

```
1    play_time = 60;
2    cur_time = 60;
```

As we mentioned earlier, we will use those two variables to store the time in seconds.

`play_time` is the total time that we can play the game. We will use this variable anytime we want to start/restart the game to set the alarm to the right value.

`cur_time` is a variable that will store the time at any moment and will be used to be displayed on screen for the player to see. We are going to use *cur*_time as the value of a new alarm that will check the victory condition, and we will also draw its value on screen.

CHAPTER 4   CARD GAME (PART 2)

So let's create a new Alarm 1 event for obj_controller and add this code to it:

```
1   /// @description Game over checks
2   cur_time = 0;
3   if(check_victory(deck))
4   {
5   global.game_state = STATES.WON;
6   }
7   else
8   {
9   global.game_state = STATES.LOST;
10  }
```

Line 1: Time's up! We're setting cur_time to 0.

Lines 3–10: We check if there are still any pairs that need to be matched using *check_victory*, and then we set the game to either the WON or LOST state, according to the result of *check_victory*.

Now that we have our alarm[1] event to check the victory condition and set the current game state, we need to connect it to our code, so that it's actually useful. We want this check to run when the time is up, so we will set it in the Create obj_controller with a value based on the value of play_time, which equals to 60, as we decided that a game is going to last 1 minute.

So just add this one line at the end of obj_controller's Create event:

```
1   alarm[1] = play_time*game_get_speed(gamespeed_fps);
```

Now nearly everything is set. We only need to visualize the time remaining, so that the player knows and sees a message when they win or lose.

To show the time, we need to create an HUD (Heads-Up Display), which is a part of the GUI (Graphical User Interface). An HUD is displayed as an overlay on screen during the game and has the task of showing the player some valuable information (in our case the time passing).

GameMaker has a special event to handle GUI drawing, which is called Draw GUI event.

Draw GUI is a sub-event of the Draw event, and it's specialized in drawing GUI elements. One of the most important differences between the two is that in the Draw GUI event, the coordinates of the screen are fixed and are not bound to the room, but to the game window. That means that if you draw a picture or a text at coordinates x=0, y=0, it will always be drawn in the upper-left corner of the screen, even if it's not correspondent to the upper-left corner of the room.

Note Draw GUI is a specialized event that is used to draw UI elements. The difference from the Draw event is that in Draw GUI the coordinates are relative to the game window, while in the Draw event they are relative to the room.

In the code for the Draw GUI event, we want to check the state we are in and update the timer if we are still playing; otherwise, we want to show a game over message according to the state we are in.

To write a message on screen, we need a font asset, which we can create by right-clicking Fonts in the Resources panel and selecting Create Font. You can use the font you like; just make sure you create two fonts, one called fnt_message of size 20 and one called fnt_timer of size 12.

Now we need to add the code. Let's create a new Draw GUI event for obj_controller and put this code inside:

```
1   /// @description draw UI
2   switch(global.game_state)
3   {
4       case STATES.PLAYING:
5       cur_time = ceil(alarm[1]/game_get_
                speed(gamespeed_fps));
```

CHAPTER 4   CARD GAME (PART 2)

```
6           break;
7
8       case STATES.WON:
9           alarm[1] = -1;
10          draw_set_font(fnt_state);
11          draw_set_color(c_red);
12          draw_text(room_width/2 - 100, room_height/2 - 100,
            "YOU WON!");
13          break;
14
15      case STATES.LOST:
16          alarm[1] = -1;
17          draw_set_font(fnt_state);
18          draw_set_color(c_red);
19          draw_text(room_width/2 - 100, room_height/2 - 100,
            "YOU LOST!");
20          break;
21
22      default:
23          break;
24  }
25
26  draw_set_font(fnt_timer);
27  draw_set_color(c_white);
28  draw_text(90, 0, "Time left: " + string(cur_time));
```

   Lines 2: This is the switch that allows us to draw different info in the HUD according to the state in which the game is.

   Lines 4–6: We update the value of cur_time, which represents the remaining time that we want to draw on screen (lines 26–28).

CHAPTER 4 CARD GAME (PART 2)

Lines 8–20: We disable alarm[1] by setting its value to -1, and then we draw on screen a message to say if the player won or lost, according to the current game state.

Lines 26–28: We draw on screen the timer using the update value of cur_time.

Note draw_set_font and draw_set_color must be called every time you want to write a text calling draw_text. In fact, those two functions allow you to set the font and the color of the text you're going to write on screen.

As a finishing touch, we want the time to be reset also when we reshuffle the cards pressing the enter key. We also want to make sure that the game state is set again to Wait (0).

So let's open up obj_controller's Key Down ⊙ Enter event and add these two lines at the end of the code:

```
1   cur_time = play_time;
2   alarm[1] = play_time * game_get_speed(gamespeed_fps);
```

Those two lines will make sure that when you press enter, the game timer will be reset to 60 seconds and that the game state will be set back to Wait (0), so that the player can play again and the victory/loss message will not be prompted anymore.

Let's run the game and see if everything's alright (Figure 4-5)!

If you followed and coded along, the game should play as expected, and now you have a complete game with victory and loss conditions that's replayable and fun!

Good job!

CHAPTER 4 CARD GAME (PART 2)

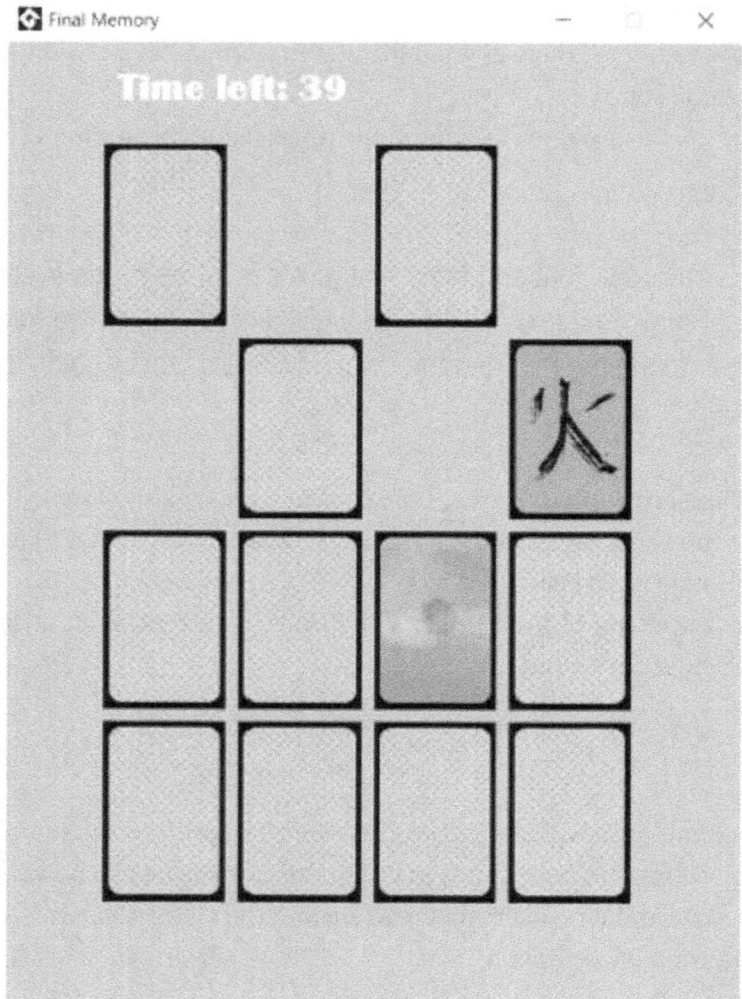

Figure 4-5. *Our complete memory game with a time-based gameplay!*

You have your very first and complete video game made with GML and GameMaker: Studio 2! Congratulations!

CHAPTER 4   CARD GAME (PART 2)

Take your time to enjoy this exciting moment and feel great, because you achieved something impressive! Just think about it: before starting to read Chapter 3, you never coded a game in GameMaker; and now you have a fully working card game with a time mode, nice graphics, and a cool gameplay!

Never forget to recognize and cheer on your achievements, because this helps you to not giving up and not feeling like you're wasting time.

Now that you have Memory, you can free your imagination and try to improve it by adding some features, some game modes, or anything else you might think about.

In the next chapter, we are going to start a new exciting project. We will code a top-down shoot 'em up game introducing a lot of new features and concepts like enemies, bullets, score, and much more!

TEST YOUR KNOWLEDGE!

1. What is a finite-state machine?
2. How can an FSM help you create your game?
3. Can you design an FSM of a vending machine?
4. What are game states?
5. Can you describe the meaning of the Wait state in the game flow?
6. Why is the design phase so important?
7. What are enumerators?
8. How can you declare and access an enumerator in GML?
9. What is the scope of enumerators?
10. Can you describe the visible property of an object?

CHAPTER 4 CARD GAME (PART 2)

11. Can you interact with an object while it's not visible (visible == false)?

12. What's an HUD?

13. What's the difference between Draw and Draw GUI?

14. What do we mean when we talk about the fun factor?

15. Why is immersion important in your game?

16. Can you think of a new feature you can add to our Memory game to make it more fun? Can you design it?

17. What is an alarm in GameMaker, and how does it work?

CHAPTER 5

Fixed Shooter

Making your first video game, you made the very first step into the world of game development! But don't settle on that! **The job of a game developer is to constantly study, play, and make games.** So, let's start a new project!

In this and the next chapter, we are going to create a game belonging to one of the most popular and important genres of the video games history: shoot 'em up!

A shoot 'em up (or shmup) game consists in the player facing multiple enemies shooting 'em up (you don't say?) and dodging their bullets.

It's still debated which design elements are canonical in a shmup game. Anyway, we are happy with the recognized basic definition: a game in which the player must face multiple enemies shooting them down and dodging their bullets. That's exactly what we are going to create in this chapter!

Anyway, it's important to do a little introduction to the genre, so that we can understand better what we are talking about.

History of the Genre

Shoot 'em up – also known as shmup or STG – is one of the most enduring and purest game genres in the history of video games. Born in 1962 with Spacewar!, the genre had its golden age in the years between 1980 and 1995. This majestic era for the genre brought to us some of the best shmups of all time; legends like Space Invaders, Galaga, the 1940 series,

CHAPTER 5　FIXED SHOOTER

Darius, Ikaruga, R-Type, Raiden, and DonPachi – but also the entire run-and-gun sub-genre (e.g., Contra and Metal Slug) – saw the light in those years.

If the 1980s were the years of the definition of the shoot 'em up genre, where games perfected and defined the standard of the genre (like scoring mechanics, waves of enemies, bullet patterns, etc.), the 1990s were the years in which those concepts were pushed to their limits: enemies greatly increased in number, and bullets started to fill the screen like never before, with a lot of colors, patterns, and flashes. Some shmups started to become something more than improvements on Space Invaders and Galaga; they became precursors of a new extreme sub-genre: bullet hell or danmaku (弾幕) in Japan.

Bullet hell is a sub-genre of shoot 'em up and focuses on the player dodging complex patterns of enemies and bullets while scoring points by killing enemies. Bullet hell games often hide some interesting mechanics like DonPachi's combo mechanic in which you have to keep the combo chain to maximize your score or Bangai-O's grazing mechanic in which you have to graze bullets without taking damage to greatly increase your counter-attack's power.

The possibilities with shoot 'em ups and their sub-genres are endless, and they surely can teach you a lot about game design and gameplay mechanics. Think about it: they are improving on the same concept of killing a lot of enemies shooting at them since 1960s, and they still are popular and one of the world's favorite genres.

It's important and very interesting to note how pure this genre remained in the years. In fact, some of the core mechanics are still there, untouched. For example, in those games, it is very important that controls are precise and smooth. Another interesting thing to note is that background story is very marginal, because gameplay is the main focus of the genre. Shoot 'em up players want to deal with a huge number of enemies and test their reflexes and dodging skills (often in fast-paced levels) and don't really care about the reason why they're doing it.

CHAPTER 5   FIXED SHOOTER

That's why it's a very interesting case of study to us! We can concentrate on game mechanics and gameplay and study some of the most interesting features that a game can have, like bullets, enemies' movements, camera scrolling, power-ups, and of course energy and ammunition management.

In this chapter, we are going to create a fixed shooter, that is, a shoot 'em up game with fixed screen (non-scrolling level) and some limitations, like the fact that enemies are lined up attacking or advancing at regular intervals of time and the player can move only left and right and has just one type of attack. Some famous fixed shooters from which we are taking the inspiration are Space Invaders (Taito, 1978) and Galaga (Namco, 1981).

The next chapter will build on the work we are going to do on this chapter, allowing us to create a top-down STG (like Ikaruga, Star Fox, DonPachi, etc.) using assets and code from our fixed shooter and improving on it adding new features like power-ups, vertical scrolling, enemies following patterns, and other exciting features like boss fights! We are going to get deeper on boos fights with a special chapter (Chapter 7) dedicated to them.

So, let's go ahead and design our shoot 'em up game starting – as usual – with a game design document!

Space Gala (GDD)

Space Gala is a single-player shoot 'em up game – specifically a fixed shooter – in which the player has to eliminate all the enemies shooting at them and survive dodging all their attacks before they get too near the home base.

CHAPTER 5   FIXED SHOOTER

Story and Setting

You are colonel Jonathan Spacepants, and you are the last hope for mankind. Your mission is to destroy the alien fleet before they reach our space station.

Gameplay

Space Gala revolves around dodging and shooting. It's very important to keep the player focused on those two activities maintaining a fast pace but also giving the player a good amount of satisfaction and motivation.

Satisfaction will be increased by smooth controls and fun combat.

Motivation can be reached by giving the player a sense of progression. Progression can be achieved by increasing the difficulty of the game from level to level, to keep the challenge going while the player improves their skills.

Victory Conditions

The game can be won by eliminating all the enemies in a level.

You can lose both by dying and allowing the enemies to advance reaching the bottom of the level.

Controls

The player can control the spaceship by using the **arrow keys** to move left and right only and the **spacebar** to attack.

It's very important, for the genre, to have precise and smooth controls. We don't want to add any friction in the player's movements.

Right Arrow: Move right.

Left Arrow: Move left.
Spacebar: Attack – a single bullet dealing standard damage.
Esc: Open the menu.

Menu

You can open/close the menu by using the Esc key. Via the menu, you can close the game, restart it, or resume the paused game.

A smaller version of the menu should be shown when the game is over to allow the player to restart or close the game.

Pacing

The sense of urgency should be the preponderant feeling in Space Gala. You need to wipe out a fleet of aliens before they reach the base and/or kill you. The aliens are continuously moving, and you need to be a fast and precise shooter to deal with them quickly.

Enemies

There is just one type of enemy:

- **Reds**: Basic enemies that move left and right and advance while randomly shooting.
  - HPs (Health Points): 1.
  - ATK (How much damage they inflict): 1.
  - Movements: They move left and right and regularly jump down by X pixels.

CHAPTER 5   FIXED SHOOTER

Game Modes

There is just one arcade game mode. The player must kill all the enemies to win the game.

Level 1

Level 1 is pretty simple. The player has to face a fleet of nasty red aliens that want to approach the space station.

The aliens will dodge the bullets by continuously moving left and right while they recharge their FTL engines to jump toward the space station. They can jump no more than 30 pixels forward, and they need to wait approximately 5 seconds before the FTL engine recharges and they can jump again.

The aliens will shoot randomly in front of them (easy to dodge).

The level is made of one group of 16 aliens.

Similar Games and Influences

Space Gala is obviously inspired by Space Invaders and Galaga.

The gameplay is more like the Space Invaders experience, with the aliens descending gradually and sporadically shooting.

Other notable games of the same genre are Centipede, Galaxian, and Moon Cresta.

Target Audience

Fixed shooter today is a niche sub-genre of STG. The audience is not very wide, but it's super passionate and cares a lot about the purity of the genre.

From GDD to the Game

Let's start by creating a new project called Space Gala. To do that, open GameMaker: Studio 2 and select File ➤ New Project from the menu bar at the top of the window.

Now that we have our new project, we need to create all the assets to get started and build our game!

Assets

We will need some sprites and other assets for our game. You can either make them yourself or download them from the companion GitHub repository of this book.

Whether you download them or made them yourself, the following is a complete list of all the assets needed in this game. Make sure that your custom assets are compatible with those or that you make the right changes to avoid any incompatibility.

spr_player

This is the sprite representing the player's spaceship.

This sprite is of dimensions 50 × 43 pixels and has the pivot point in the middle-center.

The **pivot point** is the reference point that will be used to calculate the position of the sprite. For example, if we set the pivot in the middle-center of the image, when we will move an instance using that sprite to coordinates 0,0, the center of the sprite will be exactly at coordinates 0,0, so we will be able to see only the bottom-right corner of the sprite.

To change the pivot point of a sprite, open up the sprite and head to the combo box just above the sprite preview (Figure 5-1). There you can select the point in which you want your pivot point to be. Alternatively, you can select *Custom* from the combo box and select the point yourself by clicking directly on the image in the point of the sprite you want your pivot to be.

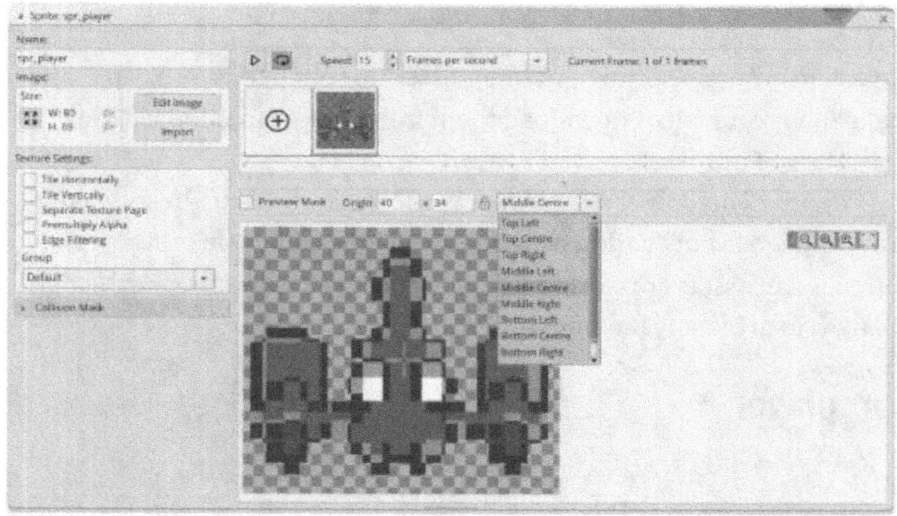

Figure 5-1. *Changing the pivot point for a sprite*

Because we want our spaceship to be hittable by enemies' bullets, we need to tell GameMaker that this specific sprite can collide with other objects. How do we do that? Using collision masks!

A sprite's collision mask is the area used to calculate if that sprite is colliding with any other sprite or not – if it does, a collision event for the object associated with that sprite is triggered.

CHAPTER 5 FIXED SHOOTER

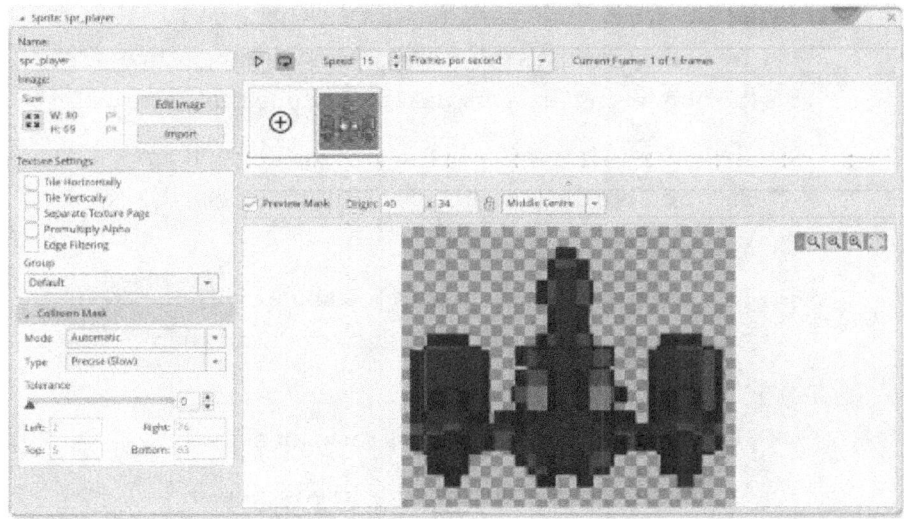

Figure 5-2. *Applying a collision mask to a sprite*

To create a collision mask for spr_player, just click the Collision Mask button to open up a new section that allows you to set up the collision mask you want (Figure 5-2). There are various options. Let's check them out:

- **Mode**: The mode decides how the mask is positioned on the image and can be of three types:

    - Automatic: GameMaker calculates by itself where to put the mask based on the image (it basically tries to fit the colored parts and ignore the transparent pixels).

    - Full Image: The mask is applied on the entirety of the image ignoring transparency.

    - Manual: You have to position the mask on the image by yourself.

125

- **Type:** The type of the mask decides the shape and nature of the mask. It's the most important thing, since it's the one setting that can make your game run slower.

    - Rectangle: The mask consists in a rectangle. If any sprite enters the coordinates of this rectangle, the collision event is triggered.

    - Rectangle with rotation: It's a rectangle collision mask that is able to rotate with the sprite to keep the right collision area.

    - Ellipse (slow): The mask consists in an ellipse.

    - Diamond (slow): A diamond-shaped collision mask – very useful to approximate plane-like objects like our spaceship!

    - Precise (slow): The mask precisely mimics the image shape (works only with Automatic and Full Image modes).

    - Precise per frame (slow): The mask precisely mimics the image shape and is recalculated once per frame (in case you rotate it or resize it).

For our spaceship, an automatic rectangle-shaped mask is more than sufficient; but if you want, you can alternatively use a diamond or precise mask; since it's just one object, it won't affect much the performance of the game.

CHAPTER 5 FIXED SHOOTER

spr_bullet_player

This is the sprite we are going to use for the player's bullets.

It's a 16 × 16-pixel sprite representing a yellow pellet.

Its pivot point is in the middle-center.

You can safely select an automatic rectangle collision mask, for this one.

spr_life

This is the sprite we are going to use to represent the player's HP.

It's a 16 × 16-pixel heart-shaped sprite.

Its pivot point is in the middle-center.

This one doesn't need a collision mask, as you might have guessed.

spr_enemy_red

This is the sprite that we will use for red alien spaceships.

It's a 16 × 18-pixel sprite with pivot point set at the bottom-center.

You can safely choose an automatic/manual rectangle collision mask; but if you feel like it, you can choose a more accurate collision mask, like ellipse or precise.

spr_background

Of course, we need a background image to give the player the idea that we are in deep space!

This is a 256 × 256-pixel image representing the space that we are going to repeat covering all of our room's surface.

Other than sprites, we will also need some fonts to manage the aesthetic of the information we are going to show on the screen (score, HP, menu, etc.).

It's up to you to choose the font type, but here you can find some interesting characteristics of those fonts.

fnt_score

The font that we will use to show information on screen like HPs (Health Points) and score.

Font Type: Arial
Style: Regular
Size: 14
Leave the rest at their default value.

fnt_messages

This is a font we will use to show messages like the current game state or the menu options.

Font: Arial
Style: Black
Size: 14
Leave the rest at their default value.

rm_level_1

Right-click the default room room0 and rename it rm_level_1. Double-click it, and the room will open revealing the Room Editor as a left sidebar.

In the Room Editor, head to Properties ➤ Room Settings and make sure that width is 1024 and height is 768.

CHAPTER 5　FIXED SHOOTER

Now go in Layers and click Background layer; a new section will appear just below the layers list named Background Layer Properties. Go ahead and click No Sprite to select spr_background. Now check both Horizontal Tile and Vertical Tile, right below it.

That's it. The room is properly set up and should show a preview of the spr_background sprite repeating itself for the entire surface of the room, making the impression that we're in front of the vastness of the universe. Cool, isn't it?

Making Features, Not Objects

We are going to create a total of five objects, for our game: the player, the game controller, one enemy, and two bullets. We will need those objects to manage every aspect of the logics of our game – from movements to shooting to the menu management. We won't cover the objects' creation by creating them one by one, but we will code following the concepts and gameplay elements we need to implement. **It's important to understand that your work is not to assemble pieces of something pre-built by someone else.** You are not just following instructions; you are understanding how to make a game by yourself. I want you to be completely independent at the end of this book, so that you can make games and learn new things by yourself, without having to ask someone else to solve a problem for you.

Your work is, and should always be, to add features to your game. So, we will cover one by one each feature and gameplay element that we need to implement for our game. I hope this will help you to understand the connection between every element that composes a game.

Let's start from the movements. In the next section, we will understand and implement the functionalities to move our spaceships with the arrow keys and to make the enemies move left and right and jump down every five seconds.

Movements

We will start from the player's avatar. Right-click Objects in the Resources sidebar, select Create Object and name it **obj_player**.

Make a new Create event for obj_player by clicking Add Event in the object's Events window and selecting Create. Now add to that event the following code:

```
1    hp = 10;
2    spd = 3;
```

Line 1: Sets the player's health to 10.

Line 2: Sets the movement speed for the player to 3 pixels. Since we are going to manage the movement in the Step event and it occurs once per frame, this means that the player will move 3 pixels per frame (3 pixels × 60 frames = 180 pixels per second).

According to our GDD, the player object should be able to move left and right smoothly without any acceleration or friction.

To do that, in the obj_player's Event window, click Add Event and select Key Down ▶ Left, to create a Key Press ▶ Left key event for obj_player and add the following code:

```
1    if (x > 0 + sprite_width/2)
2    {
3        x -= spd;
4    }
```

The code above checks if the player is still inside the left margin of the screen, and if that's the case, it moves the object by decreasing its X-coordinate by spd (that we initialized to 3). We are decrementing the value of x using a combination of operators: subtract (-) and assign (=), which will assign to *x* the result of *x − spd*.

CHAPTER 5 FIXED SHOOTER

> **Note** The concatenation of the assignment operator (=) and arithmetic operators (like +, -, *, /) creates compound assignment operators (+=, -=, *=, /=). These operators perform an arithmetic operation and then assign the result to the variable. For example, x += 5 is equivalent to x = x + 5.

The code we defined above is executed once per frame, so – as we just said before – it will be a movement of spd* 60 = 180 pixels per second. We need to add half the width of the sprite to 0 (i.e., the x margin of the room) because the pivot point of our sprite is in the middle-center – if we don't do this, only half of our sprite would be visible, since the coordinates are calculated for the pivot of the sprite and so it would be allowed to move left until the pivot reaches x = 0.

Obviously, we could have safely written x > sprite_width/2 instead of x > 0 + sprite_width/2; but to write that 0 can greatly increase the readability of the code, because it makes clear that we are referring to the room's left margin + half the size of the sprite. **Sometimes it's better to be explicit for the sake of readability**, especially if the verbosity doesn't impact the performance of the game – like in this case.

Let's do something very similar for the right arrow key. In obj_player, click Add Event and select Key Down ➤ Right and add the following code to it:

```
1   if (x <room_width - sprite_width/2)
2   {
3       x += spd;
4   }
```

The code above checks if the object is still inside the margins defined by the width of the room minus half the width of the sprite. We need to subtract half the width of the sprite to the width of the room because the

CHAPTER 5 FIXED SHOOTER

pivot point of our sprite is in the middle-center – not doing this means that we would see only half of the sprite for the same reason we had to add that value to 0 in the Key Press ➤ Left event.

Now, just to test if we're doing this good, open up rm_level_1 and drag and drop obj_player in the middle of the room. Press F5 or click the Run icon in the toolbar to compile and run the game (Figure 5-3).

If you followed the instructions, you will be able to move left and right using the left and right arrow keys, and your character will stop moving reaching the left and right margin. Cool! You made your first control movements! That's an exciting goal! Controls are very smooth and arcade-styled. You move without frictions or accelerations, and that's perfect as it is! No need to tweak it further!

Figure 5-3. *Running the game for the first time*

CHAPTER 5   FIXED SHOOTER

Now that we have our player's avatar working, we need to take care of the enemies!

Right-click Objects in the Resources sidebar and select Create Object, and then go ahead and create a new object called **obj_enemy_red**. This will be our first enemy! According to the GDD, it's a very weak enemy with just one HP, and it can deal only one damage to the player. It moves left and right and sporadically shoots a bullet toward us. That's a lot of new things! Let's start step by step! **Divide et impera** – as the Romans (and software engineers) used to say!

We want obj_enemy_red to perform a swinging movement like the one in Space Invaders and Galaga, but a little bit smoother! Our red aliens will swing left and right so that they are harder to hit and can dodge some of the player's bullets, and they will slowly advance toward the player direction.

This is a gameplay trick to make the enemies harder but without writing an AI algorithm, which requires way more effort and knowledge. Also, we don't need a very advanced AI for our enemies because they are a lot! We can be happy with the fact that they move left and right forcing the player to anticipate the shot. The fact that there are a lot of enemies to kill and that they slowly advance creates pressure – that's more than enough to make our little game challenging.

So, the aliens will move from left to right and then go back from right to left and repeat. To do this, we can calculate a complex oscillation function using trigonometry notions, or we can just move toward a direction until we reach a boundary and then invert the direction until we reach the other boundary. I think the second idea is better, because it's easier to implement and understand and I am a big fan of the KISS (Keep It Simple, Stupid) principle.

CHAPTER 5 FIXED SHOOTER

Open up obj_enemy_red and click Add Event ➤ Create to add a Create event, and then add the following code:

```
1   hp = 1;
2   atk = 1;
3   spd = 1;
4
5   dir = 1;
6   start_x = x - 25;
7   end_x = x + 25;
8
9   move_down_speed = game_get_speed(gamespeed_fps) * 5;
10  alarm[0] = move_down_speed;
```

Lines 1-2: We are creating an hp variable to keep track of the resilience of this enemy and an atk variable to know how much damage it will deal. In this case, the enemy has one HP and deals one damage point, so it would be safe to omit those two variables and just make it die when hit or deal a single damage when they hit something; but – as I'm always repeating – it's important to structure your code so that it's manageable and understandable by you and other people. It's a very good habit to write generic code that can be reused for other similar tasks – in this case, it can be used to create different enemies.

Line 3: This is the speed variable. Just like for obj_player, we are defining a variable that tells us the speed at which the alien should move. You can set it whatever value you like, but it's fine for now to keep it at 1.

Line 5: This is the variable that decides the direction toward which the alien is moving. In fact, this variable will be multiplied to spd so that we can change its value to a positive value or negative value depending on if dir equals to 1 or -1. Moving right means increasing the x value, and moving left means decreasing it.

135

Line 6: This is our left limit (25 pixels on the left of the alien's original position). The alien will move left until they reach or pass the X-coordinate; then they will invert their direction.

Line 7: This is the right limit (25 pixels on the right of the alien's original position). The alien will move right until they reach or pass the X-coordinate; then they will invert their direction.

Lines 9–10: Here we declare the variable move_down_speed to 5 seconds and use it to set alarm 0 to that value. We will use this alarm to make the alien ship move down every 5 seconds. You can safely change move_down_speed's value to whichever value you prefer, but I think that 5 seconds is a good amount of time for a first level.

Now that we have our variables set in the Create event, we need to make good use of them to manage the movements of the alien.

In obj_enemy_red, click the Add Event button and select a Step event and write up this code in it:

```
1   if (x <= start_x or x >= end_x)
2   {
3       dir *= -1;
4   }
5
6   x += spd * dir;
```

Line 1: This line checks if the object is going out of bounds relatively to the start_x and end_x variables we defined in the Create event.

Line 3: If we are going out of bounds (so the condition checked at line 1 is true), we invert the object direction by multiplying dir by -1.

Line 6: Just after we did our checks, we can safely modify the x value by adding to it spd times dir. If dir is positive, we will move right; if it's negative, we will move left.

> **Note** Multiplying a number by -1 always gives you the same number with opposite sign.
>
> Let X be any number greater than zero, then it's always true that
>
> X * -1 = -X
>
> -X * -1 = X
>
> In general, when you multiply a positive number by a negative number, you get a negative number; when you multiply a negative number by a negative number, you get a positive number.

Now we need to add the functionality for the enemy to move down. In obj_enemy_red, go ahead and create an Alarm 0 event by clicking the Add Event button and selecting Alarm ➤ Alarm 0. Now write the following code inside of the event:

```
1   y += 50;
2   alarm[0] = move_down_speed;
```

In the code above, we increase the y value by 50 so that the alien ship jumps down by 50 pixels, and then we reset the alarm to the same value so that after 5 more seconds (or whichever value you choose), the ship will jump down by another 50 pixels.

Let's test if we did everything good by dragging obj_enemy_red in the middle of room0, and press F5 or click the Run button in the toolbar to compile and execute the game (Figure 5-4).

CHAPTER 5 FIXED SHOOTER

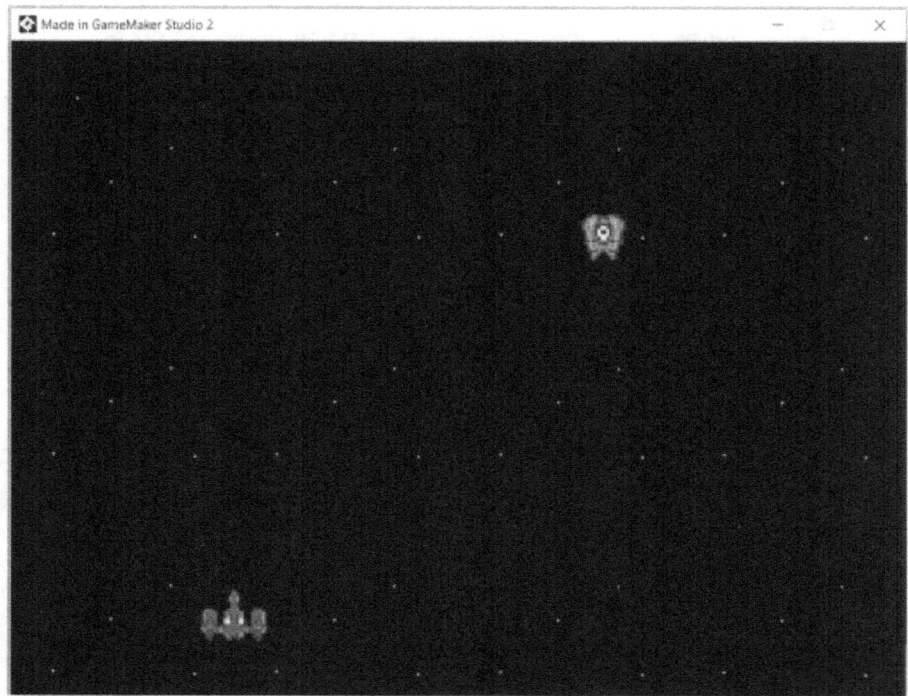

Figure 5-4. *We added to the game the swinging enemy!*

Great! Our red alien ship moves left and right, and it jumps down by 50 pixels every 5 seconds! Amazing!

Now close the game and go back to GameMaker; next up: shooting!

Shooting

The concept of shooting we are going to create is based on a variable that both the player and the aliens have: atk.

atk decides the amount of damage that an object inflicts on others. To make this work, we need to pass that value to the bullet object, so that when the bullet collides with an instance of another object, it inflicts the right damage.

Let's start by creating a bullet object.

CHAPTER 5   FIXED SHOOTER

Right-click Objects in the Resources sidebar and select Create Object to create a new object and name it **obj_bullet_player**.

This will be the bullet shot by the player when they press the spacebar.

Assign to this object spr_bullet_player and click Add Event ➤ Create and add this one line of code:

```
1    atk = 1;
2    spd = 10;
```

Line 1: We are assigning 1 to the bullet's atk variable so that it deals one damage. We will use this value to decrease the hp of the instance colliding with the bullet.

Line 2: We assign 10 to the bullet's spd variable so that we can later set its velocity by assigning this value to the speed built-in variable.

Note   Speed is a GameMaker's built-in variable that allows an instance to travel by moving by *speed* pixels per frame in the direction faced by the instance. An instance's direction is decided by the value of the built-in *direction* variable.

Note   Direction is a GameMaker's built-in variable that represents the direction faced by an instance, and it's expressed in degrees:

- **Right**: 0 degrees

- **Up**: 90 degrees

- **Left**: 180 degrees

- **Down**: 270 degrees

You can implement a rotating system, for example, by gradually changing the value of ***direction*** by pressing a key. That could be a good way to simulate how a car steering works.

139

CHAPTER 5   FIXED SHOOTER

Now that we have a bullet, we want it to give some damage, so click Add Event in the Events section of obj_bullet_player and select Collision ▶ obj_enemy_red and add the following code:

```
1   other.hp -= atk;
2   instance_destroy(id, true);
```

Line 1: other is a reserved keyword that you can use in a collision event to refer to the instance with which the collision is happening – in that case obj_enemy_red. In this line, we are subtracting atk to the colliding obj_enemy_red instance's hp variable, dealing exactly atk damage points. Since our plan is to use the shooter object's atk value, that means that the colliding obj_enemy_red instance will take a quantity of damage depending on the atk value of the shooter instance.

Line 2: After the bullet collides with the enemy instance, it gets destroyed. destroy_instance(id, val) it's a GameMaker's internal function, and it destroys the instance referred by id and then it triggers the Destroy event if val is true. We want to trigger the Destroy event so that we can show the explosion of the bullet, just after it's destroyed.

Note   destroy_instance(inst, val) is a function that destroys the instance referred by inst and triggers the Destroy event for that instance if val is true.

When you call destroy_instance without specifying the arguments like this

```
destroy_instance();
```

by default, the function destroys the caller instance and triggers its Destroy event.

As we just said, we want the bullet to explode when it's destroyed. To do that, click Add Event in the Events section of obj_bullet_player and select Destroy to create a destroy event and add this line in it:

```
1    effect_create_layer('Instances", ef_firework, x, y, 0.1,
     c_yellow);
```

The function **effect_create_layer** allows us to use the particle system embedded in GameMaker to create a cool particle effect in the room layer "Instances." In the note below, you can read a complete explanation of the function.

There is a good amount of pre-made particle effects that you can use; ef_firework makes a cool fireworks-like explosion that we can use to simulate the explosion of our bullets onto the alien ships.

In this case, effect_create_layer will make a fireworks particle effect in the exact position in which the bullet collided of size 1/10 of the original size of the effect and yellow color, since yellow is our bullet's color. Feel free to play with that value and change it accordingly to your own taste.

Note You can easily create particle effects with GameMaker by using the effect_create functions.

There are two functions:

effect_create_layer: it creates the effect in a specific layer of the room. You must specify the layer using a string referring to its name.

effect_create_depth: it creates the effect at a specific depth in the room – the depth is a real number between -16000 and +16000.

CHAPTER 5 FIXED SHOOTER

The arguments you can pass to the two functions are similar:

effect_create_layer(layer_name, type, x, y, size, color);

effect_create_depth(depth_value, type, y, y, size, color);

where

- **layer_name** is a string containing the name of the layer of the room in which you want the particle effect to show.

- **depth_value** is a real number between -16000 and +16000 representing the depth on screen at which you want the particle effect to show.

- **type** is the type of particle effect you want to create (you can find more info on the particle system and particle types in the GameMaker documentation: https://manual.gamemaker.io/monthly/en/GameMaker_Language/GML_Reference/Drawing/Particles/Particles.htm).

- **x** and **y** are the coordinates at which the effect will be created.

- **size** is the scale value of the effect (1 = full size, 2 = double size, 0.5 = half size).

- **color** is the RGB value of the color you want the effect to be drawn.

So now we have our bullet ready to be used. The only thing missing is the possibility to shoot it. Let's fix this!

Double-click obj_player to show the Object Editor and head on the Create event that we made in the previous section.

To be able to shoot and deal damage, we need to add an atk variable to the player object – as we just said. We also want to set a sort of shoot delay, so that we can decide the rate at which we are shooting the bullets – or it will shoot 60 times in a frame, which is not what we want.

CHAPTER 5 FIXED SHOOTER

Let's edit the Create event for obj_player so that it looks like this:

```
1   hp = 3;
2   spd = 10;
3   atk = 1;
4
5   can_shoot = true;
6   shoot_delay = game_get_speed(gamespeed_fps) * 0.2;
```

Line 3: We added the atk variable, so that we can control the amount of damage that our spaceship inflicts to the enemies.

Line 5: can_shoot is a Boolean variable that we will use to regulate when we can shoot and when we cannot. It will be set to false when pressing the spacebar, and it will get reset to true after shoot_delay steps, so that we will be able to shoot again.

Line 6: shoot_delay is a variable that represents the delay we want to add to our shooting. In this case, we are setting a delay of 0.2 seconds, so that our spaceship's gun will shoot five bullets per second.

Let's now make the functionality to shoot. In the Events section of obj_player's Object Editor, click *Add Event* ➤ *Key Down* ➤ *Space* to create an event that will trigger when the spacebar is held down and put this code in it:

```
1   if ( can_shoot )
2   {
3       can_shoot = false;
4       var _bullet = instance_create_layer(x, y, "Instances",
            obj_bullet_player);
5       _bullet.atk = atk;
6       _bullet.direction = point_direction(x, y, x, y-1);
7       _bullet.speed = _bullet.spd;
8
9       alarm[0] = shoot_delay;
10  }
```

CHAPTER 5 FIXED SHOOTER

Lines 1–3: We shoot bullets only if can_shoot is true. When it is, we change its value to false, so that we can implement that shoot delay we just talked about.

Line 4: We create a local variable to store the obj_bullet_player instance we are creating calling instance_create_layer at coordinates x,y in the Instances layer.

Lines 5–7: We then assign obj_player'satk value to the _bullet's atk variable. We set the bullet's direction to point straight up at a speed of spd (which is 10) pixels per second.

Line 9: Lastly we set alarm[0] to a value equal to shoot_delay. Alarm 0 has the job to set back can_shoot variable to true, so that we can attack again after shoot_delay steps.

Note point_direction(x1, y1, x2, y2) is a function that can be used to change the orientation of an object to face an imaginary line drawn between points x1,y1 and x2,y2. The function returns the value in degrees of a vector comprised between the points x1,y1 and x2,y2.

A common usage of this function is

```
direction = point_direction(x1, y1, x2, y2);
```

Last, but not least, let's create the event linked to alarm[0]. Once again, in the Events section of obj_player's Object Editor, click Add Event ➤ Alarm ➤ Alarm 0 and add this line to it:

```
1  can_shoot = true;
```

That's it! We don't need anything else. Just set the variable to true, so that we can shoot again after the right amount of time.

Now let's check that everything is working good by running the game (press F5 or click the Run icon in the toolbar).

CHAPTER 5   FIXED SHOOTER

Great! Pressing the spacebar, we can shoot yellow pellets, and they collide with the enemy making a nice particle effect (Figure 5-5)!

Figure 5-5. *We can now shoot bullets that explode when they collide with alien ships!*

That's good, but not great. A good weapon is such only if it kills; and it's not the case yet, because the enemy cannot die. So, we have to turn the enemy into a mortal being.

The bullet does actually deal damage to the enemy, because of that other.hp -= atk; line that we inserted into the bullet's collision event with the alien spaceship, but the enemy is not dying. To make it die, we need to check if enemy's HP reaches zero, and when it does, we have to destroy the enemy instance.

CHAPTER 5 FIXED SHOOTER

The best way to do it is to modify the step event of obj_enemy_red adding this code at the end of it:

```
1   if ( hp <= 0 )
2   {
3       instance_destroy();
4   }
```

The code above checks if obj_enemy_red's hp reaches 0; if it does, it calls instance_destroy and triggers the Destroy event. Remember that the default behavior of instance_destroy (that means when you call the function without arguments) destroys the current instance and triggers the Destroy event.

Time to create the Destroy event for obj_enemy_red! Click Add Event ➤ Destroy and add this code to it:

```
1   effect_create_layer("Instances", ef_explosion, x, y, 1,
        c_dkgray);
```

This one line creates a cool particle effect explosion of size 1 and color dark gray at enemy's current coordinates.

Let's test what we implemented! Press F5 or click the Run button in the toolbar to compile and run the game.

Okay, that's way better! Now we can shoot at the alien ship and make it blow up in a cool smokey explosion!

Now that we dealt with the player's shooting, we should give the ability to shoot to the enemies too.

According to the GDD, the enemies should shoot after a random amount of time. As we learned in Chapters 3 and 4, to generate random numbers, we have to initialize the random seed by calling the randomize function. We don't want to do it inside of obj_enemy_red because that means that the function will be called as many times as many enemies we put in the level. Sounds like we might use a game controller object!

CHAPTER 5 FIXED SHOOTER

Right-click Objects in the Resources sidebar, select Create Object, and name it obj_controller. This will be our game controller object.

In the Events section of obj_controller, click Add Event ➤ Create and add the randomize function call to it:

```
1   randomize();
```

Next up: we need to create the bullet object for the enemies. We can use the template of obj_bullet_player by right-clicking it and selecting Duplicate. Rename that copy as obj_bullet_enemy and double-click it to open up the Object Editor.

We just need to change a couple of things in this object, and we are good to go.

Head to the Events section of obj_bullet_player, right-click the collision event, choose Change Event, and select Collision ➤ obj_player.

Now we're all set, and the bullet is ready to be shot by the alien ships. We just need to allow the enemy to shoot.

Open the obj_enemy_red's Object Editor and select the Create event. We must make some modification to the code in this event, so that we can properly set up the random attack. Let's add this one line to the bottom of the code:

```
1   alarm[1] = game_get_speed(gamespeed_fps) * random_
    range(0.5, 5);
```

We set alarm[1] at a random time value, so that it will trigger between half a second and 5 seconds since when the instance is created.

Now click Add Event ➤ Alarm ➤ Alarm 1 and put the following code inside the event:

```
1   var _bullet = instance_create_layer(x, y, "Instances", obj_
    bullet_enemy);
2   _bullet.atk = atk;
3   _bullet.direction = point_direction(x, y, x, y+1);
```

147

```
4    _bullet.speed = bullet.spd;
5
6    alarm[1] = game_get_speed(gamespeed_fps) * random_
     range(0.5, 5);
```

Lines 1–4: Just like for obj_player, we are creating a bullet, setting its direction (pointing down), speed, and attack power.

Line 6: We reset the timer to a new random value between half a second and 5 seconds.

Now we are all set for the enemy to shoot bullets at random time, but we still cannot die. Let's double-click obj_player and create a new step event by clicking Add Event in the Events section of the Object Editor and select Step ➤ Step.

Inside the Step event, add this code:

```
1    if ( hp <= 0 )
2    {
3    instance_destroy();
4    }
```

Lines 1–4: Just like we did with obj_enemy_red, we are checking every step if hp reached 0 (or less); and if it does, we destroy the instance and trigger the Destroy event.

Now let's add the Destroy event by clicking Add Event ➤ Destroy and add this one line to it:

```
1    effect_create_above(ef_explosion, x, y, 1, c_dkgray);
```

It's the same line that we used to destroy the alien spaceship. It's more than enough to create a cool effect when our spaceship is destroyed.

Now it should be all set. We can verify it by pressing F5 (or clicking the Run button in the toolbar) and running the game.

CHAPTER 5 FIXED SHOOTER

It works! The alien ship is shooting at random intervals of time toward the bottom of the room, and if it hits the player three times, the player dies! That's all we need to play! We have all the elements for our shoot 'em up gameplay!

Now the only things we still miss are a HUD to visualize some information, the menu, and some level design! Let's deal with those features!

Designing rm_level_1

Here we are! We have our enemy prototype and our player's avatar and an empty room. We have to use those elements to make a level. The art of level design is all about creating levels that can be beautiful to look at, fun to play, and possibly narratively interesting.

In this version of the game, being that a fixed shooter, there's not much that we can do with our levels; but we can try to copy the two big names of this genre: Space Invaders and Galaga. Those two games just put a fleet of aliens at the top of the level in an ordered formation and let the battle be consumed in that limited space.

Open up rm_level_1 and Drag and Drop obj_enemy_red instances so that it looks like Figure 5-6.

CHAPTER 5 FIXED SHOOTER

Figure 5-6. *Building rm_level_1 in GameMaker's Room Editor*

Running the game, you will notice how that kind of design is more than enough to make the level challenging. In fact, depending on how often the enemies shoot, it's not so easy to dodge all those bullets and eliminate 27 enemies with just three HPs. I think we reached a good balance for that level.

We now need to think about how we can win or lose the game.

Game States

You probably noticed that in Chapters 3 and 4, when we built the Memory card game, we started from designing the game flow, and then we implemented the functionalities, while now we are going the other way around. Those are the two most common creative processes to make games.

When you have a clear idea of what you are going to do and you have a clear idea of the game flow, you should start by this and prepare the whole structure of the game from the ground up.

When you know you want to use some specific functionalities in your game (like in this case we knew we wanted some basic shmup functionalities like shooting and moving), but the game flow is still not clear, you should start by prototyping/studying the various features and functionalities you want to implement in your game – like we did here by building the moving and shooting features before thinking about the game flow.

Both those two ways to create games are viable and good. Sometimes you just need to play around with features to have an idea of what you can make; sometimes your ideas are clear, and you can immediately start planning and structuring the game flow.

I think starting from the features it's a good way to think about what you're building and to come up with interesting gameplay ideas, but this can be achievable also by preparing a basic system with all the useful functionalities already implemented and then building on it. You just have to find out which style works better for you.

That being said, since we decided we want to build a game state system to control the flow of the game, we have to create a global variable called game_state whose value can be one of the states defined by an enum representing the various states.

Space Gala's states flow is simple, as you can see in Figure 5-7. When we start up the game, we can immediately start playing. We can pause the game by pressing the Esc key; and through that menu, we can restart the game, resume it, or quit it. We can access the restart and quit functions also by losing or winning the game.

CHAPTER 5 FIXED SHOOTER

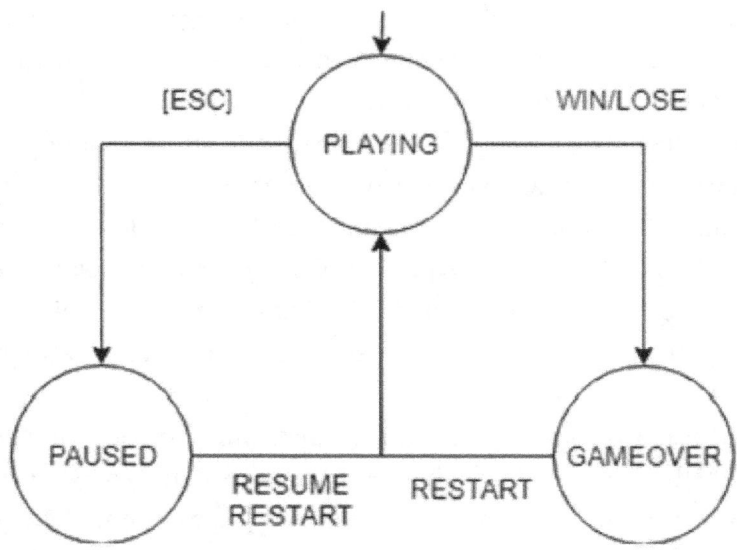

Figure 5-7. *Space Gala's states flow*

Double-click obj_controller to open up the Object Editor, and select the Create event we already added before and modify it so that it looks like this:

```
1   enum STATES {
2   PLAYING,
3   PAUSED,
4   GAMEOVER
5   };
6
7   randomize();
8
9   global.game_state = STATES.PLAYING;
10
11  game_set_speed(60, gamespeed_fps)
```

CHAPTER 5　FIXED SHOOTER

Lines 1–5: Here we define the state enum that represents all the various states our game can be in.

Line 7: As we did in the last section, we are initializing the random seed by calling randomize.

Now that we have our game state global variable, we can start using it to put the game in pause or to make the game end.

Line 9: When the game begins, the game is in playing state.

Line 11: Like we did with the Memory game, we are defining the speed of the game to 60 FPS.

Since we have a PAUSED state, we want to add the functionality for it, so go ahead and create a new Key Pressed event for obj_controller by clicking *Add Event* ▶ *Key Pressed* ▶ *Other* ▶ *Escape* and add the following code:

```
1   if ( global.game_state == STATES.PLAYING )
2   {
3       global.game_state = STATES.PAUSED;
4       show_debug_message(string(global.game_state));
5   }
6   else if ( global.game_state == STATES.PAUSED )
7   {
8       global.game_state = STATES.PLAYING;
9       show_debug_message(string(global.game_state));
10  }
```

The code above changes the state of the game from PLAYING to PAUSED and from paused to playing when we press the Esc key.

We want to change the game state also when our ship is destroyed, because that would be game over!

Double-click obj_player and open the Destroy event, and add these lines at the bottom of the code:

```
1   global.game_state = STATES.GAMEOVER;
2   show_debug_message(string(global.game_state));
```

153

CHAPTER 5   FIXED SHOOTER

Every time an instance of obj_player gets destroyed, the game state changes to states.gameover allowing us to understand that the game ended and the player shouldn't be able to play anymore.

Obviously, the game should also end when every alien gets killed by the player.

That's simpler than it seems! Just open obj_controller by double-clicking it in the Resources sidebar, and create a Step event by clicking Add Event ➤ Step ➤ Step and add the following code:

```
1   if ( !instance_exists(obj_enemy_red) )
2   {
3       global.game_state = STATES.GAMEOVER;
4   }
5   show_debug_message(string(global.game_state));
```

In the code above, we check if there is any instance of obj_enemy_red in the room; if there isn't, the game state is changed to STATES.GAMEOVER.

Doing this check in the Step event overrides the change of state we do when we press the Esc key.

Also, every time the Step event is called, we show in a debug message (shown in GameMaker's console) the code of the current game state, so that we can verify the change of the state when we run the game.

Note   By default, when we declare an enum, GameMaker assigns to each of its elements a value starting from 0 to n-1, with n being the number of the elements of the enum.

In our case

STATES.PLAYING = 0

STATES.PAUSED = 1

STATES.GAMEOVER = 2

CHAPTER 5 FIXED SHOOTER

Running the game by pressing F5, we can see that when we press the Esc key, GameMaker's console shows a text telling us whether the game is in pause or not showing the value of global.game_state (which is 0 in playing mode and 1 in pause mode). Also when we die or we kill every enemy in the room, we can see the change of the state to STATES.GAMEOVER.

You can close the game and get rid of those show_debug_message lines, as we don't need them anymore.

We have a working game state system. Now we just need to use it to regulate the flow of our game. For example, it would be great to implement a pause/resume functionality that allows both player's and enemies' spaceships to move and shoot only when the state is playing, and we also want the bullets to freeze when the state is not playing. Such system will allow us to stop the action when the game is paused or over. It would also be great to notify the player about the current game state by showing an appropriate text on the screen. Let's get on it!

Go ahead and open up obj_player's Object Editor, and modify the code inside the Key Down ➤ Left event so that it looks like this:

```
1   if (x> 0 + sprite_width/2 and global.game_state == STATES.
    PLAYING)
2   {
3     x -= spd;
4   }
```

We just added a condition to check whether the game is in the playing state; if it is, we move left the spaceship.

Now do the same for Key Down ➤ Right:

```
1   if ( x<room_width - sprite_width / 2 and global.game_state
    == STATES.PLAYING )
2   {
3     x += spd;
4   }
```

155

CHAPTER 5 FIXED SHOOTER

And of course we have to do the same also for our shooting key, by modifying the Key Down ▶ Space event like this:

```
1   if (can_shoot and global.game_state == STATES.PLAYING )
2   {
3   can_shoot = false;
4
5   var _bullet = instance_create_layer(x, y, "Instances",
    obj_bullet_player);
6   _bullet.atk = atk;
7   _bullet.direction = point_direction(x, y, x, y-1);
8   _bullet.spd = 10;
9
10  alarm[0] = shoot_delay;
11  }
```

Now, to be able to shoot, we don't need only to have can_shoot to be true. We also need that the game state is in playing mode.

This only blocks our capacity to move left and right and to shoot. Our bullets will still travel forward once shot, even if we pause the game. Let's fix this!

Thinking about what we did with the bullets, we are not changing their position by increasing/decreasing the Y-coordinate like we do with the enemies' and the player's spaceships. We make them move by changing their direction and changing their speed. That means that they travel at a fixed speed – so to make them stop, we just have to change speed value to 0.

Double-click obj_bullet_player and create a new Step event by clicking Add Event ▶ Step ▶ Step and add the following code:

```
1   if ( global.game_state == STATES.PLAYING )
2   {
3   speed = spd;
4   }
```

```
5    else
6    {
7    speed = 0;
8    }
```

The Step event will now continuously check whether the game state is in playing state or not; and if it is, it will change the speed to spd; if it's not, it will change it to 0 making the bullet stop.

Since we are now changing constantly the bullet's speed, we don't even need obj_player to do it anymore. Let's get rid of that line in obj_player's Key Down ➤ Space event and modify the code so that it looks like this:

```
1    if (can_shoot and global.game_state == STATES.PLAYING )
2    {
3    can_shoot = false;
4
5    var _bullet = instance_create_layer(x, y, "Instances",
     obj_bullet_player);
6    _bullet.atk = atk;
7    _bullet.direction = point_direction(x, y, x, y-1);
8    alarm[0] = shoot_delay;
9    }
```

We deleted the line that modified the speed of the bullet from there, since we are doing it from obj_bullet_player's step event.

Running the game (pressing F5 or clicking the Run button in the toolbar), you will now notice that the player's spaceship and its bullets will freeze where they stand when you pause the game, but the enemies and their bullets won't! We need to apply that same mechanism to the enemies and their bullets!

Double-click obj_enemy_red's and head to its Alarm 1 event and get rid of the line that modifies the speed of the bullet, so that it looks like this:

CHAPTER 5　FIXED SHOOTER

```
1   if ( global.game_state == STATES.PLAYING )
2   {
3   var _bullet = instance_create_layer(x, y, "Instances",
    obj_bullet_enemy);
4   _bullet.atk = atk;
5   _bullet.direction = point_direction(x, y, x, y+1);
6   }
7   alarm[1] = game_get_speed(gamespeed_fps) * random_
    range(0.5, 5);
```

Now double-click obj_bullet_enemy in the Resources sidebar, and substitute the content of the Step event with this code:

```
1   if ( global.game_state == STATES.PLAYING )
2   {
3   speed = spd;
4   }
5   else
6   {
7   speed = 0;
8   }
```

Well! Looks like everything is in order! Let's double-check by running the game!

The player and the enemies can shoot at each other while the game is not in pause (Figure 5-8), and they freeze when it is. Great!

Welp! That was a long run, but we didn't finish yet! We need to take care of two last things: how to open up the menu and drawing info in the HUD.

CHAPTER 5 FIXED SHOOTER

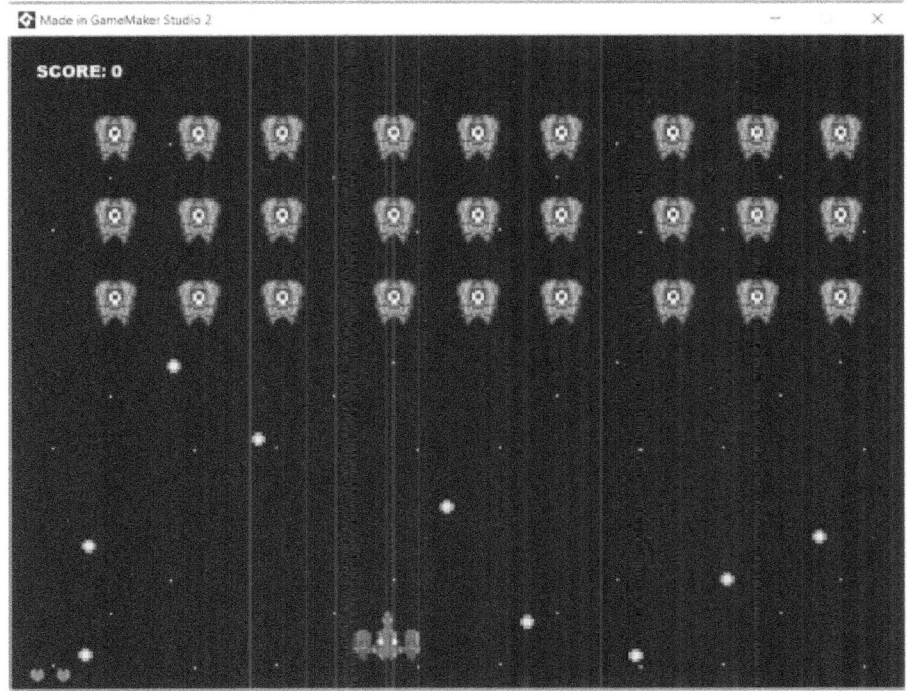

Figure 5-8. *Shooting implemented for both the player and the enemies*

Making HUDs

Our HUD will be very simple It will consist only in a couple of texts drawn on screen showing the player's score and the status of the game (whether paused or not) and some icons to show the player's HP.

We will do this – as always – using obj_controller. Let's open it up by double-clicking it in the Resources sidebar and create a new Draw GUI event by clicking Add Event ➤ Draw ➤ Draw GUI.

159

CHAPTER 5 FIXED SHOOTER

In the Draw GUI event, add the following code:

```
1   draw_set_font(fnt_messages);
2   draw_set_color(c_white);
3   draw_text(30, 30, "SCORE: " + string(score));
4
5   if ( global.game_state != STATES.PLAYING )
6   {
7       if ( global.game_state == STATES.PAUSED )
8       {
9           draw_text( 900, 30, "PAUSE" );
10      }
11      else
12      {
13          draw_text( 850, 30, "GAME OVER" );
14      }
15  }
16
17  if ( instance_exists(obj_player) )
18  {
19      var _xhp = 30;
20      repeat(obj_player.hp)
21      {
22          draw_sprite(spr_life, 0, _xhp, 750);
23          _xhp += 30;
24      }
25  }
```

Lines 1–3: As usual, we set up the game to draw a text showing our current score represented by the score built-in variable. We never change this value in the game yet, so it will remain at 0 for all the time, but we are going to fix this very soon!

CHAPTER 5 FIXED SHOOTER

Lines 5-15: In this part, we check the current state of the game; and if we are in a pause or game over state, we draw the right text on the screen to let the player know.

Line 17: It checks if an instance of obj_player exists. We need this check because we are accessing a variable belonging to obj_player. If we access a variable of an object without doing this check, there is the risk that our game can crash. In fact, accessing a variable of a nonexisting instance – for example, an instance that has been recently destroyed – will cause a fatal error in the game and a crash.

Lines 19-24: Here we are drawing a spr_life sprite on screen as many times as many HPs we have. We draw them at 30 pixels intervals from one another at the bottom of the screen. We are using our local variable xhp as the X-coordinate so that we can easily increase that value by 30 pixels without using fixed coordinates for every single icon drawn.

Now that we are dealing with the score, we should increase it every time we destroy an alien spaceship. Let's do this by editing the obj_enemy_red Destroy event and adding this line to it:

```
1    score += 100;
```

Now, when we destroy an enemy ship, our score will be increased by 100.

That's it! Run the game to check that everything is working!

Running the game, you may see that the player's HPs are shown as hearts in the bottom-left corner of the screen and the score is visible in the top-left corner of the game screen. Also, when you press the Esc key to pause the game, everything freezes, and the text PAUSE is shown in the top-right corner of the screen.

Great! That looks a lot more like a game!

CHAPTER 5   FIXED SHOOTER

What About Victory?

According to the GDD, the player wins the game when they destroy every alien spaceship in the room and loses it when they are killed, or the enemies reach the bottom of the room – meaning they reach the base.

We already added the code to change the state when we die, or all the enemies are wiped out. We only need to change the state also when they reach the bottom of the room. Nothing simpler!

Open up obj_controller and head to the Step event, and change it so it looks like this:

```
1   if ( !instance_exists(obj_enemy_red) )
2   {
3       global.game_state = STATES.GAMEOVER;
4   }
5   else
6   {
7       for ( var _i = 0; _i<instance_number(obj_enemy_red); _i++ )
8       {
9           var _enemy = instance_find(obj_enemy_red, _i);
10          if ( _enemy.y>= room_height )
11          {
12              global.game_state = STATES.GAMEOVER;
13          }
14      }
15  }
```

Lines 5–15: If there's still at least one instance of obj_enemy_red, we cycle through all the instances of obj_enemy_red in the room and check if at least one of them has the Y-coordinate greater than or equal to the height of the room; if exists such an instance, we change the game state to STATES.GAMEOVER.

> **Note** **instance_number** is a built-in function that counts how many instances of an object exist in the current room and returns that number.

For example:

`var _monsters_number = instance_number(obj_monster)`

The code above counts how many instances of obj_monster there are in the current room and returns the value into _monsters_number.

instance_find(obj, i) is a built-in function that searches for the i-th instance of the object obj looping through all the instances in the current room.

For example:

`var _second_monster = instance_find(obj_monster, 2);`

Returns into the _second_monster variable, the id of the second instance of obj_monster after searching all the instances in the room.

Running the game by pressing F5, you will see that everything is working as expected. The game over is triggered when we kill every alien, when we die, or when an alien reaches the bottom of the room. Great! But what if we want to play again? Or quit the game? Here comes the menu!

Menu

We will create a very simple menu made of texts that we can navigate with the up and down arrow keys.

Our menu should offer the functionalities to resume the paused game, restart the game, and quit it.

CHAPTER 5 FIXED SHOOTER

Double-click obj_controller in the Resources sidebar to open up the Object Editor, and add these three lines of code at the bottom of its Create event:

```
1   options = [ "RESUME", "RESTART", "QUIT" ];
2   opt_number = array_length(options);
3   menu_min = 0;
4   menu_index = 0;
```

In the code above, we create an array called options that contains the various labels for our menu options, then we store the size of the array in the opt_number variable, and we define menu_index that we will use to keep track of our position in the menu and menu_min that represents the first element of the menu. We need menu_min because we want to show RESUME as an option when we press the Esc key while playing, but we don't need it when we are showing the menu after the game is over, because there is not a game to resume. So, when pausing during the game, menu_min will be 0; but when the game is over, menu_min will be 1 – so that we can avoid the RESUME option.

The logic to move the cursor in the menu will be part of the Step event. We want the game to allow us to move in the menu only if the game is in pause or the game is over – meaning when the game is not in the playing state. If that's the case, we want to change the value of menu_index by pressing the up and down arrow keys.

Open up the code related to obj_controller's Step event, and add this code at the bottom:

```
1   if ( global.game_state != STATES.PLAYING )
2   {
3       if (global.game_state == STATES.PAUSED)
4       {
5           menu_min = 0;
6       }
```

```
7       else
8       {
9           menu_min = 1;
10      }
11
12      var _move = keyboard_check_pressed(vk_down) - keyboard_
        check_pressed(vk_up);
13      menu_index += _move;
14      if ( menu_index < menu_min )
15      {
16          menu_index = opt_number - 1;
17      }
18      else if ( menu_index > opt_number - 1 )
19      {
20          menu_index = menu_min;
21      }
22  }
```

Line 1: This code is executed only if the game is paused.

Lines 3–10: Here we change the value of menu_min to 0 or 1 (getting rid of the RESUME option in the second case) according to the value of the game state global variable.

Line 12–13: Move represents the movement we make in the menu by pressing the up or down key. keyboard_check_pressed(k) returns 1 when the key k is pressed. So if we both press the up and down arrow keys, the value of move is 1 - 1 = 0; if we press only the down arrow key, its value is 1; and if we press only the up arrow key, it is -1. We can directly sum this value to menu_index (which we do in line 4) to properly change our position in the menu according to the array options.

Lines 14–21: This is pretty straightforward. We check whether we are going out of bounds and, if we do, fix it. If we press up when we are at the topmost option in the menu, we are brought to the last one and vice versa.

CHAPTER 5 FIXED SHOOTER

It's very important to check the bounds of your arrays, because not doing this means your game will crash when you try to access an array element that does not exist.

Perfect! We only have to draw that on screen, so that we can see it!

To achieve this, we can just add some lines of code in the Step event's game state check, so that when the game is in pause, we can draw our menu on the screen.

Open up obj_controller's Draw GUI event, and modify the code so that it looks like this:

```
1    draw_set_font(fnt_messages);
2    draw_set_color(c_white);
3    draw_text(30, 30, "SCORE: " + string(score));
4
5    if ( global.game_state != STATES.PLAYING )
6    {
7        if ( global.game_state == STATES.PAUSED )
8        {
9            draw_text( 900, 30, "PAUSE" );
10       }
11       else
12       {
13           draw_text( 850, 30, "GAME OVER" );
14       }
15
16       for( var _i = menu_min; _i < opt_number; _i++ )
17       {
18           if ( menu_index == _i )
19           {
20               draw_set_color(c_white);
21           }
22           else
```

```
23              {
24                  draw_set_color(c_dkgray);
25              }
26              draw_text( 850, 600 + 30 * _i, options[_i] );
27          }
28      }
29
30      if ( instance_exists(obj_player) )
31      {
32          var _xhp = 30;
33          repeat(obj_player.hp)
34          {
35              draw_sprite(spr_life, 0, _xhp, 750);
36              _xhp += 30;
37          }
38      }
```

We totally revolutionized this code. Now we are not checking anymore only if the game state is set to paused or game over, we are firstly checking if it's not in playing mode (line 5), then we check whether the game is paused or is over, and we draw the right text in the top-right corner of the screen. At lines 16–27, we loop between the menu options, and we draw them one by one in the bottom-right corner of the screen white-coloring the option with the same index of menu_index – that means that the option we are currently pointing is the white one, while the others are grayed out. This helps the player to quickly see the selected item which is the brighter one in the list.

The last thing remaining is to do something when we select an option from the menu. We do this by creating an event triggered when we press the enter key. We will check if we are in pause mode and where are we in the menu, so that we can execute the right action.

In obj_controller, click Add Event ➤ Key Pressed ➤ Enter, and add this code to it:

```
1   if ( global.game_state != STATES.PLAYING )
2   {
3       switch( menu_index )
4       {
5           case 0:
6               global.game_state = STATES.PLAYING;
7               break;
8           case 1:
9               game_restart();
10              break;
11          case 2:
12              game_end();
13              break;
14      }
15  }
```

In the preceding code, we check if we are in a status different from STATES.PLAYING; if that's the case, we check the value of menu_index and execute the right action according to it.

Lines 5–7: If menu_index equals 0, we know that we are pointing to the first element of the array, which is Resume game. In that case, all we want is to go back to the game, and we only need to reset global.game_state to STATES.PLAYING to do that.

Lines 8–10: If menu_index equals 1, we are pointing to Restart game. To restart the game, the only thing we need to do is to call the game_restart() function. It will reinitialize everything and restart the game from the beginning.

Lines 11–13: If menu_index equals 2, we are pointing to Quit game. To close the game, we use game_end() built-in function that closes the game application.

CHAPTER 5 FIXED SHOOTER

Done! Let's check that everything works by pressing the F5 key.

Running the game, you can verify that pressing the Esc key you can access the full version of the menu with the RESUME, RESTART, and QUIT options and check that they work properly (Figure 5-9). When you both win or lose the game, you can access a menu with only the RESTART and QUIT options – just what we wanted!

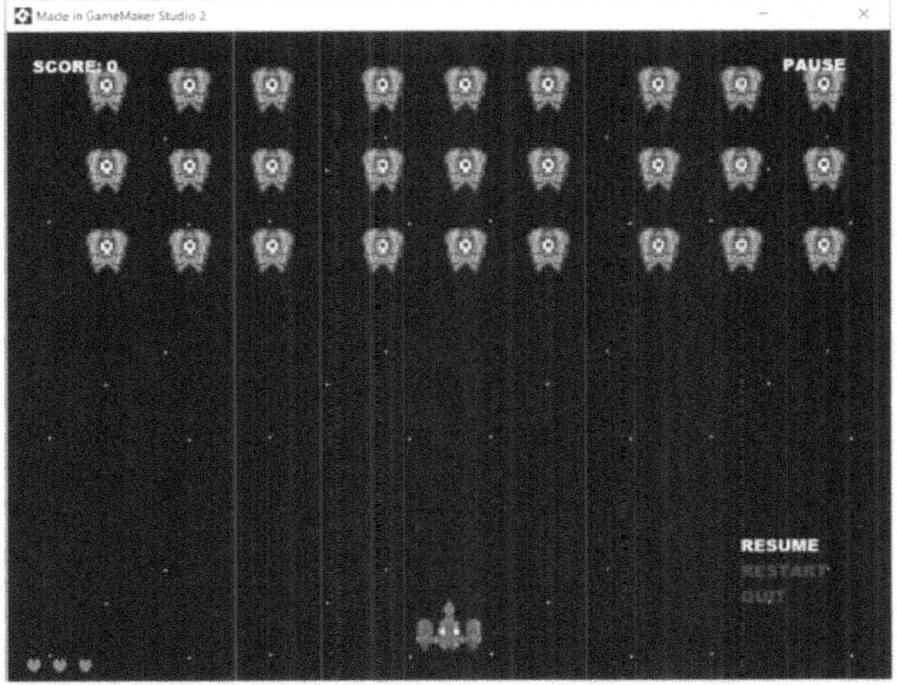

Figure 5-9. *The complete Space Gala game*

Whoah! That was a long one! But we did it! We made a complete shoot 'em up game from scratch! Can you believe it?

Enjoy the game and play with it trying to add new features! In the exercise section, you can find some interesting coding challenge that you can use to add features to the game you just created.

CHAPTER 5   FIXED SHOOTER

In the next chapter, we will extend this version of the game we just created to make it look more like a 1990s STG. We will convert the game into a scrolling shooter and add more enemies, and we will also create our first boss fight! But, coolest of all, we will take inspiration from the masterpiece of the genre, Ikaruga, and we will design and implement its iconic polarization system.

Fasten your seatbelt, we're getting deeper into the outer space!

TEST YOUR KNOWLEDGE!

1. What is a pivot point?
2. What is a collision mask?
3. What happens when the collision masks of two instances collide?
4. Can you tell the difference between an automatic rectangle and a full image rectangle collision mask?
5. Do you think it's good to always use precise masks for your sprites?
6. How does the built-in variable speed work?
7. How does the built-in variable direction work?
8. To what value should you set the direction built-in variable to make an instance face left?
9. Can you use another way to modify the value of direction?
10. How does point_direction work?
11. How does destroy_instance(inst, val) work? What is the default action when you call it without argument?

CHAPTER 5 FIXED SHOOTER

12. How can you create particle effects in GameMaker?

13. How can you count how many instances of an object are present in the room?

14. How does instance_find work?

15. Currently, the player loses the game when the enemies reach the bottom of the room. This can feel unfair to the player, since there is a moment in which they cannot fight back the enemies if not crashing into them. The limit should be raised to make the game feel less weird.

    a. At which coordinate on the Y-axis do you think the game should trigger the game over?

    b. Can you modify the game to change this feature?

16. Play some classics of the shmup genre (Space Invaders, Galaga, Centipede, 1940, etc.) and write down the best features of any one of them.

    a. Compare how these games play to how Space Gala plays. What do you think can be improved in Space Gala, after doing this comparison?

    b. Can you implement one or more of those changes?

CHAPTER 6

Shoot 'Em Up!

In the previous chapter, we began our journey into the world of shooter games starting from the classics of the fixed-shooting genre, making a game inspired by Space Invaders and Galaga.

In this chapter, we will move toward the classics of the 1990s, like R-Type and especially Ikaruga.

We will adapt the code of Space Gala so that it can implement some new features, like scrolling camera, enemies moving on patterns, enemies tracking the player and aiming while shooting, eight-direction movement, and boss fights.

Moreover, we will borrow an interesting idea from Ikaruga, which is one of the most iconic shoot 'em ups ever made. We will create a gameplay mechanic inspired by Ikaruga's polarization system.

Ikaruga had this innovative gameplay element that allowed the player to change the color of its spaceship from white to black to match the color of the enemies' bullets. In fact, in Ikaruga, your ship wouldn't get any damage if hit by a bullet of its same color. Instead, the ship would absorb the bullet to charge an attack bar for its secondary attack. This is a very original gameplay that made Ikaruga really stand out from all the rest.

We will borrow this color-switching idea to implement an additional gameplay element to make the experience more fun. The player will be able to switch between red and blue, and their bullets will change color. When the player gets hit by a bullet of the same color, it will charge a bar that once full will allow them to launch a super strong attack that will kill every visible enemy. Additionally, when shooting down enemies using bullets of their same color, the player will score bonus points.

This gameplay mechanics motivates the player to learn and master the color-switching function, but it will also raise the risk for them to receive damage, raising the level of the challenge! This will make the game more fun and exciting.

There's a lot of stuff to cover, but first let's spend some words on the design and gameplay considerations.

Fixed vs. Scrolling Shoot 'Em Up!

The first big difference between fixed and scrolling shooters is, of course, the scrolling feature. In a scrolling shooter, the level advances at a constant speed, and the player is forced to dodge and attack at a sustained pace.

Traditionally, scrolling shooters were just vertically scrolling all the levels until they reached the end. Going forward, while the genre evolved, level design became more complex, and some scrolling shooters (and not only them) became shooters on rails, where the camera followed some nonlinear path throughout a complex level. There are some interesting examples of level design, in the scrolling shooter panorama, which are very interesting to explore (e.g., R-Type or Ikaruga). In this project, we will focus on vertical scrolling shooters.

Since we are going to make a lot of changes to our game, it's appropriate that we update Space Gala's game design document. It's very important to regularly update the GDD with new features and modifications so that it reflects and tracks the changes in the game.

The first thing we need to change is the genre. Space Gala is not just a fixed shooter anymore, but it's a hybrid shoot 'em up, and in the new level that we will implement in this chapter, we will add some new mechanics.

Then, it's important to talk about the new level that we are going to include in the game.

CHAPTER 6   SHOOT 'EM UP!

Let's edit the GDD so that it includes the new features we want to implement. We will use it as a guide to follow the upgrade of Space Gala.

> **Tip** Remember to always keep your game design document updated.
>
> Every change you make on the project should be registered in the GDD to keep the whole team on the same page.

Space Gala v.2.0 (GDD)

Space Gala is a single-player hybrid shoot 'em up game – meaning that depending on the level, it may be a fixed shooter or scrolling shooter.

The objective of the player is to eliminate all the aliens shooting them down while trying to survive dodging all their attacks or taking them to boost the special attack bar.

Story and Setting

Jonathan Spacepants is back and once again he's the last hope for mankind. His mission is to destroy the alien fleet before they reach Earth's space station. After that, the orders are to advance and hunt down the remaining aliens and kill their leader.

Gameplay

Space Gala revolves around dodging and shooting. It's very important to keep the player focused on those two activities maintaining a fast pace but also giving the player a good amount of satisfaction and motivation.

Satisfaction will be increased by smooth controls and fun combat.

Motivation can be achieved by giving the player a sense of progression. Progression can be achieved by increasing the difficulty of the game from level to level, to keep the challenge going while the player improves their skills.

Color-Switching

The game implements a color-switching system similar to Ikaruga's polarization system to enhance the gameplay and offer an additional challenge.

The player can change the color of their ship from red to blue and vice versa using the X key.

Color-switching allows the player to get hit by bullets of the same color to recharge the super-attack called **X-bomb**, which is a bomb that will wipe out every enemy in the visible area.

Color-switching is also useful to raise the player's score. In fact, killing an enemy with a bullet of the same color will raise the score by 100% and double the damage inflicted.

X-Bomb Charge

The player can charge the X-bomb by being hit by bullets of the same color. Once the bar is full, pressing the spacebar, the X-bomb will be released.

The X-bomb will kill every visible enemy.

Victory Conditions

The game can be won by completing the mission for every level:

- Level 1: Kill all the enemies.
- Level 2: Kill the final boss.

You lose the game if you die or if you fail any level's mission.

Controls

The player can control the spaceship by using the **arrow keys** to move and the **Z** key to attack and **X** key to activate polarization.

It's very important, for the genre, to have precise and smooth controls. We don't want to add any friction in the player's movements.

Right Arrow: Move right.
Left Arrow: Move left.
Up Arrow: Move up.
Down Arrow: Move down.
Z: Attack – a single bullet of the color of the ship dealing standard damage.
X: Switch color.
Spacebar: Release X-bomb.
Esc: Open/close menu.

Menu

You can open/close the menu by using the Esc key. Via the menu, you can close the game, restart it, or resume the paused game.

A smaller version of the menu should be shown when the game is over to allow the player to restart or close the game.

Pacing

The sense of urgency should be the preponderant feeling in Space Gala. You need to wipe out a fleet of aliens without being killed. The aliens are continuously moving, and you need to be a fast and precise shooter to deal with them quickly.

The introduction of the color-switch system will make the pace even faster.

CHAPTER 6 SHOOT 'EM UP!

Enemies

There are three types of enemies:

- **Reds/Blues**: Basic enemies that move left and right and advance while randomly shooting – they are present only in level 1.
    - HP (Health Points): 1.
    - ATK (How much damage they inflict): 1.
    - Movements: They move left and right and regularly jump down by X pixels.
- **Red/Blue Walkers**: Advanced one-eyed enemies. They follow complex paths around the map and attack randomly the player.
    - HP: 2.
    - ATK: 1.
    - Movements: They follow complex paths around the level.
- **Red/Blue UFOs**: Turret-like enemies. They continuously aim at the player and regularly shoot them.
    - HP: 2.
    - ATK: 1.
    - Movements: They remain still and track the player's movements shooting at them.

Game Modes

There is just one arcade game mode. The player must kill all the enemies in level 1 and the boss in level 2 to win the game.

Level 1

In Level 1, the player must face a fleet of nasty red aliens that want to approach the space station.

The aliens will dodge the bullets by continuously moving left and right while they recharge their FTL engines to jump toward the space station. They can jump no more than 50 pixels forward, and they need to wait approximately 5 seconds before the FTL engine recharges, and they can jump again.

The aliens will shoot randomly in front of them creating a barrage, or a *bullet curtain* (*danmaku*弾幕), as they would say in Japan.

The level is made of one group of 16 aliens.

Level 2

Level 2 is a classic vertical scrolling level. The player travels all the length of the level dodging/absorbing bullets and killing enemies until they reach the final boss.

The level is filled with three types of enemies: reds/blues, red/blue walkers, and red/blue UFOs.

Similar Games and Influences

Space Gala is obviously inspired by Space Invaders, Galaga, and Ikaruga.

CHAPTER 6 SHOOT 'EM UP!

The gameplay of level 1 is more like the Space Invaders experience, with the aliens descending gradually and sporadically shooting, while level 2 resembles more like Ikaruga, travelling through a vertically scrolling level and having additional mechanics and enemy types.

Other notable games of the same genre are Centipede, Galaxian, and Moon Cresta.

Target Audience

The audience is a bit niche, but it's super passionate and cares a lot about the purity of the genre.

Assets

All those changes come with some additions to the assets.

Other than spr_enemy_red, we now want to add a collection of red and blue enemies so that we can implement the color-switching system and a couple more types of enemies.

We also need an original sprite for the boss and two recoloring of the bullet sprite.

spr_enemy_red

Pivot Point: Middle-center
Collision Mask: Automatic, rectangle
Size: 50 × 57

spr_enemy_blue

Pivot Point: Middle-center
Collision Mask: Automatic, rectangle
Size: 50 × 57

spr_enemy_ufo_red

Pivot Point: Middle-center
Collision Mask: Automatic, rectangle
Size: 64 × 64

spr_enemy_ufo_blue

Pivot Point: Middle-center
Collision Mask: Automatic, rectangle
Size: 64 × 64
spr_bullet_red

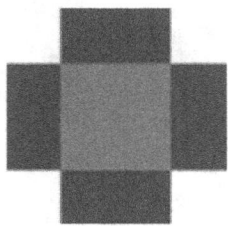

Pivot Point: Middle-center
Collision Mask: Automatic, rectangle
Size: 16 × 16
spr_bullet_blue

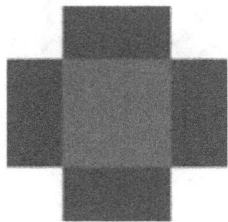

Pivot Point: Middle-center
Collision Mask: Automatic, rectangle
Size: 16 × 16
spr_player_red

Pivot Point: Middle-center
Collision Mask: Automatic, precise
Size: 80 × 69
spr_player_blue

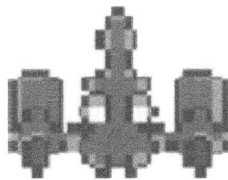

Pivot Point: Middle-center
Collision Mask: Automatic, precise
Size: 80 × 69
spr_boss

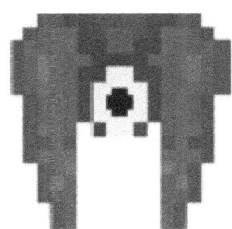

Pivot Point: Middle-center
Collision Mask: Automatic, precise
Size: 120 × 135

Sounds

Sounds are very important in a game. They can change the game's pace and make everything more enjoyable. Sounds can make a situation more realistic or atmospheric. We are creating a great game and adding a lot of nice features, but it's totally silent. In this chapter, you will learn how to add sounds to the game.

CHAPTER 6 SHOOT 'EM UP!

To create a new sound effect to use in your game, right-click Sounds in the Resources sidebar and select Create Sound, name it, and then click the label *No Sound* to select a new audio file from your computer.

You can play sounds in your game by using the audio_play_sound function; its signature is

`audio_play_sound(soundid, priority, loops)`

where

- *soundid* is the name of the sound asset that you want to play.
- *priority* is the channel priority of the sound.
- *loop* is a Boolean that tells GameMaker if the sound should be played in loop or not.

To stop playing a sound that you set to loop, you can use the function audio_stop_sound. Its signature is

`audio_stop_sound( index )`

where *index* is the name of the sound you want to stop.

Note You should use audio_play_sound and audio_stop_sound both for sound effects and to play soundtracks. The only difference between the two, from GMS2's point of view, is that sound effects are played once, while soundtracks are looped.

For this version of the game, we will introduce sound effects. As usual, you can use my sounds (that you can find in the website of this book), or you can make them yourself.

CHAPTER 6   SHOOT 'EM UP!

We will need these sound assets:

snd_menu: This will be played when moving the cursor in the menu.

snd_shoot: This sound effect will be played every time the player shoots.

snd_damage: This will be played when the player gets hit or the enemy explodes.

snd_colorswitch: This is the sound effect related to the new color-switch feature.

snd_esc: This sound effect will be used to open/close the menu.

snd_gameover: This one will be played when the player dies.

This will also be the chapter where we introduce cameras and views, so that we can decide which part of a room to show. In Space Gala, we are going to use cameras to manage the vertical scrolling of the game, so that we can let the player explore the entirety of the new level 2 and travel for all its length toward the final boss.

CHAPTER 6   SHOOT 'EM UP!

Cameras and Viewports

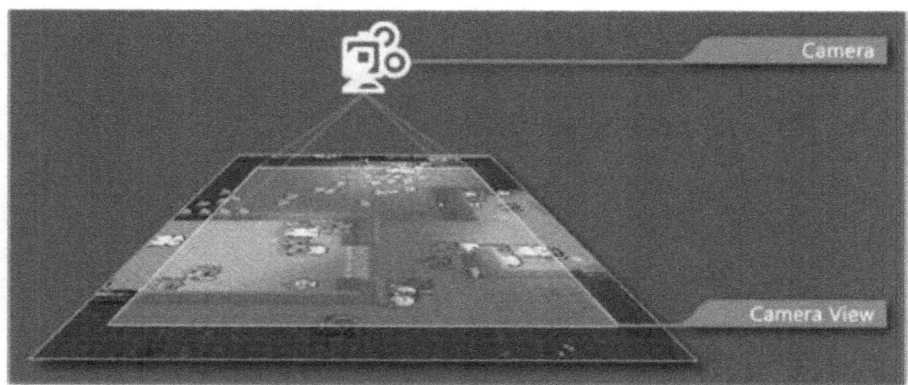

Figure 6-1. *Here's a visual explanation of the difference between Camera and Camera View*

By default, rooms in GameMaker are shown entirely into the viewport. A viewport is basically a window in your game world. You can decide which portion of the room you want to show to the player using cameras.

Cameras (Figure 6-1), in GMS2, allow you to decide which portion of the room you want to show to the player. Like real cameras, you can change their angle, move them, and use them for a lot of tasks, for example, draw HUD elements (like Minimaps or zoom-in/zoom-out sections) or create split screens or Cutscenes.

When you create a camera, you can define the view, which is the area that is visible from the camera.

Space Gala's level 2 will be a way bigger room than the one in level 1, and we want to travel through its entirety using a scrolling camera, so we need to activate viewports and cameras.

Create a new level by right-clicking Rooms in the Resources sidebar and selecting Create Room. Call the new room rm_level_2 and modify its property so that it has a width of 1024 and a height of 10000 pixels.

CHAPTER 6 SHOOT 'EM UP!

In the properties section of the Room Editor, tick *Enable Viewports* and *Clear Viewport Background*. Below, in Camera Properties, edit the fields so that the values are as follows:

- X Pos = 0
- Y Pos = 9230
- Width = 1024
- Height = 768

In Viewport Properties, change the values in the fields like this:

- X Pos = 0
- Y Pos = 0
- Width = 1024
- Height = 768

We just set the viewport and the camera. Now we can use them to show our game world. The camera will be placed at coordinates 0,9230 – meaning the bottom of the very long room we created.

We want the camera to scroll vertically from the bottom to the top of the level. To do that, we will create a camera object. This object will regulate and check all the things related to the camera management and will travel from the bottom of the room to its top, while the real camera will follow this object. Confused? Well, it's easier done than said.

Create a new object by right-clicking in the object section of the Resources sidebar and selecting Create Object.

Call the new object obj_camera and add a new Create event by clicking Add Event ▶ Create in the Object Editor. Add this code to it:

```
1   cam = view_camera[0];
2   x = room_width /2;
3   direction = point_direction(x, y, x, y-1);
4   spd = 2;
```

187

CHAPTER 6　SHOOT 'EM UP!

Line 1: We assign the camera to a variable named cam. We are doing this to make it simple to manage the camera.

Line 2: We move obj_camera to the center of the room.

Lines 3–4: We set the direction of obj_camera to face up, and then we set the spd variable to 2. We will use this variable later to update the speed of the object, so that it will start moving up.

Note　view_camera is an array that contains the eight active cameras that you can have in your game.

In fact, you can have up to eight views in your game, and for each of those views, you can only have one active camera. This means that you can only have eight active cameras at any time.

view_camera is an array that contains the cameras associated to the eight views of the game.

We need to stop camera scrolling every time the game is not in playing state and to resume when it goes back to playing mode.

To do that, create a Step event for obj_camera by clicking Add Event ➤ Step ➤ Step and put this code in it:

```
1   if ( global.game_state == STATES.PLAYING )
2   {
3       if ( instance_exists(obj_player) )
4       {
5           var _cam_x = camera_get_view_x(cam);
6           var _cam_y = camera_get_view_y(cam);
7           var _cam_w = camera_get_view_width(cam);
8           var _cam_h = camera_get_view_height(cam);
9
```

```
10          if ( _cam_y<= 0 )
11          {
12              spd = 0;
13          }
14          speed = spd;
15          obj_player.speed = spd;
16
17          if ( obj_player.x - obj_player.sprite_width/2 <=
            _cam_x )
18          {
19              obj_player.x = _cam_x + obj_player.sprite_
                width/2;
20          }
21          if ( obj_player.x + obj_player.sprite_width/2 >=
            _cam_x + _cam_w )
22          {
23              obj_player.x = _cam_x + _cam_w - obj_player.
                sprite_width/2;
24          }
25          if ( obj_player.y + obj_player.sprite_height/2 >=
            _cam_y + _cam_h )
26          {
27              obj_player.y = _cam_y + _cam_h - obj_player.
                sprite_height/2;
28          }
29          if( obj_player.y - obj_player.sprite_height/2 <=
            _cam_y )
30          {
31              obj_player.y = _cam_y + obj_player.sprite_
                height/2;
32          }
33      }
```

```
34     }
35     else
36     {
37         if ( instance_exists(obj_player) )
38         {
39             speed = 0;
40             obj_player.speed = 0;
41         }
42     }
```

The purpose of the code above is to check if the game is paused or not. If it is, the speed of the object and the player ship gets zeroed (lines 39–40); if it's not, the speed of both the camera and the player is reset to the value of the spd variable (lines 14–15). Also, when the game is not in pause, we constantly check if the ship is inside the camera view coordinates; if it's not, we put them back in. This creates some sort of bounds, so that the player cannot escape the game screen.

We need to change also the speed of the player's spaceship to the same velocity value because otherwise, eventually the player's spaceship will be carried by the screen (since it cannot go out of bounds) and so the player movements will be influenced by some sort of friction that we must absolutely avoid.

Ok, it's time to test that everything is in the right place! But before we do, we should make some modifications to both obj_player and obj_controller.

In level 1, obj_player was prevented from exiting the bounds of the screen with a simple check on the width of the room. This is not appropriate anymore, since now that we have a camera, we want the player to rely on the camera's coordinates, so that we are free to move and tilt the camera and change the room's dimensions without messing with this feature. To do that, we will change this check to the default camera view coordinates (that in level 1 coincide with the room itself, so it's safe).

Open up obj_player and select the Key Down ▶ Right event, and change its code so that it looks like this:

```
1   if ( x<camera_get_view_width(view_camera[0]) - sprite_width
    / 2 and global.game_state == STATES.PLAYING )
2   {
3       x += spd;
4   }
```

This will check whether the player exited the bounds of the camera and in that case prevents the player from moving the spaceship.

Do the same also for Key Down ▶ Left event:

```
1   if ( x> 0 + sprite_width/2 and global.game_state == STATES.
    PLAYING )
2   {
3       x -= spd;
4   }
```

Now we want to add the possibility to move up and down, but only when we are not in level 1, because that is a fixed shooter level. To do that, we will use the built-in variable *room* that tells us the name of the current room.

In the **obj_player**'s Object Editor, click *Add Event* ▶ *Key Down* ▶ *Up* and write this code in it:

```
1   if ( room != rm_level_1 and global.game_state == STATES.
    PLAYING )
2   {
3       y -= spd;
4   }
```

The code above allows the use of a key to move up, only if the player is not in level 1.

CHAPTER 6 SHOOT 'EM UP!

Let's do the same for the down arrow key clicking Add Event ➤ Key Down ➤ Down and adding this code to the newly created event:

```
1   if ( room != rm_level_1 and global.game_state == STATES.
    PLAYING   )
2   {
3     y += spd;
4   }
```

Thinking about boundaries, right now the enemies shoot at the player no matter where they are in the room. This is not optimal, because it means that even if the player can't see the enemy, the enemy will shoot at them. This is unpredictable and unmanageable for the player, meaning not fun. In this case, we can fix this issue by letting the enemies shoot only when they are in the camera boundaries.

Open up obj_enemy_red's Alarm 0 event and modify it to do these checks like in the following code:

```
1    var _cam = view_camera[0];
2    var _cam_x = camera_get_view_x(_cam);
3    var _cam_y = camera_get_view_y(_cam);
4    var _cam_w = camera_get_view_width(_cam);
5    var _cam_h = camera_get_view_height(_cam);
6
7    if ( global.game_state == STATES.PLAYING )
8    {
9    if ( x> _cam_x and x < _cam_x + _cam_w and y > _cam_y and y
     < _cam_y + _cam_h )
10   {
11   var _bullet = instance_create_layer(x, y, "Instances",
     obj_bullet_enemy);
12   _bullet.atk = atk;
```

CHAPTER 6   SHOOT 'EM UP!

```
13   _bullet.direction = direction;
14   _bullet.color = color;
15   }
16   }
17   alarm[0] = game_get_speed(gamespeed_fps) * random_
     range(0.5, 5);
```

Lines 1–5: We calculate the camera's coordinates, like we did before.

Line 9: Here we check that the enemy is within the camera visible surface; we only want to execute that code if it is.

There is a similar issue with the player's bullets. In fact, right now the player can shoot, and the bullet will travel through all the map hitting enemies out of sight. This is not good, because the player can manage to clear the area killing all the enemies while they can't even shoot (because they're out of the screen, as we just defined in the previous code block).

What we want to do is to make sure that when the bullet gets out of the camera coordinates, it gets destroyed. We can implement this by using the point_in_rectangle function.

Note   point_in_rectangle(px, py, x1, y1, x2, y2) is a built-in function that allows you to check whether a given point px,py falls in the rectangular area defined by x1,y1 and x2,y2.

We can use this function, for example, to check if the current instance is inside the camera's bounds like this:

point_in_rectangle(x, y, cam_x, cam_y, cam_x+cam_w, cam_y+cam_h)

193

To implement the check on the bullet's position, head to obj_bullet_player's Step event and append the following code:

```
1    var _cam = view_camera[0];
2    var _cam_x = camera_get_view_x(_cam);
3    var _cam_y = camera_get_view_y(_cam);
4    var _cam_w = camera_get_view_width(_cam);
5    var _cam_h = camera_get_view_height(_cam);
6    if ( notpoint_in_rectangle(x, y, _cam_x, _cam_y, _cam_x + _cam_w, _cam_y + _cam_h) )
7    {
8    instance_destroy(id, false);
9    }
```

Lines 1–5: As we already did in other situations, here we define the camera variables, so that we can access its properties.

Lines 6–9: In these lines, we use point_in_rectangle to check whether the current instance (the bullet) is inside the camera's boundaries (defined in lines 1–5). If the bullet gets out of bounds, we destroy the instance not triggering the Destroy event, because we don't want to play the particle effect when this happens (playing it would give the player wrong feedback on what's happening in the game).

We have to make some modifications also to obj_controller. In fact, right now, victory conditions of level 1 are applied also to level 2, and that's a problem, since level 2 has different rules and gameplay mechanics. The idea is that you win level 1 by killing all the enemies and level 2 by reaching the end of the level and beating the final boss. So, we must divide the two things.

CHAPTER 6 SHOOT 'EM UP!

Open up obj_controller's Step event, and change the code so that it looks like this:

```
1   if ( global.game_state != STATES.PLAYING ) // menu managing
2   {
3   if (global.game_state == STATES.PAUSED)
4   {
5   menu_min = 0;
6   }
7   else
8   {
9   menu_min = 1;
10  }
11
12  var _move = keyboard_check_pressed(vk_down) - keyboard_check_pressed(vk_up);
13  menu_index += _move;
14
15  if ( _move != 0 )
16  {
17  audio_play_sound(snd_menu, 1, false);
18  }
19
20  if ( menu_index<menu_min )
21  {
22  menu_index = opt_number - 1;
23  }
24  else if ( menu_index>opt_number - 1 )
25  {
26  menu_index = menu_min;
27  }
28  }
```

CHAPTER 6 SHOOT 'EM UP!

```
29
30  if ( room == rm_level_1 ) // check victory condition
    for level 1
31  {
32  if ( !instance_exists(obj_enemy_red) )
33  {
34  global.game_state = STATES.GAMEOVER;
35  }
36  else
37  {
38  for ( var _i = 0; _i<instance_number(obj_enemy_red); _i++ )
39  {
40  var _enemy = instance_find(obj_enemy_red, _i);
41  if ( _enemy.y>= room_height )
42  {
43  global.game_state = STATES.GAMEOVER;
44  }
45  }
46  }
47
48  if ( global.game_state == STATES.GAMEOVER and !instance_
    exists(obj_enemy_red) )
49  {
50  if (room_exists(room_next(room)))
51  {
52  room_goto_next();
53  }
54  }
55  }
```

Lines 1–28: This is our old code to manage the menu. It's still valid.

CHAPTER 6   SHOOT 'EM UP!

Lines 30-55: We moved the checks of victory and game over into the if that checks if we are in level 1 or not. In lines 48-54, we also added a check to control if we actually won (we killed every obj_enemy_red), and in that case we warp to the next room, if it exists.

Everything is in place to do our first test for the scrolling feature! We only need to drag the objects inside the room. Open up rm_level_2 and put obj_camera and obj_player at the bottom of the room by dragging them from the Resources sidebar and dropping them in the room. You must also drop obj_controller in there, but please note that while you can place obj_controller anywhere in the room, you don't want to do the same with obj_player and obj_camera. You should put them where you want your game to start since there will be the starting position of the game.

Run the game by pressing F5, and you would notice that the camera correctly scrolls vertically followed by the player's spaceship that can now move in the eight directions. Great! Let's go on!

Designing Color-Switching

We should now design and implement color-switching, our new gameplay mechanic inspired by Ikaruga.

Color-switching can be activated by pressing the X key, and it will change the color of the ship from blue to red and from red to blue if pressed again.

The ship will now shoot bullets of its same color, and hitting an enemy with a bullet of the same color will deal double damage.

When the player gets hit by a bullet of the same color, they won't get damage at all.

To manage color switching, we will use a color variable, so that we can tell whether an instance of an object is blue or red.

We will implement the various colors using enums, to enhance readability.

CHAPTER 6　SHOOT 'EM UP!

Add this code to obj_controller's Create event:

```
1   enum COLORS {
2   NONE,
3   RED,
4   BLUE
5   };
```

Now we can use this enum to assign a color to obj_player and change it when the player presses the X button.

In obj_player's Create event, add the following code:

```
1   sprite_index = spr_player_blue;
2   color = COLORS.BLUE;
```

Pretty self explanatory: we set the sprite of the player to spr_player_blue, which is the default color even for when there is no color-switching skill active. We then assign the color blue to obj_player.

Now let's create a new event by clicking Add Event ▶ Key Down ▶ Letters ▶ X. This will be our color-switching key, so let's attach this code to the event:

```
1   switch( color )
2   {
3   case COLORS.RED:
4   color = COLORS.BLUE;
5   sprite_index = spr_player_blue;
6   break;
7   case COLORS.BLUE:
8   color = COLORS.RED;
9   sprite_index = spr_player_red;
10  break;
11  }
```

The code above will check for the value of the color variable. If it is red, it changes it to blue (lines 3–6), and it also changes the sprite of obj_player to spr_player_blue; vice versa, if it's blue, it changes the value of color to red (lines 7–10) and obj_player's sprite to spr_player_red.

The next thing to implement is to change the color of the bullets according to the color of the ship.

To do that, we first have to add the color feature to the bullets. So open up obj_bullet_player, and add this line at the bottom of the Create event:

```
1   color = COLORS.NONE;
```

Let's do the same also for obj_bullet_enemy's Create event by adding the same line:

```
1   color = COLORS.NONE;
```

According to the GDD, we must also change the binding of the shooting key to Z, since now it's the key for the primary shoot, while space is the key for the secondary shoot.

Right-click Key Down ➤ Space event and select Change Event. Now choose Key Down ➤ Letters ➤ Z. Double-click it to open the code and make these modifications:

```
1   if (can_shoot and global.game_state == STATES.PLAYING )
2   {
3   can_shoot = false;
4
5   var _bullet = instance_create_layer(x, y, "Instances",
    obj_bullet_player);
6   _bullet.atk = atk;
7   _bullet.direction = direction;
8   _bullet.spd = 10;
9   _bullet.color = color;
10
```

```
11    switch(color)
12    {
13    case COLORS.RED:
14    _bullet.sprite_index = spr_bullet_red;
15    break;
16    case COLORS.BLUE:
17    _bullet.sprite_index = spr_bullet_blue;
18    break;
19    default:
20    _bullet.sprite_index = spr_bullet;
21    break;
22    }
23    audio_play_sound(snd_shoot, 1, false);
24    alarm[0] = shoot_delay;
25  }
```

Lines 11–22: Here, after we create the bullet and change its properties, we check the color of the ship (if set) and change the color of the bullet according to it – both changing the sprite and the variable.

The rest of the code is unchanged.

Now run the game by pressing F5. You will be now able to change your ship's and bullet's color by pressing the X key.

Great! But right now, the color switching feature isn't doing much difference. We should implement those mechanics we talked about. Let's start from the player's bullets. We want that when the player kills an enemy with a bullet of the same color, they get additional score. Let's make a new type of enemy for level 2, so that we can keep obj_enemy_red bound to level 1's gameplay.

Our new enemy will have some features in common with obj_enemy_red, but will be different in other things. It would be great if we could define a generic enemy object on which all the enemies will be based. Fortunately, we can do this in GameMaker by using the concept of inheritance.

Inheritance

Inheritance is an important concept of the Object-Oriented Programming paradigm. It is the mechanism of basing an object construction upon another object. Thanks to this principle, we can define a general object that acts as a blueprint to other objects derived from it. There is a specific terminology to express the hierarchy that lies at the heart of inheritance: the generic object is called the parent, while the objects that derive from it are its children.

For example, in our game, we want to create different kinds of enemies that share the same basic structure; in particular, we want that every enemy has basic stats like HP, speed, and attack power and that they all are vulnerable to the player's bullets; but we want to differentiate them in how they move and shoot. So, we can create a parent object obj_enemy that has the basic features that all the enemies share so that we can extend this template creating children objects that implement other specific types of enemies.

Figure 6-2 shows a representation of that hierarchy concept; Alien-X is the parent object that is extended by children Alien-Y and Alien-Z.

CHAPTER 6   SHOOT 'EM UP!

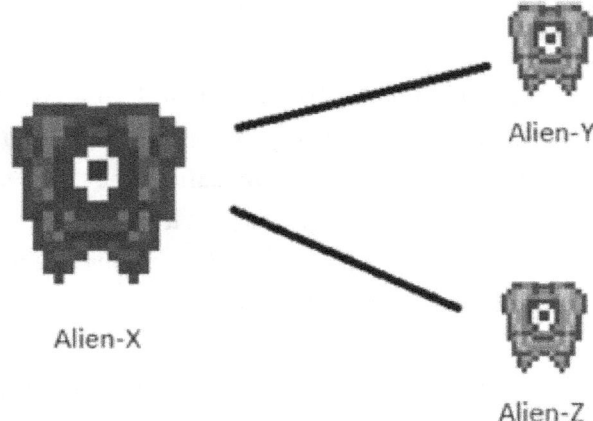

Figure 6-2. *Alien-X is the parent object that is extended by children Alien-Y and Alien-Z. Alien-Y and Alien-Z can both inherit or override Alien-X properties and events*

So, let's create our enemy parent by right-clicking Objects in the Resources sidebar and selecting Create Object. Call this new object obj_enemy. There's no need to assign a sprite to this object.

For this new object, we will create some events that implement common things that we want all our enemies to have. Let's start with the create event.

In obj_enemy, click Add Event ➤ Create and put this code in it:

```
1   hp = 1;
2   spd = 1;
3   atk = 1;
4   color = COLORS.NONE;
```

We are assigning by default to every enemy some stats like HP, attack strength, speed, and color (but the color is none by default). We can still customize those stats for every single enemy by overriding them. We will see how very shortly.

202

Now create a Step event by clicking Add Event ➤ Step ➤ Step. We will use this event to manage the HP level of the enemies, since we want every enemy to die by default when HP drops to zero. So, let's add this code to the Step event:

```
1   if ( hp<= 0 )
2   {
3   instance_destroy(id, true);
4   }
```

We also want that after they died, every enemy explodes giving a base score of 100 points. So, create a new Destroy event for obj_enemy and add these lines to it:

```
1   effect_create_above(ef_explosion, x, y, 1, c_dkgray);
2   score += 100;
```

Finally, we want to associate Alarm 0 to shooting for every enemy instance, so that we don't have to rewrite every time that alarm if we don't want to implement a more advanced shooting for our enemies.

So, in obj_enemy, click Add Event ➤ Alarm ➤ Alarm 0 and write this code in the event:

```
1   var _cam = view_camera[0];
2   var _cam_x = camera_get_view_x(_cam);
3   var _cam_y = camera_get_view_y(_cam);
4   var _cam_w = camera_get_view_width(_cam);
5   var _cam_h = camera_get_view_height(_cam);
6
7   if ( global.game_state == STATES.PLAYING )
8   {
9   if ( x > _cam_x and x < _cam_x + _cam_w and y > _cam_y and
        y < _cam_y + _cam_h )
```

```
10  {
11      var _bullet = instance_create_layer(x, y, "Instances",
        obj_bullet_enemy);
12      _bullet.atk = atk;
13      _bullet.direction = direction;
14      _bullet.color = color;
15  }
16  }
17  alarm[0] = game_get_speed(gamespeed_fps) * random_
    range(0.5, 5);
```

Now, every enemy inheriting from obj_enemy will have by default the shooting alarm to be Alarm 0, unless differently specified.

Since we are restructuring the enemies and we have our player moving in the eight directions, it's good to cover the case in which the player collides with an enemy. When this happens, we want the enemy ship to explode and the player to get standard damage. To do that, create a collision event with the player in obj_enemy, by clicking Add Event ➤ Collision ➤ obj_player, and put these two lines of code in it:

```
1   other.hp -= atk;
2   instance_destroy(id, true);
```

Now, every time an obj_enemy collides with the player, it will deal its damage to the player and then destroy itself.

Now that we have the parent object, we want to align obj_enemy_red to it, so that we can make use of obj_enemy's blueprint to implement some main features.

Firstly, let's create the parent-child relationship between obj_enemy and obj_enemy_red. Open up obj_enemy_red's Object Editor and click Parent to open the Parent view, and click *No Object* to select obj_enemy so that it will become obj_enemy_red's parent.

CHAPTER 6   SHOOT 'EM UP!

Now, open obj_enemy_red's Create event, and substitute the code with this:

```
1   event_inherited();
2
3   color = COLORS.RED;
4   dir = 1;
5   start_x = x - 25;
6   end_x = x + 25;
7
8   move_down_speed = game_get_speed(gamespeed_fps) * 5;
9
10  alarm[0] = game_get_speed(gamespeed_fps) * random_range(0.5, 5);
11  alarm[1] = move_down_speed;
```

Line 1: Here we are telling GameMaker that we want this object to inherit completely all the code included in its parent's Create event. So it means that to have this line, it's like having copy-pasted all the code in obj_enemy's Create event.

We have to modify also obj_enemy_red's Step event so that it will inherit obj_enemy's behavior and implement its own movement policy. So open up obj_enemy_red's Step event, and substitute the code managing the HP dropping with event_inherited. The result will look like this:

```
1   event_inherited();
2
3   if ( global.game_state == STATES.PLAYING )
4   {
5   if ( x<= start_x or x >= end_x )
6   {
7   dir *= -1;
8   }
```

205

```
 9
10    x += spd * dir;
11  }
```

Lastly, let's get rid of Destroy and Alarm 0 events, since we want obj_enemy_red to only use the code in obj_enemy without further modifications.

Now that we have obj_enemy acting as a blueprint for all the enemies, we should use it also to manage collisions with bullets, so that we don't have to rewrite the same code for every enemy we make.

Double-click obj_bullet_player and right-click the collision event with obj_enemy_red, choose Change Event, and choose Collision ➤ obj_enemy.

All done! Now the bullets will damage and kill every object inheriting from obj_enemy. To double-check, feel free to press F5 and test your new code.

Color Shooting

To add the possibility of enemies to shoot bullets of their own color, it's convenient to add this functionality to every enemy, so that we don't have to rewrite the same code over and over.

Tip It's a very good practice to try not to write the same code multiple times. This principle is commonly referred to as DRY (Don't Repeat Yourself). If you know that a piece of code will need to be used multiple times, try to think of how you can avoid it and write it once and use it everywhere.

Let's start adding the color feature to the enemies by modifying the code in the Alarm 0 event of obj_enemy as follows:

```
1   var _cam = view_camera[0];
2   var _cam_x = camera_get_view_x(_cam);
3   var _cam_y = camera_get_view_y(_cam);
4   var _cam_w = camera_get_view_width(_cam);
5   var _cam_h = camera_get_view_height(_cam);
6
7   if ( global.game_state == STATES.PLAYING )
8   {
9       if ( x> _cam_x and x < _cam_x + _cam_w and y > _cam_y
        and y < _cam_y + _cam_h )
10      {
11          var _bullet = instance_create_layer(x, y,
            "Instances", obj_bullet_enemy);
12          _bullet.atk = atk;
13          _bullet.direction = direction;
14          _bullet.color = color;
15          switch( color )
16          {
17              case COLORS.RED:
18                  _bullet.sprite_index = spr_bullet_red;
19                  break;
20              case COLORS.BLUE:
21                  _bullet.sprite_index = spr_bullet_blue;
22                  break;
23              default:
24                  _bullet.sprite_index = spr_bullet;
25                  break;
26          }
27      }
28  }
29  alarm[0] = game_get_speed(gamespeed_fps) * random_
    range(0.5, 5);
```

CHAPTER 6　SHOOT 'EM UP!

Lines 14–26: We assign obj_enemy's color's value to bullet's color; and then, according to that value, we change the bullet's sprite.

Now that we are applying color-based shooting to every enemy, we want this feature to be active only with enemies that are not in rm_level_1. In fact, it's total nonsense to have that feature there, since the final goal of color-switching is to recharge the super-attack, but that would be overkill in rm_level_1. So we need to make a little modification to obj_enemy_red's Create event. Instead of having this line

```
1   color = colors.red;
```

change it to this:

```
1   if ( room == rm_level_1 )
2   {
3     color = COLORS.NONE;
4   }
5   else
6   {
7     color = COLORS.RED;
8   }
```

Adding this control, obj_enemy_red will shoot red bullets only if it's not in level 1.

We have another feature that we want to activate only in level 1, and this is the jumping down action that we implemented using Alarm 0. Open up obj_enemy_red's Alarm 1 event, and add the check for level 1 like shown in the code below:

```
1   if ( room == rm_level_1 and global.game_state == STATES.PLAYING )
2   {
3     y += 50;
4   }
5   alarm[1] = move_down_speed;
```

Now this code will be triggered only if we are in level 1 (line 1).

We should do the same modification we did in obj_enemy_red Create event to obj_player. Let's open it up by double-clicking it in the Resources sidebar. Head to its Create event and change this line

```
1    color = colors.blue;
```

into this:

```
1    if ( room == rm_level_1 )
2    {
3        color = colors.none;
4    }
5    else
6    {
7        color = colors.blue;
8    }
```

Great! Now we have our color-switching feature active only for levels that are not level 1!

You can test it by running the game in level 1 and verifying that you cannot switch color with your ship and both you and the enemies shoot yellow bullets.

Now that we have this cleared out, let's add more fun to the game, by adding more enemies that we can use to fill level 2.

More Enemies

We have color-switching and enemy hierarchy implemented. Now we can start thinking of adding more enemies to increase both fun and challenge. In particular, we will add these enemies:

CHAPTER 6   SHOOT 'EM UP!

- **Blues**: Just like obj_enemy_red, but blue!
- **Red/Blue Walkers**: This kind of enemy will follow a predesigned path and shoot red/blue bullets.
- **Red/Blue UFOs**: Red/blue UFOs that track the position of the player and shoot bullets of their same color.

Ain't Nothing but the Blues

Blues are just needed to balance the presence of the reds in level 2, since color switching will be active. In fact, having this feature with only one type of enemies wouldn't make much sense.

They are pretty simple to make: just duplicate obj_enemy_red by right-clicking it in the Resources sidebar and choosing Duplicate.

Rename the duplicated object as obj_enemy_blue, and open it up by double-clicking it.

The only things we should change are the sprite that should be changed to spr_enemy_blue and the value of the color in the Create event. Opening the Create event, we need to change the code that defines the color variable like this:

```
1  if ( room == rm_level_1 )
2  {
3  color = COLORS.NONE;
4  }
5  else
6  {
7  color = COLORS.BLUE;
8  }
```

The only interesting line, here, is line 7 that we changed according to the enemy's color.

That's it! We have a new enemy that will shoot blue bullets!

Before trying this in level 2, we have to make sure that when the player's ship has the same color of the colliding obj_bullet_enemy instance, they're not getting damage.

Double-click obj_bullet_enemy, open the Collision event with the player, and change the code to this:

```
1   if ( room == rm_level_1 )
2   {
3   other.hp -= atk;
4   }
5   else
6   {
7   if ( color != other.color )
8   {
9   other.hp -= atk;
10  }
11  else // same color, so not getting damage
12  {
13  // TO DO: super attack charge
14  }
15  }
16  instance_destroy();
```

What we did here was to prevent the use of color-based damage for level 1 and add it only on other levels.

Don't worry, we will take care of line 13 very soon!

Let's create a test level to see that everything is working. Right-click Rooms in the Resources sidebar, and select Create Room and call it rm_test.

CHAPTER 6 SHOOT 'EM UP!

Open up rm_test and Drag and Drop these instances in it:

- obj_player
- obj_enemy_red
- obj_enemy_blue
- obj_controller

Now press F5! You should see that getting hit by a bullet of your ship's same color is not a threat anymore. You will get your ship damaged only by different colored bullets.

Also, shooting to an enemy with a bullet of its color will get you 100 more points!

Walkers on Paths

In your game, you may want, at a certain point, to let one of your objects to follow a predefined path. For example, in a top-down RPG, you may want some characters to walk back and forth on a street or things like that. GameMaker has a very useful tool called Paths that you can use to do just that.

Paths are a series of points in a room connected to one another by a line or a curve, and they represent a way that your instances can walk back and forth.

We will use those useful tools to create interesting patterns that our enemies can follow while the player traverses the level. We will call those enemies walkers.

To create our first walker, right-click Objects in the Resources sidebar, and select Create Object. Rename the newly created object obj_enemy_walker_red, and set its sprite as spr_enemy_red since it's not important for the player to recognize the difference between a base red enemy and a red walker. The only difference between the two is the pattern they follow moving.

CHAPTER 6 SHOOT 'EM UP!

We want this enemy to be child of obj_enemy, so click Parent and select obj_enemy as its parent.

Now, double-click the newly created obj_enemy_walker_red, and create a new Create event with this code inside:

```
1   event_inherited();
2   color = colors.red;
```

There's no need to check if we are in room 1 or not, since this kind of enemy won't be present there.

We now want to create a path for obj_enemy_walker_red to follow, so let's open up rm_level_2. In the Room Editor, click Create New Path Layer as shown in Figure 6-3.

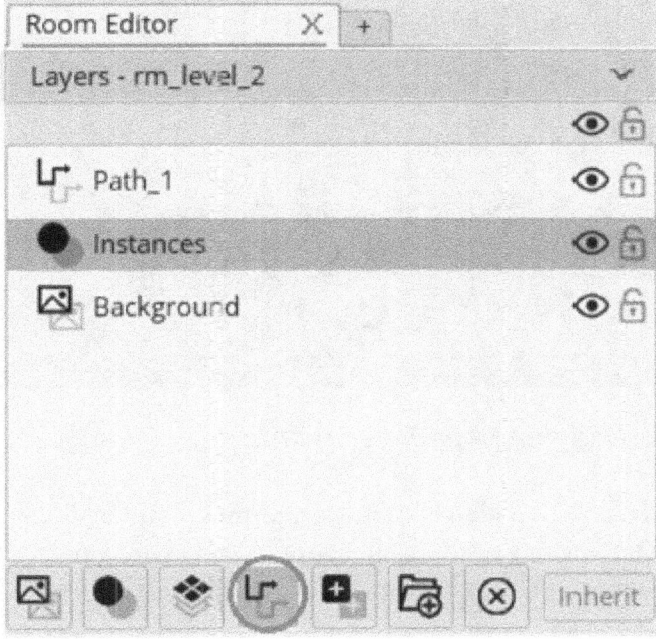

Figure 6-3. *The button circled on the bottom of the picture allows you to create a new path layer*

CHAPTER 6   SHOOT 'EM UP!

Creating a path layer will open a new section in the Room Editor called Path_1 Layer Properties. From there, click Select Path and click Create New. You're now in creating mode, and you can create a path by clicking points directly in the room.

Create a path (Figure 6-4) of your choice that you want one (or more) of your walkers to follow. When you are done drawing the path, you can change some details like the smoothness of the curve and if it's closed or not.

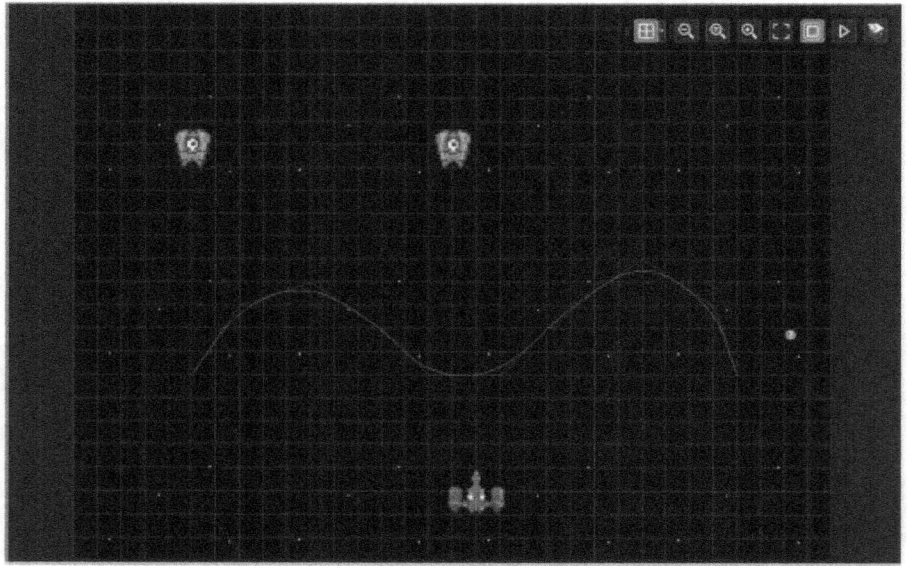

Figure 6-4. *Designing a path in a room*

A closed path is a path where the last point is connected to the first one; GameMaker will automatically draw a line between that path's first and last points.

After you designed your path, give it a name – for example, pth_path0 – by renaming it. Now we only need to assign this path to obj_enemy_walker_red.

Open up obj_enemy_walker_red's Object Editor, and add this line of code at the bottom of the Create event:

```
1    spd = 3;
2    path_start(pth_path0, spd, path_action_restart, false);
```

Calling path_start, you can assign a path to an object, and decide how it will traverse it.

The signature of path_start is

```
path_start( path_name, obj_speed, path_action, path_absolute )
```

where

- *path_name* is the name of the path.
- *obj_speed* is the speed at which you want the object to traverse the path.
- *path_action* is the action you want to be executed after the object traversed the path – like walking back to the reverse path, starting over again from the first point, and so on. See the documentation for more details.
- *path_absolute* tells GameMaker if you want the object to walk the path following the exact coordinates you specified or if you prefer to walk relatively from the coordinates of the object.

In our case, we want obj_enemy_walker_red to traverse pth_path0 at speed spd (i.e., equal to 3), we want it to walk back the reversed path after it reaches the last point of the path, and we want it to do it relatively to its starting coordinates.

Place an obj_enemy_walker_red instance in the room, and press F5 or select Run from the toolbar to compile and run the game. You will see that obj_enemy_walker_red is traversing the path you designed at the speed you specified in its Create event.

215

CHAPTER 6 SHOOT 'EM UP!

Great! We have a new type of enemy! Let's make also a blue one!

To make a blue walker, you just need to duplicate obj_enemy_walker_red by right-clicking it and selecting Duplicate.

Remember to change its color to blue both in the sprite by choosing spr_enemy_blue and in the Create event by changing the value of color like this:

```
1   event_inherited();
2   color = COLORS.BLUE;
3   spd = 3;
4   path_start(pth_path0, spd, path_action_reverse, false);
```

Now we have a blue walker. You can have fun making paths and assigning them to different kinds of walkers by duplicating them. Designing nice paths can greatly enhance the game experience and increase the challenge for the player, so free your imagination!

Unidentified Flying…Instance!

Our third enemy is a turret type. It tracks the movements of the player and shoots at them at regular intervals.

Create a new object by right-clicking Objects and selecting Create Object, and call it obj_enemy_ufo_red. Chooseobj_enemy as its parent.

Now create a new Create event for obj_enemy_ufo_red, and put the following code inside:

```
1   event_inherited();
2   spd = 1;
3   color = COLORS.RED;
4   alarm[0] = game_get_speed(gamespeed_fps) * spd;
```

We set the Create event so that it will inherit all the stats from obj_enemy, but we are changing some of them. We are setting the color as red and the speed as 1. We will use the speed not to move, but to shoot. We want the turret to shoot every second, so we are setting the alarm with spd.

Since we want the ufo to shoot every second, we have to modify the shooting rate in Alarm 0's event, because the default value is calculated randomly (in obj_enemy).

So create a new Alarm 0 event for obj_enemy_ufo_red and, after inheriting the parent's event, set Alarm 0 to the right value, like this:

```
1   event_inherited();
2   alarm[0] = game_get_speed(gamespeed_fps) * spd;
```

Now we want to make sure that the ufo follows the player around aiming at their spaceship. We can do this using the Step event. Once per frame, we will check the position of the enemy ship, and set the direction of obj_enemy_ufo_red to point at it.

Let's do it by creating a step event clicking Add Event ▶ Step ▶ Step and adding this code:

```
1   event_inherited();
2
3   if ( instance_exists(obj_player) )
4   {
5   var _dir = point_direction(x,y, obj_player.x, obj_player.y);
6   direction = _dir;
7   image_angle = _dir;
8   }
```

After inheriting the event of obj_enemy at line 1, we are checking that the player exists at line 3; and if it does, we set obj_enemy_ufo_red's direction so that it faces obj_player. We also rotate the sprite by using image_angle (line 7) so that also the sprite faces the player's direction.

CHAPTER 6   SHOOT 'EM UP!

Let's test our UFO by putting it into the room and running the game pressing F5.

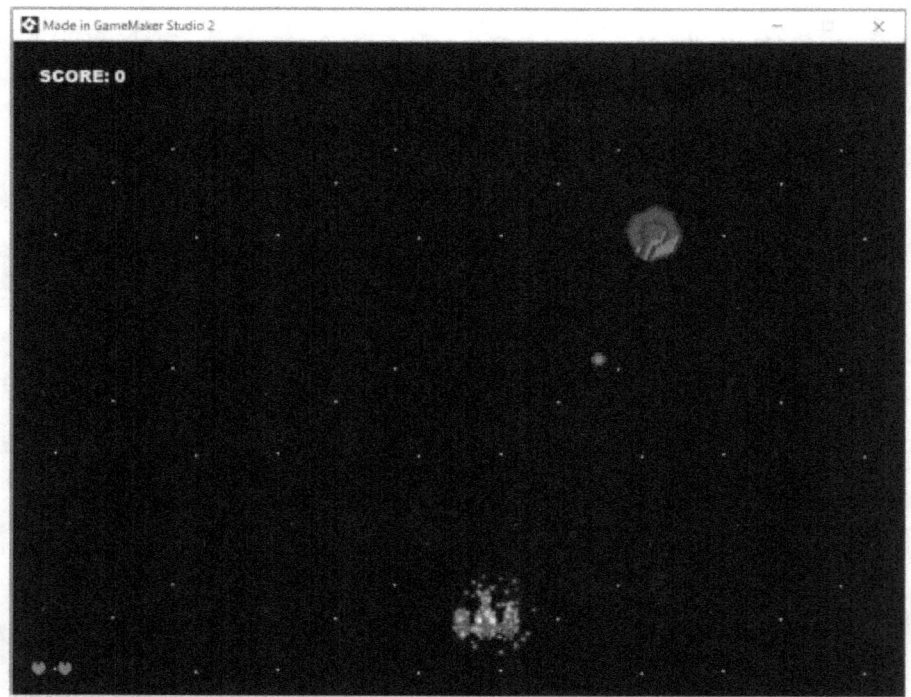

Figure 6-5. *UFOs will track the player's movements and aim to them while shooting*

Great! While the player moves, the UFO tracks their movements and shoots aiming at them (Figure 6-5) – just what we wanted.

Now let's create a blue ufo too, by duplicating obj_enemy_ufo_red. You can do that by right-clicking it in the Resources sidebar and choosing Duplicate. Rename it obj_enemy_ufo_blue and open up its Object Editor.

Let's edit its sprite by choosing spr_enemy_ufo_blue and its Create event by changing its color value to blue like this:

```
1    event_inherited();
2    spd = 1;
3    color = COLORS.BLUE;
4    alarm[0] = game_get_speed(gamespeed_fps) * spd;
```

Cool! Now we have two UFOs ready to hunt down the player's spaceship! We only need a super weapon to put them in their place!

Super-Attack

Following the design we made in our GDD, the color-switching feature has the main objective of charging the special attack that will blow up every enemy visible to the camera.

We will assign this attack to the spacebar, and this will be available only when a controller variable gets to 100, representing a 100% charge of the special engine that triggers the bomb.

We need to define a controller variable for the special attack, and we can do this in the Create event of obj_player. Let's open up obj_player's Object Editor, and add this line to the bottom of the event:

```
1    super_attack = 0;
```

Now, we want to create the event to trigger this attack, so let's create a Key Pressed event for the spacebar, by selecting Add Event ▶ Key Pressed ▶ Space on obj_player, and add this code to it:

```
1    if (super_attack >= 100)
2    {
3        with ( obj_enemy )
4        {
5            var _cam = view_camera[0];
6            var _cam_x = camera_get_view_x(_cam);
7            var _cam_y = camera_get_view_y(_cam);
```

CHAPTER 6 SHOOT 'EM UP!

```
8            var _cam_w = camera_get_view_width( _cam );
9            var _cam_h = camera_get_view_height( _cam );
10
11           if ( point_in_rectangle( x, y, _cam_x, _cam_y,
                 _cam_x + _cam_w, _cam_y + _cam_h ) )
12           {
13               instance_destroy();
14           }
15       }
16
17       super_attack = 0;
18   }
```

Line 1: We want to execute this code only when the attack is fully charged (when it reaches 100).

Line 3: Here we use the **with** reserved word that allows us to temporarily change the context. In this case, we can consider all the code between the brackets as if it was being executed inside the obj_enemy instance. This allows us to simplify the code and, for example, to call functions like instance_destroy in the context of obj_enemy, rather than obj_player, where this code resides.

Lines 5–9: Here we calculate the coordinates of the visible portion of the screen like we did for our obj_camera. We are not using the same coordinates by taking them from that object, because we want that feature to not be dependent on obj_camera.

Lines 11–18: We destroy only the enemies inside the boundaries of the camera.

Now that we have the attack, we need to visualize its data and add the functionality to charge it by absorbing enemies' bullets.

To do that, we will use obj_controller's Draw GUI event, since we are using it for every other HUD element.

CHAPTER 6   SHOOT 'EM UP!

Open up obj_controller's Draw GUI, and edit its code so that it looks like this:

```
1   draw_set_font(fnt_messages);
2   draw_set_color(c_white);
3   draw_text(30, 30, "SCORE: " + string(score));
4
5   if ( global.game_state != STATES.PLAYING )
6   {
7       if ( global.game_state == STATES.PAUSED )
8       {
9           draw_text( 900, 30, "PAUSE" );
10      }
11      else
12      {
13          draw_text( 850, 30, "GAME OVER" );
14      }
15
16      for( var _i = menu_min; _i < opt_number; _i++ )
17      {
18          if ( menu_index == _i )
19          {
20              draw_set_color(c_white);
21          }
22          else
23          {
24              draw_set_color(c_dkgray);
25          }
26          draw_text( 850, 600 + 30 * _i, options[_i] );
27      }
28  }
29
```

```
30  if ( instance_exists(obj_player) )
31  {
32      var _xhp = 30;
33      repeat(obj_player.hp)
34      {
35          draw_sprite(spr_life, 0, _xhp, camera_get_view_
            height(view_camera[0])-30);
36          _xhp += 30;
37      }
38
39      draw_set_font(fnt_messages);
40      draw_set_color(c_white);
41      draw_text(30, 60, "X-BOMB: " + string(obj_player.super_
        attack) + "%");
42  }
```

Lines 39–41: These are the only lines we modified. We just set a font and a color for the text, and then we wrote the label X-BOMB followed by the value of super_attack variable. Last thing to do is to charge it up!

We will manage the charging in the collision event between the player and the enemy's bullet. So open up obj_bullet_enemy's collision event with obj_player. We only have to add one line where we put that placeholder comment. The new code of the collision event will be this:

```
1  if ( room == rm_level_1 )
2  {
3      other.hp -= atk;
4  }
5  else
6  {
7      if ( color != other.color )
```

```
 8      {
 9          other.hp -= atk;
10      }
11      else
12      {
13          if ( other.super_attack< 100-10 )
14          {
15              other.super_attack += 10;
16          }
17          else
18          {
19              other.super_attack = 100;
20          }
21      }
22  }
23  instance_destroy(id, true);
```

Lines 13–20 are the part we changed. For every bullet colliding with the player, if it has the same color of the player's ship, the super-attack gets charged by 10. We do an extra check to see if the variable is going over 100 and fix it if it does.

Ok, now the whole system is working! We just have to double-check if we did everything alright!

Run the game by pressing F5 or clicking the Run button in the toolbar!

Great! When the ship gets hit by bullets of the same color, it charges (Figure 6-6) the special attack; and when it reaches 100%, we can use it by pressing the spacebar wiping out every enemy in the area (Figure 6-7)!

CHAPTER 6   SHOOT 'EM UP!

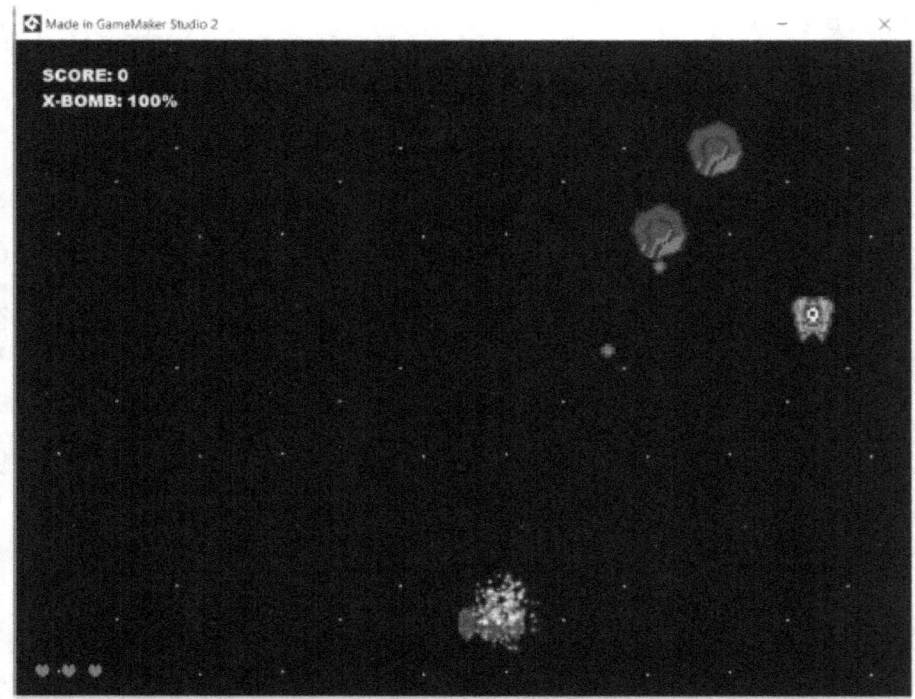

Figure 6-6. *The X-bomb charge reaches 100%, thanks to the collision with bullets of the player's same color*

CHAPTER 6   SHOOT 'EM UP!

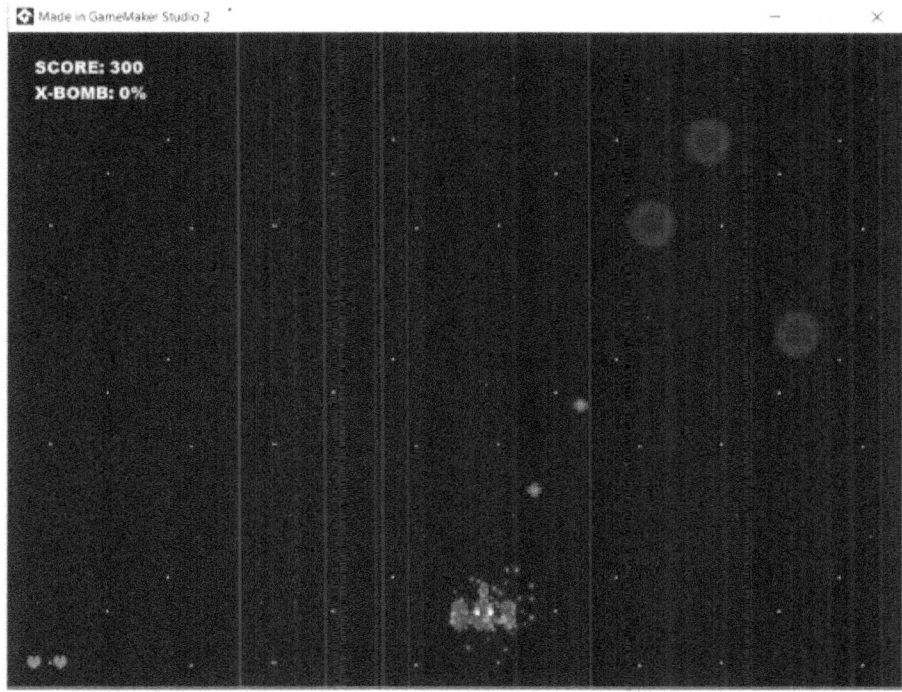

Figure 6-7. *The X-bomb, when triggered, destroys every enemy in the visible area*

How to Design a Good Shmup Level

Shoot 'em ups are games very much based on gameplay mechanics. The most important thing to do is to find a good gameplay mechanic that can drag forward all your game. Level design, for any of the levels you design, should be based on the concept of highlighting this principal mechanic.

In Space Gala, we should design level 2 to exploit the new powers we are giving to the player. First of all, we should introduce the player to the feature, by making so that the first part of the level alternates blue and red enemies. Then we should start mixing them in small quantities. The end of the level should feature at least a couple of sections with a big number of blue and red enemies following interesting patterns, so that the player can feel the tension of the fast pace of our game and they will be forced to master their color-switching skills.

Try to design a level following those guidelines. If you have problems coming up with something meaningful, you can check the level I made in the project for this chapter on the GitHub page of the book.

Boss Fighting

Boss fights are one of the most important and fun elements in a video game. We will talk extensively about them in the next chapter. For now, let's just focus on how to make a boss in our game.

Shoot 'em ups have probably the most interesting boss fights. They are often made of phases, in which the boss changes moveset and/or attacks, and they mix various styles. There are bosses that use a lot of different and artistic bullet patterns, there are bosses that spawn minions, and so on.

Our boss will start by aiming at the player and shooting normal bullets. Then, after reaching half of its HP, it will grow bigger and start spawning turrets.

Let's start by creating a new obj_boss object by right-clicking Objects in the Resources sidebar and choosing Create Object.

Set spr_boss as obj_boss's sprite and select obj_enemy as its parent. Now you should see all the events inherited from obj_enemy in the Events panel of the Object Editor.

Right-click the inherited Create event and choose Inherit Event. Now you can access the code. We will use this event to set some important variables and start the attack timer:

```
1    event_inherited();
2
3    maxhp = 10;
4    hp = maxhp;
```

```
5    str = 1;
6    atk_delay = 2;
7
8    phase = 0;
9
10   alarm[0] = game_get_speed(gamespeed_fps) * atk_delay;
```

Lines 3-4: Setting the HP for the boss. We will use maxhp in later calculations.

Lines 5-6: Setting the strength of the attack and the attack delay (for the first phase).

Line 8: We will use this variable to keep track of the various phases of the boss.

Line 9: As usual, alarm 0 is the one used to attack.

Inherit also the Step event by right-clicking it and selecting Inherit Event. We want to keep the check on the HP, but we want to also add a tracking feature and the phase management:

```
1    event_inherited();
2
3    if ( instance_exists(obj_player) )
4    {
5        var _dir = point_direction(x,y, obj_player.x,
                    obj_player.y);
6        direction = _dir;
7    }
8
9    if ( hp<maxhp/2 and phase == 0)
10   {
11       phase = 1;
12       alarm[1] = game_get_speed(gamespeed_fps) * 0.1;
13   }
```

Lines 3-7: This code will rotate constantly the direction of the boss to face the player. This won't affect the boss sprite.

Lines 9-13: These lines change the phase of the boss to 1 when the HP drops to half of the maximum HP (maxhp/2). When the boss is in phase 1 (phase == 1), it grows bigger and then starts spawning UFOs.

Now, we have to implement the growth of the boss. Let's do it by creating a new Alarm 1 event by clicking Add Event ➤ Alarm ➤ Alarm 1. This is the alarm that will rule the growth of the boss. Add this code to the event:

```
1   if(sprite_width< 120 * 3)
2   {
3       if ( global.game_state == STATES.PLAYING )
4       {
5           image_xscale += 0.1;
6           image_yscale += 0.1;
7       }
8       alarm[1] = game_get_speed(gamespeed_fps) * 0.1;
9   }
10  else
11  {
12      atk_delay = 1;
13      alarm[2] = game_get_speed(gamespeed_fps) * 2;
14  }
```

Lines 1-9: This code makes the boss grow bigger until it reaches three times its original width (120 pixels).

Lines 10-14: After the boss finishes growing, it sets its attack delay to 1 (meaning one bullet per second). After this, it sets Alarm 2 so that it starts spawning one UFO every 4 seconds.

Finally, let's create a new Alarm 2 event to manage the UFO spawning by clicking Add Event ➤ Alarm ➤ Alarm 2. Put the following code in the event:

```
1   if ( global.game_state == STATES.PLAYING )
2   {
3       var _cam = view_camera[0];
4       var _cam_x = camera_get_view_x(_cam);
5       var _cam_y = camera_get_view_y(_cam);
6       var _cam_w = camera_get_view_width(_cam);
7       var _cam_h = camera_get_view_height(_cam);
8
9       var _minion_x = random_range( _cam_x, _cam_x +
        _cam_w );
10      var _minion_y = random_range( (_cam_y + _cam_h)/2,
        _cam_y + _cam_h );
11      instance_create_layer(_minion_x, _minion_y,
        "Instances", obj_enemy_ufo_red);
12  }
13  alarm[2] = game_get_speed(gamespeed_fps) * 2;
```

Lines 3–7: As usual, we calculate the coordinates of the cam.

Lines 10–11: These lines calculate random coordinates in the lower half of the screen and spawn an UFO in there.

That's it! Now we just need to do some little adjustment. We want the player to not destroy the boss when colliding with it, and we want the boss to make three explosions and give 1000 points as score, when killed.

Let's start with the collision. Right-click obj_boss's collision event with obj_player and choose Override Event and write this code in it:

```
1   other.hp -= atk;
```

The code above will damage only the player when they collide with the boss.

Now, let's take care of obj_boss's Destroy event.

CHAPTER 6 SHOOT 'EM UP!

Override also the Destroy event and write the code below in it:

```
1   effect_create_above(ef_explosion, x-30, y, 1, c_fuchsia);
2   effect_create_above(ef_explosion, x, y, 2, c_purple);
3   effect_create_above(ef_explosion, x+30, y, 1, c_fuchsia);
4   score += 1000;
```

Here we are! Put the boss at the end of level 2 and test the game by pressing F5 (Figure 6-8 shows the boss fight in action).

If you followed me until now, everything should work properly!

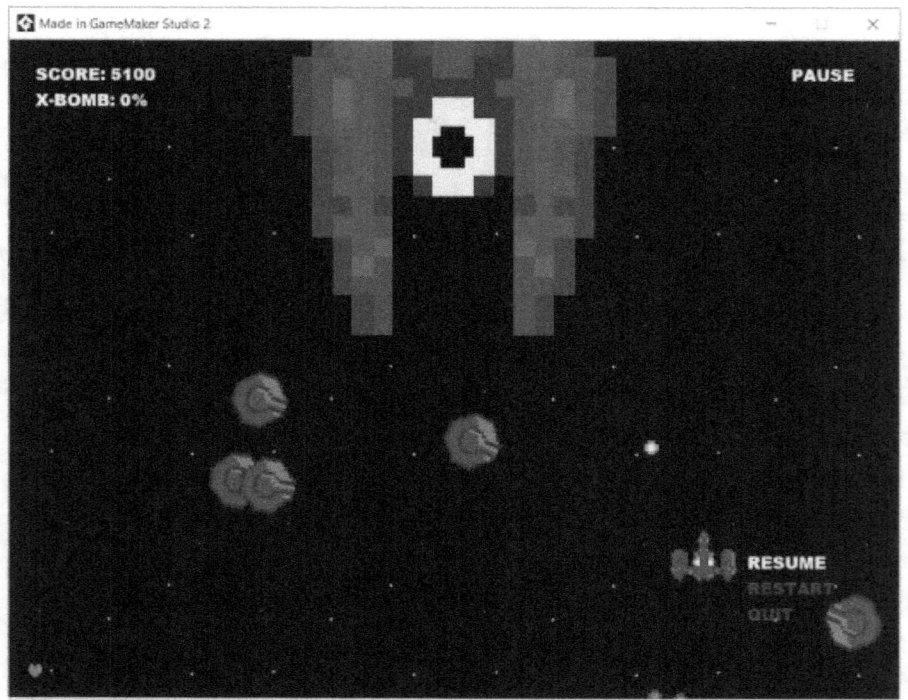

Figure 6-8. *In the middle of phase 2!*

Great! The game is complete!

We have an interesting gameplay and a variety of enemies! More importantly, we have a boss!

This game is a template that you can use to play, learn, and experiment! Free your imagination and try to make new levels or even extend the game with brand-new features!

Only by experimenting by yourself you can channel the game designer that's in you!

Conclusion

Space Gala started very small and became a game full of features and with an interesting gameplay. You learned so much in this chapter! We created a scrolling shooter filled with different kinds of enemies; we developed a chargeable special weapon, thanks to a color-switching system that allows the player to absorb bullets of their same color; we learned how to create paths and make NPCs follow them; and finally we made our very first boss fight!

This is amazing, and you should spend some time cheering to your determination and accomplishment!

Before diving into the next chapter, you should experiment with your new game and try to create some new exciting features (don't forget to update your GDD, if you do)!

In the next chapter, we will talk further about boss fights, and we will analyze some of the most important and iconic of the video games history, to better learn how we can do better and how a boss fight can be both challenging and fun!

TEST YOUR KNOWLEDGE!
---

1. How do you play an audio file in GM?
2. What is a viewport? How many of them can you have in GM?
3. What is a camera? How many of them can you have in GM?

CHAPTER 6   SHOOT 'EM UP!

4. What is an active camera? How many of them can you have in GM?

5. What is the difference between a viewport and a camera?

6. How can you access active cameras in GML?

7. How can you get the properties (position and size) of a camera?

8. How can you check if an instance of an object exists in a room?

9. How can you check if an instance is inside the boundaries of a specific active camera?

10. Can you improve color-switching by adding a new bonus or malus?

11. Do you think that adding more colors to color switching would be beneficial to gameplay? Why?

12. Can you explain the concept of inheritance?

13. Why is inheritance advantageous?

14. Can bullets benefit from inheritance?

15. Right now we are reusing obj_enemy_red from the previous game. This can be isolated in a separated enemy object not featuring the color property. Can you improve the hierarchy of obj_enemy by creating the colorless object?

16. What is a path in GMS? How can you create one?

17. How do you assign a path to an instance?

18. Are paths always walked at the coordinates at which they are drawn when created?

19. How can you make an instance track the position of another instance?

20. Can you come up with a new kind of enemy?

21. Enemies are quite weak until now. Make them stronger to increase the challenge. How does this affect the level design?

22. What are the best features of a shmup level?

23. Design a new level for Space Gala trying to make the color-switching feature shine.

24. What are the key features that a boss fight should have?

25. Design and implement a third phase for obj_boss.

26. Analyze DonPachi's combo mechanic, Bangai-O's grazing mechanic, and Ikaruga's polarization system.

    Can you tell what makes them so interesting and fun?

27. Play a shmup game (you can pick one of those listed), and write down what you liked and what you didn't like in the gameplay.

    How would you fix the things you didn't like?

    Can you integrate the things you liked in Space Gala?

CHAPTER 7

Designing Bosses

Video games are probably the most complex media around. They consist of a huge variety of components and tell stories in many ways: through environmental storytelling, cutscenes, and player interactions with characters. Among the most interesting and often complex characters are the bosses – the ones that get in the players' way.

Bosses are special characters that stand out from regular enemies both narratively and gameplay-wise. They are often found at the end of a level or area and play a crucial role in the player's progression and the story. Bosses often serve as teachers, helping players learn mechanics or master techniques. The best bosses make this learning process fun and significant in terms of storytelling and pathos. But what makes a boss fight fun?

The meaning of fun is debated across psychology and game design. One widely accepted theory is presented by Raph Koster in his book *A Theory of Fun*. He suggests that a game is fun if it teaches the player something at their own pace. When a game stops teaching or makes learning too difficult, it ceases to be fun. This principle applies particularly to boss fights.

A good boss fight should be challenging but not unfair. It can be intimidating but must also be rewarding and fair. The challenge and preparation required should always be matched by the value of the reward. Additionally, the outcome should be influenced by the player's preparation, knowledge, equipment, or other factors within the player's control.

CHAPTER 7   DESIGNING BOSSES

Boss fights are especially engaging when they teach new gameplay mechanics, allowing players to learn throughout the encounter. This could involve learning a new technique, move, item, or broader concepts like outsmarting enemies or using the environment to their advantage. The ability to face a challenge with critical thinking gives players a sense of control and makes their choices feel meaningful.

A great example of this is the Draygon boss fight in **Super Metroid** (Nintendo, 1994). Draygon is a huge beast that is hard to dodge, making nearly all its attacks hit the player. The player can defeat it by either mastering the controls or outsmarting the beast. During the most dangerous moment in the fight, when Draygon grabs Samus and flies around the map, Samus can set herself free by using the grappling hook to channel electricity into Draygon through a sparking machinery. Outsmarting such a powerful enemy gives the player a strong sense of satisfaction and makes the boss fight memorable.

The Draygon fight also teaches players about using game mechanics in innovative ways. By using the grappling hook trick, players learn that they can interact with the environment using their weapons and tools, opening up new ways to approach challenges. This lesson is key to both defeating Draygon and playing the rest of the game effectively.

Not only does the Draygon fight teach gameplay mechanics, but it also enhances the game's narrative. The sense of danger and urgency during the fight, combined with the player's ultimate victory, makes Samus feel like a true hero. This boss fight helps to establish the game's atmosphere and keeps players immersed.

Another example of autonomy in boss fights is the Ceaseless Discharge in **Dark Souls** (FromSoftware, 2009). This optional boss, a massive demon made of lava, can be beaten either by engaging in a challenging fight or by tricking it into falling into a pit. The narrative behind this boss fight, involving the demon's love for his dead sister, adds emotional depth and makes players empathize with him. This emotional connection often

CHAPTER 7 DESIGNING BOSSES

leads players to avoid the fight altogether, demonstrating how meaningful storytelling can enhance player engagement.

Both Draygon and Ceaseless Discharge teach us how to create memorable boss fights by leveraging game mechanics, providing a sense of autonomy, and integrating narrative elements. These fights show that giving players the freedom to approach challenges in different ways and creating emotional connections can make boss fights more engaging and satisfying.

Teaching and Experimenting

One of the video game series that gets everyone to agree is The Legend of Zelda. The Zelda series is an endless source of game design lessons, especially when it comes to boss fights. One of the most interesting boss fights is the first boss fight in "The Legend of Zelda: A Link to the Past". This fight features six Armos Knights that jump around the room in various patterns, trying to collide with and damage the player. Due to how Link attacks and the knights move, it's very difficult to dodge and attack them with the sword. However, just before the boss fight, there's a chest containing a bow. Using the bow allows the player to stay at a distance and easily eliminate the knights one by one, turning a challenging boss fight into an easy task. This teaches players how to use new items through boss fights: you get a new item, test it on easy foes, and then your skills are tested in a boss fight. After defeating the boss, the game knows you've mastered that technique and can add complexity to the gameplay.

Learning and being tested is good and makes a challenge fun, but the ability to face situations autonomously and creatively is also very important. This is achieved by letting the player experiment and face challenges in different, nonstandard ways. It's important to teach techniques in boss fights, but it's equally important not to force the player into one way of completing a challenge. Give them the possibility to succeed in different ways, even if it means more effort.

CHAPTER 7   DESIGNING BOSSES

One of the best examples of autonomy and experimentation in a boss fight is The End in **Metal Gear Solid 3: Snake Eater** (Konami, 2004). This fight is a sniper challenge against the veteran sniper nicknamed The End. He's hiding in the forest with full camouflage, constantly aiming and shooting at the player. The standard way to take him down is by using binoculars to search for the glint of his sniper rifle's lens or by using the directional microphone to listen for his heavy breathing and, after locating him, taking him down. This fight is super fun and educational since you get to test every important skill in the game: observing, planning, camouflaging, stealth, and more. You also learn how to use important tools that can help you outside the boss fight. Outsmarting the best sniper around using what you have is satisfying and memorable.

There are a couple of tricks to avoid the fight, making this probably the most interesting boss fight in the game. You can avoid facing The End by sniping him earlier in the game or by saving the game when the fight starts and loading it one week later (one week in real time, not in the game). In the second method, since The End is very old, he will die of natural causes, allowing you to proceed without problems. It's a bit of a dark Easter egg, but undeniably brilliant!

As you can see, good boss fights always offer possibilities, challenges, motivation, and lessons to learn.

Motivation!

There are boss fights that break all the rules we've talked about but are still memorable. These fights rely heavily on narrative and give players strong motivation to fight by leveraging their emotions and sense of connection to the game world and its characters.

One brilliant example is the Mother Brain boss fight in **Super Metroid**. Mother Brain is the source of all the chaos in the game, which is a good enough reason to defeat her. But just before the fight, she kills the baby

CHAPTER 7 DESIGNING BOSSES

Metroid you've been protecting. This act of cruelty ignites the player's rage, making the fight intensely personal. You're equipped with a vaporizing laser, and shattering her brain becomes one of the most satisfying experiences in gaming. The fight is easy, but the emotional drive makes it unforgettable.

Creating this kind of motivation involves building a narrative setting, fostering relationships between the player and NPCs, and then introducing dramatic events. Players are engaged because they care about the characters and know their actions matter. This engagement keeps them playing, even if the challenge is tough. The harder and more fun the challenge, combined with strong motivation, the more memorable the boss fight.

Another contemporary example of a boss fight that leverages social relatedness is in **Undertale** (Toby Fox, 2015). Undertale is filled with charismatic characters, and the relationship between them and the player is key. The game has three different endings based on how you interact with NPCs and bosses: pacifist, genocide, and neutral. One of the most notable boss fights is against Sans, unlocked only in the genocide run. Sans breaks all the good design rules: he deals damage over time and attacks without warning. These attacks are fast and hard to dodge, and he even mocks you, suggesting you give up. Beating him requires intense training and memorization of his attacks, but the fight is incredibly satisfying because it aligns with the game's core theme of determination.

Sans' fight is unfair by design but memorable because it ties into the player's emotional investment and the overarching narrative of determination. Undertale teaches game designers how to create charismatic and fun bosses by leveraging players' need for social relatedness to boost their motivation and immersion. The unfairness of Sans' fight makes it memorable because the player cares deeply about their journey and reasons for fighting. This is a crucial lesson: players will engage deeply with a game if their actions feel meaningful and connected to the story.

239

CHAPTER 7 DESIGNING BOSSES

How Can We Use This?

In Space Gala, we created a simple boss fight that doesn't quite compare to the likes of Draygon, Sans, or other memorable bosses. Our one-eyed space monster might be a bit scary, but it lacks the depth and emotional impact. The main thing it does well is reinforce the core gameplay mechanics of Space Gala: dodging and shooting. And that's important! A good boss fight should teach or reinforce gameplay mechanics, just like the Armos Knights in A Link to the Past. To beat our one-eyed boss, players need to dodge bullets and UFOs while constantly shooting. It's functional but not memorable. So, how can we make it better and more enjoyable?

One idea is to introduce new behavior. Maybe the monster gets tired after following the player around and, when it's exhausted, closes its eye, stops spawning UFOs, and stops shooting. This would give the player a chance to clear the area of UFOs before the monster resumes its attack. Another option is to add narrative depth. Maybe the monster is the leader of the alien vanguard, and defeating it delays the invasion. Giving the boss a purpose or backstory can make the fight more engaging.

There are many ways to improve this boss fight. Right now, you have a basic project that you can build on and enhance with new tools, weapons, mechanics, or narrative elements. Designing a game experience is the most delicate phase of game development and determines whether the game is just a pastime or an exciting, memorable experience.

From our discussion, we can say that a fun boss fight should challenge the player and teach or reinforce a gameplay mechanic. It should leverage the player's emotions and psychological needs, like the need to relate to the game world and its characters and the meaningfulness of their actions. Players should be able to choose their own style and pursue their objectives without feeling forced into a specific narrative or gameplay path.

CHAPTER 7 DESIGNING BOSSES

To conclude, a good boss fight should keep the player immersed in the gameplay and provide a reason to keep playing – whether it's narrative motivation or fun gameplay. Ideally, it should also serve as a final test of the skills and mechanics the player has mastered throughout the game, enhancing their sense of competence and achievement.

Tip   You should try to think about all the most interesting and memorable boss fights you found in your gaming experience and ask yourself: What makes this boss fight memorable? Asking and answering these questions will help you to develop a sort of awareness in terms of good game design and will allow you to create better game experiences.

Try to use this knowledge to improve Space Gala and its boss fight!

In the next chapter, we will start a new adventure exploring the platformer genre, which is one of the most important. We will create a single-screen platformer that will be extended to a scrolling platformer in Chapter 9 – just like we did with Space Gala. Exploring the huge world of 2D platforming will give us the opportunity to learn some very important concepts of game design and development like gravity, jump, 2D movements, special platforms, power-ups, different kinds of enemies, and so on.

That's going to be a lot of fun!

CHAPTER 8

Single-Screen Platformer

In the previous chapters, we built from scratch a couple of shoot 'em up games basing our design on the classics of the genre. We got inspiration from giants like Galaga, Space Invaders, and Ikaruga. We explored the genre in its entirety and its evolution through the years learning precious lessons about how to design and develop a good and fun STG. We studied and reproduced important and iconic features that shaped the genre, and we improved on our own design from chapter to chapter. Finally, we talked extensively about boss fight design, and we saw some important cases from the industry.

In this chapter and the next, we are going to follow the same creative process by creating a basic game and improving it following the historical evolution of the 2D platformer game genre.

In this chapter, we will create a single-screen platformer taking inspiration from games like Space Panic (Universal, 1980), Donkey Kong (DK; Nintendo, 1981), Pitfall! (Activision, 1982), Lode Runner (Brøderbund Software, 1983), The Fairyland Story (Taito, 1985), Mario Bros. (Nintendo, 1985), and Bubble Bobble (Taito, 1986). Our game will be a single-screen platformer in which the player has to collect items scattered in the level moving between the platforms by jumping and climbing ladders while avoiding enemies and get to the end of the level.

CHAPTER 8   SINGLE-SCREEN PLATFORMER

With this project, we will have the possibility to understand the nature and the evolution of the genre while learning how to create from scratch common game mechanics like jumping, climbing ladders, creating power-ups and items, and managing a side-scrolling camera. We will then focus our attention on the design of the genre, what's important, and how to make it fun. Fasten your seatbelt and get ready, once again, to make games!

When you think about video games, probably the first idea that comes to your mind is platformer games – those games where you control a character that has to walk through the whole level from one side of the screen to the other picking items, crushing enemies, and saving princesses.

Platformers are one of the most important and one of the oldest game genre of the history of the medium. They are actually a sub-genre of the action game genre; and even if now it's synonym with jumping on platforms (so much that jumping on platforms is actually known as platforming), in the beginnings of the genre, it was mostly about climbing ladders and trekking through small single-screen levels.

We are going to study platformers and not action games in general because it's a singularity in the video games history. In fact, it's the only sub-genre that is constantly on the frontline of the gaming experimentation. Always evolving, platformers defined the various gaming eras by introducing new iconic gameplay elements – a totally opposite approach compared to STG games!

There are a lot of platformer games that revolutionized the video games industry! For example, Super Mario Bros. introduced side-scrolling and metamorphosis; Sonic the Hedgehog added (a kind of) physics to movements and platforming; Tomb Raider created the first worldwide recognized female heroine; Crash Bandicoot mixed traditional platforming with plenty of mini-games; Super Mario 64 set the de facto standard on 3D platforming with cutting-edge camera and movement controls; and Prince of Persia: The Sands of Time revolutionized the genre with its rewind system. Even now, the platformer genre is a vibrant one, full of revolutionary ideas and always dragging the gameplay evolution forward.

CHAPTER 8   SINGLE-SCREEN PLATFORMER

It all started with Space Panic (Universal, 1980), an arcade game in which the player had to dig holes in the ground to trap the enemies and then hit them with the shovel to kill them off. The possibility to move between the platforms using ladders made this the first platformer game of the history.

Space Panic didn't feature neither jump nor screen scrolling. At the time, jump and gravity were two complex concepts to add to a game, and screen scrolling was unaffordable in many cases for technological reasons.

One year after the release of Space Panic, Nintendo published the game that started not one but two IPs: Donkey Kong (Nintendo, 1981).

Donkey Kong was so important in many ways! Firstly, it was the beginning of both Donkey Kong and Mario; secondly, it was the game that everybody recognizes as the true first platformer. In fact, even if Space Panic was the first, the one that everybody remembers is Donkey Kong. This is probably because it implemented all the determining characteristics of the 2D single-screen platformer like jumping to move between platforms, ladders, power-ups, and obstacles. From Donkey Kong, the platformer genre became more about jumping than climbing ladders.

The first half of the 1980s was mostly made of similar-looking single-screen platformers that were about killing all the enemies in the room to move forward or going from point A to point B. Apart from Nintendo, with the already mentioned Donkey Kong and Mario Bros. games, many other developers, especially in Japan, were producing games with this kind of gameplay; one above all is Taito that published many blockbusters like The Fairyland Story and Bubble Bobble.

It's interesting to dedicate some words to Mario Bros., though, because it introduced a couple of interesting features. In fact, this first prototype of the adventures of the Italian plumber featured complex interactions with the enemies that could be jumped on making them fall on their back and then could be kicked – a mechanic that became iconic since then. The game also featured a nice cooperative gameplay that became the de facto standard in singlescreen platformers.

CHAPTER 8   SINGLE-SCREEN PLATFORMER

We now have a clearer idea of what are the main characteristics of the genre, but what is important to a platformer to be fun? What do we want to take from those classics to shape our game?

The game we are going to create will be a single-screen platformer. This choice has a double benefit: it's easy to make (which is good, since you are learning), and it's also very interesting from a game design point of view! In fact, it's not easy to create an interesting gameplay or level in a space so small! But it's when you have to face hard challenges that you can really learn and test your design skills!

The game will use both the jumping and ladder climbing systems. Since we have a limited space, it's important to give the player more options to move and the level designer more elements to create interesting levels.

The game, as we said, will be about collecting items. The player should collect all the objects in the room to go to the next level.

The player can win the game by collecting all the items for all the levels and can lose it dying three times.

Let's put all this on a game design document that we will use as a reference while developing the game!

Cherry Caves

Cherry Caves is a single player 2D platformer game about collecting items in a set of labyrinthine caves. It's inspired by the classics of the first half of the 1980s – the single-screen platformer era.

Story and Setting

In 20XX, the Earth saw the extinction of cherries that now can be found only by extracting them from old snacks and illicit traffics. Cherries are now even more expensive than the most precious metal in the world and the purest diamond.

CHAPTER 8 SINGLE-SCREEN PLATFORMER

You heard the voice that cherries are naturally growing in a cave populated by strange alien creatures in the form of big colored balls.

Fearless and with a great desire of tasting cherries and becoming rich by reselling them, you decide to adventure in the deeps of the Cherry Caves.

Gameplay

The goal in Cherry Caves is to collect all the cherries in every level and get to the exit.

While trying to collect all the cherries, the player will be put in danger by strange enemies bouncing around the level.

Victory Condition

Each level is completed by reaching the goal represented by a yellow star (Figure 8-1).

Figure 8-1. *The yellow star, representing the goal that needs to be reached in the level*

The level can be completed only by collecting all the cherries in it (Figure 8-2). Until that moment, the star will remain grayed out (Figure 8-3).

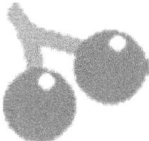

Figure 8-2. *Icon of the cherries, the item that needs to be collected in order to complete the level*

CHAPTER 8 SINGLE-SCREEN PLATFORMER

The player can lose the game by getting hit by the enemies three times. Every time the player gets hit, they restart from the starting point of the current level.

Note The player has only one possibility of getting hit before restarting the level, because levels are very small and to have more than one possibility to get hit would have lowered the challenge too much.

Controls

Controls are pretty standard with the arrow keys to move and the spacebar to jump.

Left: Move left.
Right: Move right.
Up: If on the ladder, climb up.
Down: If on the ladder, climb down.
Spacebar: Jump.
Esc: Open/close menu.

Enemies

Enemies, from a coding point of view, are very similar. They don't attack; they just move following patterns. The design of the level is what makes them a threat to the player. Anyway, just to differentiate a bit, there are two different enemies that you can find in the caves:

- **Purple Balls**: These strange balls only bump following a vertical pattern. They are found usually in small spaces blocking the way to some juicy cherry treasure.

CHAPTER 8 SINGLE-SCREEN PLATFORMER

- **Green Balls**: These strange green balls follow more complex and longer patterns and can give a serious headache to an unprepared explorer.

Assets

To create Cherry Caves, first of all, we need some assets. So open up GameMaker, and let's create a bunch of new resources that we will use to build our game!

Sprites

To create a new sprite, right-click Objects in the Resources sidebar, and select Create Object. Do this for all the following sprites!

spr_player_idle

Size: 50 × 64
Pivot Point: Middle-center
Collision Mask: Automatic, Rectangle

spr_player_walk

This is an animated sprite. You can make one by simply creating a single spr_player_walk sprite and adding two images to it using the *Import* key or by creating images individually in the Sprite Editor.

249

CHAPTER 8   SINGLE-SCREEN PLATFORMER

Size: 50 × 64
Pivot Point: Middle-center
Collision Mask: Automatic, Rectangle
Speed: 4

spr_player_climb

Size: 50 × 64
Pivot Point: Middle-center
Collision Mask: Automatic, Rectangle

spr_block_red

Size: 64 × 64
Pivot Point: Middle-center
Collision Mask: Automatic, Rectangle

spr_block_brown

Size: 64 × 64
Pivot Point: Middle-center
Collision Mask: Automatic, Rectangle

spr_ladder

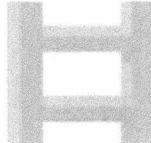

Size: 64 × 64
Pivot Point: Middle-center
Collision Mask: Automatic, Rectangle

spr_ball_purple

Size: 64 × 64
Pivot Point: Middle-center
Collision Mask: Automatic, Rectangle

CHAPTER 8   SINGLE-SCREEN PLATFORMER

spr_ball_green

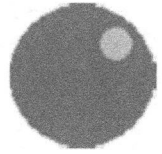

Size: 64 × 64
Pivot Point: Middle-center
Collision Mask: Automatic, Rectangle

spr_cherry

Size: 64 × 64
Pivot Point: Middle-center
Collision Mask: Automatic, Rectangle

spr_goal

Size: 64 × 64
Pivot Point: Middle-center
Collision Mask: Automatic, Rectangle

Fonts

To create a font, right-click Fonts in the Resources sidebar, and select Create Font.

fnt_score

For this font, I am using the preinstalled Consolas font with style regular and size 20. If you are not a Windows user or you don't have Consolas installed on your computer, just pick the font you like better to show the score in your game.

Sounds

snd_menu: This sound effect will be played when opening the menu and moving the cursor.
    snd_goal: This one will be played when touching the goal.
    snd_cherry: This is played when picking a cherry.
    snd_jump: A sound effect played when jumping.
    snd_damage: This effect will be played when taking damage.

How to Create a Hero

Berry will be our first recognizable hero! We already made three games, but none of them featured a recognizable character. Berry, with his blueberry hair and chibi style, aims for that title! Let's help him by creating him!

To create Berry, right-click Objects in the Resources sidebar and select Create Object. Name it obj_player and select spr_player_idle as its default sprite.

A platformer is not such if you can't move! So, let's give Berry the ability to walk!

CHAPTER 8 SINGLE-SCREEN PLATFORMER

The concepts we are going to use to let the player walk are just the same that we applied to Space Gala. Anyway, this time we will not use separated events for every key, but we will manage everything in the Step event by using GML.

Before we dive into the coding in the Step event, we need to create some useful variable that we will need later.

Create a new Event by clicking Add Event and selecting **Create**.

In this event, we will create the usual *spd* variable. You already know that one; it will store the value of the speed at which we want the player to move. Additionally, we will also create a *hsp* which is the horizontal speed, representing the combination of the absolute speed value and the direction of our character (left or right).

So, easy as it sounds, add this line to obj_player's Create event:

```
1   spd = 4;
2   hsp = 0;
```

Ok, now we can focus on the main event of this object: the step event.

Create a new step event by clicking Add Event ➤ Step ➤ Step in the Object Editor.

To check whether the player is pressing a key, without using the dedicated events, we must use a family of dedicated functions which are shown and explained below.

keyboard_check(key_code): This function checks whether the key with code key_code is held down or not. It takes a keyboard code as input and returns a Boolean value that tells whether the player pressed or not the key.

The key_code is a number that represents a keyboard key for the system. GameMaker provides you with all the key codes you may need. Check the documentation for more details.

CHAPTER 8   SINGLE-SCREEN PLATFORMER

keyboard_check_pressed(key_code): This function checks whether the key with code key_code has just been pressed. Just like keyboard_check, it takes as input a key code and returns a Boolean telling the programmer if the key was actually pressed or not.

keyboard_check_released(key_code): This function checks whether the key with code key_code has just been released. It takes as input a key code and returns a Boolean telling the programmer if the key was actually pressed or not.

For our purpose, we will use keyboard_check to check if the player pressed the arrow keys to move, because we want the player to continue moving while holding down the key.

So, let's write up some code in that empty Step event:

```
1   var _keyleft = keyboard_check(vk_left);
2   var _keyright = keyboard_check(vk_right);
3
4   var _move = _keyright - _keyleft;
5   hsp = spd * _move;
6
7   if ( _move != 0 )
8   {
9       image_xscale = _move;
10      sprite_index = spr_player_walk;
11  }
12  else
13  {
14      sprite_index = spr_player_idle;
15  }
16
17  x += hsp;
```

Lines 1–2: We use _keyleft and _keyright to store the result of the function calls that check if the player pressed the left or right keys.

255

Lines 4–5: We declared a new temporary variable called _move. In this variable, we are storing the difference between the values of _keyleft and _keyright (note that the numeric value of true is 1 and the value of false is 0) so that if we are pressing right, move is equal to 1 - 0 = 1 and when we are pressing left, move is equal to 0 - 1 = -1. You will see in a bit how this can be useful.

The variable hsp, as already said, represents the horizontal speed, which is the velocity at which the player is moving on the X-axis. When hsp is 0, the player is not moving left or right; when it's greater than 0, the player is moving right; when it's less than 0, the player is moving left.

Since we are very smart, we are using move to understand the direction toward which the player wants to move by multiplying the value of the speed to move. This will save us from writing an if statement.

Lines 7–16: Here we check that the player is moving by checking that move is different from 0. If the player is moving, we want the sprite to face the right direction. To do that, we are using the image_xscale property which tells GameMaker to draw the sprite normally (when image_xscale equals 1) or flipped (when image_xscale equals -1). We could have accomplished this also by creating two sprites, one for the left and one for the right; and you should still do this if you want your character to have two different looks when looking left and when looking right, but this is not the case.

We also want the player to change the sprite accordingly to the fact that it's moving or not. This is why we change the sprite to spr_player_walking when move is not zero; else, we change it to spr_player_idle.

Line 17: At the end, we add the value of hsp to x, effectively moving obj_player on the X-axis.

Now open up the first room – that I renamed room0 – and drag obj_player and drop it in the middle of the level. Run the game, and you will see that Berry moves left and right (Figure 8-3), but it doesn't stop and goes outbound. Let's fix this!

CHAPTER 8 SINGLE-SCREEN PLATFORMER

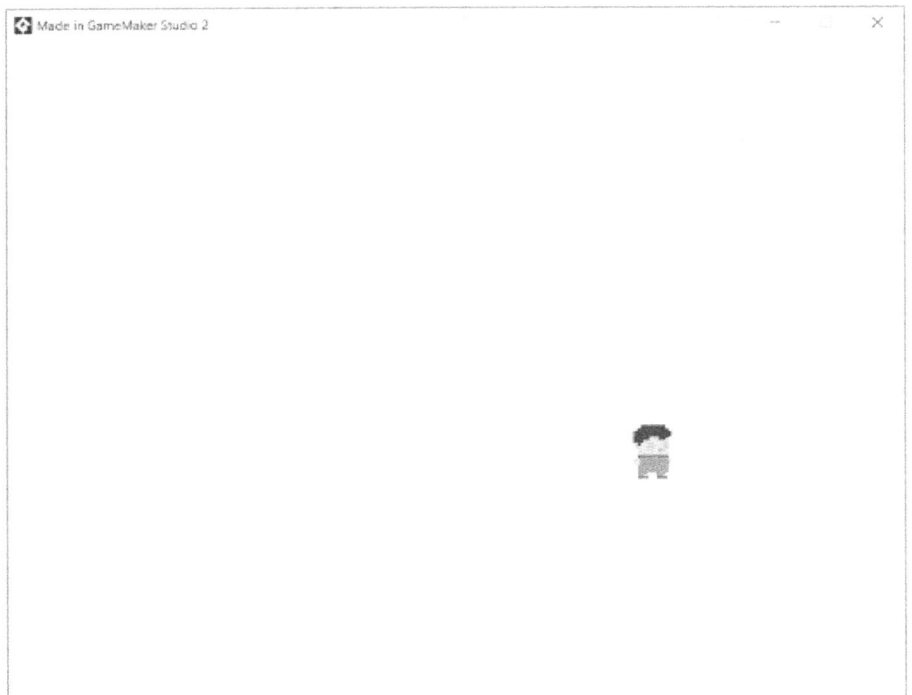

Figure 8-3. *Berry moves left and right, but doesn't stop when the room ends*

Setting the Boundaries

In Space Gala, we defined where the player could go and where they could not by setting some boundaries related to the dimension of the camera. We could do this also this time, but instead, we will create an object that we will use to block the way of our player. This block will be used both as a delimiter and as the ground on which the player can walk. Having the blocks to also delimit the screen boundaries allows us to better define the level from an aesthetic point of view and to save us some lines of code (which is always good).

CHAPTER 8   SINGLE-SCREEN PLATFORMER

In Cherry Caves, we will use two kinds of blocks that from a coding perspective are the same thing, but they feature two different sprites (spr_block_brown and spr_block_red). This will help us in the task of making levels feel more colorful and different from one another. Often this technique was used in blockbuster games like Taito's Bubble Bobble or even other game genres like Namco's Pac-Man.

To have those two kinds of blocks means that we should create two different objects; but since we want them to behave in the same way, we should make a third object that we will use as the parent, so that we can code all the logic around that one object and have it inherited to the other two.

Figure 8-4 shows the hierarchy that we will use with the three block objects.

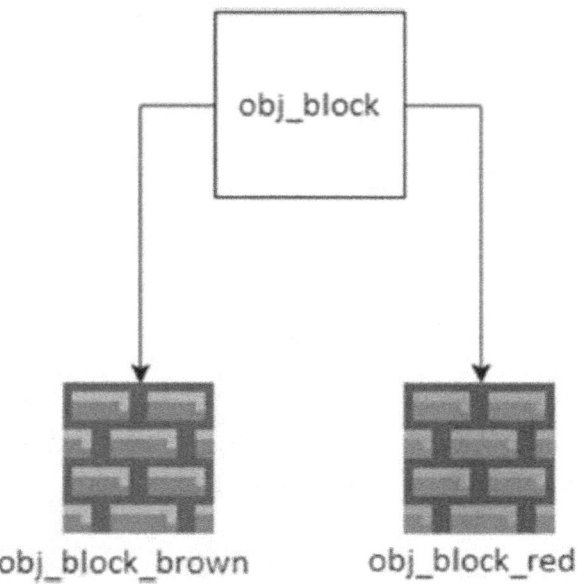

Figure 8-4. Blocks hierarchy

CHAPTER 8 SINGLE-SCREEN PLATFORMER

Let's create the three objects by right-clicking Objects in the Resources sidebar and selecting Create Object. Name the first obj_block and assign no sprite to it, name the second obj_block_brown and give it the spr_block_brown sprite, and then give the third one the name of obj_block_red and the spr_block_red ground.

Add obj_block as parent for both obj_block_red and obj_block_brown. To do so, open their Object Editor and click Parent and choose obj_block.

Anyway, we won't use any of those objects to program the logic. We will continue using the obj_player's step event.

So open up obj_player's Object Editor and select the Step event. Add to the bottom of the event these lines:

```
1  if ( place_meeting(x+hsp, y, obj_block) )
2  {
3    while ( not place_meeting(x+sign(hsp), y, obj_block) )
4    {
5      x += sign(hsp);
6    }
7    hsp = 0;
8  }
9  x += hsp;
```

Line 1: place_meeting(x, y, object) moves the current instance to the provided *x,y* coordinates, then checks if there's a collision with *object*, and finally moves the instance back to its original coordinates.

It's a function to check collisions just like the dedicated event we used in Space Gala to check collisions between the enemies, the player, and the bullets.

We are checking collisions in the step event instead of using a dedicated event, because we need to tweak a bit the collision checking. In fact, in line 1, we are not just checking the current coordinates at which obj_player's instance is; instead we are checking if we will collide with an instance of obj_block (or its children) after advancing *hsp* pixels on the X-axis.

259

CHAPTER 8   SINGLE-SCREEN PLATFORMER

Lines 3–7: If obj_player is going to collide after *hsp* pixels, since we want a pixel-perfect collision, we start a loop in which we add 1 pixel in the right direction (using the sign function, explained in detail later) on the X-axis to obj_player and check if it collides with obj_block (or its children). Until it doesn't, we continue adding 1 pixel on the X-coordinate. When obj_player eventually collides with obj_block (or its children), we stop doing this and set hsp to 0 so that obj_player won't move anymore.

Here we created a pixel-perfect collision system to use obj_block instances as walls that block horizontally the player.

Line 9: We update *x* as the last thing, so that all the modifications we are making with the collision checking have effect on *hsp* and on the value of *x*.

Note   In the previous code, to check for the sign of hsp, we used the sign function.

sign(num) is a function that given a number num returns 1 if num is greater than 0, -1 if it's less than zero, and 0 if it's equal to 0.

Now open up room0 and add two instances of obj_block_brown or obj_block_red to the left and right side of obj_player instance. Running the game, you can verify that obj_player will collide with the blocks being unable to pass over them (Figure 8-5).

CHAPTER 8 SINGLE-SCREEN PLATFORMER

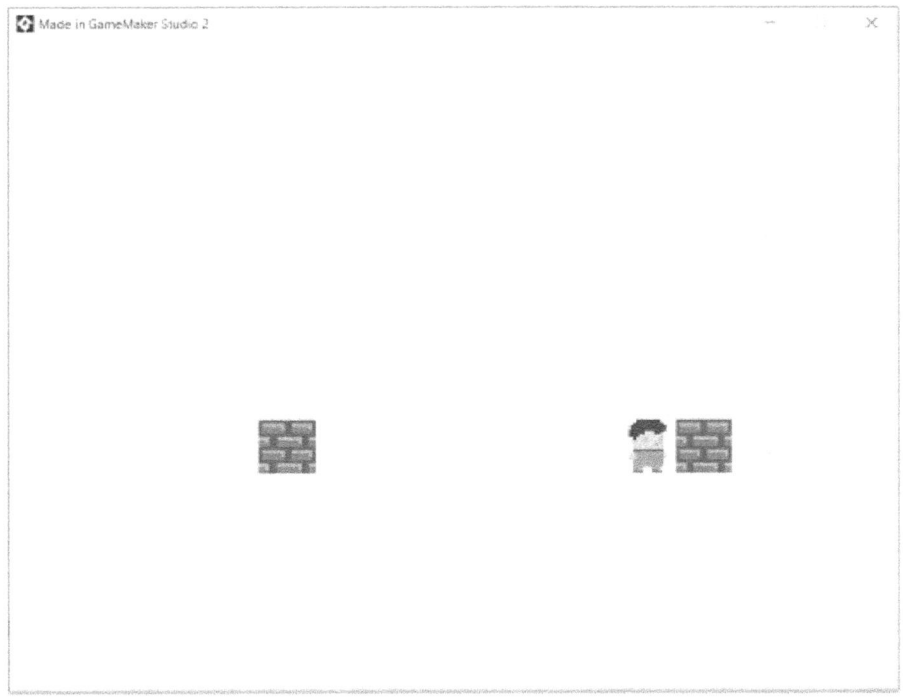

Figure 8-5. *Now we can block Berry using children of obj_block (in this case obj_block_brown)*

Something is not right, though. Berry shouldn't be allowed to float in the air; he should be subject to gravity.

GameMaker comes with its own physics system that can simulate a fairly accurate physical system. It has also a gravity system, and it's very good if you want to make a game like Angry Birds. That's not our case. In fact, in a platformer, just like in a shmup, it's very important for the system to have pixel-perfect movements and a very arcade playstyle. Platformer gamers don't want to slip over a platform because of friction and acceleration, they don't want to have an accurate physics system when colliding, and so on. What is important in a platformer game is precision,

261

CHAPTER 8 SINGLE-SCREEN PLATFORMER

and this can be achieved only by moving things the old way. That's why we won't use GameMaker physics system, but instead we are going to learn how to create an arcade gravity system in the old-school way.

Everything That Goes Up Comes Down

Gravity represents the acceleration of any mass falling on the ground, and in fact also in games it's represented as a value that adds constantly to the y-position of an object (generally the player's avatar). There's a difference though: in real life, acceleration increases the velocity of a falling object, that keeps going faster and faster, while in video games, this doesn't generally happen – especially in arcade games. In arcade games, gravity is treated as if it was the speed at which an object is falling, rather than the acceleration.

While an object is not on a blocking surface, it falls down, and its position is updated by adding to its Y-coordinate a fixed amount of pixels equal to the gravity value.

We will use a variable to represent gravity and to update the player's Y-coordinate. We will then apply the same principle we used for the horizontal collision with obj_block, on the Y-axis, so that obj_player will be blocked by obj_block (or one of its children) and it will stop falling. We will track if the player is grounded or not by using a Boolean variable.

So, first of all, let's add *grv* (for gravity) and *grounded* to the Create event of obj_player:

```
1    grv = 0.5;
2    grounded = false;
3
```

And now let's open up again obj_player's step event and add some code at the bottom of the file:

```
1   vsp = vsp + grv;
2   if (place_meeting(x, y+vsp, obj_block))
3   {
4   while (not place_meeting(x, y+sign(vsp), obj_blcck))
5   {
6   y += sign(vsp);
7   }
8   vsp = 0;
9   grounded = true;
10  }
11  else
12  {
13  grounded = false;
14  }
15  y += vsp;
```

Line 1: Here we are doing with vsp (vertical speed) the same thing we did with hsp; but instead of adding speed and multiplying it by the direction we want to move to, we just add the gravity value to vsp, which is the vertical speed.

Line 2: Here we check if obj_player will collide with an instance of (or derived from) obj_block after vsp pixels on the Y-axis. This is the same concept we applied to the previous piece of code to calculate horizontal collisions with obj_block.

Lines 4-9: Like in the previous code, when we see that adding vsp pixels to the Y-coordinate of obj_player will result in a collision with obj_block, we update y by adding 1 pixel in the direction of vsp (just like we did with x and hsp). When obj_player finally reaches obj_block, vsp gets set to 0 and grounded to true. In fact, when obj_player perfectly collides with obj_block, this means that Berry touched the ground, so he's grounded.

CHAPTER 8 SINGLE-SCREEN PLATFORMER

Line 13: If obj_player is not touching obj_block anymore, grounded gets set to false, meaning that the player is floating and should be affected by gravity (hence, vsp shouldn't be set to 0, like we do in case of collision (line 8).

Line 15: After all these checks, the Y-coordinate gets finally updated by adding to it a vsp number of pixels effectively moving (or not) the player's avatar.

Time to test! Open up room0 and add some instances of obj_block_brown all around the borders of the room and put obj_player in the middle of it and run the game. You will see that Berry will fall to the ground and can move around but he can't go over the blocks (Figure 8-6).

A gravity system is not very useful if you cannot jump! That's the next thing we are going to cover!

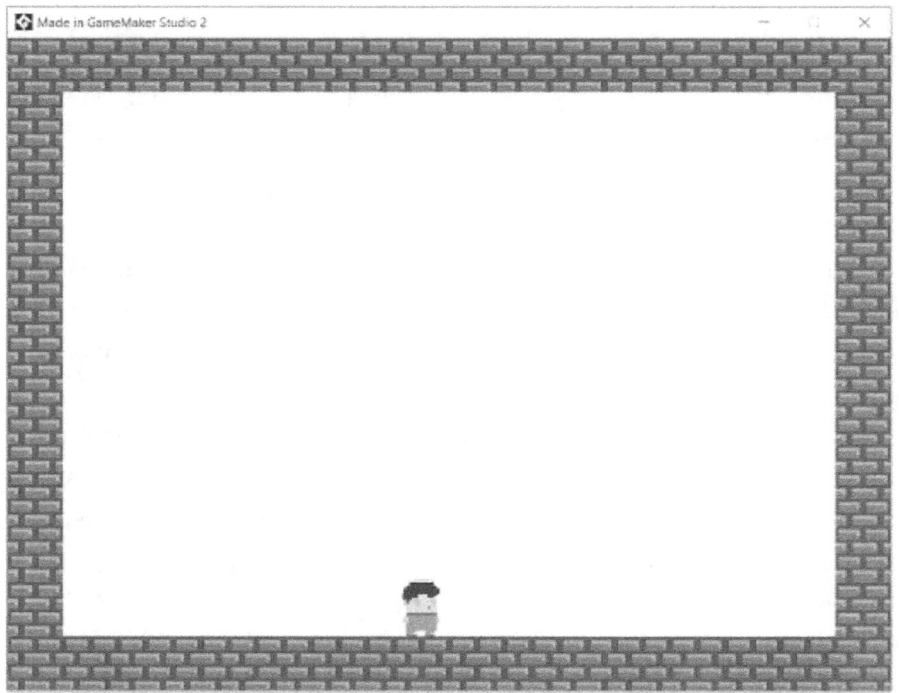

Figure 8-6. *Gravity affects Berry, making him fall on the ground represented by the blocks*

Get a Jump on Gravity!

Jumping is way simpler than you could think. In fact, if falling means adding pixels to the Y-coordinate, jumping means the opposite: subtracting pixels from the Y-coordinate. This is what we do when jumping. We will check whether the player pressed the spacebar key, and if they did, we subtract a fixed value to the Y-coordinate.

First, we should add to obj_player's Create event the jspd variable representing the jump speed which is the power of the jump:

```
1   jspd = 10;
```

Then open up obj_player's Step event, and let's add the logic we talked about by adding this line at the top of the code:

```
1   var jumping = keyboard_check_pressed(vk_space);
```

And this code at the bottom of obj_player's Step event, just before updating the Y-coordinate:

```
1   if ( grounded and jumping )
2   {
3   vsp = -jspd;
4   grounded = false;
5   sprite_index = spr_player_idle;
6   }
```

That's it! Now running the game, you should be able to see that pressing the spacebar, the player will be able to jump and fall back on the ground (Figure 8-7)!

CHAPTER 8　SINGLE-SCREEN PLATFORMER

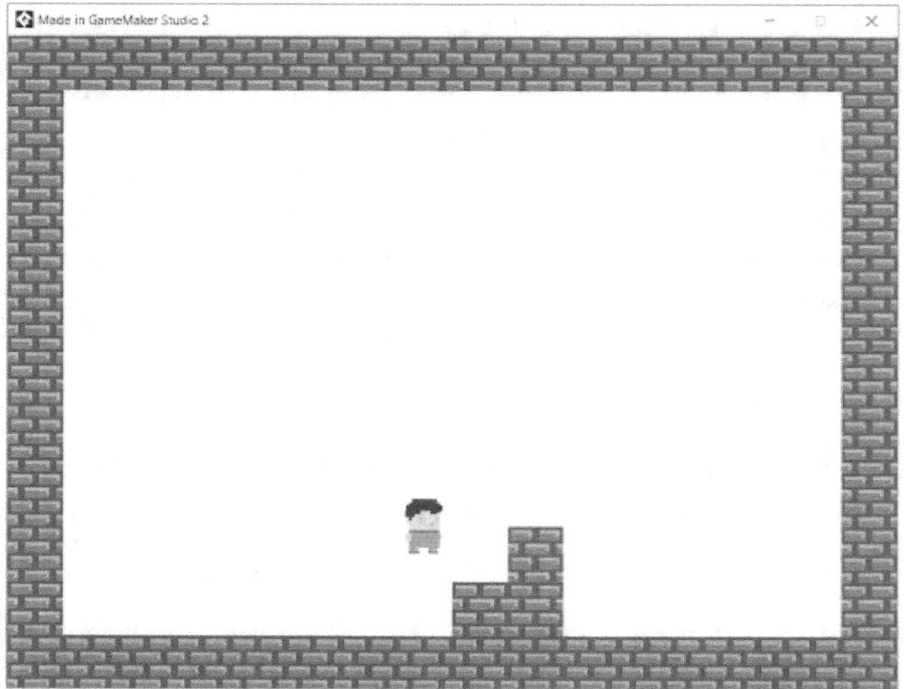

Figure 8-7. *Berry can now jump and fall back on the floor*

Climbing the Ladder

We are halfway from finishing our game. We want to add yet another feature! We want the player to be able to climb ladders, a very important feature in single-screen platformers.

To manage gravity, we will use a climbing controller variable that will be switched to true when the player is on a ladder and to false when they're not.

This variable will allow us to better manage animations and gravity.

We also need to check if the player is pressing the up and down arrow keys, because we want the player to climb the ladder only when they're standing in front of it and pressing the up or down button. By doing this, the player will change the status of the climbing variable; and from that moment, pressing the up or down key will mean moving up or down, not being affected by gravity anymore. Gravity will return to affect the player position after they climbed down the ladder.

So, first, let's add the climbing variable to the obj_player Create event:

```
1   climbing = false;
```

We initialize it with the false value because we assume that every level should not start being on a ladder.

We are going to change some bits of code we wrote for obj_player's Step event, and add some more. Following, you will find obj_player's Step event new code, after the modifications and additions – let's analyze it:

```
1   var _keyleft = keyboard_check ( vk_left );
2   var _keyright = keyboard_check ( vk_right );
3   var _keyup = keyboard_check ( vk_up );
4   var _keydown = keyboard_check ( vk_down );
5   var _jumping = keyboard_check_pressed ( vk_space );
6
7   var _move = _keyright - _keyleft;
8   var _vmove = _keydown - _keyup;
9   hsp = _move * spd;
10  vsp = vsp + grv;
11
12  // WALKING
13  if (_move != 0)
14  {
15  image_xscale = _move;
16  if ( grounded )
17  {
18  sprite_index = spr_player_walk;
19  }
```

```
20  }
21  else
22  {
23  if ( not climbing )
24  {
25  sprite_index = spr_player_idle;
26  }
27  }
28
29  // JUMP
30  if ( grounded and jumping )
31  {
32  vsp = -jspd;
33  grounded = false;
34  sprite_index = spr_player_idle;
35  }
36
37  // CLIMBING
38  if ( place_meeting(x, y+1, obj_ladder) )
39  {
40  if (vmove < 0) or(vmove == 0 and climbing) or(vmove > 0 and place_meeting(x,y+sprite_height,obj_ladder))
41  {
42  climbing = true;
43  }
44  else
45  {
46  climbing = false;
47  }
48  }
49  else
```

CHAPTER 8 SINGLE-SCREEN PLATFORMER

```
50  {
51  climbing = false;
52  }
53
54  if ( climbing )
55  {
56      vsp = vmove * spd;
57    sprite_index = spr_player_climb;
58  }
59
60  // HORIZONTAL COLLISION WITH BLOCKS
61  if ( place_meeting(x-hsp, y, obj_block) )
62  {
63      while ( not place_meeting(x+sign(hsp), y, obj_block) )
64      {
65      x += sign(hsp);
66    }
67      hsp = 0;
68  }
69  x += hsp;
70
71
72  // VERTICAL COLLISION WITH BLOCKS
73  if ( place_meeting(x, y + vsp, obj_block ) )
74  {
75      if (not ladder)
76    {
77      while ( not place_meeting(x, y+sign(vsp), obj_block) )
78          {
79              y += sign(vsp);
80          }
```

269

CHAPTER 8   SINGLE-SCREEN PLATFORMER

```
81              vsp = 0;
82              grounded = true;
83          }
84      }
85      else
86      {
87          grounded = false;
88      }
89      y += vsp;
```

Lines 1–5: Here we check the keyboard inputs using the keyboard_ check functions instead of the dedicated events.

Lines 7–8: move and vmove just decide the horizontal and vertical direction toward which the player should move based on the player's input.

Lines 9–10: hsp and vsp are, respectively, the horizontal and vertical speed variables. They count how many pixels the player should move horizontally and vertically. This value will be affected by later calculations, but it's also dependent on the player's input checked at lines 1–5.

Lines 13–20: Here we check if the player is moving left or right. If they are, we flip the avatar in the right direction using image_xscale (note that a value of 1 means that the sprite is left at the original orientation, while -1 flips it in the opposite direction); and then, if the player is grounded, we change the sprite of obj_player to spr_player_walk that shows a walking animation. We change the sprite only if the player is grounded, because we don't want Berry to look like he's walking in the air, when he's jumping or falling.

Lines 21–27: If the player is not moving left or right, we check that he's not climbing, and then we change obj_player's sprite to spr_player_idle that shows Berry idle.

Lines 30–35: This is our jumping code. We check if the player is grounded and jumping (hence pressing the spacebar), and if they are, we make obj_player go up by changing vsp to a negative value of -jspd. Then we set the grounded variable to false, since we are not anymore on the ground; and then we change the sprite of obj_player to spr_player_idle, so that we have the illusion that Berry is jumping feet together.

Lines 38–52: This is new! Here we manage the climbing mechanic. First, we check if obj_player is colliding with an instance of obj_ladder. We do it by moving testing at coordinates x,y+1 because we want to include the case in which the player has the ladder just under their feet.

If this condition is true, it means the player is touching a ladder or has it at their feet, so we must determine the various cases that can trigger the climbing mode of the player's character.

We said that we want obj_player to keep climbing the ladder when

- The player is pressing the up key (vmove< 0) in front of a ladder.

- The player is pressing the down key (vmove> 0), and there is a ladder just under obj_player. In that case, obj_ladder is at coordinates x, y+sprite_height (just one block under the player).

- The player is not moving up or down, but they already are in climbing mode (they were just climbing the ladder and stopped before reaching the ground).

If one of those three conditions (line 40) is true, we set the climbing variable to true; else, we set it to false.

Finally, if the player is not touching the ladder at all (line 51), we set climbing to false.

Lines 54–58: If the player is on the ladder (after the calculation we made in lines 38–52), we don't want to be affected by gravity anymore, so we just set vsp to a value that's equal to the player's movement speed (represented by spd) times the direction in which the player wants to climb (represented by vmove). We also change the sprite of obj_player to spr_player_climb.

Lines 61–70: This is our code to check the collisions with obj_block on the X-axis (moving horizontally). Nothing has changed, so we can move on.

Lines 73–89: This is the code that checks the collisions with obj_block on the Y-axis (moving vertically). Also, this one is unchanged, so there's nothing to add.

Controlling the Game Flow

We have a working platforming system, but this alone doesn't make a game.

According to the GDD, Cherry Caves is a game involving the collection of cherries for all the levels. Those cherries will unlock the exit of the game. The collection of cherries is made harder by enemies that will block Berry's way. When he gets hit by those enemies, the level will restart. Berry can be hit only three times. After that he will die for good, and the game will be over.

We will manage the game flow using the game state system we used also in Space Gala. Since Cherry Caves' flow is pretty simple, we will borrow most of the states from Space Gala. Figure 8-8 shows the Cherry Caves' game flow as a finite-state machine. Let's describe them:

- **PLAYING**: This state represents the playing phase of the game. The game is ready to get inputs from the player, and every object acts normally.

- **PAUSED**: In paused state, every object gets deactivated, and the player can access the menu to resume, restart, or quit the game.

CHAPTER 8 SINGLE-SCREEN PLATFORMER

- **DEAD**: The player has been hit by an enemy. Therefore, they lose a life and restart the room from the starting point.

- **GAMEOVER**: The player has been hit for the third time. The game is over, and the player can only restart the game or quit.

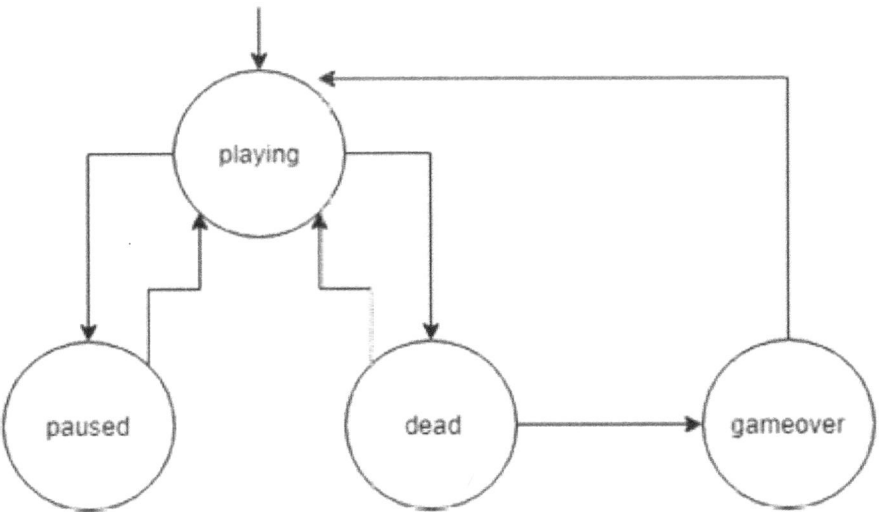

Figure 8-8. *The FSM representing the game flow for Cherry Caves*

Let's explore the various transitions:

- **From PLAYING to PAUSED**: Triggered by pressing the Esc key. It opens the pause menu.

- **From PAUSED to PLAYING**: Triggered by pressing the Esc key. It closes the pause menu.

- **From PLAYING to DEAD**: Triggered by being hit by an enemy. It restarts the room and subtracts one life.

CHAPTER 8   SINGLE-SCREEN PLATFORMER

- **From DEAD to PLAYING**: Triggered by being hit by an enemy and not having finished all the lives. The room is restarted, and the status is set to playing again.

- **From DEAD to GAMEOVER**: Triggered by being hit by an enemy and having finished all the lives or by having completed all the levels. The game over screen is shown, and the player can decide to restart or quit the game.

- **From GAMEOVER to PLAYING**: Triggered when the player, after a game over, decides to restart the game. It restarts the game from the first room.

Now we have a clearer idea of the game flow, and we can go back to coding.

To implement the game controller and manage all those states, we will use a game controller object, as we did in Space Gala.

Let's create the obj_controller and its Create event. Then add the following code:

```
1   enum STATES {
2   PLAYING,
3   PAUSED,
4   DEAD,
5   GAMEOVER
6   };
7   global.game_state = STATES.PLAYING;
8
9   game_set_speed(60, gamespeed_fps);
10
11  global.cherries = 0;
12  global.cherries_max = instance_number(obj_cherry);
13  global.startx = obj_player.x;
```

```
14  global.starty = obj_player.y;
15
16  options = [ "RESUME", "RESTART", "QUIT" ];
17  opt_number = array_length(options);
18  menu_index = 0;
19
20  if ( room == room0 )
21  {
22  lives = 3;
23  }
```

Lines 1–7: We create the states data structure, as we did for Space Gala. Then we set up the starting state as states.playing.

Lines 11–12: *cherries* is the global variable that counts the number of cherries picked up by the player, while cherries_max counts the number of cherry objects present in the room by using instance_number function.

Note instance_number(obj) takes as input an object and returns how many instances of that object are present in the current room.

Lines 13–14: startx and starty are the starting position of obj_player in the level. We will use them to reset the player to the original position once they die.

We could have used the room_reset function to reset the whole level, but it's not optimal, since some global variables (e.g., score) are kept, while others (e.g., lives) are reset; so since the behavior of room_reset is not consistent, we avoid using it under this circumstance.

Lines 16–18: This is the code to set up the pause menu, as we already saw in Space Gala. The options are the same: resume, restart, and quit. Resume will resume the game, restart will restart it from the first room, and quit will close the application.

Lines 20–23: These lines set the number of lives to three when you start the game from the first room. When lives reach 0, the game is over.

Everything is set up, and the obj_controller is ready to manage all the mechanics we planned to implement.

Firstly, let's deal with the various states. When the game enters in the paused state, we want to stop everything and show the menu. Differently from Space Gala, this time we will manage everything concerning the logic inside the Step event avoiding relying on keyboard management events. This will allow us to have more control on the code that will not be scattered around. You may prefer the modular style that GameMaker suggests, but it's really a matter of taste and personal preference. There's not a golden rule, for this aspect.

So, let's create a Step event for obj_controller and put some code in it. As usual, we will comment the following code:

```
1    var _esc_pressed = keyboard_check_pressed(vk_escape);
2    var _enter_pressed = keyboard_check_pressed(vk_enter);
3    var _move = keyboard_check_pressed(vk_down) - keyboard_
     check_pressed(vk_up);
4
5    if ( _esc_pressed )
6    {
7    if ( global.game_state == STATES.PLAYING )
8    {
9    global.game_state = STATES.PAUSED;
10   audio_play_sound(snd_menu, 1, false);
11   instance_deactivate_all(1);
12   }
13   else if ( global.game_state == STATES.PAUSED )
14   {
15   global.game_state = STATES.PLAYING;
16   instance_activate_all();
```

```
17  }
18  }
19
20  if ( global.game_state == STATES.PAUSED )
21  {
22  menu_index += _move;
23
24  if ( _move != 0 )
25  {
26  audio_play_sound(snd_menu, 1, false);
27  }
28
29  if ( menu_index < 0 )
30  {
31  menu_index = opt_number - 1;
32  }
33  else if ( menu_index > opt_number - 1 )
34  {
35  menu_index = 0;
36  }
37
38  if ( _enter_pressed )
39  {
40  switch( menu_index )
41  {
42  case 0:
43  global.game_state = STATES.PLAYING;
44  instance_activate_all();
45  break;
46  case 1:
47  game_restart();
```

```
48     break;
49   case 2:
50     game_end();
51     break;
52   }
53 }
54 }
```

Lines 1–3: These lines just make some keyboard checks that we need later. We are using keyboard_check_pressed instead of the dedicated events.

Lines 5–18: When the escape key is pressed, if the active state is playing, we change it to paused, play a sound, and deactivate all instances using instance_deactivate_all; if the active state is paused, we change it to playing and reactivate all the instances in the room.

> **Note** You can activate or deactivate all the instances in the game by using instance_activate_all and instance_deactivate_all.
>
> instance_activate_all() activates all the instances in the room.
>
> instance_deactivate_all(notme) deactivates all the instances in the room. It takes one parameter that says whether we want the current instance to remain active or not. If the parameter is true, the current instance (the one which called the function) will not be deactivated.

Lines 20–54: Here we check if the active state is paused. If it is, we access the functions of the menu that works exactly like the one in Space Gala. The only difference is that we added the keyboard control for the enter key in there using the result of the keyboard_check_pressed function stored in the enter_pressed variable (lines 38–52).

When the player chooses the first option (resume), all the instances get reactivated and the state changed to playing.

If the player chooses the second option (restart), the game gets reset by calling game_restart().

If the player chooses the third option (quit), we call game_end() and quit the application.

This code is the same we used in Space Gala and allows us to manage the simple menu we designed in the previous chapters to access the three main functions (resume, restart, quit).

To visualize the menu, we should now draw the various graphical elements using the Draw GUI event, as we did in Space Gala.

Let's create a Draw GUI event for obj_controller and add this code in it:

```
1   if ( global.game_state == STATES.PAUSED )
2   {
3       draw_set_color(c_white);
4       draw_set_font(fnt_score);
5       draw_text(room_width/2, room_height/2, "PAUSE");
6
7       for( var _i = 0; _i < opt_number; _i++ )
8       {
9           if ( menu_index == _i )
10          {
11              draw_set_color(c_white);
12          }
13          else
14          {
15              draw_set_color(c_dkgray);
16          }
17          draw_text( 1200, 700 + 30 * _i, options[_i] );
18      }
19  }
```

CHAPTER 8   SINGLE-SCREEN PLATFORMER

In the code above, when the active state is PAUSED, we draw a PAUSE writing at the center of the screen, and we show the menu in the bottom-right corner.

We want to do something similar for the game over state. We want the screen to go black and show the menu with just the options to restart and quit the game, so let's open again obj_controller's Step event and add this code to the bottom:

```
1   if ( global.game_state == STATES.GAMEOVER )
2   {
3       instance_deactivate_all(1);
4       menu_index += _move;
5
6       if ( _move != 0 )
7       {
8           audio_play_sound(snd_menu, 1, false);
9       }
10
11      if ( menu_index < 1 )
12      {
13          menu_index = opt_number - 1;
14      }
15      else if ( menu_index > opt_number - 1 )
16      {
17          menu_index = 1;
18      }
19
20      if ( _enter_pressed )
21      {
22          switch( menu_index )
23          {
24              case 1:
```

```
25                  game_restart();
26                  break;
27              case 2:
28                  game_end();
29                  break;
30          }
31      }
32  }
```

Similarly to what we did for the paused state, we should add some code to the Draw GUI event to visualize the menu. The only difference is that at lines 6–13, we check if there are still lives: if it's the case, it means that the game is over because the player won, so we write a victory message; else, we write a game over message. Let's write this code to the bottom of obj_controller's Draw GUI event:

```
1   if ( global.game_state == STATES.GAMEOVER )
2   {
3       draw_set_color(c_white);
4       draw_set_font(fnt_score);
5
6       if ( lives<= 0 )
7       {
8           draw_text(room_width/2, room_height/2,
            "GAME OVER");
9       }
10      else
11      {
12          draw_text(room_width/2, room_height/2, "YOU WON!");
13      }
14
```

CHAPTER 8 SINGLE-SCREEN PLATFORMER

```
15      for( var _i = 1; _i<opt_number; _i++ )
16      {
17          if ( menu_index == _i )
18          {
19              draw_set_color(c_white);
20          }
21          else
22          {
23              draw_set_color(c_dkgray);
24          }
25          draw_text( 1200, 700 + 30 * _i, options[_i] );
26      }
27  }
```

HUD

It's important for the player to constantly be updated about some information like the number of lives remaining, the current score, and of course the number of cherries collected so far.

A simple way to manage it is to add all those information in the top of the window, creating a simple HUD with all that info in line.

The number of lives will be represented by a little version of spr_player_idle and a text showing the value of the lives variable; the number of cherries will be shown using a little version of the spr_cherry sprite and using global.cherries and global.cherries_max, while the score, as usual, will be a text showing the value of the score variable.

The result will be the status bar in Figure 8-9, which is simple, but effective. All the information is available to the player, and every entry has a clear semantic.

Figure 8-9. *Cherry Caves' HUD*

The HUD will be created in obj_controller's Draw GUI event, as every GUI-related element. So, let's open up that event and add these lines on the top of the code:

```
1   draw_set_color(c_black);
2   draw_rectangle(0, 0, room_width, 40, false);
3
4   draw_set_color(c_white);
5   draw_set_font(fnt_score);
6   draw_text(20, 10, "SCORE: " + string(score));
7
8   draw_set_color(c_white);
9   draw_sprite_ext(spr_cherry, -1, (room_width/2)-32, 20, 0.5,
    0.5, 0, c_white, 1);
10  draw_text(room_width/2, 10, string(global.cherries) + "/" +
    string(global.cherries_max));
11
12  draw_set_color(c_white);
13  draw_sprite_ext(spr_player_idle, -1, room_width-110, 20,
    0.5, 0.5, 0, c_white, 1);
14  draw_text(room_width-100, 10, " X " + string(lives));
```

Lines 1-2: This is new, but easy. We are drawing a rectangle using the draw_rectangle function.

Note You can draw shapes on the screen by using some specific built-in functions. In the preceding code, we used one of those functions to draw a rectangle.

draw_rectangle(x1, y1, x2, y2, ol) draws the rectangle defined by the points x1,y1 and x2,y2. The rectangle consists just in the outline if ol is true, and it's filled in if ol is false.

CHAPTER 8   SINGLE-SCREEN PLATFORMER

Lines 4–6: As we already did in the previous projects, these lines will show the current score in our HUD.

Lines 8–11: This is how the cherries' number is shown. We first draw the sprite by resizing it of 1/2 its dimension, and then we show the numbers next to the icon.

Lines 12–14: Similar to lines 8–11, we show the number of lives next to a resized idle image of Berry.

You can now run the game to check that the HUD and the pause system both work well. The result will be the one in Figure 8-10.

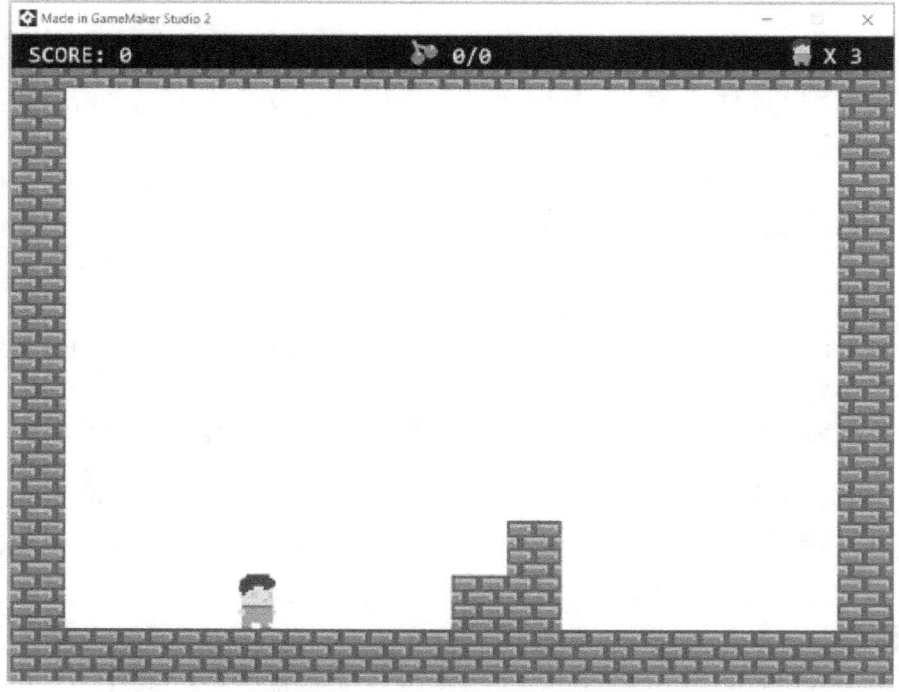

Figure 8-10. *Cherry Caves' test level with the HUD*

Anyway, we can't check the game over functionality or the collecting feature, since we don't have any enemy or cherry in our game! Let's fix this!

CHAPTER 8   SINGLE-SCREEN PLATFORMER

How to Die

This will be one of the easiest sections in the whole book. In fact, we structured the game so neatly that enemies and death are just a matter of setting variables and collisions.

First, let's talk a bit about the terrible ball-shaped enemies.

Cherry Caves' enemies are bouncing balls that follow some patterns conveniently with the design of the level. For the first level, we will create a basic ball-enemy bouncing on a vertical trajectory. For the second level, we will create a second ball-enemy following a more complex path simulating the bouncing down to various platforms. Since all the enemies have the same effects on the gameplay, we want to manage them using inheritance. We will create a ball-enemy parent with which we will manage all the interactions with the player, so that we can create as many ball-enemies as we like without being forced to rewrite the same mechanics and interactions every time.

Let's create a couple of new objects called obj_ball and obj_ball_purple. Give to the second the sprite spr_ball_purple and set its parent to be obj_ball.

This will be the first enemy type. We will code its bouncing behavior by making it move upward until it finds a wall; then it will invert the direction and start moving downward until it finds another wall forcing it to move upward again and so on.

Add a Create event for obj_ball_purple and initialize those two variables:

```
1    spd = 4;
2    dir = -1;
```

The enemy will move at a speed of 4 pixels per step, while the dir variable will track the direction.

285

CHAPTER 8　SINGLE-SCREEN PLATFORMER

Now we need the logic! Create a Step event and add this code:

```
1   if ( global.game_state == STATES.PLAYING )
2   {
3       y += spd * dir;
4
5       if ( place_meeting(x, y, obj_block) )
6       {
7           dir *= -1;
8       }
9   }
```

First, we check if the game state is in the playing state (line 1); then we increase the y value by spd*dir (line 3), which means that we are moving the instance by spd pixels in the direction defined by dir (left if dir is less than zero and right otherwise). Finally, we check for a collision with obj_block at line 5: if the collision occurs, we invert the direction of the instance (line 7).

Easy, right? You can test that everything's fine by putting some obj_block_red or obj_block_brown and a couple of obj_ball_purple in a room. You should verify that the instances of obj_ball_purple bounce up and down blocked only by instances of obj_block_red or obj_block_brown.

The only thing that's missing for our enemy is the ability to kill the player. We can manage this by creating an interaction between obj_player and obj_ball based on collisions.

Open up obj_player and add a new collision event by selecting Add Event ▶ Collision ▶ obj_ball.

In this event, we don't need to do much, since we will manage all the logics of death in the obj_controller Step event, so let's just add a status change and destroy the player object:

```
1   global.game_state = STATES.DEAD;
2   instance_destroy();
```

In the destroy event, we will just play a death jingle. Create a Destroy event for obj_player and add this one line in it:

```
1    audio_play_sound(snd_damage, 1, false);
```

When the player gets hit, as we said, we want to make them start again from the initial position (that we saved using global.startx and global.starty) until they run out of lives. Open up obj_controller's Step event, and add this code at the bottom to manage the dead state:

```
1    if ( global.game_state == STATES.DEAD )
2    {
3        lives--;
4        alarm[0] = game_get_speed(gamespeed_fps) * 1;
5        global.game_state = STATES.PLAYING;
6
7        if lives <= 0
8        {
9        global.game_state = STATES.GAMEOVER;
10       }
11   }
```

In the preceding code, we check whether the active state is dead. If it is, we decrease by one the global variable lives, change back the state to playing, and set the alarm 0 to 1 second. The alarm 0 event will deal the task to relocate the player on the original coordinates. We also check if the player has still lives (line 7). If they haven't, the active state becomes game over.

We must now create an Alarm event to manage the respawn of the player. Click Add Event ▶ Alarm ▶ Alarm 0 and add this line of code:

```
1    instance_create_layer(global.startx,global.starty,
     "Instances", obj_player);
```

CHAPTER 8 SINGLE-SCREEN PLATFORMER

Great! Now Berry can die! Well, I don't know if this is a good thing for him, but it definitely is for us! Let's try out the game to check that everything is working great.

The only thing we are missing right now is the possibility to collect cherries. Let's work on it!

Cherry-Picking

Collecting cherries, as per GDD, is the main goal in Cherry Caves. In this section, we will create the cherry object that we will use to score and unlock the next level.

Create a new obj_cherry object and give it the spr_cherry sprite. The player can pick up this item by colliding with it, and when they do, the score is updated as well as the number of cherries picked (monitored by global.cherries). So, we will just need three events:

- **Create**: In which we will set the pts variable which is the amount of points gained by picking the item
- **Collision with obj_player**: That will destroy the instance, add pts to score, and increase global.cherries
- **Destroy**: That will play a simple particle animation and play a sound

Let's start by adding the Create event for obj_cherry. Inside this event, we just need to add this line:

```
1    pts = 100;
```

Now add a collision event with obj_player by clicking Add Event ➤ Collision ➤ obj_player and write this code in it:

CHAPTER 8 SINGLE-SCREEN PLATFORMER

```
1   score += pts;
2   global.cherries++;
3   instance_destroy();
```

The preceding code adds the amount of points we just set up in the Create event to the score variable, increases the number of picked cherries, and destroys the instance.

Finally, the Destroy event will just play a jingle and a particle animation:

```
1   effect_create_layer("Instances", ef_firework, x, y,
    1, c_red);
2   audio_play_sound(snd_cherry, 1, false);
```

Great! Now let's try this out by adding the cherries to the room. Because of how we coded obj_controller, it will count the number of cherries in the room and automatically set the maximum number of cherries that should be picked to pass the level. Picking them up, the number of picked cherries in the HUD will update as well as the score.

Anyway, we can't leave the room both because we don't have a goal object and because we don't have a second level. Well, we don't either have the first one. Let's fix all those issues one by one.

Through Cherries, to the Star

To win the game, as we said, the player should collect all the cherries in all the levels, and then they can access the exit of the level.

The exit is represented by a yellow star that will show up only when the player collects all the cherries in the room.

The logic behind the goal object is pretty simple: it's invisible and inactive until global.cherries is equal to global.cherries_max; then it turns active and visible; and when colliding with the player, it will warp them to the next level.

289

CHAPTER 8 SINGLE-SCREEN PLATFORMER

Let's create a new object and call it obj_goal and add a Create event. This event will be responsible to initialize the active and goal_reached variables which are used to manage the status of the instance depending on if the player collected all the cherries. Add this line in obj_goal's Create event:

```
1  active = false;
2  goal_reached = false;
```

Create a Step event and add this code:

```
1  if ( global.cherries == global.cherries_max and not goal_
     reached )
2  {
3      active = true;
4  }
5
6  visible = active;
```

To constantly check the status of the game, we need to check in the step event whether global.cherries has reached global.cherries_max (line 1). If the player collected all the cherries and we haven't yet triggered the goal, we want the instance to be activated (line 3). From the status of the active variable depends the visibility of the object (line 6).

Now, the most important piece of code of all is the collision with obj_player. When the player hits the goal, we want to deactivate the goal instance, play a victory sound and a little particle effect, and after a second, warp the player to the next room.

Add a new collision event with obj_player and put this code in it:

```
1  if ( active )
2  {
3      alarm[0] = game_get_speed(gamespeed_fps) * 1;
4      active = false;
```

CHAPTER 8 SINGLE-SCREEN PLATFORMER

```
5       goal_reached = true;
6       effect_create_layer("Instances", ef_firework, x, y, 1,
        c_yellow);
7       audio_play_sound(snd_goal,1,false);
8   }
```

The Alarm event will check if there is a room after the current one. If there is, the player gets warped to it; if there's not, the game will end showing the game over screen. So go ahead and create an Alarm0 event for obj_goal and add this code to it:

```
1   if ( room_next(room) != -1 )
2   {
3       room_goto_next();
4   }
5   else
6   {
7       global.game_state = STATES.GAMEOVER;
8   }
```

Great! Now everything is in place! We just need to add a new room to test it!

Create a new room of the same dimensions (1440 × 900) of room0 and call it room1. Add in this new room just an obj_block_red border and ground, the player, and obj_controller. Now run the game; it should start from room0 (if not, check the order of the rooms in the Resources sidebar: room0 should be on top of room1). Collect all the cherries in the room and run for the goal. Once you hit the goal, you should be teleported to room1.

Well, those rooms are a bit shallow, anyway. Let's design some better ones.

CHAPTER 8   SINGLE-SCREEN PLATFORMER

Level Design: The Art of Creating Worlds

Level design is more a matter of taste, experience, and convenience, but there are some good advice you can use. Especially with genres like single-screen 2D platformers, there are some easy checks you can do when you're designing a level:

- **Check the Jumps:** A common mistake is to not check jumps for good. Sometimes, if you're not very expert in level design, you can fall victim of the enthusiasm and design a very good level but with way too hard jumps. Maybe you know that a particular jump can be done, but it's very hard to do, and you should be super precise. If it's not intentional for the jump to be so hard or if it's in the early phases of the game, avoid it.

- **Hard Is Good, Too Hard Is Not:** The same should be applied to the toughness and density of enemies. A hectic level is good, even a hard one, but pay attention to not make everything too difficult or you will get the opposite effect: instead of challenging the player, you will bore them, and they won't play at all.

- **Make It Cool:** One of the most important things of a level is good looking. Levels should be nice to look at. They should be harmonious, have a purpose, and/or tell a story. The industry is full of games that tell stories only by using good level design. Make your levels interesting and worth playing.

- **Don't Make It Too Easy:** A thing that should always be avoided is to make things too easy for the player. No one wants to waste time playing a game too easy. Gamers want to be challenged and want to feel like they're improving. Try to make levels that reward the player, but making them earn that reward. An easy way to accomplish this is by making an enemy protect a valuable item or by hiding items in fake walls.

Designing Caves

Back to our game, we should make something easy for room0 that can teach the basic mechanics without saying a thing. How can we do this?

Figure 8-11 shows an example of room0. This is a pretty good first level because it has some training area like (1) that has the purpose of letting the player take confidence with the controls and (2) that is useful to learn the ladder mechanic without any danger.

(3) is a good place for a first tentative scoring of points by collecting cherries. It's an isolated cherry guarded by a single easy-to-dodge ball. Also, there are two ways to reach that place: the first is by jumping the steps in front of the red ball and the second is by climbing the ladder and jumping from the platform. The conformation of the level in (4) suggests both the possibilities.

After picking the first cherry, the player can go easy to (5) and then reach the goal at (6).

CHAPTER 8 SINGLE-SCREEN PLATFORMER

Figure 8-11. *room0 in Cherry Caves*

A level designed trying to respect all those rules will help the player understand the basics of the game. A good understanding of the fundamental mechanics is crucial to introduce more interesting challenges in the next levels.

Level 2!

A second level should reinforce the concepts just learned in the first.

For example, you can build something like Figure 8-12. You can see that the starting point (1) is protected, so that we are still giving a safe start to the player; but just a second later, we introduce a pit (2) to start making the player uncomfortable and ready to face dangers. There is an easy to pick cherry at (3) that has the purpose to motivate the player to pick the other two. A little gift is always a good encouragement.

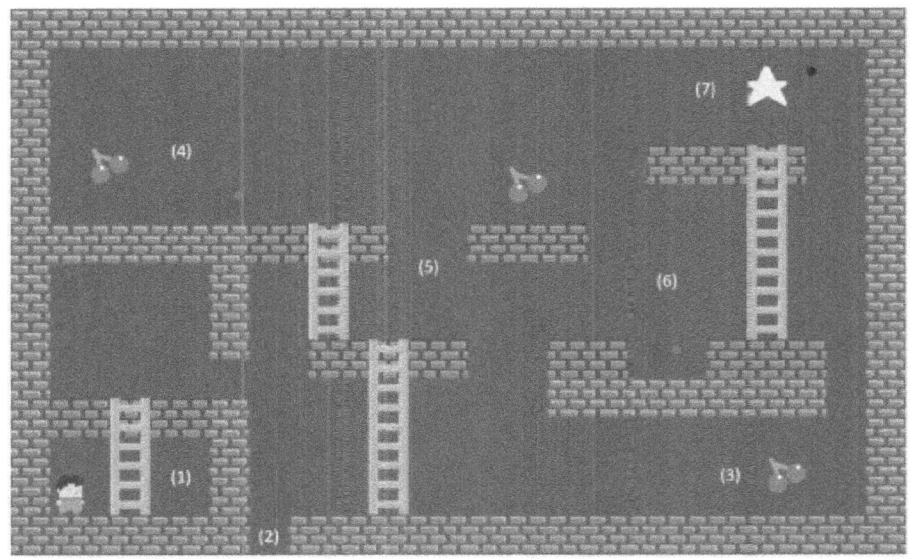

Figure 8-12. *room1 in Cherry Caves*

At (4) there is a danger similar to the one the player experienced in room0, while at (5) they need to decide which way is better to use: the upper or the lower. Both look like feasible but dangerous. For the first time, the player can choose how to act. At (6), there is a not so easy passage, and at (7) there is finally the goal.

This level reinforces all the concepts learned in the previous level and introduces some new, like the possibility to choose and pits in which the player can fall off.

Actually, there is a way to make this level even more interesting! We could introduce a ball-enemy that rolls from (7) down to the pit at (2) passing from (5).

That sounds interesting! Let's do it!

Select Path Layer in the Room Editor for room1 and design a path that rolls down the level into the pit, as in Figure 8-13, and call it pth_path_ greenball.

CHAPTER 8 SINGLE-SCREEN PLATFORMER

Figure 8-13. *The path for obj_green_ball in room1*

Now create a new object and call it obj_green_ball and set its parent as obj_ball.

Add a Create event for this object and put this line in it:

```
1   path_start(pth_path_greenball, 3, path_action_stop, true);
```

This line will make the ball start the path you just design as soon as it is created.

We want the object to be destroyed when it goes out of bounds. Since the path ends out of the screen, we can make a check on the Y-coordinates of the object in the Step event.

Create a Step event and add this code in it so that when the ball reaches a y value greater than the room height, it gets destroyed:

```
1   if ( y >= room_height )
2   {
3       instance_destroy();
4   }
```

CHAPTER 8 SINGLE-SCREEN PLATFORMER

Now we want that every 2 seconds, a new ball is created and follows the same path. To do that, we can use an alarm in obj_controller.

Create a new Alarm 1 event for obj_controller and put this code in it:

```
1   if global.game_state == STATES.PLAYING
2   {
3       instance_create_layer(x,y, "Instances", obj_
        ball_green);
4   }
5   alarm[1] = game_get_speed(gamespeed_fps) * 2;
```

Now that we have this event, we want it to be triggered when we enter the level, so let's add this code at the bottom of obj_controller's Create event:

```
1   if ( room == room1 )
2   {
3       alarm[1] = game_get_speed(gamespeed_fps) * c.1;
4   }
```

Great! Now you can run the game and test that everything is working great! The balls are generated once every 2 seconds, and they follow the path down the pit (Figure 8-14).

297

CHAPTER 8   SINGLE-SCREEN PLATFORMER

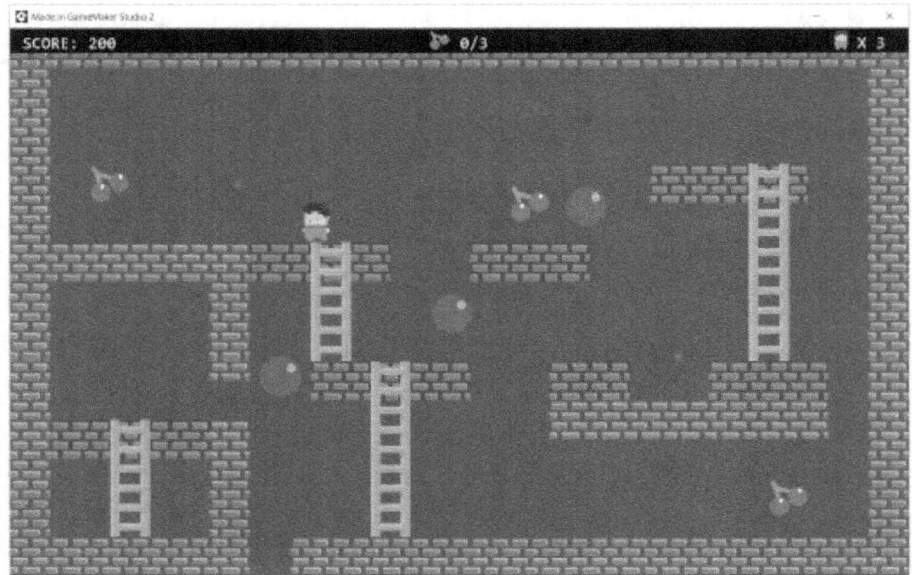

Figure 8-14. *room1 completed and working!*

We concluded this exciting chapter by creating a nice and fun single-screen 2D platformer. It's very old-school, but it has a lot of potential!

In fact, I challenge you to play out with it by designing new levels and enemies and maybe adding new items to collect!

Feel free to explore, create, and play, because this is the spirit to become a great GameMaker!

In the next chapter, we will go further and expand this project to make it become a scrolling platformer in the style of the end of 1980s/early 1990s classics like Super Mario Bros. and Sonic the Hedgehog.

TEST YOUR KNOWLEDGE!

1. What are the most important characteristics of a platformer?
2. How can you check if the player pressed a key using only GML?

3. How can you flip a sprite?

4. How does the place_meeting function work?

5. How does the sign function work?

6. Can you describe how we implemented gravity?

7. Can you modify the code so that you can perform a double jump?

8. Can you describe how we implemented the ability to climb ladders?

9. Describe Cherry Caves' game flow. Why do we need the dead state?

10. How can you activate or deactivate all the instances of the game at once?

11. Try to play around with the HUD trying different ayouts. Which one is the best? Why?

12. What are the good level design principles?

13. Can you design a third level following the good level design principles we definec?

CHAPTER 9

Scrolling Platformer

In Chapter 8, we saw how to create a single-screen platformer (SSP) implementing some interesting features and tackling some challenging new problems like gravity management, jumping, climbing on ladders, and picking up collectibles to clear the level. We also talked about level design and how to make things more interesting by positioning things in smart ways.

In this chapter, we are going to extend that project by adding some new features to turn Cherry Caves 1 (CC1) into a scrolling platformer in the style of Super Mario Bros. The new project will be called Cherry Caves 2 (CC2) and will be heavily based on CC1 both from a technical and narrative point of view.

We will use this opportunity to compare single-screen platformers to side-scrolling platformers and learn how to implement all those new and juicy features that made the fortune of the genre from SMB on.

At the end of the 1980s, scrolling platformers started to conquer the market becoming one of the most popular types of game. Most of the success of this genre is thanks to Super Mario Bros. (Nintendo, 1985). The game by Nintendo revolutionized the entire gaming industry giving the players a game so good that's still subject of study for game designers. What makes this game so good? Why is the platforming genre so successful? Let's dive into the exciting world of side-scrolling platformers to answer to these questions and to understand how to create good and fun games!

CHAPTER 9   SCROLLING PLATFORMER

As usual, let's start from the game design document.

Cherry Caves is a single-player 2D side-scrolling platformer game inspired by classics like Super Mario Bros.

The player will guide Berry through his second adventure. This time the goal is not collecting all the cherries, but just reaching the end of each level.

Story and Setting

After his descent to and return from the Cherry Caves, Berry brought cherries back to humanity, and the mankind returned to grow them. Berry was celebrated like a hero.

However, Berry underestimated the dangers that lay in the Cherry Caves; in fact, the strange green and purple balls were the eggs of an octopus-like alien race attracted by the unique taste of cherries, and since there are no more cherries in the underground, the squishy aliens are invading the surface to get them!

Led by a great sense of responsibility (and a bit of guilt), Berry decides to fight back using the secret power of cherries!

Gameplay

The goal in Cherry Caves 2 is to reach the end of each level, like what happens in classic 2D side-scrolling platformers. So, differently from the first game, this one is very focused on platforming itself and collecting items is just a plus.

The ball-enemies are gone. In this second game, the enemies are octopus aliens who have similar behavior but are implemented in a slightly different way.

CHAPTER 9　SCROLLING PLATFORMER

Victory Condition

Each level is completed by reaching its end represented, like in the first game, by a yellow **star** (Figure 9-1).

Every time Berry gets hit, he dies and loses a life; then the level is restarted.

The player can die three times before the game is over.

Figure 9-1. *Star (goal)*

Items

CC2 features **cherries** (Figure 9-2) not as mere collectibles, but as a power-up. In fact, picking cherries will boost Berry making him invulnerable and lethal to all the enemies for a small amount of time.

Figure 9-2. *Cherry (power-up)*

Coins (Figure 9-3) are a new addition to the game. They are just collectible items scattered in the levels. When the player picks a coin up, their score grows.

CHAPTER 9　SCROLLING PLATFORMER

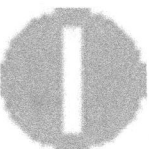

Figure 9-3. Coin (collectible)

Note　To try and balance out the difficulty, the player can be hit just once before they die like in Super Mario Bros. (if we don't count power-ups).

In this project, collectibles only have the effect of growing your score. Anyway, a good thing to do would be to give a meaning to collectibles and to allow the player to unlock or buy something in exchange, as a reward for the effort. We will talk more about this in Chapter 10.

Controls

Controls are the same to the ones in Cherry Caves.
　Keyboard
　Left: Move left.
　Right: Move right.
　Up: Move up (ladder).
　Down: Move down (ladder).
　Spacebar: Jump.
　Esc: Open/close menu.
　Enter: Confirm (menu).

Enemies

In CC2, you have a new kind of enemies, more detailed from an aesthetic point of view and with different patterns compared to those in CC1.

The new enemies are alien octopuses. There are two kinds of enemies:

- **Green Octopus** (Figure 9-4): These strange green octopus aliens hatched from green balls/eggs, and they just move back and forth. Don't touch them!

Figure 9-4. *Green Octopus – they like to walk around!*

- **Purple Octopus** (Figure 9-5): These purple octopus aliens can jump very high and can cling to the ceiling. Beware of their fall! They hatched from purple balls/eggs.

Figure 9-5. *Purple Octopus – they like to jump around!*

Attack

This time Berry is not so vulnerable. In fact, not only he can destroy octopuses by eating a cherry and becoming invincible, but he can also jump on enemies' heads and squash them.

CHAPTER 9 SCROLLING PLATFORMER

Miscellaneous

Other cool additions in CC2 are the platforms. You can now use special platforms to reach new places. There are three different kinds of platforms:

- **Falling Platforms** (Figure 9-6): Very unstable platforms. They tend to fall down when the player touches them.

Figure 9-6. Falling platform – you touch it; it falls down

- **Moving Platforms** (Figure 9-7): They move back and forth and can be used by the player to access certain hidden places. You can see a lot of them in games like Super Mario Bros. and the original Mega Man series.

Figure 9-7. Moving platform – it moves back and forth

- **Trampoline Platforms** (Figure 9-8): They're like real-world trampolines and make the player's character jump constantly. When the player presses the jump button at the right time, the platform makes the player jump even higher to reach very high places.

Figure 9-8. Trampoline – you can use it to jump higher!

Similar Games

CC2 is a very standard 2D side-scrolling platformer and plays like Super Mario Bros. (Nintendo, 1987).

Other similar games are Rayman (Ubisoft, 1995), Alex Kidd in Miracle World (SEGA, 1986), Donkey Kong Country (Nintendo, 1994), Super Mario Bros. 3 (Nintendo, 1993), DuckTales (Capcom, 1989), and Klonoa: Door to Phantomile (Namco, 1997).

Assets

As usual, let's list the assets needed for this chapter. They are basically the same to Cherry Caves, with some new addition. Since the new game will be made starting from the base of Cherry Caves, I will only list the new assets.

spr_land

This is our first tile set. We will learn how to work with tile sets to build our levels faster and make them look more beautiful. Tile sets are also a good way to not fill rooms with objects to design a level like we did in Cherry Caves, which makes them a good way to create levels saving computing resources.

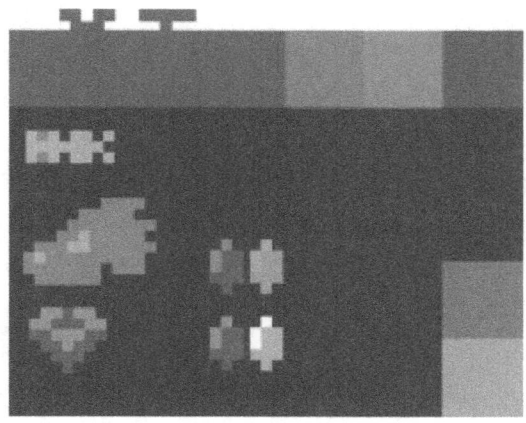

Size: 416 × 352
Pivot Point: Top-left (not important)
Collision Mask: Automatic, Rectangle (not important)

spr_skybg

This image is just a blue image that we will use for the sky in our levels.

Size: 400 × 300 (not important, since it will be repeated as a pattern)
Pivot Point: Middle-center (not important)
Collision Mask: Automatic, rectangle (not important)

spr_platform_falling

This is the sprite we will use for the falling platforms.

Size: 64 × 32
Pivot Point: Top-center
Collision Mask: Automatic, rectangle

spr_platform_trampoline

This is the sprite we will use for the trampoline platforms.

Size: 64 × 32
Pivot Point: Top-center
Collision Mask: Automatic, rectangle

spr_platform_moving

This is the sprite we will use for the moving platforms.

Size: 64 × 32
Pivot Point: Top-center
Collision Mask: Automatic, rectangle

CHAPTER 9   SCROLLING PLATFORMER

spr_octopus_green

These are the sprites we are going to use for green octopus aliens. Together they make a nice animation that simulates their squishy crawl.

Size: 64 × 64
Pivot Point: Middle-center
Collision Mask: Automatic, rectangle
Animation Speed: 4

spr_octopus_purple

These are the sprites we are going to use for the purple octopus aliens, the ones that jump and cling to the ceiling. These two sprites form the jumping animation, which is all we need for them.

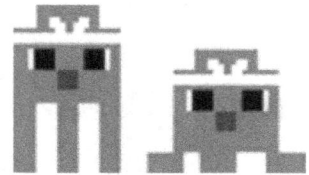

Size: 64 × 64
Pivot Point: Middle-center
Collision Mask: Automatic, rectangle
Animation Speed: 4

spr_titlescreen

This is the image that we will use in the title screen.

Size: 1280 × 720
Pivot Point: Top-left
Collision Mask: Automatic, rectangle (not important)

spr_coin

This is the sprite of the coins, the new collectibles of CC2. You should import these four images in the order shown here to create the illusion of a rotating coin

Size: 32 × 32
Pivot Point: Middle-center
Collision Mask: Automatic, rectangle
Animation Speed: 8

CHAPTER 9   SCROLLING PLATFORMER

spr_terrain

This sprite will be used to create new blocks that we will use just to mark the impassable places.

Size: 64 × 64
Pivot Point: Middle-center
Collision Mask: Automatic, rectangle

Fonts

We need just one more font. This font will be used to draw "PRESS START" in the title screen.

fnt_title

For this font, I am using the preinstalled Impact font with style regular and size 20.

Sounds

Other than the sound effects we already had in Cherry Caves 1, we will also need the following new assets:

> **snd_coin**: This sound effect will be played when the player picks a coin up.

snd_frenzy: This sound effect will be looped when the player picks a cherry and becomes invincible for a small amount of time.

snd_squash: This sound effect will be played when the player kills an enemy.

The More You Do It …

… the better you get! And the more you create games, the more you align to the standards of modern gaming. Cherry Caves was a fun game with a lot of potential; but the ideas that we want to implement in this chapter will put our game closer to standards of modern blockbusters like New Super Mario Bros. 2, Shovel Knight, Celeste, Hollow Knight (HK), and Rayman Legends.

This major update to Cherry Caves will be easier to make, very interesting to discuss, and lots of fun to play! Why easier? Well, because we are starting with a working 2D platformer "engine," and we just need to implement some new content and quality of life (QoL) features – the hard and boring part is already done! You will be amazed by how easier it is to create a game when you already have a good base. This is why you should always work in a modular fashion! Reinventing the wheel is almost never a good idea.

So, let's begin!

First, duplicate your Cherry Cave project. We will use a copy of that project to build upon it, so that we don't have to make the same things twice.

To duplicate a project in GMS2, just open it and select File ➤ Save As in the menu at the top of the window, to save a copy of the project in another location. Select the location you want, and call the new copy Cherry Caves 2.

CHAPTER 9　SCROLLING PLATFORMER

Ok, now let's start working on the new copy of the project! The first thing we want to do is to get rid of all the rooms we previously created. We will create new rooms in this chapter, and we don't really need those we created in Chapter 8, since they are made with a style that is more right for a SSP than a scrolling platformer.

A golden rule of game design is to always remember the genre you are working on, when you design new content. A good content for a genre can be extremely wrong for another genre.

Title Screen

Title screens are the first thing you see in a game. They are very important, more than you think! In fact, they are the first thing to set the tone of the game. You may have noted that title screens always match the atmosphere of the game you're going to play, so that you can enter in the right mood to enjoy the game at its best. This is a big part of the immersion process, one of the factors that put the player in a cognitive flow status.

Cognitive flow is a status of energized focus that happens when someone is fully immersed into an activity. This status can be influenced by a lot of factors like the atmosphere of the game (boosted by aesthetics and narrative), the gameplay, the difficulty level, and the skills of the player.

A good title screen can totally help the player to enter in the right mood for the game. An appropriate title screen can give the game credibility and help the player to immerse in the experience, facilitating the triggering of the cognitive flow status.

This is a good enough reason to create a title screen for our game!

In particular, the title screen I created (Figure 9-9) tries to communicate the main topic of the game: the invasion of those strange octopuses aiming for the cherries. Let's analyze it!

CHAPTER 9 SCROLLING PLATFORMER

First thing to note is that, according to the GDD, in this game we can see the sky. It might feel a bit weird because the title is still Cherry Caves 2, but we're not in the caves anymore, but the Cherry Caves still have a lot of influence in the story; in fact they are the source of the alien invasion.

The point of view of the image is from the bottom: this gives us the impression of being in a disadvantageous position, like if we are dominated.

The octopuses dominate the scene by overlooking us. This gives the impression that they are dominating us.

Another thing to note is that one of them (the green one) watches angered in our direction, meaning that they're not friendly, while the other (the purple one) is trying to pick the cherry from the game title, which tells us that they want the cherries.

Putting it all together, we can tell that those strange octopuses are angered with us because we stole their cherries (in Cherry Caves 1), and now they are here to take them back and punish us.

Figure 9-9. *The title screen of Cherry Caves 2 introduces us to the story of the game*

CHAPTER 9   SCROLLING PLATFORMER

Let's start by creating a new room named *title* by right-clicking Rooms in the Resources sidebar and selecting Create Room.

Double-click the newly created room, and it will open the Room Editor. Head to the Layers panel and select the Background layer as in Figure 9-10.

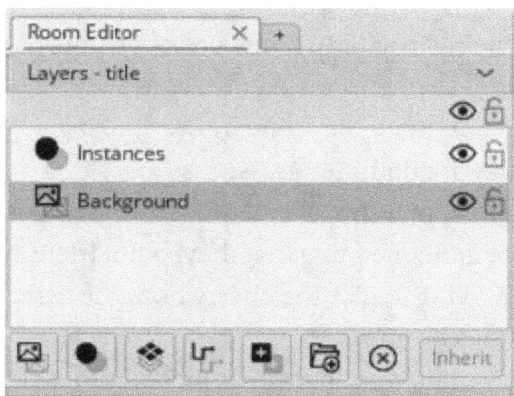

Figure 9-10. *Select the Background layer in the Room Editor*

Once you selected the Background layer, head to the Background Layer Properties panel (just under the Layers list) and select spr_titlescreen as sprite by clicking the three-dot button. Don't forget to also tick the Stretch box, so that the background image will be displayed also on bigger screens. The result should look like Figure 9-11.

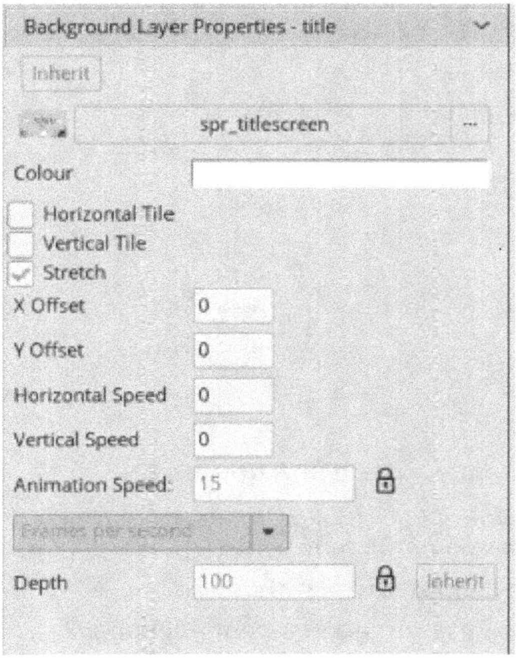

Figure 9-11. Select spr_titlescreen as Background layer's sprite from the Background Layer Properties panel

Finally, go to Properties panel, just under the Background Layer Properties panel, and set the width of the room to 1280 and its height to 720 like in Figure 9-12.

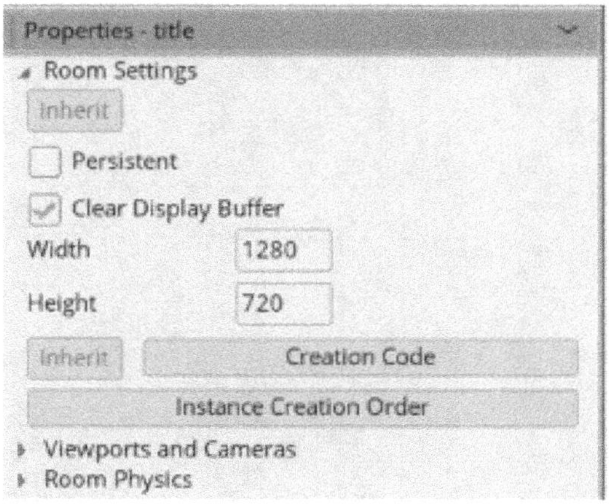

CHAPTER 9   SCROLLING PLATFORMER

Figure 9-12. Set the room's width and height

Ok, now we have our title screen, but it doesn't really do anything, and of course it doesn't allow us to play the game.

We can fix this by creating a new controller object – just like obj_controller – specifically for the task of managing this title screen.

The title controller will allow us to create a blinking *PRESS START* label, and it will manage the keys input to start or quit the game, and we will also implement the possibility to go fullscreen pressing F12 or the F key.

Create a new object by right-clicking Objects in the Resources sidebar and selecting *Create Object*. Call the new object obj_controller_title and open up its Object Editor.

Just like obj_controller, this object won't have a sprite.

Let's start from the easy things: keys management.

Create a new Step event for obj_controller_title and write the following code in it:

```
1   if keyboard_check_pressed(vk_enter) or keyboard_check_
    pressed(vk_space)
2   {
```

```
3     room_goto_next();
4   }
5
6   if (keyboard_check_pressed(ord("F")) or keyboard_check_
    pressed(vk_f12))
7   {
8       window_set_fullscreen(!window_get_fullscreen());
9   }
10
11  if (keyboard_check_pressed(vk_escape))
12  {
13      game_end();
14  }
```

Lines 1-4: Pressing the enter or the space key will allow the player to go to the next room (that will be the first level of the game). We are using keyboard_check_pressed, but really any function of the keyboard_check family would do, in this case

Lines 6-9: Here's the new bit! F and F12 are the fullscreen toggle keys. You can activate or deactivate fullscreen by pressing one of those keys. To do it, we are using window_set_fullscreen(bool), which is a function that takes a Boolean argument and activates (if *bool* is true) or deactivates (if *bool* is false) the fullscreen mode. To do the toggle trick, we are passing as an argument to this function the negative of the current status of the screen. In fact, windows_get_fullscreen returns true if the game is in fullscreen mode and false if it's not. By negating it with the unary operator NOT (!), we are just saying that we want to set the fullscreen mode if it's not set and we want to deactivate it if it's set.

This is a trick you can reuse anytime you need to implement a toggle: just negate the current status.

Lines 11-14: Finally, by pressing the escape key, the game just ends using the function game_end().

CHAPTER 9   SCROLLING PLATFORMER

The next thing we want to add is the blinking text. It's a nice addition that makes the screen feel less boring and static and reminds of some classic platformers that did this, like Mega Man (Capcom, 1987) and Power Blade (Taito, 1990).

To create a blinking text, we need a timer that will toggle a Boolean variable. This Boolean variable will be used to decide if the text should be shown or not.

The diagram in Figure 9-13 shows the logics of the algorithm we are going to write.

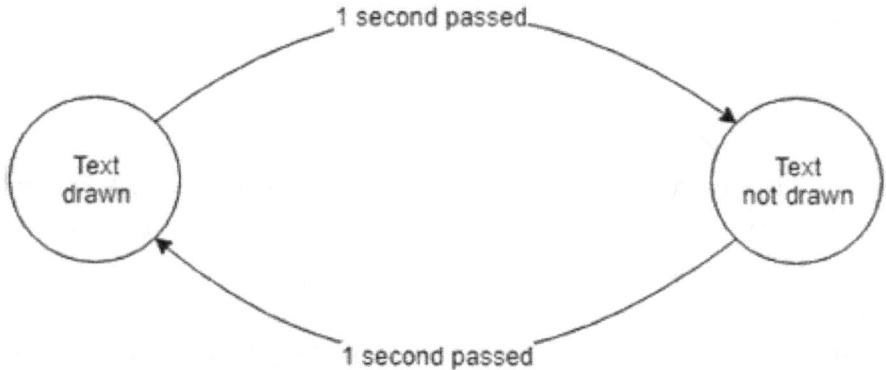

Figure 9-13. *FSM representing the logic behind the blinking effect of the "Press Start" text*

So we need a controller variable, a speed variable (to decide the blinking speed), and an alarm.

Let's start by adding a Create event to obj_controller_title by clicking Add Event in the Events panel of the Object Editor. In this new event, add this code:

```
1   game_set_speed(60, gamespeed_fps);
2   blink_speed = 2;
3   alarm[0] = game_get_speed(gamespeed_fps) * blink_speed;
4   press_start = true;
5   var _width = 1280;
```

CHAPTER 9 SCROLLING PLATFORMER

```
6    var _height = 720;
7    display_set_gui_size(_width, _height);
8    window_set_fullscreen(true);
```

Line 2: This is our blinking speed variable. The text will blink once per second (you can adjust this following your taste).

Line 3: This is our controller variable. We set it to true because we want to start the game with the text visible.

Line 4: Here we set up the alarm to be triggered after one second.

Lines 5–8: In these lines, we force the resolution of the game to 720 p (line 9), and then we activate the fullscreen mode.

Tip Using display_set_gui_size(width, height) with hardcoded width and height values is very useful when you want to quickly make your game compatible with many screen resolutions. Anyway, if you want some better compatibility avoiding black stripes at the borders of your screen, you will need to add the possibility to set a custom resolution by allowing the player to select from a list the right values of width and height to pass to display_set_gui_size.

The code for the alarm is straightforward. We just negate the control variable and reset the alarm so that it will trigger again in a second.

Create a new Alarm event by clicking Add Event ➤ Alarm ➤ Alarm 0 and write the following code in the event:

```
1    press_start= !press_start;
2    alarm[0] = game_get_speed(gamespeed_fps) * blink_speed;
```

In the code above, as we said, we negate the control variable (line 1) by assigning its own negated value to it (just like we did previously with the fullscreen key), and then we reset alarm 0 to trigger again in 1 second (line 2).

CHAPTER 9 SCROLLING PLATFORMER

We're nearly done! We only have to actually draw (or not) the text. As usual, we will do it in the Draw GUI event. Create a Draw GUI event by clicking Add Event ➤ Draw ➤ Draw GUI, and write the following code in the event:

```
1    var _cam_w = display_get_gui_width();
2    var _cam_h = display_get_gui_height();
3    x = (_cam_w/2)-50;
4    y = _cam_h-100;
5
6    if press_start
7    {
8        draw_set_color(c_red);
9        draw_set_font(fnt_title);
10       draw_text(x, y, "PRESS START");
11   }
```

Lines 1–4: We change the coordinates of the object calculating the position using the width and height of the display. To do that, we use display_get_gui_width and display_get_gui_height.

Lines 6–11: Here we check if the control variable is true (line 6), and if it is, we draw the text at coordinates x,y (the ones at which the object has been repositioned in lines 3 and 4) using the font fnt_title (line 9) of color red (line 8).

Ok, now it's all done. We just have to test it! Drag and Drop obj_controller_title in the room, in the position in which you want the text to be drawn, then save and run the game by pressing F5 or clicking the Run button in the toolbar. It should open up the title screen with the blinking text PRESS START (Figure 9-14). Of course by pressing the enter key, we will get an error, because we don't have a next room to join; but you can test out that the fullscreen toggle is correctly working and that by pressing the escape key you will be able to quit the game. Well done!

Figure 9-14. *Now the title screen features a nice blinking PRESS START text*

Tiles and Level Design

In the previous chapter, we created levels just placing blocks and ladders, like in the SSP classics. This was the way to do it back in the days, but with the technology advancements, more memory was available to devs and so more colors and more possibilities to shape new and varied worlds. With all those possibilities, a single image wasn't enough anymore, so tile sets were created.

Tile sets are images that collect various tiles of the same size that can be used to build game worlds. Tile sets revolutionized level design because they reduced the quantity of tiles to load to build a level but still allowing the designer to create diverse levels. Tile-based levels have the advantage to have the level organized as a grid of N × M tiles of the same size. This makes easier to manage distances and movements and of course have a sense of distance that can be expressed in scale in Minimaps or that can be exploited to recreate realistic locations.

CHAPTER 9   SCROLLING PLATFORMER

The first tile-based game was Galaxian (Namco, 1979), a fixed shooter that implemented a tiled (using tiles of 8 × 8 pixels) scrolling background (just the background, not the level). This technology became the basis of later blockbusters like Donkey Kong (Nintendo, 1981) and revolutionized the industry. In fact, back in the days, to make games was one of the most difficult things for a developer. Game developers didn't have many tools that we have now like modern game engines and powerful computers; they had to save on every bit of memory and directly program their games for every single piece of hardware. Having a new technology that allowed to save on the execution time needed to load images in memory was a great thing that allowed games to be faster and more colorful and also allowed game designers to express themselves and their ideas better.

Tile sets are a great addition to a GameMaker's toolbox, and, of course, they are available in GameMaker. The tile set we are going to use is the one in Figure 9-15, and it's made of *32 × 32-pixel* tiles, and the total size of the image is *416 × 352 pixels*.

To use our tile set, we should first create a sprite associated to the image representing the tile set, as we said in the *"Assets"* section.

The new sprite, as we already said, is called *spr_land* and will be the base to create the tile set. Change its tile width.

Right-click Tile Sets in the Resources sidebar and select Create Tile Set to open the Tile Set Editor. Rename the new tile set *ts_land* and assign *spr_land* (Figure 9-15) to it.

CHAPTER 9   SCROLLING PLATFORMER

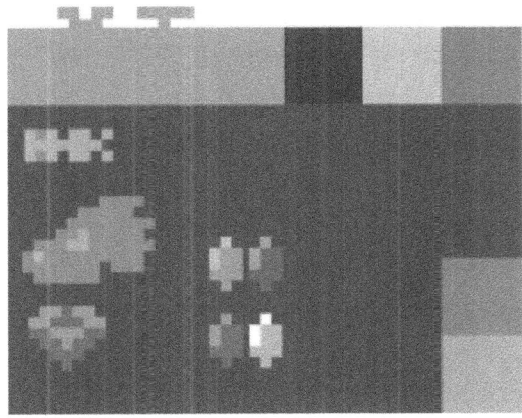

Figure 9-15.   *The tile set that we will use in this project (tiles of size 32 × 32 pixels)*

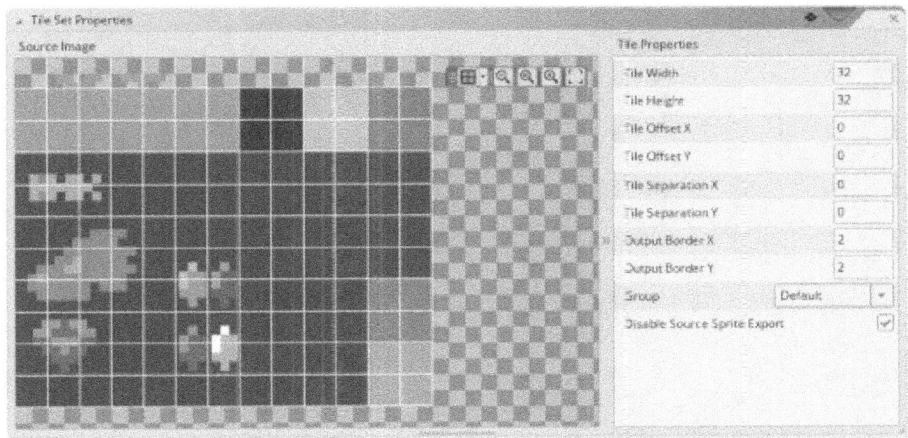

Figure 9-16.   *Tile Set Properties window*

In the Tile Properties section of the Tile Set Properties window (Figure 9-16), change both the width and height of the tile to 32 pixels, as shown in Figure 9-16. We will work on the level design using tiles of 32 × 32 pixels.

325

CHAPTER 9 SCROLLING PLATFORMER

We are now ready to build the first level of the game! Let's create a new room called room0. This new room should feature some more layers, compared to our first project (Chapter 8).

We will need three instance layers: one for enemies, items, and the player, one for the blocks that build the level like ladders and red and brown blocks, and one for the objects that we will use to delimit the impassable parts of the level (this layer will not be visible, once in game).

We will also need, of course, a tile layer that we will use to build the aesthetic of the room.

Let's start from this one!

Create a new tile layer by clicking Create New Tile Layer button in the Layers panel in the Room Editor as shown in Figure 9-17.

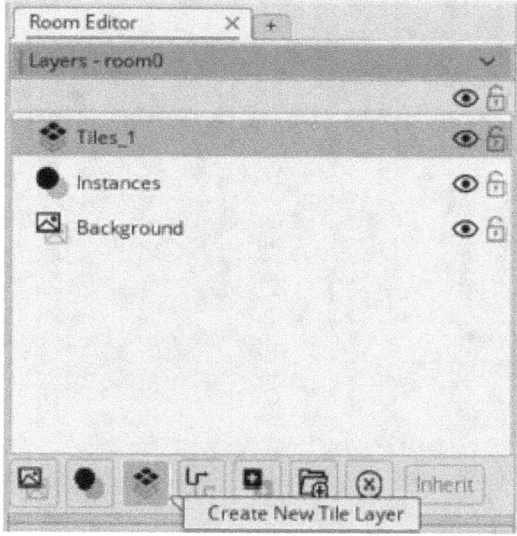

Figure 9-17. *Press the "Create New Tile Layer" button to create a new Tile Layer in the selected room*

CHAPTER 9 SCROLLING PLATFORMER

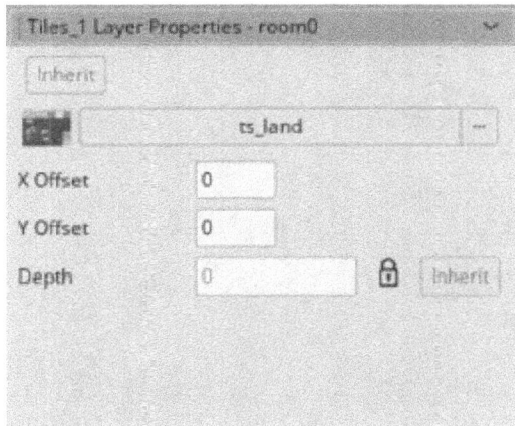

Figure 9-18. *From this Properties view, you can change some details about your Tile Set Layer and assign a Tile Set to it*

In Tiles_1 Layer Properties, add a new tile set by clicking the three-dot button and choosing ts_land, as shown in Figure 9-18.

Now that the tile set is loaded and the tile layer is selected, a new panel labeled Room Editor (Figure 9-19) should open on the right side of GMS2.

327

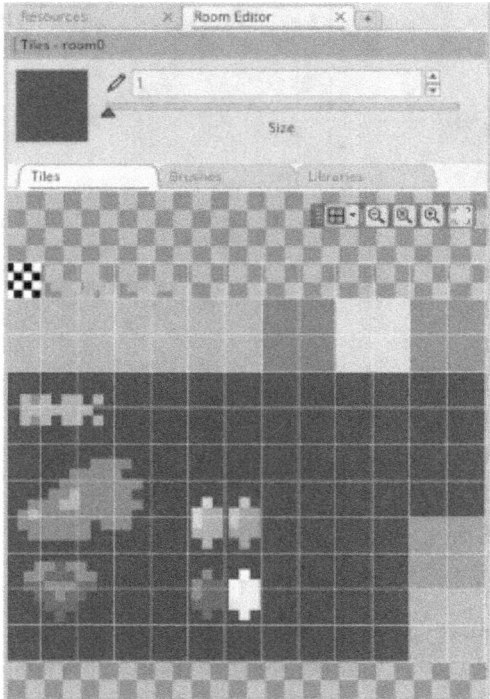

Figure 9-19. *Room Editor panel, that allows you to "paint" your level with your tile set!*

This new panel features three tabs:

- **Tiles**: Where you can select one or more tiles to draw your level.

- **Brushes**: Where you can compose brushes to design your level using some specific tile patterns created by selecting some areas from the tile set.

- **Libraries**: Which allow you to add to the room premade animated tiles and auto-tiles. Animated tiles are exactly what they sound: tiles that are animated, for example, the water in games like Final Fantasy, The

Legend of Zelda, or Pokèmon. Auto-tiles are a tile set that allow you to create tiles that automatically connect to each other when they are placed together. They are widely used to create sand pits, rivers, lakes, and so on.

Note Auto-tiles are widely used in top-down games, like The Legend of Zelda, Final Fantasy, Pokèmon, and basically all the top-down RPGs that you can think of. Anyway, we are not going to cover them in this book since they're not very popular in platformers. If, after reading this book, your objective is to create a top-down RPG, I strongly recommend you to check auto-tiling on GameMaker's official documentation (`https://gamemaker.io/en/tutorials/tile-set-editor`). It can add a lot to your game's aesthetic.

To start drawing the level using tiles, the first thing to do is to adjust the grid of the room by opening the grid options in the grid toolbar and setting both Grid X and Grid Y to 32 pixels, as shown in Figure 9-20.

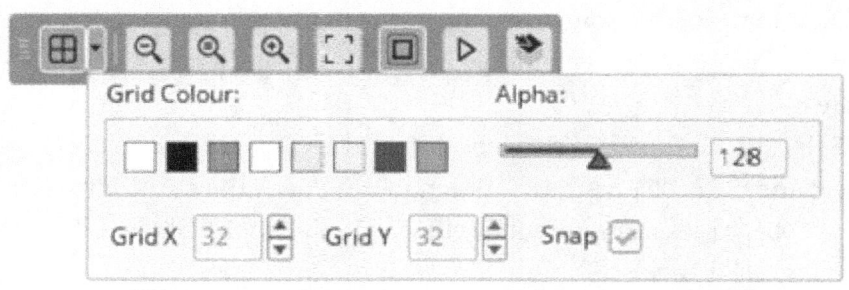

Figure 9-20. *The grid toolbar showing various options*

CHAPTER 9 SCROLLING PLATFORMER

Select the first tab, Tiles, and select the green tile and draw a line of grass. Just under this green line, draw a thick brown area that goes down to the bottom of the room like in Figure 9-21.

Figure 9-21. *Our level starts to take shape!*

Now that we have something like Figure 9-21, we should delimit the areas in which our hero can move. We will do it using a new object. Let's create it!

Select the Resources sidebar and right-click Objects and select Create Object and call it `obj_terrain`. Assign to this object the `spr_terrain` sprite and set `obj_block` as its parent by clicking Parent in the Object Editor and selecting `obj_block`.

Now we have an object that we can use to delimit walkable areas in our levels.

Open up again the Room Editor and create a new Instance Layer and name it *Blockers*.

CHAPTER 9 SCROLLING PLATFORMER

With the Blockers layer selected, Drag and Drop an `obj_terrain` object and stretch it so that it covers completely the grassland (and underlying ground) you created with the tiles as shown in Figure 9-22.

Figure 9-22. *Adding blockers to the ground tiles*

We don't want obj_terrain to be shown on screen; we just want to use its collision mask. To do that, we can make the whole Blockers layer invisible by clicking the open eye icon in the Layers list in the Room Editor (Figure 9-23).

331

CHAPTER 9   SCROLLING PLATFORMER

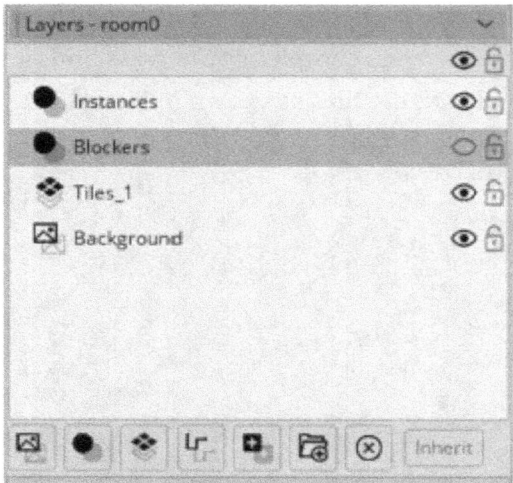

Figure 9-23. *Blockers layer is now invisible (the eye icon is now a closed eye)*

Now that the Blockers layer is invisible, the grassland we have drawn previously is visible once again. Drag and Drop obj_player into the room, just above the grassland, and run the game.

The title screen will appear. Pressing the enter key or the spacebar, the new room (room0) will be loaded, and the player will gently fall on the grass. Great! It works!

We just learned how to design aesthetically complex levels without using a ton of objects to manage collisions, which is a very efficient way to do it! It's a big save of memory and execution time. This will make our games lighter and faster, and it will also allow us to create levels faster.

We can use obj_terrain also to delimit the borders of the screen (Figure 9-24). In fact, you can place instances also outside the room grid. This is a fast way to delimit the borders of the screen without writing a single line of code at the price of just three instances (because generally you want to leave the player fall into pits and die and you don't need to block this fall).

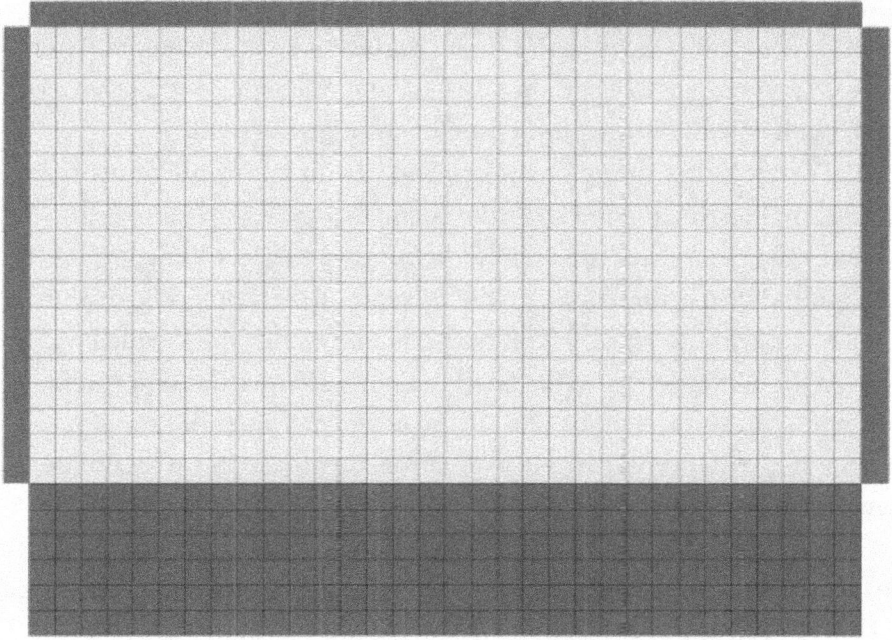

Figure 9-24. *Blockers limiting the area in which the player can move freely*

> **Note** You can add instances to a layer only if it is visible. So, remember to always make the Blockers layer visible when you want to add new instances of obj_terrain to it.

Scrolling Camera

A scrolling platformer is not such if it's not scrolling, so let's fix that!

We saw how to create a scrolling level in Chapter 6, when we created the scrolling level for Space Gala. We are going to follow a similar process, but with some little differences.

CHAPTER 9 SCROLLING PLATFORMER

As we learned during the development of Space Gala, to create a scrolling level, we need to activate viewports and create a camera. The camera will zoom in to a certain position, and this time it won't move by itself, but it will follow the player moving through the level.

Let's start by activating viewports. You can do this by opening up room0 and heading to the Properties section in the Room Editor left sidebar. Once there, tick the Enable Viewports and Clear Viewport Background boxes; then open up the Viewport 0 section by clicking the small black arrow beside the Viewport 0 label and tick the Visible box. Now, in the Viewport 0 section, head to Camera Properties and change the Width to 1280 and Height to 720. Do the same for Viewport Properties.

Figure 9-25 summarizes the settings needed to correctly set up the viewport and camera.

As we said, we want this camera to follow an instance of obj_player, so we will use the built-in function accessible directly from the Room Editor. In fact, in the Viewport 0 section, just under the Viewport Properties section, there is a section called Object Following (Figure 9-26). Click the three-dot button, select obj_player, and set Horizontal Border to 512 (which is half the width of the camera) and Vertical Border to 384 (which is half the height of the camera). The horizontal and vertical borders tell GameMaker how much space at least there must be between the instance and the horizontal and vertical borders of the camera. Tweaking with these values allows you to choose how strict the camera should follow the player – if you set those values to 0, the camera will move only when obj_player reaches the borders of the camera.

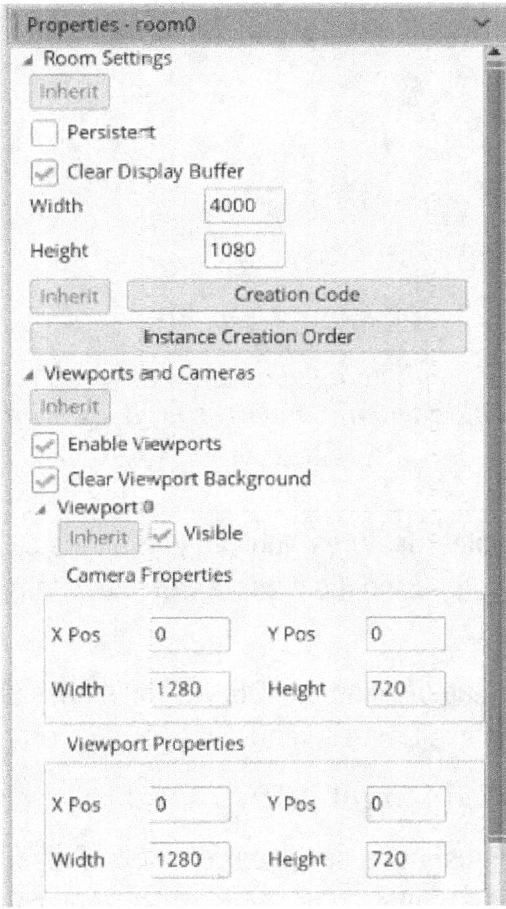

CHAPTER 9   SCROLLING PLATFORMER

Figure 9-25. Settings for the viewport and camera for room0

335

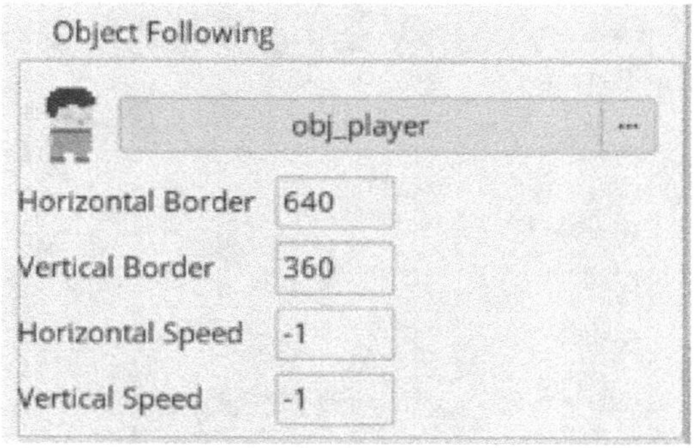

CHAPTER 9   SCROLLING PLATFORMER

```
Object Following
[icon]  obj_player           ...
Horizontal Border  640
Vertical Border    360
Horizontal Speed   -1
Vertical Speed     -1
```

Figure 9-26. *Object Following allows you to set up the camera to follow a specific object when it moves around the room*

Note   As many other features, you can turn on the camera following feature also via code using the camera_set_view_target(camera, object).

For example, instead of using the IDE, we could have added this line in the obj_controller's Create event:

`camera_set_view_target(view_camera[0], obj_player);`

I'm using the IDE just because it's easier and because – in my opinion – it's always better to not write code, if you can avoid it by using a GUI made just for that job.

Save and run the game! It's easy to notice that the game has zoomed in to Berry and it's following him moving back and forth the platform we made! This is officially a side-scrolling platformer now!

Fixing and Re-adapting

Before we go further creating the game, we should make some modifications to the existing code. In fact, there are some objects which are just useless right now and some other that need to be tweaked a bit to work in this new project.

Let's start by deleting obj_ball_red and obj_ball_green. We don't need them anymore; we will create brand-new enemies for this game.

Since balls are not a thing anymore, let's also rename obj_ball to a more appropriate obj_enemy.

Since we deleted the lines related to obj_ball_green, we need to also delete the Alarm 1 event from obj_controller, because it was used to respawn instances of obj_ball_green to the top of the level.

Now head to obj_controller's Create event. Get rid of the lines defining global variables global.cherries, global.cherries_max, global.startx, and global.starty. We won't need those variables anymore since we are drastically changing mechanics

In fact, to complete a level, we don't want the player to collect all the cherries anymore. We just want them to walk all the way to the end.

We don't need startx and starty global variables either, because when the player dies, we want to reset all the level, and we don't want to maintain some sort of memory of the state of the game (collected cherries and others) as we did before. The objective of the game, now, is just to get over the platforming challenges; so, when the player dies, the game should reset any object, enemy killed, and so on.

In the Create event, delete also the lines about room0 and room1. The code for room0 is not good anymore. We will initialize the lives variable in the title screen, so that we can set as the first room whatever room we like and won't have any problem with lives. The code about room1, instead, was intended to work with obj_ball_green that we don't have anymore.

CHAPTER 9 SCROLLING PLATFORMER

As we stated before and in the GDD, the goal of this game is just to reach the star at the end of the level, so we should make a little modification also to obj_goal, since it's programmed to activate itself only when the player picks every cherry in the level. Let's double-click obj_goal in the Resources sidebar to open it up. Head to the Step event and delete everything except this one line:

```
1    visible = active;
```

That's it! Now obj_goal is ready to be used in Cherry Caves 2!

We now need to add a new global variable called global.money and assign the value of the global built-in variable score to it. We will use this variable to reset the value of score when the player dies, so that we will set the value of the coins that the player had when starting the level (otherwise, score won't be reset and will continue to basically reward the player for dying by adding more and more points for each death).

The Create event of obj_controller should now look like this:

```
1    enum STATES {
2        PLAYING,
3        PAUSED,
4        DEAD,
5        GAMEOVER
6    };
7    global.game_state = STATES.PLAYING;
8
9    global.money = score;
10
11   options = [ "RESUME", "RESTART", "QUIT" ];
12   opt_number = array_length(options);
13   menu_index = 0;
14   game_set_speed(60, gamespeed_fps);
```

CHAPTER 9   SCROLLING PLATFORMER

Now open the title room and, in the left sidebar in the Properties section, click Creation Code and add this line in it:

```
1   lives =3;
2   global.game_state = STATES.PLAYING;
```

A room's creation code is a piece of code that is going to be executed when the room is created. It's useful to initialize variables and settings, like we did. Now, every time we enter the title screen, lives will be initialized to 3.

Now go back to obj_controller and head to the Step event and scroll all the way down to the section in which we check for the game state paused. In this section, we need to change the effects of the reset and quit options. Edit those lines like this:

```
1   if ( global.game_state == STATES.PAUSED )
2   {
3       menu_index += _move;
4
5       if ( _move != 0 )
6       {
7           audio_play_sound(snd_menu, 1, false);
8       }
9
10      if ( menu_index < 0 )
11      {
12          menu_index = opt_number - 1;
13      }
14      else if ( menu_index > opt_number - 1 )
15      {
16          menu_index = 0;
17      }
18
```

CHAPTER 9 SCROLLING PLATFORMER

```
19      if ( _enter_pressed )
20      {
21          switch( menu_index )
22          {
23              case 0:
24                  global.game_state = STATES.PLAYING;
25                  instance_activate_all();
26                  break;
27              case 1:
28                  room_restart();
29                  score = global.money;
30                  break;
31              case 2:
32                  game_restart();
33                  break;
34          }
35      }
36  }
```

Just following this section we just modified, there are the STATES.DEAD and STATES.GAMEOVER sections. We need to make great changes to those two. In fact, we don't want anymore the game to show a menu when the player dies, but we just want the text GAME OVER to be shown; and then, if the player presses the spacebar or enter, we want to go back to the title screen.

So modify that section so that it looks like this:

```
1   if ( global.game_state == STATES.DEAD )
2   {
3       global.game_state = STATES.PLAYING;
4       alarm[0] = game_get_speed(gamespeed_fps) * 1;
5   }
6
```

```
7    if ( global.game_state == STATES.GAMEOVER )
8    {
9        instance_deactivate_all(1);
10       if ( _enter_pressed )
11       {
12           game_restart();
13       }
14   }
```

Now let's move to the Alarm 0 event that we need to change completely. We don't want the game to respawn the player at the starting position as it was before when they die; we want the game to reset the room and the score. So open the Alarm 0 event and get rid of the code inside it and substitute it with this:

```
1    lives--;
2    if lives <= 0
3    {
4        global.game_state = STATES.GAMEOVER;
5    }
6    else
7    {
8        room_restart();
9        global.game_state = STATES.PLAYING;
10       score = global.money;
11   }
```

Finally, the biggest edit of all, we need to change the code that draws the HUD. In the previous chapter, we used the size of the room to place items on the screen. This can't be done anymore, since now we are using cameras and viewports which are way smaller than our levels.

CHAPTER 9 SCROLLING PLATFORMER

So, to draw the HUD, we will use now the size of the camera. This means that instead of using room_width, we must use display_get_gui_width(), and instead of room_height we must use display_get_gui_height().

We need to eliminate the part of the HUD in which we show the number of the cherries collected, and we also want to eliminate the possibility to show the menu when the game state is set on game over, so we need to get rid of that code.

Finally, we want to add a little touch to the pause and game over screens. Since now the level will be made not only by objects but also by tiles, using the instance_deactivate_all() function will make disappear all the objects from the screen and freeze them; but it won't make disappear the tiles, so we would have a bad effect by leaving things like they are right now. To overcome to this problem, we could simply draw a black rectangle to cover the scene, just before starting to draw the menu and status texts.

To draw a rectangle on the screen, we can use the draw_rectangle function that we already used to draw the black band for the HUD.

After those modifications, the code inside the Draw GUI event should look like this:

```
1   var _cam_w = display_get_gui_width();
2   var _cam_h = display_get_gui_height();
3
4   draw_set_color(c_black);
5   draw_rectangle(0, 0, _cam_w, 40, false);
6
7   draw_set_color(c_white);
8   draw_set_font(fnt_score);
9   draw_text(20, 10, "SCORE: " + string(score));
10
11  draw_set_color(c_white);
12  draw_sprite_ext(spr_player_idle, -1, _cam_w-100, 20, 0.5,
    0.5, 0, c_white, 1);
```

```
13    draw_text(_cam_w-100, 10, " X " + string(lives));
14
15    if ( global.game_state == STATES.PAUSED )
16    {
17        draw_set_color(c_black);
18        draw_rectangle(0, 0, _cam_w, _cam_h, 0);
19
20        draw_set_color(c_white);
21        draw_set_font(fnt_score);
22        draw_text(_cam_w/2, _cam_h/2, "PAUSE");
23
24        for( var _i = 0; _i<opt_number; _i++ )
25        {
26            if ( menu_index == _i )
27            {
28                draw_set_color(c_red);
29            }
30            else
31            {
32                draw_set_color(c_white);
33            }
34            draw_text(_cam_w-200, _cam_h-200 + 30 * _i,
              options[_i] );
35        }
36    }
37
38    if ( global.game_state == STATES.GAMEOVER )
39    {
40        draw_set_color(c_black);
41        draw_rectangle(0, 0, _cam_w, _cam_h, 0);
42
```

```
43      draw_set_color(c_white);
44      draw_set_font(fnt_score);
45
46      if ( lives<= 0 )
47      {
48          draw_text(_cam_w/2, _cam_h/2, "GAME OVER");
49      }
50      else
51      {
52          draw_text(_cam_w/2, _cam_h/2, "YOU WON!");
53      }
54  }
```

Ok, now everything's alright. But before we move forward, let's make also a little modification to obj_player. We want to have some death pits that will instantly kill Berry if he falls in them. To do this, open up obj_player's Step event and add this code to the bottom:

```
1   if (y >room_height)
2   {
3       global.game_state = STATES.DEAD;
4       instance_destroy();
5   }
```

This code will just check if the y variable of obj_player becomes greater than the height of the room; and if it does, it means that the player went down out of the screen, and so it changes the game state to STATES.DEAD and destroys the obj_player instance by calling instance_destroy().

You can now Drag and Drop an instance of obj_controller and check that it's now correctly working and showing the HUD and letting you fall into pits and die! How nice!

Ok, now everything is in the right place, and we can continue creating our game!

Different Ways to Move

One of the funniest things in platformers is that there are different ways to traverse the level. One of those ways is by using different kinds of platforms. There are a whole lot of different platforms like elevators, moving platforms, rotating platforms, trampolines, and so on. In this section, we will implement three kinds of platforms to have some more tools to build fun levels.

The first kind of platform we will make is a trampoline. This special kind of platform, when walked on, bounces the player ceaselessly and allows them to jump even higher by pressing the jump button. One of the first examples of trampolines appeared in Super Mario Bros. (Nintendo, 1987), and it was crucial to reach high places and secrets. Another game that makes a large use of trampolines is Sonic the Hedgehog (SEGA, 1990) that uses them to send Sonic flying through the distance to reach some more advanced point of the level.

The trampoline platform works in an interesting way. Every time the player collides with it, the trampoline triggers the jump action into the player, just like if they pressed the jump button. When the player presses the jump button while bouncing on the trampoline, an additional force will be summed to the standard jump force of the player making them jump higher.

Create a new object and call it obj_platform_trampoline and associate to it the sprite spr_platform_trampoline.

Set obj_block as the parent to obj_platform_trampoline, since we want the player to be able to jump on it and not fall through it.

Add a Create event to obj_platform_trampoline by selecting Add Event ▶ Create in the Object Editor, and add this one line to it:

```
1    jump_force = 6;
```

This variable represents the additional jump force that we will impress in the player, when they press the jump button.

CHAPTER 9   SCROLLING PLATFORMER

Now create a Step event and add this code inside it:

```
1   if (place_meeting(x, y-1, obj_player))
2   {
3       obj_player.force_jump = true;
4       if (keyboard_check(vk_space))
5       {
6           obj_player.jspd_bounce= jump_force;
7       }
8   }
```

Lines 1–3: This line checks if the player is on the platform; if they are, a Boolean variable inside obj_player, force_jump, will be set to true. It will trigger the jump function.

Lines 4–7: This code checks if the player is pressing the spacebar. If they are, a variable called jspd_bounce, inside obj_player, is set to the value of jump_force. This new variable, jspd_bounce, will be summed to jspd that decides the height of the jump inside obj_player.

Of course, those two variables (jspd_bounce and force_jump) are not present right now in obj_player. So, let's add them, so that we can add the trampoline to the game!

Open up obj_player and add those two lines to its Create event:

```
1   jspd_bounce = 0;
2   force_jump = false;
```

Now open up its Step event and modify the jump section so that it looks like this:

```
1   // JUMP
2   if ( grounded and _jumping or force_jump)
3   {
4       force_jump = false;
5       vsp = -(jspd + jspd_bounce);
```

```
6        jspd_bounce = 0;
7        grounded = false;
8        obj_player.sprite_index = spr_player_idle;
9        audio_play_sound(snd_jump, 1, false);
10   }
```

Line 2: We added as a trigger for the jump the condition that force_jump is true. So now the jump will trigger both if the player is grounded and is pressing the jump button and if the force_jump variable becomes true.

Line 4: When the jump function is triggered, force_jump is set to false (so it won't jump endlessly).

Line 5: The vertical speed of the player is calculated by adding the standard jump force jspd to jspd_bounce that can be changed by the trampoline object.

Line 6: Just after being used, the jspd_bounce must be reset to 0; otherwise, the jump will be higher and higher.

Lines 7–9: These two lines are just as they were before. We just change the sprite to the idle sprite and play the jump sound.

It's all in place! We just have to Drag and Drop an instance of obj_platform_trampoline into the room and test it by running the game (Figure 9-27)!

The second type of platform is the falling or disappearing platform. This is a classic of platforming games. You can find it literally in any platformer game ever (even 3D!).

Falling (disappearing) platforms are basically platforms that, when in collision with the player, just fall down after a certain amount of time. This type of platforms is a very interesting addition to level design, since they both add a challenge and a way to reach distant places. Often, after a session of platforming on those platforms, the player is rewarded with a precious object or a secret.

CHAPTER 9   SCROLLING PLATFORMER

Falling platforms are actually conceptually easy. They just wait to collide with the player, and when they do, they start to move down until they reach the end of the map; at this point, a new platform is generated in the original position of the one that is falling, and the falling platform is destroyed.

So, let's create a new object called obj_platform_falling and assign to it spr_platform_falling.

Add a Create event to the newly created object and write this code in it:

```
1   triggered = false;
2   startx = x;
3   starty = y;
```

The code above initializes a controller variable that we will use to control the generation of the new platform, and it sets the starting coordinates that we will use to generate the new platform in the right place.

Add a Step event to obj_platform_falling and add this code in it:

```
1   if ( place_meeting(x, y-1, obj_player) and !triggered )
2   {
3       alarm[0] = game_get_speed(gamespeed_fps) * 1;
4       triggered = true;
5   }
```

The code above just checks for the collision with the player (when they are just above the platform) and triggers only if the triggered variable is set to false. If those conditions are satisfied, an alarm is set to 1 second, and the triggered variable is set to true.

We need the alarm to make the platform fall after a second, so that we will give the player the possibility to escape.

Add a new Alarm 0 event to obj_platform_falling and add this code to it:

```
1   move_towards_point(x, y+1, 10);
2   alarm[1] = game_get_speed(gamespeed_fps) * 0.5;
```

Line 1: We move the platform downward at a speed of 10 pixels per frame.

Line 2: We set another alarm to trigger in half a second.

The new alarm 1 will be used to generate the new platform and destroy the falling one. Add a new Alarm 1 event to obj_platform_falling and add these lines to it:

```
1   if not place_meeting(startx, starty, obj_player)
2   {
3       instance_create_layer(startx, starty, "Instances",
            obj_platform_falling);
4       instance_destroy();
5   }
6   else
7   {
8       visible = false;
9       alarm[1] = game_get_speed(gamespeed_fps) * 0.2;
10  }
```

Lines 1–5: When the alarm triggers, we check if the player's character is where the new platform should be created, because we don't want to pin them creating a platform where they stand. If the area is free, a new platform is created at the original coordinates, and the falling platform is destroyed for good; otherwise, the falling platform becomes invisible, and the alarm gets reset, so that we can check again in 0 2 seconds.

CHAPTER 9   SCROLLING PLATFORMER

You can personalize this platform by adding a particle effect in the Destroy event, so that it looks like the platform crashed to the ground.

Now let's test the new platform by dragging and dropping it in room0, possibly in the pit we created while drawing the level.

Save and run the game! The platform should be there waiting for the player to walk on it. When they do, the platform waits a second and then falls down (Figure 9-28), and a brand-new platform is generated in its place. Awesome!

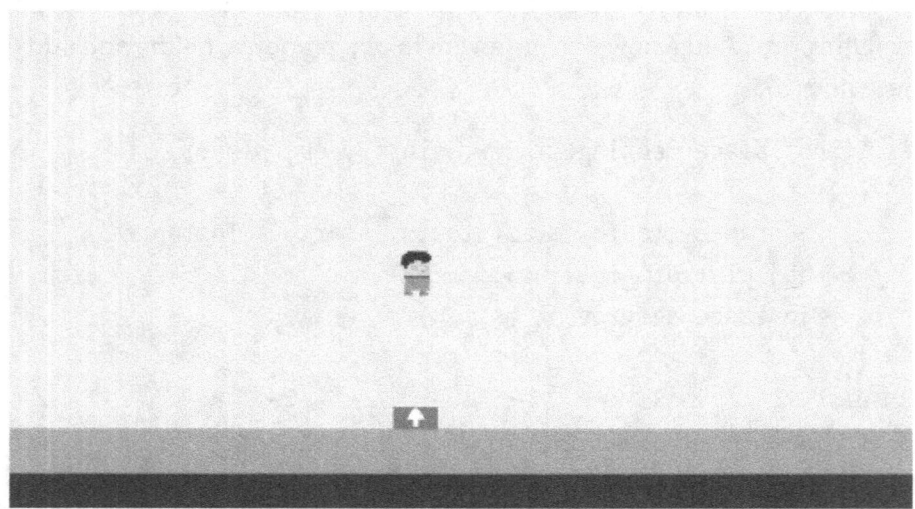

Figure 9-27. *Berry having fun on his new trampoline!*

CHAPTER 9   SCROLLING PLATFORMER

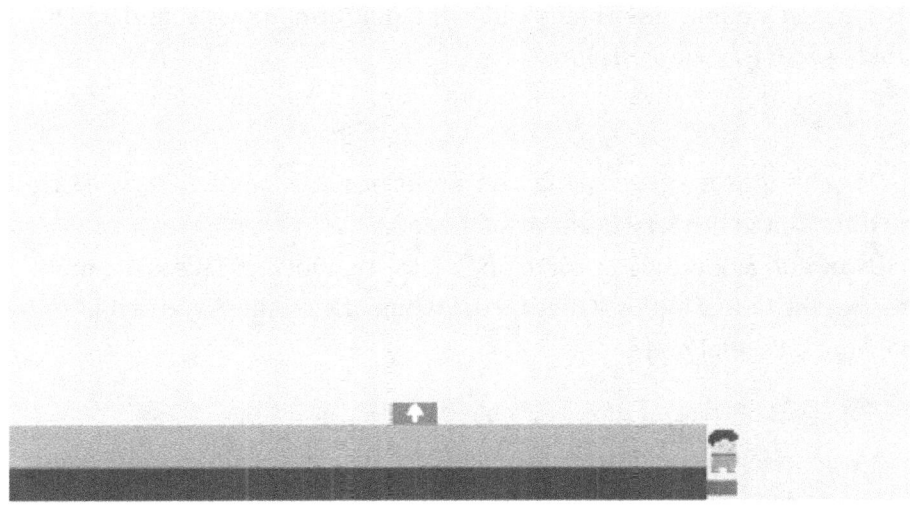

Figure 9-28. *Berry is falling with the falling platform...oops!*

Last, but not least, one of the most useful and fun platforms you can find in a platformer game is the moving platform. It's a super-useful platform that moves back and forth allowing the player to reach distant places giving also a bit of a challenge, because the player is forced to jump on it while it's moving.

The movement of the platform is easy to implement, but the problem is that just moving the platform won't move also the player who's on it. In fact, we assume they will just because in the real world that's how it works. But our game doesn't work with real-world physics. Don't forget that everything moving or falling is programmed to do it and there is not a physics engine that's governing forces. We can put any object in the middle of the map, and it won't fall. Only the player's avatar will, because we programmed it to do it.

So, we need to simulate physics even with moving platforms. How can we do this? Well, we can borrow the idea we used to create trampolines and apply a horizontal movement in the direction in which the platform is moving when the player is on the moving platform.

Let's create this new object, call it obj_platform_moving, and add a Create event to it with this line:

```
1   speed = 2;
```

We change the speed so that the platform starts moving. We will invert the direction in the Step event when needed.

Now add a new Step event to obj_platform_moving. This is the main event of the object and will feature the whole mechanic. So, add this code in it, and let's analyze it:

```
1   if (place_meeting(x, y, obj_block))
2   {
3       speed *= -1;
4   }
5
6   if place_meeting(x, y-1, obj_player) or place_meeting(x-1,
    y, obj_player) or place_meeting(x+1, y, obj_player)
7   {
8       obj_player.hsp_carry = speed;
9   }
```

Lines 1–4: We are letting the platform move in a direction until it finds an instance of obj_block. When this happens, the platform inverts its direction (line 3).

Lines 6–9: Here we check if the player is on the platform. If they are, the value of the movement of the platform is assigned to obj_player'shsp_carry variable which sums up to the horizontal movement of the player's character.

There's a little problem with this platform. Right now, it works right only if we put it between two instances of obj_block. This means that we cannot make some interesting platforming sessions where the player has to jump between many moving platforms without having the possibility to rest on a solid instance of obj_block_red or obj_block_brown. We can

CHAPTER 9 SCROLLING PLATFORMER

fix this and gain some more level design possibilities by creating a special object which will work as an invisible marker for our moving platforms.

Create a new object called obj_marker and assign to it a square sprite. It can be whatever sprite you want, since it's going to be invisible. In fact, tick on the box labeled *Invisible* in the object's Object Editor.

Now go back to obj_platform_moving's Step event and modify the code like this:

```
1   if (place_meeting(x, y, obj_block) or place_meeting(x, y,
    obj_marker))
2   {
3       speed *= -1;
4   }
5
6   if place_meeting(x, y-1, obj_player) or place_meeting(x-1,
    y, obj_player) or place_meeting(x+1, y, obj_player)
7   {
8       obj_player.hsp_carry = speed;
9   }
```

All set, now you can place the moving platform between two instances of obj_marker, and the platform will go back and forth between them.

To make all this work properly, though, we have to create the hsp_carry variable into obj_player, like we did with jspd_bounce; and we have to add this value to the horizontal movement of the object.

Let's open up obj_player and head to its Create event and add this line:

```
1   hsp_carry = 0;
```

Now open the Step event and add these lines just before the horizontal collision check:

```
1   hsp += hsp_carry;
2   hsp_carry = 0;
```

353

CHAPTER 9   SCROLLING PLATFORMER

Cool! Looks like it's all ready to test this out!

Add an instance of obj_platform_moving to room0 and test that it's correctly working. You should be able to move back and forth together with the platform (Figure 9-29).

Figure 9-29.   *The moving platform is correctly working!*

Cool! We created three new platforms that we can use to design fun and challenging levels!

Now we just need some enemy to fight or to escape from!

Gotta Squash 'Em All!

In Cherry Caves (Chapter 8), we created very simple enemies that just rolled around in the level. You couldn't possibly fight them, but they could kill you with just a touch. Not fair, right? Let's create some enemies that can be fun to face.

Our new enemies are the octopus aliens we already talked about in the GDD and, as we already said, will have two simple patterns: moving left

CHAPTER 9 SCROLLING PLATFORMER

and right and jumping up and down. The big difference, anyway, is that they can be killed by jumping on their heads.

Let's start by creating a new object named obj_octopus_green. Assign to this object spr_octopus_green and set obj_enemy as its parent.

Add a create event to this object and initialize those two variables in it:

```
1   dir = 1;
2   spd = 4;
```

dir is, as always, the direction in which the enemy will move, and spd is the speed at which it will move.

The enemy we are creating will move in a direction until they find an instance of obj_block; when it finds it, it will change direction and continue moving.

To implement this behavior, we need a Step event. Let's add it to obj_octopus_green and add this code to it:

```
1   if ( global.game_state == STATES.PLAYING )
2   {
3       if (place_meeting(x, y, obj_block) or place_meeting(x,
        y, obj_marker))
4       {
5           dir *= -1;
6           image_xscale = image_xscale *-1;
7       }
8       x += spd * dir;
9   }
```

The code above checks whether the game is in playing status; and if it is, it moves of spd*dir pixels on the X axis until it finds an instance of obj_block or obj_marker (line 3). When this happens, the object inverts the moving direction by multiplying dir by -1 (line 5), and it flips its own sprite using image_xscale.

355

Finally, as always, add a Destroy event with a particle effect to make it more gory:

```
1   effect_create_above(ef_firework, x, y, 1, c_purple);
2   audio_play_sound(snd_squash, 1, false);
```

Ok, the enemy is ready! The only thing left is the interaction with the player. We will code it into obj_player, by using the collision with obj_enemy.

Double-click obj_player and open up the collision event with obj_enemy. In this event, add the following code to create the possibility to squash squids!

```
1    if (( y + sprite_height/2 ) < other.y)
2    {
3        instance_destroy(other);
4        force_jump = true;
5    }
6    else
7    {
8        global.game_state = STATES.DEAD;
9        instance_destroy();
10   }
```

Lines 1–5: In these lines, we check if, when the collision happens, the instance of obj_enemy is just below the player. If that's the case, the enemy gets destroyed and the player bounces.

Lines 6–10: If, when the collision happens, the enemy is not below the player, this means that the enemy is touching the player and so the player should die; so, the game state gets changed to STATES.DEAD, and the player instance is destroyed.

CHAPTER 9   SCROLLING PLATFORMER

That's it! Open up room0 and add an instance of obj_octopus_green and put it between two blocks (instances of obj_block) or two markers (instances of obj_marker) as shown in Figure 9-30, and test what we did until now!

The enemy will move back and forth between the two blocks or markers (Figure 9-30) and kill the player when touched. If the player jumps on it, the enemy dies in a purple gore explosion.

Figure 9-30. *The enemy has been placed between two instances of obj_marker (the magenta squares)*

The second kind of enemy that we want to create is the purple octopus. This is an octopus that jumps very high and clings on the ceiling; then, it slowly falls down to the ground again – and repeat.

To create such a goofy enemy, create a new object called obj_octopus_purple and set as its parent obj_enemy.

Add a Create event to this new object and add this code to it:

```
1   dir = -1;
2   spd = 4;
3   wait = false;
```

Lines 1 and 2, as usual, are about direction and speed that we will use to program the up and down patterns, while the wait Boolean variable is used to make the octopus wait a bit before it falls on the floor or jumps on the ceiling again, so that we can give the impression that it's really jumping, grabbing on the ceiling, and falling down again.

The majority of the logics is, as usual, in the Step event. Let's add one to this object and put this code in it:

```
1   if ( global.game_state == STATES.PLAYING )
2   {
3       y += spd * dir;
4
5       if ( place_meeting(x, y, obj_block) and !wait )
6       {
7           wait = true;
8           spd = 0;
9
10          image_yscale = image_yscale *-1;
11          image_index = 0;
12          alarm[0] = game_get_speed(gamespeed_fps) * 1;
13      }
14  }
```

Lines 1–3: As usual, if the game is in the playing state, the instance moves spd∗dir pixels.

Lines 5–13: We want the instance to stop when it collides with a block and flip vertically its sprite, so that it gives the impression to be attached to the surface, and then we set alarm 0 to 1 second. Alarm 0 will make the octopus move again in the opposite direction and reset the wait variable, so that the octopus can splash on another surface.

Create an Alarm 0 event and add this code in it:

```
1   spd = 4;
2   dir *= -1;
3   image_index = 1;
4   wait = false;
```

Lines 1–2: After 1 second, the movement speed of the octopus is set back to 4 (the original value) and the direction is inverted, so that it can move in the opposite direction.

Lines 4–5: The image index is set to the appropriate frame, and the wait variable is set to false, so that the condition in the Step event can be triggered again when the instance will find another obj_block instance.

Once again, let's add a Destroy event with a particle animation, just like we did in obj_octopus_green using the same line of code:

```
1   effect_create_above(ef_firework, x, y, 1, c_purple);
2   audio_play_sound(snc_squash, 1, false);
```

Ok, it's done! Let's test it by dragging and dropping it in room0 and placing a block some tiles over it. Starting the game, the octopus will start to jump up and down splashing and grappling to the block and falling down again (Figure 9-31). This kind of enemy can be killed when it's on the ground, before it jumps up to grab the ceiling (or the block), just like obj_octopus_green.

CHAPTER 9   SCROLLING PLATFORMER

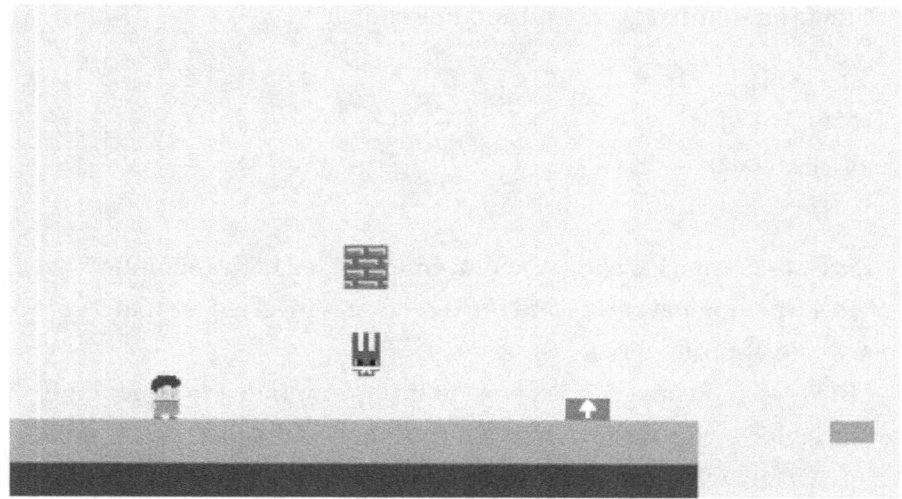

Figure 9-31. *The purple octopus having the best time by jumping up and down the bricks block*

We created a new enemy! It was very easy to make, but it feels original and very different from the other one. It uses some tricks that make it feel more alive than obj_octopus_green, so it's a very good addition.

This is a very good example of how you can create enemies and interactions with little effort.

Tip Very often, good game design is not about creating complex things, but things that feel credible and appropriate. The objective of a good design is to immerse, entertain, and amuse the player; and you can do it often with simple things.

Items and Power-Ups

A very important feature of platformer games is the possibility to interact with items and power-ups. Items are usually objects that can be used to do something. The most popular items are collectibles like coins that are often used to buy things from merchants and special items like keys that are used to open special doors and unravel other hidden parts of the game world.

Power-ups are another kind of beast. They allow the player to gain temporary bonuses and powers and so to face levels, enemies, and all the game's challenges in different ways. This adds a layer of variety that makes the player feel in control of their decisions; and this leads them to experiment, play in different ways, and have fun with the game, which is our primary objective as GameMakers, so yay! Let's create some items for our game!

Coins

Coins are the most common collectible items in video games. Started just to track the score, they became a way to mark the path that the player is supposed to follow, like breadcrumbs. Nearly every platformer has some sort of coins used with this scope in mind or as a currency to buy items from in-game merchants or shops.

We are going to implement our own coins too! Our coins will have a nice rotating animation and will jump up when picked up (like in Super Mario Bros.). The only effect that these coins will have will be to grow the score and to mark the path to follow to get to the end of the level.

Let's start by creating a new object named obj_coin. Assign to it the spr_coin sprite and add a Create event. In this event, write up this single line of code:

```
1  value = 1;
2  can_score = true;
```

CHAPTER 9 SCROLLING PLATFORMER

Line 1: We have the value of the coin. When picked up, it will add 1 to the score.

Line 2: We have a controller value that we will use to avoid that a coin can score more than once because of a prolonged collision with the player.

Add also a collision event with obj_player by clicking Add Event ➤ Collision ➤ obj_player, and add this code in it:

```
1   if (can_score)
2   {
3       can_score = false;
4       score += value;
5       image_speed = 0;
6       image_index = 2;
7       image_xscale = 0.5;
8       move_towards_point(x, y-1, 10);
9       alarm[0] = game_get_speed(gamespeed_fps) * 0.1;
10      audio_play_sound(snd_coin, 1, false);
11  }
```

In the code above, we check if the coin can score. If it can, we set the controller value to false, so that it can't score more than once. Then we increase the score of the player by the value of the coin. Finally, we play an animation by scaling the sprite and moving it upward (5-7) and finally destroying it thanks to an alarm (line 9).

Create an Alarm 0 event and add a call to instance_destroy() in it:

```
1   instance_destroy();
```

Coins done! Let's put them in the room and test them (Figure 9-32). By running the game, you should see them rotating, and when picked up, they get pulled up in the air and then vanish.

Figure 9-32. Coins in a pattern in our example level

Cherries

Cherries are our power-up for this game.

As per the GDD, they allow the player to become invincible for a small amount of time. During this invincibility phase, Berry can kill every enemy by just touching them.

Creating this power-up is very simple. Firstly, we need to create a powered_up Boolean variable that tells us whether Berry is powered up or not.

Open up obj_player's Create event and add this line at the bottom:

```
1    powered_up = false;
```

Now, add a collision event with obj_cherry by clicking Add Event ➤ Collision ➤ obj_cherry. When obj_player touches an instance of obj_cherry, we want obj_player to enter in powered-up mode for a small amount of time. Let's say 5 seconds. So we need to set up an alarm that can

CHAPTER 9 SCROLLING PLATFORMER

switch off powered_up and so deactivate the powered-up status. Add these two lines of code in the collision event:

```
1   powered_up = true;
2   audio_play_sound(snd_frenzy, 10, true);
3   alarm[0] = game_get_speed(gamespeed_fps) * 5;
```

Now create an Alarm 0 event and add this line in it:

```
1   powered_up = false;
2   audio_stop_sound(snd_frenzy);
```

When the player touches a cherry, the powered-up status is triggered, but we have to add some effects to it. Let's start by creating a fun colorfrenzy animation on Berry, just like the effect of the Super Star in Super Mario Bros.

Open up the Step event of obj_player and add this code just below the code that manages the ladder:

```
1   if ( powered_up )
2   {
3       image_blend = make_color_rgb(random(255), random(255), random(255));
4   }
5   else
6   {
7       image_blend = -1;
8   }
```

To create the rainbow color-frenzy effect, we use image blend, which is a property of any sprite that applies a filter to the image. We are applying to it a random color created using the make_color_rgb() function by generating three random values for red, blue, and green using the random() function. This effect is applied once per frame, so the result is a crazy succession of random colors.

When the powered_up variable is false, we set back image_blend to -1, which means no filter gets applied to the image.

Now we only need to add the code to kill every enemy when the player is powered up.

Open up the obj_player's collision event with obj_enemy and change the code as follows:

```
1   if ( !powered_up )
2   {
3       if (( y + sprite_height/2 ) <other.y)
4       {
5           instance_destroy(other);
6           force_jump = true;
7       }
8       else
9       {
10          global.game_state = STATES.DEAD;
11          instance_destroy();
12      }
13  }
14  else
15  {
16      instance_destroy(other);
17  }
```

We added the check to the status of the powered_up variable. If it's true, we instantly kill every enemy (lines 14–17). If the player is not powered up, the same check that we did before is executed.

Everything is in the right place, and you just need to test this out.

Drag and Drop a cherry into room0 and run the game. You will verify that picking up the cherry will put Berry in a frenzy mode for 5 seconds, and in this state he will be able to kill every enemy by just touching them (Figure 9-33).

CHAPTER 9   SCROLLING PLATFORMER

Figure 9-33. *When powered up, Berry can kill enemies by just touching them!*

Creating the First Level

Now that we have a complete 2D platformer engine, the only thing left is to create a nice first level.

The first level is always an interesting challenge. It's the first time the player enters the game world you are creating, and so it's the first time your creation embraces them. It's easy to make an overwhelming or underwhelming first level. Many inexperienced level designers tend to put too many or too few elements into the first level or to not place them properly. What should be clear to the level designer is that the first level should be introducing both the atmosphere and the possibilities that the game offers.

In our case, we have to introduce the player to the colorful world of Cherry Caves and its crazy characters, but also to the game mechanics and the various elements we created, like the different platforms and the power-up.

CHAPTER 9   SCROLLING PLATFORMER

We can actually put everything in the first level, and we will. The important thing is just to place things in a harmonious way, so that the level feels natural and linear and not chaotic.

The first thing we want to introduce to the player is the jump function. So we just put a pile of blocks in front of them (Figure 9-34). They will try the keys and jump through it. This will make the player feel competent because they figured out how to get over that first obstacle without explanations.

Figure 9-34.   *The first section of the level teaches you to jump*

Once the player learned how to jump, they should learn how to climb ladders; but maybe we can contextualize this, by creating a little structure made of bricks that we can climb with the ladder. We can use this opportunity to introduce the concept that risking can be rewarding. So, just under this brick structure, we could add an optional cherry that the player can try to pick up by facing both a falling platform and a jumpy octopus (Figure 9-35).

The fact that this is an optional way is made clear by the line of coins that are just on the top of the structure. The level design screams "climb up there and pick the coins," but it also silently offers the player the possibility

CHAPTER 9   SCROLLING PLATFORMER

to get an object that the player suspects may be of some importance in the game (because, you know, the game has cherry in the title, so cherries must be relevant, somehow).

In this small space, we introduced five concepts of the game, but it doesn't feel confusing. It's very clear, and the player doesn't feel forced to face the octopus to get the cherry. They can avoid getting in there and just climb the ladder, pick up the coins, and kill the easy-to-kill octopus. Because of how the second octopus is positioned, the player will probably kill it by accident by falling on their head and discovering that you can squash enemies by jumping on their heads.

Figure 9-35. *This section of the level teaches the player about the power-up powers and that they can kill octopuses by jumping or falling on their head*

After that condensed learning session, the player would probably enjoy a platforming session without further distractions. So, we could, for example, put some pits here and there or some suspended platforms to jump on (Figure 9-36).

CHAPTER 9   SCROLLING PLATFORMER

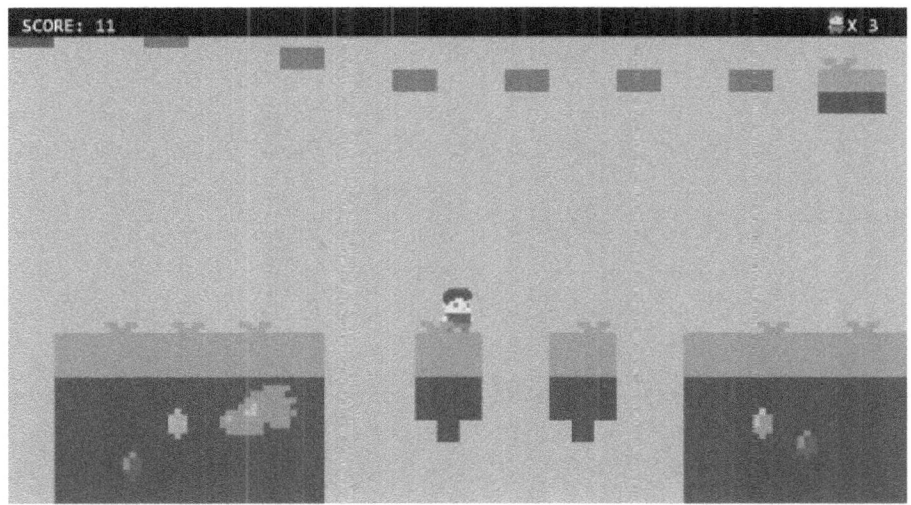

Figure 9-36. *Pits and platforms, to teach the player various platforming dynamics*

An interesting idea is to create a suspended path above the ground that can be reached only using a trampoline and then present the player a platforming session using falling platforms (Figure 9-37).

After that demanding platforming session, we can present to the player the more comfortable moving platform (Figure 9-38) and then finally the star that allows them to complete the level (Figure 9-39).

CHAPTER 9 SCROLLING PLATFORMER

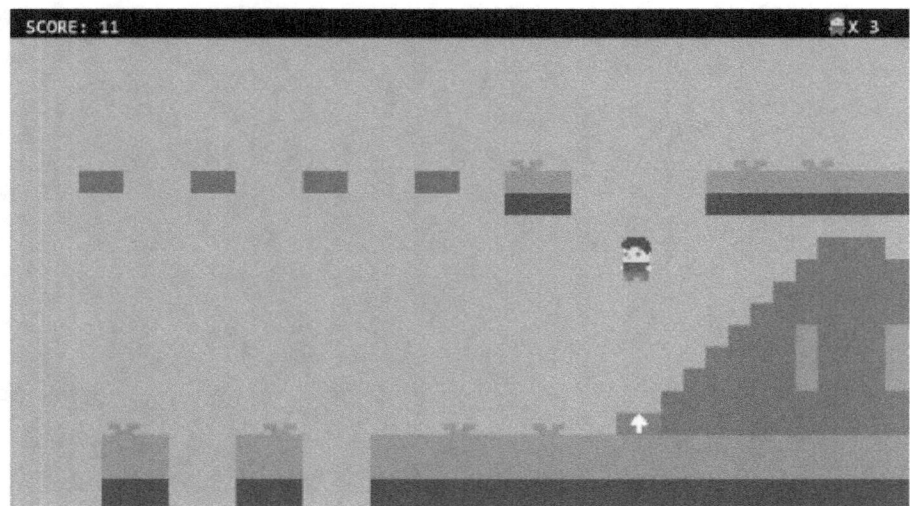

Figure 9-37. *Introducing the player to the trampoline!*

Figure 9-38. *And in the end our star: the moving platform!*

CHAPTER 9 SCROLLING PLATFORMER

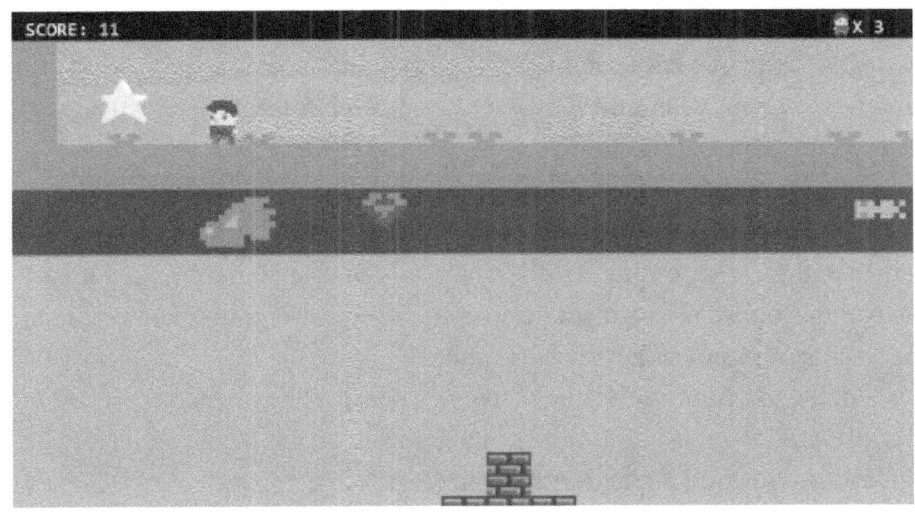

Figure 9-39. *The level ends with the star, just like in the original Cherry Caves*

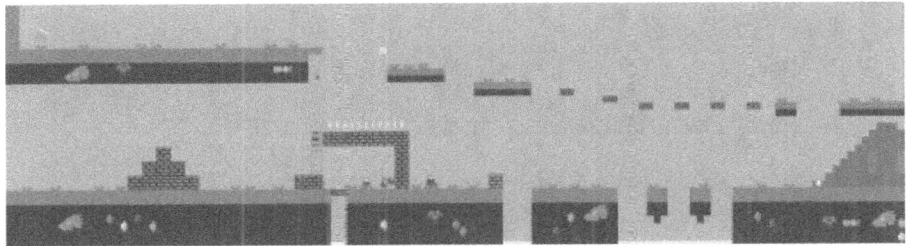

Figure 9-40. *The first level of Cherry Caves 2*

The proposed first level is represented in its entirety in Figure 9-40, and it's a room of size 4000 × 1080.

Enjoy this new game we just created building on top of Chapter 8, improving the gameplay and adding new features while learning more things about game development and GML programming.

CHAPTER 9 SCROLLING PLATFORMER

I invite you to experiment and think about new ways to entertain the player with the gameplay elements you built. Try to create interesting and fun encounters with enemies, puzzles, and platforming sessions using the tools we built in this chapter.

In the next chapter, we will continue our discussion about good platformers' design. We will explore the most popular and important games of the genre, trying to understand which one of them nailed it. We will talk about all the most important aspects of a good platformer, increasing our knowledge on the matter.

Finally, in Chapters 11 and 12, we will use all the knowledge we accumulated to create a metroidvania game, which will borrow a lot from our studies on good platformers' design.

TEST YOUR KNOWLEDGE!

1. Why is the title screen so important to a game?
2. How can you add a background image to a room?
3. How can you set the fullscreen mode in your game?
4. How can you force a specific resolution in your game?
5. What is a tile set?
6. How can you create a tile set in GameMaker?
7. Why are tile sets good to create levels?
8. Tile sets cannot be used to manage collisions; so how can you stop your player from falling, if you use them to build your levels?
9. How can you set the camera to follow an object?
10. Can you describe how the trampoline platform works?

11. Elevators are another common type of platform in video games. They move up and down and can be used by the player's character to reach high places. Using the principles explained for the moving platform, can you create an elevator platform?

12. In Cherry Caves 2, you take damage when you touch an enemy, but you can kill them by jumping on their head. Can you explain how this system works from a technical point of view?

13. How does the image_blend property works?

14. What do you think can be improved in the level we created at the end of the chapter?

15. Can you create a second level that reinforces the basic gameplay concepts of the game by offering some more complex challenges?

CHAPTER 10

Designing Platformers

In Chapter 9, we mentioned the importance of the cognitive flow in a game. We identified the cognitive flow in that condition in which the player is totally immersed into the activity of playing. While in this status, the player senses a loss of self-awareness and extreme focus on the task and loses track of the time passing. In this phase, the player is constantly learning, and this gives them amusement.

As game designers, we want the player to enter and remain in the cognitive flow, and we can accomplish this task by leveraging on game design and making use of some interesting tips.

Controls Are Key

In platformers, the feeling of controls is the most important thing. In fact, controls not only define how you interact with the game, but they're also responsible of your own immersion in it. Games with tight controls let you forget quickly that you are playing a game and put you straight into the cognitive flow. You feel confident and natural while traversing the game world, and you are ready to face challenges more and more difficult. In fact, even when you have to accomplish a hard task, knowing that you can count on your instinct and the fairness of the controls and the game system makes you feel like you can do that and gives you the motivation you need to complete the task.

CHAPTER 10   DESIGNING PLATFORMERS

In particular, the movement of the player should be precise and responsive. The golden rule is to make the character move when the button is pressed and make it stop as soon as the button is released. This will give the player control over the entity of the jump; and so, it will make the player feel into the game, moving naturally and instinctively, boosting their capacity to immerse in the game.

The same principle is used to develop the perfect jump. In fact, for most of the gamers, jumping should be dynamic, allowing the player to choose the height of the jump. This translates into the natural instinct of impressing the right amount of force in the jump to accomplish different tasks.

Jumping at different heights gives the player more possibilities in both exploration and movement. In general, this allows the level designer to create levels that push the player to constant problem-solving making the experience fun and challenging. The golden rule is to regulate the height of the jump according to the amount of time the player holds the jump button.

In our platformer games (Cherry Caves and Cherry Caves 2), the jump is very basic: you always jump at the same height, no matter how much you press the button. This is going to change in Chapter 11, where we will create the perfect jump!

Other than choosing the height of the jump, the player should be able to move in the air just like they move on the ground. Adjusting the falling trajectory is crucial for precise platforming. Giving the player the power to move while in midair, they will feel a sense of autonomy and control that will keep them focused on the game and so in that state of cognitive flow that we discussed in previous chapters.

All those characteristics were introduced by Super Mario Bros. (Nintendo, 1985), and since that moment, they started to be implemented in nearly all the platformers and became the difference between good platformers and bad platformers.

CHAPTER 10 DESIGNING PLATFORMERS

One of the best modern examples of controls made right is Super Meat Boy (Team Meat, 2010). The game became famous for featuring a very challenging platforming and ultraprecise controls. Playing Super Meat Boy is a matter of raw instinct and precision. Every second playing it is a second improving at it. The player develops the skills needed to win the level just with repetition and training, and the controls are so tight and well made that you will never end up blaming the game to be unfair. Every death is entirely your fault. And this takes us to the next important requisite of a good platformer: fairness.

It's My Fault!

When you play a game, it's crucial to feel that you're playing in a fair environment with consistent rules. This is important to take decisions and create your strategy, which can only be done based on the rules of the game. If the player can't understand the rules, they can't learn and become better at the game, thus never being able to advance. This makes the game pretty pointless, doesn't it? That's why it's so important that the player feels like they're playing in a fair environment and that if they lose, it's because they did wrong and not because the game is buggy or glitchy or behaves randomly.

This feeling of unfairness, in platformers, can be found in mainly two activities: moving around and colliding to objects.

As we already saw, a platformer's gamer expects to move in a certain way, with a certain precision. It's not acceptable to slip over a pit because of the imprecision of the controls, and it's not acceptable to have just a standard jump height or to be unable to move in midair. This is the first thing to check out when designing a good platformer game: to give the player the tools to effectively move around the map in freedom.

Collisions are the second important thing to keep under control. A good collision mask is not always the one that best fits the sprite, but it's the one that reflects the perception of the player. As shown in Figure 10-1, a good collision mask covers not the entirety of the sprite, but just the main section of the body, often leaving out the arms and legs.

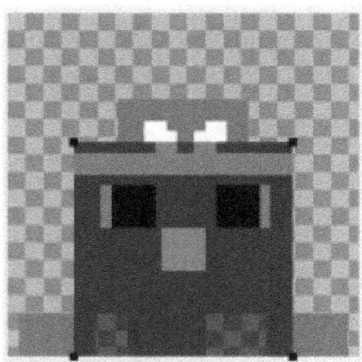

Figure 10-1. *A fair collision mask for our purple octopus!*

Together with controls and collision masks, the camera plays an important role in determining the fairness of the game. The camera should always show you everything you need to see in the game to play and win.

When a game camera fails at its job, it's likely that the player will pay the consequences. When the player gets punished because of the camera, the player feels cheated and frustrated by the whole game system. It's a very bad feeling that causes the player to label the game as bad and give it up.

We can observe a bad example of camera management in the first Dark Souls. The camera system in Dark Souls 1 (DS1) is mostly manual, but the problem with it is that in some frantic combat situations, the camera totally glitches and starts to play against you – often causing your death.

I agree. Dark Souls is a 3D game, and it's not even a platformer; but that's not so important, in this case, since the concepts that we are talking

CHAPTER 10 DESIGNING PLATFORMERS

about are applicable to a wide variety of genres. In fact, regardless of the game genre, a good camera system should always put the player in the condition of being aware of the environment around them so that they can take the appropriate action.

Back in the golden era of platformers, there were games like Mega Man, Double Dragon, Ghost 'n Goblins, and Contra that because of their 4:3 aspect ratio and low resolution (256 × 240 pixels) didn't show much space behind and in front of the character. Because of that technological limit, the player had the problem of having very little time to react to incoming enemies, and that felt unfair. If this wasn't enough, some games also featured an unfair enemy-spawning logic. For example, in Ghost 'n Goblins, the enemies had a chance of spawning under the feet of the player, dealing instant damage. This is a terrible design choice! The player should always be able to avoid damage and win the game. It's very important to think about how to avoid unpleasant situations when dealing with randomized situation, like this one. In this case, it would have been enough to check the position of the player just before spawning the enemy, making sure that the player was not there. We did exactly the same thing in Cherry Caves 2 with the falling platform, to avoid creating it on the player's character. Sometimes even little precautions like that can change the perception of a game from fair to unfair and vice versa.

Keep It Simple!

Platformers are often very fast games, and sometimes they even grow in complexity. Just think about the metroidvania sub-genre: it's a platformer in which the player moves by jumping and climbing, but it also features RPG elements like character's statistics, equipment, inventory, and map. Because of the quantity of the information to show and the pace of the game, it's important to have a clean and simple HUD that can display all

CHAPTER 10   DESIGNING PLATFORMERS

the information needed without overwhelming the player or confusing them. The player must be able to quickly locate themselves on the map, manage the inventory, understand statistics, and so on. This is crucial in a good game: keep the user interface simple!

We did a good job with this in all the games we created, by always showing information in the simplest way possible.

An example of a simple and clear HUD in a commercial game is the one featured by Diablo III (Blizzard Entertainment, 2012).

The HUD only covers the bottom of the screen and consists in the following:

- A sphere containing blood, which represents the player's health
- A sphere containing the main resources used by the player to attack (e.g., Mana, Fury, Spirit, Arcane Power, etc.)
- A long horizontal bar filling as the player gets experience, which represents the progress toward the next level
- A set of buttons representing the active skills, labeled with the key that you can use to activate them
- A heal button labeled with the key you can use to heal
- A teleport button that you can use to teleport back to the encampment (safe place)
- A set of buttons that open some game screens (e.g., character view, inventory, skills view, quest journal, and main menu)

It's a very simple and intuitive interface; all you need to know to play the game is right in the bottom of the screen. It doesn't feel confusing or tricky to understand; with just a glimpse, you can tell the amount of hits you can take and if you can heal or attack. You can build a strategy in a matter of seconds thanks to the clarity of the interface. This is so crucial, if the game has fast-paced combat and challenging battles, like Diablo III.

Power-Ups, Items, and Gear

Either if your game is a classic platformer like Super Mario Bros. or a complex metroidvania in the style of Castlevania: Symphony of the Night (Konami, 1997), your game needs some items to be enjoyable. Special items like power-ups, gadgets, or even gear and equipment add a lot of variety to the game and allow the player to face the challenges and advance the story in their own style, by choosing the path that better fits them.

Items, gear, and power-ups are extremely important to add diversification to basic tasks of the game, and they help the player to feel in charge and in autonomy, keeping them in the status of cognitive flow.

Super Mario Bros. 3 does a great job at that by offering the player a big number of power-ups. Every power-up gives Mario new powers that he can use to defeat enemies or to overcome some tricky area.

The variety and effectiveness of each power-up give the player a lot of possibilities to take on problems in different ways allowing the player to choose the one that best suits their own playstyle. Power-ups give the player the freedom to experiment and play with the rules, which leads to amusement and fun.

Interesting Collections

A thing that too many platformers do wrong are collectibles. Too many games treat them just as things to pick up while traversing a level and don't understand what collectibles really represent: rewards.

Collectibles are the reward a player is given for exploring a level, for winning a challenge, for killing a hard enemy, or for finding a secret in the level. They are things earned with commitment and skills; they can't be pointless! They must have a meaning or a purpose. Some interesting applications for collectibles are to unlock a bonus level, gift the player some rare item or skill, or even advance a specific plotline. They can't be collected just for the sake of it.

A good example is Klonoa: Door to Phantomile, in which by saving all the Phantomilians, you are rewarded with a challenging time-based extra level and a new Cutscene. Completing the extra level, you will unlock Lephise's Jukebox that allows you to play the entire soundtrack song by song – which I personally saw as an awesome reward, back in the days. Apart from my personal opinion, that's a good example of how to reward for collecting items. It adds new content (a whole new level with a brand-new game mode), it gives more details about the background story of one of the characters of the game (the Cutscene), and it even unlocks the whole OST (Original Soundtrack). Other than that, the act of saving all the Phantomilians is not even annoying, because you find them trapped along the way and they are rarely hidden. The only thing that the game asks of you to save them all is using your skills. If you have good double/chain jump skills, you can get to any Phantomilians in the game.

Moreover, the extra level that you receive by saving all the Phantomilians is a very good example of gameplay-based level design. It's built all around chain/double jump skills, and it's a lot of fun to play and replay, since it features a leaderboard with all the completion times registered. The extra piece of story told through this level and the extra Cutscene is just plain fan service, which is probably one of the most appropriate rewards you can deliver to a person who loved the game so much and got to its very end. The game also rewards you with the full soundtrack that you can play using Lephise's own gramophone whenever you want.

Klonoa shows an example of how you can deliver an interesting collectible experience without stressing the player or forcing them to ask for help (like Googling for those guides about how to collect every item), but betting everything on skills and rewarding them fairly for their efforts.

Another example of collectibles done right can be found in Batman: Arkham Asylum (Rocksteady Studios, 2009). In this modern classic of the Dark Knight, you have the optional task to collect the Riddler Trophies. They are scattered all over Gotham, and collecting all of them takes you a step closer to the Riddler himself. Every time the player collects a Riddler Trophy, they get a new clue about the location of the Riddler, and when they collect all of them, the location of the Riddler's hideout is unveiled. This achievement unlocks the Riddler's boss fight.

This is a wonderful example of how collectibles should be done because collecting them all unlocks new game content, and even if the trophies are hidden, they are never impossible to find; in fact, you just have to pay attention to the environment.

The positioning of collectibles is crucial to their positive or negative perception in the eyes of the player. For example, a bad way to do it is to scatter them in huge open world maps. This is bad because open world maps take long to explore, especially if there isn't a good way to fast travel. In fact, exploring those maps can take so long that it has become very common, in open world games, to implement fast travel via some kind of teleport or offering the player mounts to move faster.

If a level is very big, collectibles should be placed conveniently to guide the player through the relevant paths and areas, so that they don't end up getting lost. Moreover, when it's about very big areas, items and collectibles should be abundant.

We can see a great example of that principle put in practice in Super Mario Odyssey, where there are tons of collectibles all over the world and you never feel like there's not much to do. The map never feels empty. Moreover, the game features fast and fun ways to move at different speeds. This allows even huge levels to be traversed in a small amount of time and without feeling stressed or having the impression of wasting time. It's very important, for the player, to be able to move at their own pace.

On the other hand, Yooka-Laylee (Team17, 2017) features very big levels, but even if they are beautiful to watch, they're not very fun to traverse. In fact, Yooka moves very slowly and doesn't have any skill or options to move faster. This makes the experience feel very slow; and this, combined with bad positioning and variety regarding collectibles, can cause lost of interest and motivation for many players.

A famous example of collectibles done wrong can be found in Donkey Kong 64 (DK64; Nintendo, 2010). DK64 features five different collectibles: one for each Kong that you can play with. Every Kong can only pick up its own type of collectible. This means that to collect them all, you are forced to repeat the same level five times. This mechanics is repeated for other kinds of game objects like switches, secret areas, and even boss fights. It's good to give the player variety and allowing for backtracking, but if the level remains aesthetically the same and plays the same and the only thing different is the color of the collectibles, there's something wrong!

Other than that, the positioning of collectibles in DK64 sometimes feels a bit random. It's always a good idea, instead, to place collectibles and items along the right way that the player has to follow. This makes the collection less tedious and also tells the player where they should go.

This takes us to the last topic: level design. How important is it, in a platformer? And how should a level be, to be enjoyable?

World Makers

Level design is a hard task. It's the art of creating credible and recognizable places which are fun to traverse.

In the platformer genres, there are way too many games that feature huge and not memorable levels. The player is forced to explore very big places that totally lack recognizable landmarks or some way to orient

CHAPTER 10 DESIGNING PLATFORMERS

yourself while exploring. Some of those games intelligently turn around the problem by implementing a pop-up map or a Minimap in a corner of the screen; some others don't address the problem at all and end up being perceived as dull or frustrating.

A good example of memorable levels filled with landmarks is the levels found in Gex: Deep Cover Gecko (Crystal Dynamics, 1999). They are all built around a theme: there is the pirate level, the one inspired by a Japanese anime, the one set in the ancient Egypt, the Christmas level, and so on. They are all open world levels, but they never feel confusing, both because they're not too big and because they're full of landmarks. The whole game looks like a theme park, where you can go around and play various mini-games interwoven by fun platforming sessions. In fact, every level offers many puzzles and different activities in the form of mini-games that you have to deal with to advance.

A classic example of a game featuring good level design is Super Mario 64 (Nintendo, 1998). In fact, every level has a unique setting filled with recognizable landmarks and, more importantly, a clear purpose. Just take Bob-omb Battlefield as an example; it's built around the boss fight with King Bob-omb that waits for you at the top of a hill. Around this hill, there is the rest of the level that mostly consists in a path that runs from the start of the level to the top of the hill. That can look like a lazy level design, but it's perceived as a fun and well-designed level because while you walk that path, you are introduced to a lot of game mechanics that you will need to use in the rest of the game.

The level starts with the classic goombas trying to chase you. You already know them: you jump on their heads, and they're gone. Then, there are the bob-ombs that you can't defeat with a jump, so you try other buttons, and it turns out that you can grab them and throw them away. Going further, you get in contact with coins and question mark blocks that work pretty much like Super Mario Bros. Finally, you find yourself in front of a big bad Chain Chomp, which is a big bomb chained to a wooden pole behaving as a guard dog; and as soon as you get close, it will

385

attack trying to bite Mario. There are two things you can do to overcome this situation: you can try to escape by using a forward jump to quickly surpass it and get to the next area, or you can use the ground-pound move to stick the wooden pole into the ground freeing the Chain Chomp that will eventually run away breaking a jail that contains a collectible. In so little space, Nintendo managed to put a lot of information teaching the player some basics of the game, like how Chain Chomp works and how to solve some environmental puzzles. This is not only just a good learning moment, but it's also a fun memorable moment (and place) in which the player is rewarded with a collectible. While freeing the Chain Chomp, you are not thinking about the fact that you have to get the collectible; you are only thinking about how to get rid of that beast. The collectible is just your reward for solving the puzzle. It's like if the game congratulates with the player telling them that this is how you have to play this game. When level design can communicate so much information that clearly, you understand how powerful even the simplest asset in your game world can be and how big is your responsibility toward the fun factor of the game.

Level design in Super Mario 64 is often built around rewards and environmental puzzles. This makes the level memorable and fun and offers the level designer a good criterion to place collectibles making them an extra reward that doesn't turn the act of collecting into an annoying or repetitive task.

All the information you gathered while climbing the king's hill will be very useful to win the boss fight. In fact, being King Bob-omb a bob-omb himself, you know that you can grab him and throw him away. After some throws, he will surrender and beg you to stop.

Bob-omb Battlefield is a level built not only around a theme, but around a series of concepts that need to be taught to the player. That's why it's so good!

The design lesson to learn, analyzing Bob-omb Battlefield and Gex: Deep Cover Gecko, is that when you design your own levels, you should always try to think of them as real places in the fictional world of your game. Anyway, good and coherent aesthetics alone doesn't make a good game! Other than choosing a theme to give an aesthetic personality to your level, you also need to build the level around one or more gameplay mechanics.

Start creating the main area of the level (e.g., King Bob-omb's hill) and think about what the player needs to know to face that challenge or – more generally – to enjoy that piece of gameplay. Context will naturally grow around it, bringing ideas for decorative elements, paths to follow, puzzles, and platforming challenges.

For example, if you want to introduce the player to a new kind of mechanics – let's say the wall jump – design the piece of level that uses that technique at its best, and then build the rest of the level in function to that special moment of gameplay. As all the learning processes, it starts with a good preparation which can be made by adding some easier and safer wall jumps along the way. Following this process, you will end up with a nice level that teaches a new technique step by step giving the player the time they need to grok the new skill.

At the end of Chapter 9, we built our first level for Cherry Caves 2 by thinking about how to introduce the various gameplay elements we built, and this is a very good way to design games. If you don't have a narrative concept to explain or it's not the primary focus of the game, bet everything on gameplay elements by teaching them to the player one by one and increasing the difficulty step by step.

A sublime example of this level design philosophy can be found in Celeste (Matt Makes Games, 2018), where every level builds upon the concepts learned previously.

Celeste teaches you, one level at a time, how to use every skill of the game one by one and how to combine them to accomplish what in the beginning seemed impossible. The game also reinforces this concept of accomplishing hard tasks by mastering the fundamentals with the narrative expedient of the mountain climbing – which you can accomplish by focusing on doing right small simple actions.

All the levels in Celeste are challenges, and they're purely built around gameplay. That makes them not memorable, but extremely fun and challenging. Games like this save a lot on aesthetics and invest even more on gameplay mechanics. In fact, to make the level feel fun and enjoyable, the player must have access to a wide array of skills and abilities to combine one another to solve puzzles and platforming sessions. Momentum, gripping, wall jump, dash – they are all explained one by one in levels that grow more and more challenging and skill-demanding intertwining gameplay concepts together.

When we talk about games built around pure platforming, it's easy to fall into some bad habits, like repeating ideas or making symmetrical levels or levels that are way too linear. Symmetrical levels are bad because they force you to walk along a path and then repeating it reversed. This can be fun for a level or two, but on the long run, it can become tedious and annoying. Instead, try to design asymmetrical areas where each section of the level focuses on one action, skill, or gameplay moment, not on the shape of the level itself. Symmetry is nice to look at, but it hardly makes a fun level.

Conclusion

Don't worry if this may appear overwhelming or too difficult and don't mind too much if your first level designs are not super good. Level design, like nearly everything in life, is an art that requires time and practice to be mastered. While creating levels, you will constantly learn new things and become better at it. So don't give up and keep on creating games!

In the next chapter, we will go further into the platforming genre by analyzing and implementing a metroidvania game! We will learn how to create even more interesting gameplay elements like wall jump, dash, and a Minimap, and we will address the problem of backtracking in level design, which is one of the defining characteristics of the genre.

CHAPTER 11

Metroidvania (Part 1)

We covered many different genres and sub-genres, and you learned how to create a card game, a fixed shooter, a scrolling shoot 'em up, a singlescreen platformer, and a scrolling platformer. Each of these projects taught you an important lesson about game design and development. Let's summarize a bit what we saw in the previous chapters:

- Memory (Chapters 3 and 4) taught you randomization, variables, loops, and data structures.

- Space Gala and Space Gala 2 taught you how to manage shooting, bullets, collisions, health, score, enemies, and basic enemies AI and how to create basic boss fights.

- Cherry Caves and Cherry Caves 2 taught you about jumping, ground collisions, gravity, power-ups, menus, and some more about enemies with basic AI. We also started to think about how to design good levels and to foster players' motivation and engagement creating feature-rich games.

In this and the next chapter, we are going to put all this knowledge together to study and implement a project based on one of the most interesting and complex game genres around: metroidvania.

The game will be called *Isolation*. The setting is a labyrinth of tunnels and caves on an alien planet. The player, using a map and some skills like wall jump and dash, will explore those strange places in search for the exit.

CHAPTER 11 METROIDVANIA (PART 1)

The idea behind the gameplay of a metroidvania is simple, but the development is not. In fact, it requires some complex mechanics and features like maps, Minimaps, exploration skills, and also items, equipment, and an inventory menu to manage your items. A metroidvania game also requires a system of checkpoints to save the game and let the player continue the exploration.

History

Metroidvania is a sub-genre of action-adventure video games strongly based on exploration and platforming which often features also complex combat mechanics and RPG elements.

The word metroidvania is a portmanteau of two video game titles: Metroid and Castlevania. In particular, the word refers to Super Metroid (Nintendo, 1994) and Castlevania: Symphony of the Night (Konami, 1997), which are the two fathers of the genre.

The focus of the genre is on the exploration of complex structures, an activity that requires skills and/or items to be completed, thus forcing the player to backtrack. In fact, one peculiarity of metroidvania games is that they allow the player to unlock new areas only by acquiring special items like keys or weapons or by gaining new exploration skills that allow to get to places that were out of reach before.

A classic example of this mechanic can be found in games featuring doors that can be opened only with a particular key or games that feature areas reachable only with particular skills like double jump, wall jump, dash, and so on.

The way the level designer places those key items or the moment in which they choose to unlock some skills greatly affects the player's perception of the exploration and how much fun and engagement the game will give to the player.

Apart from the classic examples of Super Metroid and Castlevania: Symphony of the Night, some (more modern) very good examples of exploration and backtracking done right are Hollow Knight (Team Cherry, 2017) and Iconoclast (Konjak, 2018).

Hollow Knight does an incredible job in immersing the player in a world with deep lore and wonderful atmosphere dragging them into a huge world of interconnected underground tunnels that tell the story of a great lost kingdom. In HK, backtracking can be felt as a real consequence of finding clues that open new paths in discovering the history of this ancient world.

Iconoclast has a very original and fun way to traverse areas by solving puzzles that make a great use of key objects and skills to unlock paths. It's interesting how classic environmental puzzles make the game so fresh and different from all the other metroidvania games.

In this chapter, we will create the first part of our metroidvania called Isolation. We will implement just a subset of the features of the project; namely, we will create firstly a platforming base for the game (managing gravity, jump, and basic movements) by quickly recreating some features we already saw in Cherry Caves chapters; then we will enhance the platforming adding wall jump and dash. After, we will create the menu system to manage the different states of the game, and finally we will create a couple of rooms and a warping system to travel through them.

Isolation (Game Design Document)

Isolation is a single-player metroidvania game inspired by games like Super Metroid, Castlevania: Symphony of the Night, and Hollow Knight.

The player impersonates Maria, an archaeologist specialized in alien research isolated on an alien planet. Her objective is to escape the labyrinthic underground world in which she's trapped and find her expedition team.

CHAPTER 11   METROIDVANIA (PART 1)

Story and Setting

Maria was part of an explorative expedition on an alien world. While she was studying some rocks in the area, something went wrong, the tunnel collapsed, and she was divided from her team. Now she's alone, isolated, trying to find the way back.

Gameplay

The game revolves mainly around exploration and action combat. By using the items found along the way, the player will be able to upgrade Maria's gear and fight the enemies.

Victory Condition

Like in every metroidvania game, victory is achieved when the end of the maze is reached or the main enemy is killed.

The version of the game we will develop will be – of course – very short for the standard of a metroidvania. We will only concentrate on creating the game system, and so this time we won't have a victory condition. The game we will create will only be a prototype to show you the main features of the game system.

Controls

Isolation supports both keyboard and gamepads.
> **Keyboard**
> **Left**: Move left.
> **Right**: Move right.
> **Z**: Jump.
> **X**: Dash.
> **C**: Attack.

CHAPTER 11   METROIDVANIA (PART 1)

Esc: Pause/unpause the game.
I: Open the inventory.
Tab: Open the map.
Enter: Confirm (menu).
Gamepad
Left Analog/Direction Pad: Move left.
Right Analog/Direction Pad: Move right.
Face 1 Button: Jump.
Right Shoulder Button: Dash.
Face 3 Button: Attack.
Start: Pause/unpause the game.
Face 4 Button: Open the inventory.
Select: Open the map.
Face 1 Button: Confirm (menu).

Note that the face buttons on a gamepad are the ones that you can find at the right of the pad and are commonly bound to actions. There are two main configurations on modern controllers: one based on Xbox gamepads and one based on PlayStation gamepads. So, depending on which one of the two kinds of gamepads you have, the face buttons map like in Table 11-1.

Table 11-1. Face buttons

	Xbox controller	**PlayStation controller**
Face 1	A	Cross
Face 2	B	Circle
Face 3	X	Square
Face 4	Y	Triangle

CHAPTER 11 METROIDVANIA (PART 1)

Enemies

Isolation will feature one of the enemies from Cherry Caves 2: the green octopus (Figure 11-1) which moves back and forth horizontally.

The focus of this chapter is not on how to code interesting foes – we covered it in Chapters 5, 6, 8, and 9 – but on exploration and platforming features, so this is enough for our purpose.

Figure 11-1. *Green octopus*

Enemies have a passive AI, meaning they won't attack or search for the player, but will just move around being a physical obstacle to the player's exploration.

Attack

Maria has a highly technological gun, which is the standard equipment of space archeologists.

This special pistol can be upgraded with certain materials that she will find along the way changing the effectiveness of the weapon.

Maria can pick up and equip those upgrades by accessing the inventory system.

Skills

Maria will have two main skills:

- **Dash**, which consists in a quick step forward
- **Wall jump**, which consists in a jump stepping on a wall, allowing her to reach higher places

CHAPTER 11 METROIDVANIA (PART 1)

Maps

Isolation features a map system that will help the player to keep track of their exploring progresses in real time.

The map system is divided in a complete map accessible by pressing the Tab key on a keyboard or Select on a gamepad and a Minimap that is always visible during the game.

While the complete map, as the name suggests, shows the place in its entirety (meaning all the rooms), the Minimap only shows the current room and the adjacent rooms, as shown in Figure 11-2.

Figure 11-2. *The portion of the area shown on the Minimap and on the full map. The light-colored rectangle is the current room, the darker rectangles are the adjacent rooms*

Inventory

Isolation features an inventory system to store and equip all the items that Maria picks up.

We will concentrate more on the technical implementation of the inventory, so the aesthetical aspect will not be central. The inventory will be pretty simple, being just a list of items which updates anytime Maria picks an item.

CHAPTER 11 METROIDVANIA (PART 1)

The player can navigate the list with up and down buttons (both gamepad or keyboard) and equip an item by pressing the confirmation button (Face 1 on gamepad and Z on keyboard).

Similar Games

Isolation is based on Super Metroid for both mechanics and atmosphere, but has some inspiration also from Castlevania: Symphony of the Night (concerning the possibility to upgrade the equipment).

Some other similar games are Hollow Knight and Axiom Verge.

Assets

The following is the list of assets we are going to use for this project, plus – as usual – instructions on sprites' characteristics.

spr_player_idle

This represents Maria in idle position (not moving).

Size: 64 × 64
Pivot Point: Middle-center
Collision Mask: Automatic, rectangle

spr_player_walk

This sprite will be used for Maria's walking animation.

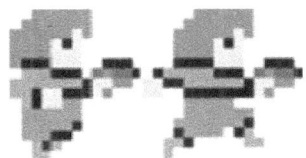

Size: 64 × 64
Pivot Point: Middle-center
Collision Mask: Automatic, rectangle

spr_player_jump

This will be used for Maria's jump animation (ascending).

Size: 64 × 64
Pivot Point: Middle-center
Collision Mask: Automatic, rectangle

spr_player_jump_fall/spr_player_dash

To represent both the fall after a jump and Maria's dashing skill, we will use the same image. You can use a single sprite to do so, but I strongly suggest you to create two different sprites, so that if you want to substitute the image for an action but not the one for the other, you can without touching the code. My code will use two different sprites with the same image.

CHAPTER 11   METROIDVANIA (PART 1)

Size: 64 × 64
Pivot Point: Middle-center
Collision Mask: Automatic, rectangle

spr_player_wallslide

This sprite represents Maria during a wall slide, which consists in sliding down while touching a wall. It's the starting state to perform a wall jump.

Size: 64 × 64
Pivot Point: Middle-center
Collision Mask: Automatic, rectangle

spr_heart

This heart will be used to represent Maria's HP in the HUD.

Size: 64 × 64
Pivot Point: Top-left
Collision Mask: Automatic, rectangle

spr_warp

This sprite will be used to mark the warp zones. We just need its collision box. The sprite won't be visible.

Size: 64 × 64
Pivot Point: Top-left
Collision Mask: Automatic, rectangle

spr_marker

This sprite will be used to mark the boundaries that the green octopus cannot pass.

Size: 32 × 32
Pivot Point: Top-left
Collision Mask: Automatic, rectangle

CHAPTER 11   METROIDVANIA (PART 1)

spr_upgrade

This sprite will be used to represent upgrades for the pistol that can be picked up by Maria and equipped.

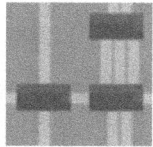

Size: 64 × 64
Pivot Point: Middle-center
Collision Mask: Automatic, rectangle

spr_cure

This sprite will be used to represent cures which are consumable objects that restore HPs.

Size: 64 × 64
Pivot Point: Middle-center
Collision Mask: Automatic, rectangle

spr_octopus_green

This is the kind of enemy moving back and forth.

Size: 64 × 64
Pivot Point: Middle-center
Collision Mask: Automatic, rectangle
Animation Speed: 4

spr_ground_brown

This sprite will be used to create the ground and wall tiles. Since we are in a cavern, it seems legit to use the same sprite for both.

Size: 64 × 64
Pivot Point: Top-left
Collision Mask: Automatic, rectangle

spr_checkpoint_inactive

This is the checkpoint platform when not active. The player should walk on it to activate it.

Size: 64 × 64
Pivot Point: Bottom-center
Collision Mask: Automatic, rectangle

CHAPTER 11   METROIDVANIA (PART 1)

spr_checkpoint_active

This is the checkpoint platform when active (when the player collides with it).

Size: 64 × 64
Pivot Point: Bottom-center
Collision Mask: Automatic, rectangle

spr_bullet_heavy

This sprite represents a bullet of a heavy weapon.

Size: 16 × 16
Pivot Point: Middle-center
Collision Mask: Automatic, rectangle

spr_bullet_light

This sprite will be used to represent a bullet of a light weapon.
Size: 16 × 16
Pivot Point: Middle-center
Collision Mask: Automatic, rectangle

Fonts

fnt_text

This is the font used to create small standard texts.
> **Font**: Consolas
> **Style**: Regular
> **Size**: 18

fnt_menu_h1

This is the font used for headers in menus.
> **Font**: Consolas
> **Style**: Bold
> **Size**: 32

fnt_menu_h2

This is the font used for smaller headers in menus.
> **Font**: Consolas
> **Style**: Bold
> **Size**: 22

Sounds

snd_item

This is the sound effect we will play when picking up an item. We will use it in Chapter 12.

snd_jump

This is the sound effect we will play when the jump button is pressed.

snd_dash

This is the sound effect we will play when the character's player dashes.

snd_shoot

This sound effect will be played when shooting with the gun. We will use it in Chapter 12.

snd_kill

This sound effect will be played when Maria kills an enemy. We will use it in Chapter 12.

snd_hit

This is the sound effect we will play when Maria gets hit. We will use it in Chapter 12.

snd_menu

This sound effect will be played when navigating through the menu.

Creating the Platforming Base

Metroidvania, as we already said, is a sub-genre of action-adventure platformers. This means that to create one, we must first build a platforming base upon which we can add features.

Since we already created a platformer in Chapters 8 and 9, I am not going to explain in detail what we are doing. Don't worry, I will show you the code and explain what it does, as always, but I'm going to do it in less detail.

CHAPTER 11 METROIDVANIA (PART 1)

The platforming base of a metroidvania is an interesting one, and it's made mixing the concepts of the two genres we already talked about: single-screen platformers and scrolling platformers.

In fact, since metroidvania games are made of big areas, it's not reasonable to load such big levels into the memory all at once; so, they use the trick of combining SSP with scrolling platformers. Basically, areas are divided into sections, so the player walks as a scrolling platformer in one section at a time, allowing the game to load just a little part of the area at a time and still giving the player the idea that they're traversing a very big place.

This is a technique that first came out with Pitfall! (Activision, 1982) which tried to evade the impossibility to build a scrolling platformer (because of technological impediments) creating the illusion of horizontal travelling connecting various rooms to one another. So, when the player walked to the right border of the screen, a new section of the area was drawn, and the player teleported to the left border of the screen, giving the illusion of progression.

Let's start working on our new project by creating a new object named `obj_player`.

Associate the new object to spr_player_idle and tick the Persistent option as shown in Figure 11-3.

CHAPTER 11   METROIDVANIA (PART 1)

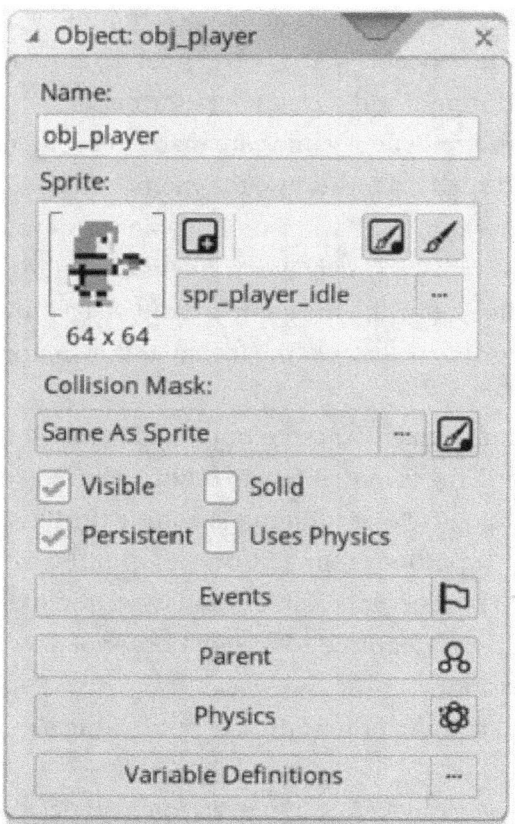

Figure 11-3. *The new object obj_player at a glance*

Every instance, in GameMaker, is created when you enter a room and destroyed when you quit it.

Warning!   When you change room, all the instances are destroyed, but their destroy event is not triggered! Use the Room End event (Other Events ➤ Room End) to perform actions when you leave the current room.

Since our game will feature several rooms, we don't want to lose all the information we have on our character, like HPs, items, and so on. So, to prevent this, we make obj_player a persistent object, meaning that it will not be destroyed when changing rooms, but will be preserved until the game is closed or the instance_destroy() function is called.

Add a Create event to obj_player and set some variables:

```
1   // stats
2   spd = 6;
3   hsp = 0;
4   vsp = 0;
5
6   // moving and jumping
7   direction = 0;
8   facing_dir = 1;
```

Line 2-4: As usual, spd is the speed at which the player can move, while hsp and vsp are the horizontal and vertical speed of the character that we will use for movements and jumping/falling.

Line 7: Here we assign the starting value of the built-in variable direction. We are setting it now for convenience, but we will use it in the next chapter to set the direction of the bullets shot.

The direction variable is set to 0 at the start to be aligned to the starting position of the player (facing right). It's a recognized tradition to start platformers always facing right, because it gives the sense of progression and suggests the player to move forward; but if you plan to make your player start facing left, change this value to 180. If you feel like you're using magic numbers, you can set the value using the point_direction function as we did in Space Gala.

Line 6: This is a variable we are going to use to keep track of the facing direction of the player, since the format of direction is not very comfortable to do some quick math. This variable will be set to 1 when facing right and to -1 when facing left.

Now, create a Step event, and let's start coding the controls of our avatar:

```
1   // --- CONTROLS HANDLING --- //
2   var _move_left = keyboard_check ( vk_left );
3   var _move_right = keyboard_check ( vk_right );
4
5   // set move and speed variables
6   var _move = _move_right - _move_left;
7   hsp = _move * spd;
8
9   if _move != 0
10  {
11      sprite_index = spr_player_walk;
12      facing_dir = _move;
13      image_xscale = facing_dir;
14      direction = point_direction(x, y, x + _move, y);
15  }
16  else
17  {
18      sprite_index = spr_player_idle;
19  }
20
21  // horizontal movement
22  x += hsp;
```

Lines 2–3: We use two Boolean variables to keep track of the user's input.

Lines 6–7: We set up the horizontal speed according to the moving direction defined by the user's input.

CHAPTER 11   METROIDVANIA (PART 1)

Lines 9-15: If the player is moving (move is either 1 or -1), we set the *direction* and *facing_dir* variables accordingly, change the sprite to the walk sprite, and scale it to face the right direction.

Line 18: If the player is not moving, we change the sprite to the idle sprite.

Line 22: Finally, we set x to the new value defined by the horizontal movement represented by hsp.

Running the game, you will be able to verify that the character is correctly moving when pressing the arrow keys.

Gamepad Support!

Keyboard controls are not enough! For our games to be more enjoyable, it's time we start supporting gamepads. GameMaker Studio 2 allows us to do it very easily thanks to some specialized functions. Let's explore them!

Note   GameMaker supports both XInput and DirectInput gamepads, but we are going to cover only XInput which is the de facto standard. Xbox pads and PlayStation pads both support XInput.

GameMaker supports up to four XInput gamepads. The gamepads are indexed from 0 to 3, and you can detect when they are plugged in or out by listening to an asynchronous system event.

Since Isolation is a single-player game that supports both keyboard and gamepads, we have no interest in this. We will always use the gamepad indexed 0.

GameMaker offers a list of functions to handle buttons and analog sticks very similarly to how mouse and keyboards are handled.

For example, to check the status of a button on the gamepad, you can use one of these functions:

- gamepad_button_check(gamepad_id, button_code)

409

CHAPTER 11   METROIDVANIA (PART 1)

- gamepad_button_check_pressed(gamepad_id, button_code)
- gamepad_button_check_released(gamepad_id, button_code)

As you can see, those functions are very similar to keyboard-related functions. This will make everything easier!

In the functions presented earlier, the gamepad_id is the index of the connected gamepad (from 0 to 3, as we already said), while the button_code is a unique value which identifies a button on the pad.

Figure 11-4 shows a map of the codes of each button and analog that composes a gamepad.

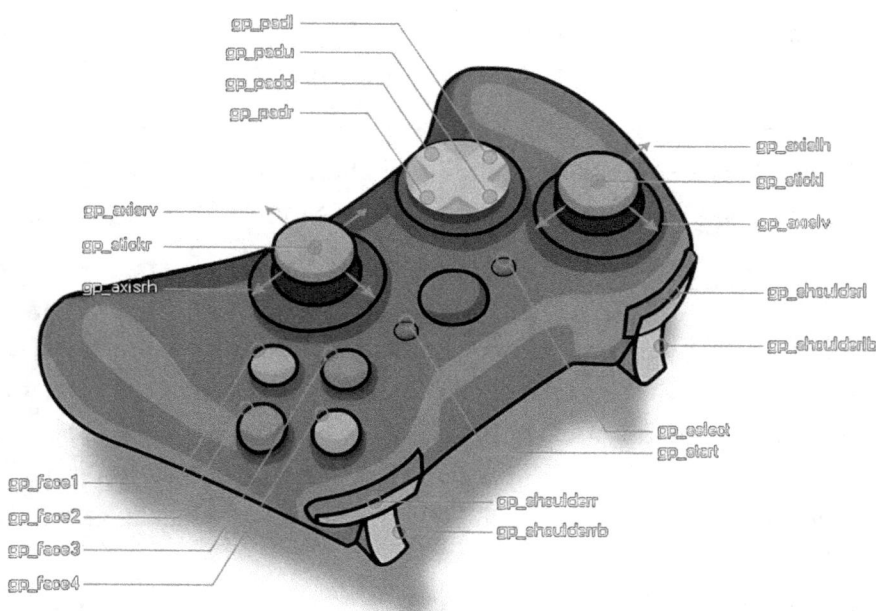

Figure 11-4. *A visual scheme of gamepad mapping on GameMaker Studio 2*

CHAPTER 11 METROIDVANIA (PART 1)

The first thing we need to do, to add gamepad support to our game, is to initialize the gamepad analog deadzone. It's important to set the deadzone of an analog stick, if you don't want your game to react to every micromovement of the analog. Having an excessively sensible analog in a platformer can be troublesome since it could cause the avatar to move when the player doesn't intend to.

We can do this in obj_player's Create event with this single line:

```
1   gamepad_set_axis_deadzone(0, 0.5);
```

Next, we have to handle the actual input, and we can do it modifying the initial part of the code in obj_player's Step event:

```
1   // --- CONTROLS HANDLING --- //
2   var _haxis = gamepad_axis_value(0, gp_axislh);
3
4   var _move_left = keyboard_check ( vk_left ) or gamepad_button_check(0, gp_padl) or (_haxis < 0);
5   var _move_right = keyboard_check ( vk_right ) or gamepad_button_check(0, gp_padr) or (_haxis > 0);
```

Line 2: Here we set the haxis variable which keeps track of the position in which we move the analog stick on the horizontal axis (either left or right). To do so, we pass to the gamepad_axis_value function, the code gp_axislh which tells the function to return the position of the left analog on the horizontal axis.

Lines 4–5: Now we set move_left and move_right to true not only according to keyboard input but also checking if D-pad (direction pad) buttons were pressed or if the left analog was used.

Now save and run the game to check that inputs are correctly working!

Take your time to taste the emotion of playing your game with a gamepad. It's a special feeling, isn't it?

CHAPTER 11   METROIDVANIA (PART 1)

Gravity, No Escaping!

We definitely need gravity in our game world, to make it a real platformer. We already know how, thanks to the work we made in Chapters 8 and 9, so let's do this quickly.

First, let's add a couple of variables to obj_player's Create event:

```
1   grv = 0.8;
2   grounded = false;
```

Line 1: This variable represents the gravity our character is affected by.
Line 2: This variable tells us if the object is touching the ground or not.

Now we must apply the gravity on our player's movements. Just append this code to obj_player's Step event:

```
1   // apply gravity
2   vsp = vsp + grv;
3
4   // vertical movement
5   y += vsp;
```

At line 2 we apply gravity to the vertical speed of obj_player, while at line 5 we commit the changes to be reflected on the actual position of the object on the Y-axis.

Next step is to create an object that can stop obj_player fall when colliding and program obj_player to manage this collision.

Go ahead and create a new object called obj_block and add no sprite to it. Then create another object and call it obj_ground_brown and associate it with spr_ground_brown by settingobj_block as a parent for obj_ground_brown. This is crucial to make obj_ground_brown an effective blocking object for obj_player.

Now let's go back to obj_player's Step event, and add this code just before the line that updates the x variable:

```
1   // HORIZONTAL COLLISION WITH BLOCKS
2   if (place_meeting(x+hsp, y, obj_block))
3   {
4       while(not place_meeting(x+sign(hsp), y, obj_block))
5       {
6           x += sign(hsp);
7       }
8       hsp = 0;
9   }
```

The code above is borrowed from Cherry Caves and manages the horizontal collision with obj_block instances. I am not going to explain this in detail, since we already saw this code in previous projects. If you need some more explanation, go back to Chapter 8 and find out the section where we first introduced this way of handling collisions with blocks.

Let's do the same for the vertical collisions, and insert this code just before we update the y variable:

```
1   // VERTICAL COLLISION WITH BLOCKS
2   if (place_meeting(x, y + vsp, obj_block))
3   {
4       while(not place_meeting(x,y+sign(vsp), obj_block))
5       {
6           y += sign(vsp);
7       }
8       vsp = 0;
9       grounded = true;
10  }
11  else
12  {
13      grounded = false;
14  }
```

CHAPTER 11   METROIDVANIA (PART 1)

The code above handles vertical collisions with obj_block instances and sets the grounded variable to true or false accordingly.

You can now position some instances of obj_block_brown and an instance of obj_player in a room and check that everything is working by running the game.

Making the Leap

We have most of the platforming system working. We just need to add the jump, so that we can move properly between platforms.

As we saw in Chapters 8 and 9, we need just three variables and a handful of lines of code to accomplish that.

Head to obj_player's Create event, and add a new variable declaration at the bottom of the code:

```
1   jspd = 18;
```

We will use this variable to apply a force that can contrast the gravity and make our avatar jump.

Open up obj_player's Step event, and in the controls handling section, just below the initialization of move_left and move_right variables, add these two lines:

```
1   var _jumping = keyboard_check_pressed(ord("Z")) or
    gamepad_button_check_pressed(0, gp_face1);
2   var _jump_released = keyboard_check_released(ord("Z"))
    or gamepad_button_check_released(0, gp_face1);
```

Those two lines check whether the jump button has been pressed or released. We will use this information in the next chunk of code to manage the jumping and stop the raising of our avatar when the button is released. This will give us total control on the character's jump allowing us for creation of fun and challenging platforming sessions in our levels.

CHAPTER 11 METROIDVANIA (PART 1)

Now, just above the section that manages collisions with obj_block instances, insert this code to manage jumping:

```
1   // JUMP
2   if (_jumping and grounded)
3   {
4       grounded = false;
5       vsp = -jspd;
6   
7       sprite_index = spr_player_jump;
8       audio_play_sound(snd_jump, 1, false);
9   }
10  
11  if (jump_released)
12  {
13      vsp *= 0.5;
14  }
```

The code above is also borrowed from Cherry Caves, and it's very straightforward. When the character is grounded and the jump button is pressed, a negative force is applied to its vertical speed. Being the force greater than the gravity applied to the vertical speed, the character will move upward, jumping. While jumping, the grounded variable turns to false, so that the player cannot jump anymore until they reach again the ground.

When the jump button is released, the jumping force gets halved so that the raising stops quickly and the character begins its fall as soon as the vsp variable reaches 0.

Save and run the game to check that everything is in place (Figure 11-5). The character should be able to move and jump on platforms correctly with both keyboard and gamepad. Great!

CHAPTER 11 METROIDVANIA (PART 1)

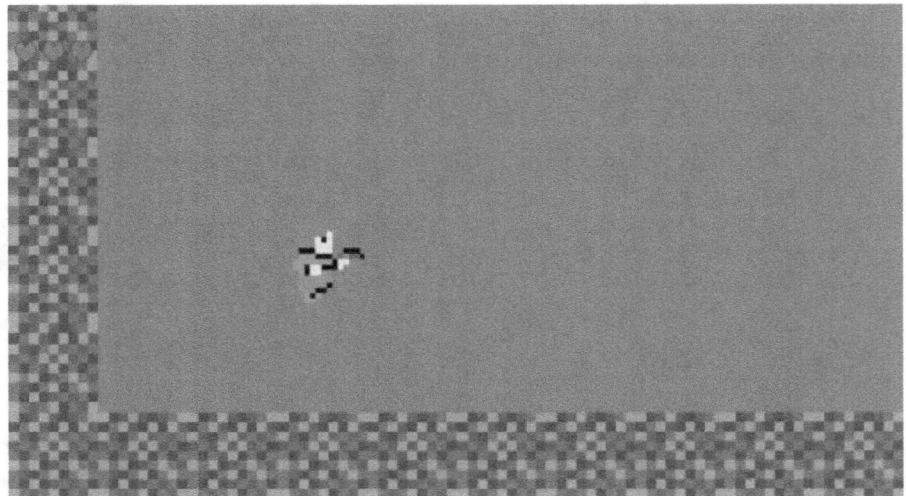

Figure 11-5. *Finally, Maria can happily jump!*

Another Kick in the Wall

A very loved feature of metroidvania games and action-adventure platformers in general is wall jump (or wall kick). Widely known thanks to the Mega Man series, wall jump allows the player to use walls to gain an additional jump starting from the moment the player's character touches the wall.

This skill is widely used in metroidvania and action-adventure platformers, because it allows the player to have much more freedom and to reach places that were unreachable before by bouncing between walls or directly climbing it with some chained wall jumps.

Wall jump is often connected to another skill: wall slide. This one is a very interesting perk that allows the player's character to grab a wall and gently slide downward. This is a huge help to avoid the leap of faith problem (meaning that the player has to make some jumps without knowing what's below) in level design without making obvious what lies on the bottom of an area.

CHAPTER 11   METROIDVANIA (PART 1)

Some games, known as rage games, do use level design patterns like *leaps of faith* to trick the player into taking the wrong decision and die. I personally think that this is bad because it makes the player feel like the whole experience is unfair. Most of the people don't like to play unfair games that don't give you the possibility to control your performance, and this is one of the feelings that breaks the magic of the cognitive flow status.

With wall slide, the player's character will slow down the fall by sliding on the wall allowing them to see what's below and eventually jump to safety with a wall jump.

We are going to implement wall kick by dividing the effort in two phases:

1. We check if the player's character is touching a wall while not grounded. If they are, we check whether the player has pressed the jump button; and, in this case, we set the coordinates at which the character should be rebound horizontally and perform a jump in the usual way.

2. When phase 1 executes, we start moving the player's character toward the rebound goal we set in phase 1. When the coordinates are reached or the avatar touches the ground, we stop moving it and end phase.

Let's start by defining the variables we will need. Go ahead and open the Create event in obj_player and append this code to it:

```
1   // wall jump/slide
2   can_wall_jump = true;
3   wall_jump = false;
4   wall_slide_friction = 0.5;
5   wj_goal_x = x;
6   already_walljumping = false;
```

Let's explain the meaning of those variables one by one:

- **can_wall_jump** is a controller variable that we will use to check whether the player has unlocked the wall jump skill or not.

- **wall_jump** tells us if the player's character can wall jump or not. This will be set to true when the player's character touches the wall and to false when they move from it.

- **wall_slide_friction** is used to store the value of the friction that we apply to the fall of the player's character when touching a wall (wall sliding). You can change this accordingly to your preference.

- **wj_goal_x** is the coordinate on the X-axis that the avatar should reach after performing a wall jump.

- **already_walljumping** is the trigger to start phase 2, as we described earlier.

Now, in obj_player's Step event, we want to add the code that tells us when the player is not grounded and is touching the wall. To do so, we need to check for the collision with an obj_block instance just a pixel next to the player's character, in the direction they're facing.

So add this code in obj_player's Step event, just above the jump code:

```
1   // Check if touching a wall -> activate wall slide/jump
2   if (not grounded and can_wall_jump and place_meeting
    (x+facing_dir, y, obj_block))
3   {
4       sprite_index = spr_player_wallslide;
5       wall_jump = true;
6       if (vsp> 0)
```

```
7       {
8           vsp -= wall_slide_friction;
9       }
10  }
11  else
12  {
13      wall_jump = false;
14  }
```

In the code above, we check whether the player's character is not grounded, can perform a wall jump, and is touching the wall using the facing_dir variable to make sure to check the collision in the direction the player's character is facing (line 2). If the condition at line 2 is not satisfied, the player cannot wall jump, so we set the wall_jump variable to false (line 13). However, if the condition at line 2 is satisfied, instead, we change the sprite to the appropriate wall slide sprite (line 4) and set the wall_jump variable to true (line 5), so that the player can wall jump, and finally, we check whether we are descending or not, and we apply the right friction to the fall (lines 6–9). In fact, we don't want the avatar to slow down also when jumping; we want them to slow down only when descending while touching the wall. To do that, we have to check whether the value of vsp is positive (line 6), in which case, we know that we are moving downward (remember that the Y-axis has the 0 on the top of the screen, and moving down from that point, it means increasing the value of the y coordinate).

Now, to implement the last part of the wall jump, we need to modify the jump code. Go ahead and substitute the block of code that manages the jump in obj_player's Step event with this code:

```
1   // JUMP
2   if (_jumping and (grounded or wall_jump))
3   {
4       grounded = false;
5       vsp = -jspd;
```

CHAPTER 11   METROIDVANIA (PART 1)

```
6
7         // WALL JUMP PHASE 1
8         if(wall_jump)
9         {
10            dash_recharging = false;
11            effect_create_layer("Instances", ef_smoke, x, y,
              1, c_white);
12            facing_dir *= -1;
13            image_xscale = facing_dir;
14            direction = point_direction(x, y, x +
              facing_dir, y);
15            wj_goal_x = x + 80 * facing_dir;
16            already_walljumping = true;
17            wall_jump = false;
18        }
19        sprite_index = spr_player_jump;
20        audio_play_sound(snd_jump, 1, false);
21    }
22
23    if (_jump_released)
24    {
25        vsp *= 0.5;
26    }
27
28    if(not grounded and not wall_jump and (vsp> 1))
29    {
30        sprite_index = spr_player_jump_fall;
31    }
```

Line 2: We added to the trigger condition a check upon the value of wall_jump that we potentially set to true in the previous block of code (the one handling the collision with obj_block).

420

Line 5: We perform the jump. This line of code is executed both when the player jumps grounded and when they perform a wall kick.

Lines 8–17: If the value of wall_jump is set to true, meaning that we are performing a wall jump and not a simple grounded jump, we invert the direction faced by the avatar, to simulate the propulsion in the opposite direction given by the wall kick. Then we set the position on the X-axis to which we want our avatar to move (line 22), we set the trigger variable already_jumping to true (line 23), and finally we switch off the wall_jump variable (line 24). Phase 1 done!

Lines 19–20: We assign the jump sprite to obj_player and play a jump sound.

Lines 23–26: We check if the jump button has been released. If that's the case, we stop the ascension.

Lines 28–31: We have a little icing on the cake. We check if the avatar is descending and it's not wall sliding. If that's the case, we change the sprite to spr_player_jump_fall. This gives the avatar some more personality and credibility and makes the game feel a bit more visually pleasing.

Ok, it's time for phase 2! As we said, phase 2 is going to constantly move the avatar toward a goal position calculated in phase 1. We also borrow the code to check if we are going to hit a wall while moving. It's highly probable that we will hit a wall after a wall jump, since to bounce between walls is its primary purpose.

Let's add some code under the section that we just wrote in the Step event of obj_player:

```
1   // WALLJUMP PHASE 2
2   if (already_walljumping)
3   {
4       var _wj_move = spd * facing_dir;
5       if ( place_meeting ( x+_wj_move, y, obj_block ) )
6       {
```

```
7            while ( notplace_meeting ( x+sign(_wj_move), y,
             obj_block ) )
8            {
9                x += sign(_wj_move);
10           }
11           _wj_move = 0;
12           already_walljumping = false;
13       }
14       x += _wj_move;
15       already_walljumping = already_walljumping and
         ((facing_dir> 0 and wj_goal_x> x) or
         (facing_dir< 0 and wj_goal_x< x));
16   }
```

Line 4: We calculate the position on the X-axis that we want the player's character to move to.

Lines 5–13: That's the code we borrowed to check if we are going to hit a wall after the wall kick. As you can see, if that's the case, after we approached the wall, we set wj_move to 0 and already_walljumping to false so that this piece of code won't be executed again.

Line 14: Here we update the X-coordinate using wj_move. This happens constantly until already_walljumping turns to false.

Line 15: After every iteration, we update the value of already_walljumping. If the avatar reached the goal or already_walljumping has been set to false (line 12), this means that we don't need to move the avatar anymore and that we can set the variable to false (or leave it to false).

Done! It was a bit tricky, but we did it!

CHAPTER 11 METROIDVANIA (PART 1)

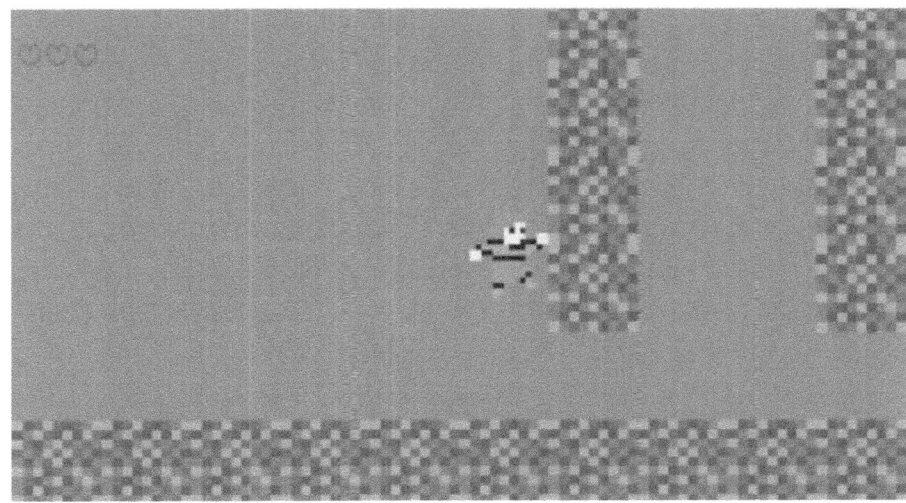

Figure 11-6. *Maria can now wall slide and jump like a modern pink-haired ninja!*

Save and run the game and enjoy your new shiny wall kick skill (Figure 11-6)! This is a great addition to any platformer that aims at exploration and complex platforming sessions!

Now let's talk about another super-important feature that's a must-have for any good metroidvania game: dash!

Moving Forward with a Dash

Dash is another skill made great by the Mega Man series. It's a feature that firstly appeared in Mega Man X, but there was a similar thing since Mega Man 3: sliding. The only difference between the two skills is that a dash can be performed in midair as well as on the ground, while a slide is only possible when on the ground. Also, a dash is exclusively used to navigate through the level quickly, while the sliding is used mostly to traverse low passages or to avoid some attacks, other than moving quickly.

CHAPTER 11   METROIDVANIA (PART 1)

Since sliding seems to have been abandoned after Crash Bandicoot and dashing has a huge following that makes it a must-have feature in nearly every single metroidvania game, we are going to concentrate only on the latter.

The dashing logic is very similar to the one we used to implement the wall jump. We basically want the player's character to be able to perform a dash every time they are grounded. This means that if they jump, they can perform just a single dash, before they touch the ground again. Touching a wall, even while wall sliding, will grant the player a dash.

The dashing movement is a fast progression forward to cover a certain distance that must be always the same. May the distance covered by a dash change, the player wouldn't be able to use it to precisely move in the level, making it a useless skill, because complex and engaging platforming always puts precision before speed. Well, except for Sonic!

To accomplish this, we divide the handling of dashing in two phases, as we did for wall jump:

1. Phase 1 starts when the player presses the dash key. In that moment, we save the current position of the avatar, set the goal – which is the position at which we want to move the avatar with the dash – and set to true a Boolean variable named already_dashing that starts the second phase.

2. Phase 2 is activated when the already_dashing variable is true. In this phase, we borrow the code to manage pixel-perfect collisions with obj_block instances and use it to check whether we are going to hit a wall, just as we did for wall jump. We also want to suspend gravity and every force that can move the player's character vertically. We want the dash to be a pure horizontal quick movement, so we leave the avatar floating for a split second and then restore gravity. To do so, we will use an alarm.

CHAPTER 11 METRO DVANIA (PART 1)

Let's start from the beginning opening up once again obj_player's Create event and declaring those variables:

```
1    // dash
2    can_dash = true;
3    already_dashing = false;
4    dash_recharging = false;
5    dash_speed = 25;
6    dash_power = 200;
7    dash_move = 0;
```

Let's see what those variables do:

- **can_dash**, just as can_wall_jump, tells us if the player is allowed to use that skill or not. You may want to deactivate it temporarily for gameplay purposes.

- **already_dashing** is the controller variable we will use to access phase 2.

- **dash_recharging** is used to avoid the possibility of spamming the dash mechanic.

- **dash_speed** is the variable that represents the speed at which we are moving while dashing.

- **dash_power** is the distance in pixel that we can cover with a single dash.

- **dash_move** is a variable we will use to move horizontally the avatar according to the dash.

Now open up obj_player's Step event and add this line just below the definition of the jump_released variable, in the controls handling section:

```
1    var _dashing = can_dash and (keyboard_check_pressed(ord
     ("X")) or gamepad_button_check_pressed(c, gp_shoulderrb));
```

425

CHAPTER 11   METROIDVANIA (PART 1)

Now position the cursor just below the block of code that handles the wall jump.

Append the following code which implements the first phase of dashing:

```
1   // DASH - PHASE 1
2   if (_dashing and not (already_dashing or dash_recharging))
3   {
4       _dash_goal = x + dash_power * facing_dir;
5       already_dashing = true;
6
7       effect_create_layer("Instances", ef_smoke, x, y, 1, c_white);
8       audio_play_sound(snd_dash, 1, false);
9       sprite_index = spr_player_dash;
10  }
```

In the code above, as we said, we check if the player wants to perform a dash (meaning they pressed the dash key); and if they did, we set the dash goal (line 4), set the controller variable to true at line 5 (so that we can access phase 2), create a nice particle effect of a dust cloud to transmit the sense of speed (line 7), and play a sound effect (line 8). Finally, we change the active sprite to the dashing sprite (line 9).

Phase 2 is a little bit longer, but it's very similar to wall jump's phase 2, so you shouldn't have problems understanding what's happening:

```
1   // DASH - PHASE 2
2   if (already_dashing and not dash_recharging)
3   {
4       // floating after _dashing
5       vsp = 0;
6       jspd = 0;
7       grv = 0;
```

```
8
9        dash_move = dash_speed * facing_dir;
10       if (place_meeting(x+dash_move, y, obj_block))
11       {
12           while(not place_meeting(x+sign(dash_move), y,
             obj_block))
13           {
14               x += sign(dash_move);
15           }
16           dash_move = 0;
17           already_dashing = false;
18           dash_recharging = true;
19       }
20       x += dash_move;
21
22       already_dashing = already_dashing and
         ((facing_dir> 0 and _dash_goal> x) or
         (facing_dir< 0 and _dash_goal< x));
23
24       dash_recharging = not already_dashing;
25
26       if (not already_dashing)
27       {
28           alarm[0] = game_get_speed(gamespeed_fps) * 0.2;
29       }
30   }
```

Line 2: As we already said, we check if we are allowed to dash and the dash skill is not recharging (e.g., we already have performed a dash in midair and touched no wall nor the ground).

Lines 5-7: We reset any force that moves our player vertically, since, while dashing, we want them to move exclusively horizontally.

Line 9: We calculate how much the avatar should move in this iteration by using dash_speed.

Lines 10-19: We check if we are going to hit a wall while dashing or not. If that's the case, we stop dashing by resetting dash_move and already_dashing, and we set to true the dash_recharging variable – which means that to perform another dash, we have to touch the ground.

Line 20: We finally move the avatar of dash_move pixels.

Line 22: We set the controller variable already_dashing accordingly, just like we did with wall jump's phase 2.

Line 24: Here we set dash_recharging to true if we finished dashing – namely, already_dashing was set to false.

Lines 26-29: If we finished dashing, we start the alarm setting it to 0.2 seconds. That alarm just sets gravity and all the variables related to vertical movement to their original value, so that we can fall down 0.2 seconds after the dash.

Now let's create the actual alarm. Add an Alarm 0 event to obj_player and just add these three lines in it:

```
1    // Restore gravity and jump speed after dashing
2    grv = 0.8;
3    jspd = 18;
```

One last thing! Pick the piece of code related to vertical collisions with blocks, in the obj_player's Step event, and change it like this:

```
1    // VERTICAL COLLISION WITH BLOCKS
2
3    if (place_meeting(x, y + vsp, obj_block ))
4    {
5        while (not place_meeting(x, y+sign(vsp), obj_block))
6        {
7            y += sign(vsp);
8        }
```

```
9       vsp = 0;
10      grounded = true;
11      dash_recharging = false;
12  }
13  else
14  {
15      grounded = false;
16  }
17
18  y += vsp;
```

We just added a single line (line 11) in which we set dash_recharging to false, when the avatar touches the floor. This line is crucial to make the dash work properly.

Ok, that was a lot of work! It's time to save and run the game to check that everything works fine!

You should be able to dash your way around and wall jump like a ninja (Figure 11-7)! That's great! We just created a super-fun platforming system that gives us a huge amount of game design possibilities! We're half the way!

CHAPTER 11   METROIDVANIA (PART 1)

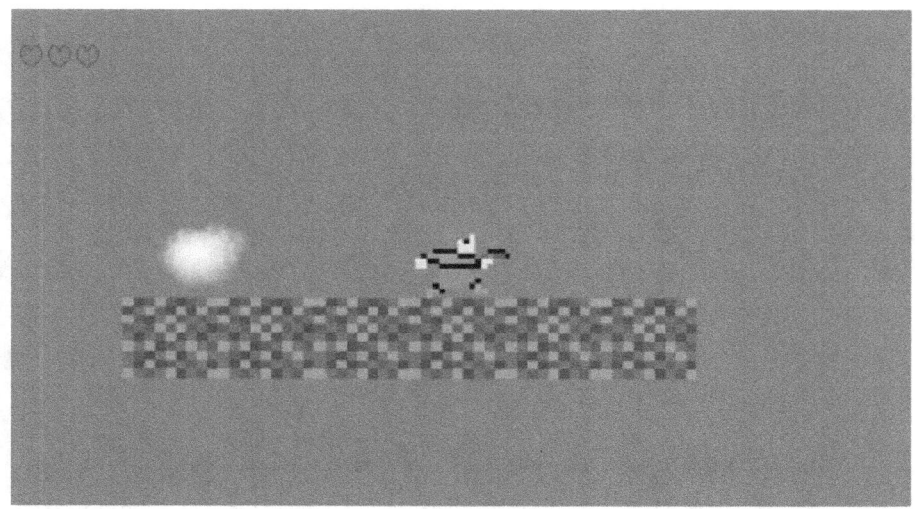

Figure 11-7. *The dash skill, combined with wall jump and wall sliding, adds a plethora of game design possibilities*

The Game Flow

I know! I know! This is the most boring part! But we need a system on which we can base our code for the map, so, let's start creating a game state system!

We saw this in all our projects, and it's probably the most powerful piece of code we are writing. It's boring just because it never changes a bit – which is also its greatness: a universal piece of code that's good for every situation!

Defining the game flow, we want to regulate the heartbeat of our game by creating statuses that tell us what we are supposed to do and display.

In Isolation, we go back to the three-state structure – just like in Space Gala – since we don't need the lives mechanic that we introduced in Cherry Caves which forced us to create an additional state (STATES.DEAD).

CHAPTER 11 METRO DVANIA (PART 1)

In Isolation, we don't want the mechanic we used in previous games where getting a hit meant to die. Maria is a tough girl and can manage to take some hits without giving up. We will introduce the concept of health. Maria will lose health for every hit she takes, and when she dies, she dies for good, possibly respawning at the last checkpoint. So, we just need a game over state.

Regarding the STATES.PAUSED state, we are going to use it for the pause menu, the full map of the area, and the inventory.

The playing state is still the state that we are going to use to play the game. Figure 11-8 shows Isolation's game flow as an FSM.

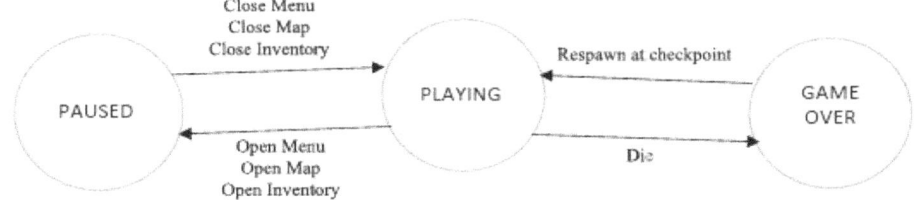

Figure 11-8. *Isolation's game flow*

Ok, let's get started! We will implement the game states shown in Figure 11-8 by reusing some code from the previous projects.

Create a new object called obj_controller, make it persistent, and add a Create event containing this code:

```
1    // GAME STATES
2    enum STATES {
3        PLAYING,
4        PAUSED,
5        GAMEOVER
6    };
7
8    global.game_state = STATES.PLAYING;
9
```

CHAPTER 11   METROIDVANIA (PART 1)

```
10  // MENU
11  options = [ "RESUME", "RESTART", "QUIT" ];
12  opt_number = array_length(options);
13  menu_index = 0;
14  cur_moved = false;
15  menu_open = false;
16
17  // resolution
18  var _width = 1280;
19  var _height = 720;
20  display_set_gui_size(_width, _height);
21
22  game_set_speed(60, gamespeed_fps);
```

Lines 1–5: Here we define the enum structure containing the various states of our game.

Line 8: We set the initial state to playing.

Lines 10–15: This is our usual code to manage the options in the pause menu. Nothing really new here.

Lines 18–20: Like in previous projects, we are forcing the resolution for compatibility.

Now let's create a Step event for obj_controller, and write this code to manage the state switch:

```
1  // --- CAPTURE CONTROLS --- //
2  var _vaxis = gamepad_axis_value(0, gp_axislv);
3
4  var _esc_pressed = keyboard_check_pressed(vk_escape) or
   gamepad_button_check_pressed(0, gp_start);
5  var _enter_pressed = keyboard_check_pressed(vk_enter) or
   gamepad_button_check_pressed(0, gp_face1);
```

```
6    var _move = (keyboard_check_pressed( vk_down ) or
     gamepad_button_check_pressed(0, gp_padd) or
     (_vaxis> 0)) - (keyboard_check_pressed(vk_up) or
     gamepad_button_check_pressed(0, gp_padu) or
     (_vaxis< 0)) ;
7    var _f_pressed = keyboard_check_pressed(ord("F")) or
     keyboard_check_pressed(vk_f12);
8
9    // Cursor _move
10   if (_move != 0)
11   {
12       audio_play_sound(snd_menu, 1, false);
13       if (cur_moved)
14       {
15           _move = 0;
16       }
17       cur_moved = true;
18   }
19   else
20   {
21       cur_moved = false;
22   }
23
24   // Fullscreen setting
25   if (_f_pressed)
26   {
27       window_set_fullscreen(not window_get_fullscreen());
28   }
29
30   // --- MENU --- //
31   if (_esc_pressed)
```

CHAPTER 11 METROIDVANIA (PART 1)

```
32    {
33        audio_play_sound(snd_menu, 1, false);
34        if ( global.game_state == STATES.PLAYING )
35        {
36        global.game_state = STATES.PAUSED;
37        menu_open = true;
38        }
39        else if (global.game_state == STATES.PAUSED)
40        {
41            global.game_state = STATES.PLAYING;
42            menu_open = false;
43        }
44    }
45
46    if (menu_open)
47    {
48        menu_index += _move;
49
50        if (_move != 0)
51        {
52            audio_play_sound(snd_menu, 1, false);
53        }
54
55        if (menu_index< 0)
56        {
57            menu_index = opt_number - 1;
58        }
59        else if (menu_index>opt_number - 1)
60        {
61            menu_index = 0;
62        }
```

```
63
64      if (_enter_pressed)
65      {
66          switch(menu_index)
67          {
68              case 0:
69                  global.game_state = STATES.PLAYING;
70                  instance_activate_all();
71                  break;
72              case 1:
73                  game_restart();
74                  break;
75              case 2:
76                  game_end();
77                  break;
78          }
79      }
80  }
81
82  // -- GAME OVER --- //
83  if (global.game_state == STATES.GAMEOVER)
84  {
85      instance_deactivate_all(1);
86      if (_enter_pressed)
87      {
88          game_restart();
89      }
90  }
```

We already saw all this many times in our previous projects, so let's not spend too much time on it and let's comment it quickly.

CHAPTER 11   METROIDVANIA (PART 1)

Lines 2–7: Those are the variables storing the information on user inputs. They are used to open and close the menu, to move the cursor through the various options, and to select the desired option.

Lines 10–22: It's a piece of code that regulates the input navigating through the options of the menu. When the cursor is moved the first time, cur_moved is set to true, so that in the next frame, cur_moved is true and move gets set to 0, so it won't move. This goes on until the player releases the button/key. When they do, cur_moved is reset to false, and the cursor can be moved again.

Lines 25–28: This code allows the player to put the game to fullscreen or windowed mode.

Lines 31–44: This is the code that manages the opening and closure of the pause menu and uses the states to understand whether the menu was opened or not.

Lines 46–80: This code manages the menu and the navigation between the available options and their selection (lines 64–79). We already saw it in detail in the previous chapters. If you feel uncertain about what this code does, feel free to pause this chapter to go back and check that piece of code.

Lines 83–90: Finally, this is the piece of code that handles the game over status. When the game is over, there's no choice, you press enter, and the game restarts.

Ok, now we only have to deal with the draw event to actually see the menu.

Let's create a Draw GUI event for obj_controller and add this code in it:

```
1   // --- SCREEN SETTINGS --- //
2   var _cam_w = display_get_gui_width();
3   var _cam_h = display_get_gui_height();
4
5   // --- DRAW LIFE --- //
6   if instance_exists(obj_player)
```

```
7   {
8       for(var _i = 0; _i<obj_player.hp; _i++)
9       {
10          draw_sprite_ext(spr_heart, -1, 10 + (40 * _i), 50,
                2, 2, 0, c_white, 1);
11      }
12  }
13
14  // --- DRAW MENU --- //
15  if (menu_open)
16  {
17      draw_set_alpha(0.5);
18      draw_set_color(c_black);
19      draw_rectangle(0, 0, _cam_w, _cam_h, 0);
20
21      draw_set_alpha(1);
22      draw_set_color(c_white);
23      draw_set_font(fnt_text);
24      draw_text(_cam_w/2, _cam_h/2, "PAUSE");
25
26      for(var _i = 0; _i<opt_number; _i++)
27      {
28          if (menu_index == _i)
29          {
30              draw_set_color(c_white);
31          }
32          else
33          {
34              draw_set_color(c_gray);
35          }
```

CHAPTER 11　METROIDVANIA (PART 1)

```
36              draw_text(_cam_w-200, _cam_h-200 + 30*_i,
                    options[_i]);
37          }
38     }
39
40     // --- DRAW GAME OVER SCREEN --- //
41     if (global.game_state == STATES.GAMEOVER)
42     {
43         draw_set_color(c_black);
44         draw_rectangle(0, 0, _cam_w, _cam_h, 0);
45
46         draw_set_color(c_white);
47         draw_set_font(fnt_text);
48
49         draw_text(_cam_w/2, _cam_h/2, "GAME OVER");
50     }
```

As we did with the step event, let's analyze quickly also this code block.

Lines 2-3: We capture the size of the screen.

Lines 6-12: This code draws on the top-left corner as many hearts as HPs the player's character has.

Lines 15-38: This code draws the menu with a semi-transparent black cover and the three options, plus the write PAUSE in the middle of the screen.

Lines 41-50: Draws the write GAME OVER in the middle of the screen, when the player loses.

Ok, now nearly everything is done. We just need to add a single line at the top of obj_player's Step event:

```
1   if (global.game_state == STATES.PAUSED) exit;
```

This line makes sure that if the game is in pause, nothing about our avatar changes, and it will remain frozen where it stands.

Now you can save and run the game and check that the pause menu actually pauses the game.

We have a nice platformer with interesting exploration mechanics, a fully working state system, and a pause menu. The last thing we need to conclude this chapter is some rooms to travel to and a working map system to keep track of the movements of the player.

Warped!

Until now, we only traveled through rooms without the possibility to go back. The avatar walked through a level, reached the end, and then spawned to the next room – never going back.

This makes sense if you're working on a game in the style of Super Mario Bros., but if you're creating an exploration-based game, you may want your character to be able to walk back and forth, traversing the same path multiple times.

This means that we cannot use blindly the room_next() or room_goto() function anymore. We need to warp the character to a certain position in a certain room depending on how we exit a room. For example, if we leave a room from the far-right door, we expect to warp in the next room starting from the far left. But if we decide to move the other way and exit from the far left, we expect to enter the next room from the far right.

The first thing that comes to mind, using our skills and knowledge until now, is to create a unique object for every warp; but this feels wrong, doesn't it? Well, your coder sense is tingling for a good reason: it's very wrong!

To achieve this goal, we need to create a single warp object and change some variables instance by instance from the Room Editor.

CHAPTER 11 METROIDVANIA (PART 1)

> **Note** In this chapter, we are not covering level design in detail. We did it in the previous chapter, and I am assuming you're now able to set up the first room featuring a basic layout based on block objects like Cherry Caves 1 or a tiled one, if you prefer like in Cherry Caves 2.
>
> If you didn't already, set up your first room as you like, using the things learned in Chapters 8 and 9 and activate a viewport and a camera for the room. As we said at the beginning of the chapter, every room will be a small side-scrolling room.

Let's start by creating a second room called room1. Create some basic floor and make sure you leave an entrance at both the left and right borders. Those will be our entrances/exits for this room. Edit room0 accordingly to achieve the same goal: having two entrances/exits. The result should be something like Figure 11-9.

CHAPTER 11 METROIDVANIA (PART 1)

Figure 11-9. *First room for our metroidvania*

Now let's create a warp object called obj_warp. Assign spr_warp to it and make it not visible by ticking the right box.

The only event we need for this object is the interaction with the player. So, click Add Event ➤ Collision ➤ obj_player, and insert this code in it:

```
1   if room_exists(target_room)
2   {
3       other.x = target_x;
4       other.y = target_y;
5       other.dashing = false;
6       other.already_dashing = false;
7       room_goto(target_room);
8   }
```

To travel between rooms, we are going to use three variables: target_room which is the room we want to warp the character to and target_x and target_y which are the x and y coordinates of the new position in the new room.

So, we check if the target room exists (line 1), and if it does, we change the obj_player's coordinates to the new target coordinates (lines 3–4), and we teleport to the next room (line 7). We also need to stop dashing, in case the player is dashing, because the warp changes the player's position, making the calculation of the dash goal inconsistent.

Figure 11-10. *The room with the two obj_warp instances at the two entrances*

Now that we have our obj_warp ready, let's position two instances of it in room0, one for each exit (Figure 11-10).

CHAPTER 11 METRO DVANIA (PART 1)

Now double-click the far-left instance, and a small window will pop up. This is the Instance Editor. You can modify every single instance you place in a room to personalize how they act. This allows you to create a general object with many behaviors and change the behavior according to your needs, right in the Room Editor.

With the Instance Editor open, click Creation Code. The creation code is a piece of code that is executed every time once when that instance is created.

In the creation code, place this code that initializes the variables we are going to use to move to the next room:

```
1   target_room = room1;
2   target_x = room_width-100;
3   target_y = 670;
```

Please note that the value of my target_y is 670 because of the height of my room (768 pixels) and the 64×64 floor tiles. If you made a room with a different height or you want to spawn the avatar at a different height, change this accordingly.

Now do the same with the far-left instance and add this to its creation code:

```
1   target_room = room1;
2   target_x = 100;
3   target_y = 670;
```

Before we check that everything is working right, let's add a couple of warps also in room1.

Add them to the room just as we did for room0: one at the left entrance and one at the right entrance.

Double-click the left warp and add this creation code to it:

```
1   target_room = room0;
2   target_x = room_width-100;
3   target_y = 670;
```

443

Now double-click the right warp and add the following creation code:

```
1  target_room = room0;
2  target_x = 100;
3  target_y = 670;
```

Ok, now we are all set! Save and run the game and enjoy your fully working warping system!

Conclusion

In this chapter, we created a solid foundation for a nice action-adventure platformer. To make it a true metroidvania, we need some more features, like a map, an inventory to carry our items, and maybe some enemies and a cool combat system.

In the next chapter, we will cover all those features, and we will also implement a saving system for our game, so that, when we die, we can keep playing from the last checkpoint we visited!

TEST YOUR KNOWLEDGE!

1. Which kinds of gamepads are supported by GMS2?
2. How can you handle input from an XInput gamepad?
3. How do you set up the deadzone of the analog stick of a XInput gamepad?
4. What is a wall jump? Why it's so important in an explorationbased game?
5. How does a wall jump work, from a technical point of view?

6. Can you modify the wall jump skill so that after the first wall jump, if the character finds another wall while rebounding, they automatically perform another wall jump?

7. How does wall sliding work?

8. Why is wall sliding important from a level design point of view?

9. What is a dash?

10. How does a dash work, from a technical point of view?

11. Can you modify the dash code to change it into a backstep like the one in Castlevania: Symphony of the Night?

12. How does the warp system work? Why is it better than the methods we used so far to manage room entrances/exits?

CHAPTER 12

Metroidvania (Part 2)

In the previous chapter, we laid the groundwork for our platforming game, setting the stage for our metroidvania adventure. Now, it's time to bring our game to life by adding essential features that every metroidvania must have. Here's what we'll cover in this chapter:

- **Map Screen**: Navigate the world with ease.
- **Minimap**: Get a quick overview of your surroundings.
- **Inventory Screen**: Manage your items and equipment.
- **Items**: Discover and collect various items.
- **Equipment**: Gear up and enhance your abilities.
- **Combat System**: Engage in battles influenced by your equipment.
- **Enemies**: Face off against various foes.
- **Save Game**: Save your progress and continue your adventure later.
- **Checkpoints**: Restart from strategic points within the game.

By the end of this chapter, our metroidvania will be fully equipped with these fundamental features, ready for players to explore and conquer. Let's dive in!

CHAPTER 12   METROIDVANIA (PART 2)

We will extensively utilize data structures, which we covered in Chapters 3 and 4 during the card game project, to develop our map and inventory systems. For our combat system and enemy design, we'll draw inspiration from Space Gala and Cherry Caves.

To implement the saving system and checkpoints, we will delve into file management using GML and the JSON standard. JSON, a widely used object notation introduced by JavaScript, represents data in an attribute-value format, making it ideal for our needs.

Let's get started on bringing these critical components to life!

About Maps

A good map can make or break your journey, both in games and in real life. A game with extensive exploration that lacks a map fails to meet the player's needs. From ARPGs to platformers, strategy games to shooters, nearly any genre benefits from a map. Whenever exploration and discovery are involved, a well-designed map is essential. If players can choose their paths or need to backtrack, a map is crucial.

Maps in video games come in many forms, from highly detailed to basic and minimalistic. The style of your map can be influenced by both narrative and gameplay considerations. For example, in DOOM (id Software, 1993) and DOOM 2 (id Software, 1994), the maps are simple line drawings. This fits the narrative of a space marine using a portable pocket computer as standard equipment. In contrast, DOOM's world map is far more detailed, showing all areas visited and those yet to explore. This map is for the player, providing a gameplay moment outside the narrative scope, allowing them to review progress and plan ahead.

This approach serves a dual purpose: it provides a break from intense gameplay, letting players relax and prepare for the next challenge. It's a clever design technique that balances difficulty with moments of respite.

Action-adventure games, especially metroidvanias, rely heavily on maps. Typically, these games offer two types of maps: a small, always-accessible HUD map and a detailed full map available on a separate screen. Some games prioritize immersion with maps that suit the narrative, while others focus on readability and clarity to prevent confusion and maintain pace.

A great example of a hybrid map is Hollow Knight's. Its map is both complex and aesthetically detailed, allowing players to add pins for points of interest like boss fights, NPCs, stores, and checkpoints. The maps in Hollow Knight are obtained from a map maker found while exploring, adding a narrative layer that enhances immersion. Additionally, players can update their maps at benches (checkpoints) if they have a pen, marking new discoveries and emphasizing the importance of exploration.

Regardless of how detailed and beautiful a map is, it relies on underlying data structures to represent room interconnections. In this chapter, we will create a basic map system for our game using GameMaker's DS Grid data structure, a powerful and versatile tool for this purpose.

Map Makers, Grids, and Semaphores

To create Isolation's map, as we said, we will use a grid.

Grids, or DS Grids, are basically two-dimensional arrays with some more features and dedicated utility functions.

CHAPTER 12   METROIDVANIA (PART 2)

	ds_grid x axis									
	0	1	2	3	4	5	6	7	8	9
0	4	3	6	4	4	8	2	6	5	1
1	5	3	7	0	4	6	8	1	4	8
2	0	4	5	1	4	0	1	1	7	5
3	4	8	2	9	1	2	4	3	8	6
4	2	2	0	2	2	6	9	3	2	0
5	5	1	1	8	5	7	3	3	0	5
6	4	7	7	0	2	7	4	6	4	0
7	3	3	3	8	9	4	8	7	4	7
8	9	3	6	1	1	0	0	6	4	3
9	2	1	6	2	4	7	2	1	8	0

(ds_grid y axis on the left)

Figure 12-1. *A basic example of a DS Grid*

In Figure 12-1, you can see what a DS Grid looks like. Think of it as a table, similar to the coordinate system of your screen, with X and Y axes. Both your screen and DS Grids use Cartesian coordinate systems (CCSs). In a CCS, each point is identified by a pair of coordinates (x, y), where x (the X-axis index) represents the column and y (the Y-axis index) represents the row.

DS Grids offer several advantages over common arrays, including the ability to perform quick searches by value, resize the grid, sort and shuffle elements, and operate on specific regions of the grid.

To create a new DS Grid, use the "ds_grid_create" function, specifying the grid's width and height. The width corresponds to the number of columns, and the height corresponds to the number of rows:

```
var my_grid = ds_grid_create(width, height);
```

CHAPTER 12   METROIDVANIA (PART 2)

This function takes the width (number of columns) and height (number of rows) of the DS Grid you want to create as inputs and returns a real number representing the ID of the newly created DS Grid.

You can access an element in a DS Grid using either the "ds_grid_get" function or the "#" accessor.

To access an element using "ds_grid_get," specify the grid ID and the element's X and Y coordinates:

```
var val = ds_grid_get(my_grid, x, y);
```

Alternatively, use the "#" accessor to achieve the same result:

```
var val = my_grid[# x, y];
```

Both methods are equivalent, so you can choose whichever approach you prefer.

If you want to set the value of the grid element at the *x,y* coordinates, you can do this either using the "#" accessor or using the function "ds_grid_set":

```
ds_grid_set(my_grid, x, y, new_value);
```

or

```
my_grid[# x, y] = new_value;
```

Again, those methods are equivalent, it's just a matter of preference.

You can search for a specific value in a DS Grid and retrieve its coordinates using "ds_grid_value_x" and "ds_grid_value_y":

```
var row = ds_grid_value_x(my_grid, reg_x0, reg_y0, reg_x1, reg_y1, my_val);

var col = ds_grid_value_y(my_grid, reg_x0, reg_y0, reg_x1, reg_y1, my_val);
```

CHAPTER 12   METROIDVANIA (PART 2)

In these functions, you must specify the region of the DS Grid to search by providing the start (reg_x0, reg_y0) and end (reg_x1, reg_y1) coordinates of the region. The search will only be conducted within this specified area. Figure 12-2 illustrates an example of a DS Grid region.

By using these powerful features, you can efficiently manage and manipulate data within your DS Grid, enhancing your game's functionality and performance.

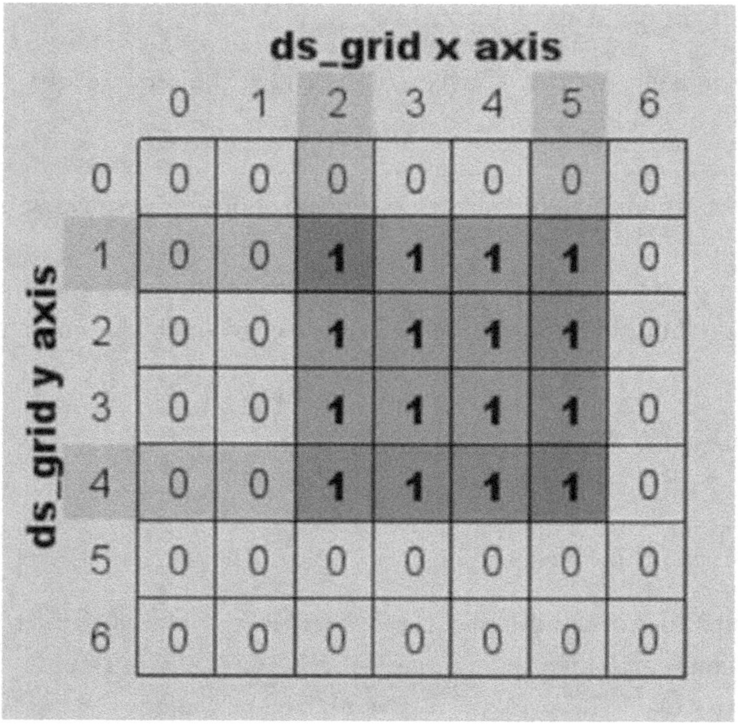

Figure 12-2. *The pink square is a grid region inside a DS Grid. This specific region starts at (1,2) and ends at (4,5)*

We will use the grid to represent the rooms' arrangement and visualize both the full and minimaps, showing where the player is located. Let's start by creating a new object called obj_map and making it persistent so that it retains information when the player's character changes rooms.

1. Create a new object named obj_map.

2. Set the Persistent property to true, ensuring the map information is maintained across room changes.

3. Add a Create event to obj_map. In this event, define the DS Grid to represent the map in the game:

```
1   map_h = 1;
2   map_w = 2;
3   map = ds_grid_create(map_w, map_h);
4   map[# 0,0] = room_get_name(room0);
5   map[# 1,0] = room_get_name(room1);
6
7   open_map = false;
```

At **lines 1** and **2**, we define map_w and map_h, which are the width (number of columns) and height (number of rows) that compose the DS Grid map.

We use those values at **line 3** to create the DS Grid using the ds_grid_create function, as we saw earlier.

Then we assign the two rooms we created in the previous chapter to two elements in the 1 × 2 DS Grid we just created, so that the first element at position 0,0 is room0 and the second element at position 0,1 is room1 (Figure 12-3).

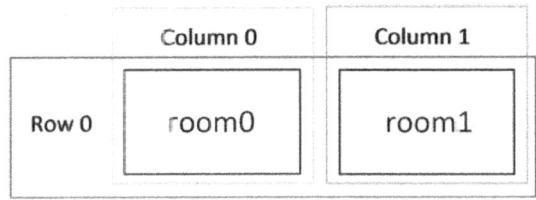

Figure 12-3. *An example of how we represent rooms with a DS Grid. Rooms with the same row value are on the same floor; rooms with the same column value and different row value are stacked on each other*

CHAPTER 12 METROIDVANIA (PART 2)

Each element in the grid that has a value different from zero represents a room. The zeroed elements do not represent rooms and will not be drawn on the screen. This allows for the creation of maps with interesting and complex shapes.

Lastly, at line 7, we initialize a control variable named "open_map" and set it to "false." This variable will be used to track whether the map is currently open or closed, similar to how "menu_open" is used in "obj_controller" to manage the menu state.

This setup ensures that the DS Grid correctly represents the rooms in your game and updates the minimap and full map to reflect the player's location accurately.

Just as we managed the pause menu in `obj_controller`, we need a Step event for `obj_map` to handle the player's input for opening and closing the map, calculate the player's position within the grid, and manage the game state by toggling the `open_map` variable accordingly.

However, we face a challenge: we already have a pause menu that appears when pressing the Esc key, controlled by `obj_controller`. How can we manage this situation?

This is a common problem in computer science and programming known as a race condition. A race condition occurs when two processes attempt to access and modify the same resource simultaneously, leading to unpredictable results. When dealing with race conditions, a concurrency algorithm is needed to schedule the activities and ensure they do not interfere with each other.

Concurrency arises when two activities try to access the same resource at the same time, which can be particularly problematic if they both attempt to modify that resource. Let's consider an example to illustrate this:

CHAPTER 12   METROIDVANIA (PART 2)

Imagine Bob and Alice share a bank account. Both can access the account and withdraw money. When they attempt a withdrawal, the ATM checks the account balance, asks how much they want to withdraw, and then dispenses the money.

Now, suppose there are $50 in the account. Bob and Alice both decide to withdraw $40 simultaneously. Each ATM reads the available balance and sees that there is enough money. Both ATMs then dispense $40 to Bob and Alice, respectively. The problem is that they end up withdrawing a total of $80 from an account that only had $50, leaving an incorrect balance (Figure 12-4). This scenario exemplifies an unaddressed race condition.

Figure 12-4. *Alice and Bob both receive $40 from the ATM, even if they have just $50 in their shared account. This is because the race condition wasn't addressed by the ATM programmer*

To avoid this in our game, we need to implement a way to handle input and state changes such that only one menu (either the pause menu or the map) can be open at a time. This can be done by checking the state of the other menu before allowing the current menu to open, ensuring there is no conflict.

Going back to our obj_map's Step event, we must handle the opening and closing of the map screen similarly to how we handle the pause menu, but with the introduction of the semaphore variable.

Here's the code to do it:

```
1   var _map_key = keyboard_check_pressed(vk_tab) or gamepad_
    button_check_pressed(0, gp_select);
2
3   if (_map_key)
4   {
5       audio_play_sound(snd_menu, 1, false);
6       if (open_map)
7       {
8           open_map = false;
9           global.can_pause = true;
10          global.game_state = STATES.PLAYING;
11      }
12      else
13      {
14          if (not global.can_pause) exit;
15          open_map = true;
16          global.can_pause = false;
17          global.game_state = STATES.PAUSED;
18      }
19  }
```

CHAPTER 12 METROIDVANIA (PART 2)

Line 1: We check for the player's input. We want the map to open when the player presses the Tab key on the keyboard or the Select button on a gamepad.

Lines 3–19: We manage the opening and closing function of the map screen, just like we did for the pause menu in obj_controller's Step event.

When the map key is pressed, if the map is already open, we close it by changing the value of open_map to false, reset to true the value of the global variable can_pause (so that we can open again the map or the pause menu), and change the state of the game to the playing state, so the action can be resumed (lines 6–11).

When the map key is pressed, if the map is not already open, we check if there is another menu open by checking the value of global.can_pause. If there actually is another menu open, we give up trying to open the map and stop executing the code (line 14). Otherwise, if no other menu screen is being displayed, we can take the control of the screen by setting global.can_pause and open_map to true and change the state of the game to paused (lines 15–17).

We must add the semaphore also to manage the pause menu in obj_controller. So, head to obj_controller's Create event and append this line to the code:

```
1    global.can_pause = true;
```

Now, in obj_controller's Step event, change the code related to the menu so that it looks like this:

```
1    // --- MENU --- //
2    if (esc_pressed)
3    {
4        audio_play_sound(snd_menu, 1, false);
5        if ( global.game_state == STATES.PLAYING and global.can_pause )
```

```
6      {
7           global.game_state = STATES.PAUSED;
8           audio_play_sound(snd_menu, 1, false);
9           menu_open = true;
10          global.can_pause = false;
11      }
12      else if ( global.game_state == STATES.PAUSED and menu_open )
13      {
14          global.game_state = STATES.PLAYING;
15          menu_open = false;
16          global.can_pause = true;
17      }
18 }
19
20 if ( menu_open )
21 {
22     menu_index += move;
23
24     if ( move != 0 )
25     {
26         audio_play_sound(snd_menu, 1, false);
27     }
28
29     if ( menu_index < 0 )
30     {
31         menu_index = opt_number - 1;
32     }
33     else if ( menu_index > opt_number - 1 )
34     {
35         menu_index = 0;
36     }
```

```
37
38      if ( enter_pressed )
39      {
40          switch( menu_index )
41          {
42              case 0: // resume
43                  menu_open = false;
44                  global.game_state = STATES.PLAYING;
45                  global.can_pause = true;
46                  break;
47              case 1: // new game
48                  game_restart();
49                  break;
50              case 2: // quit
51                  game_end();
52                  break;
53          }
54      }
55  }
```

The condition to open the pause menu is that no other menu is already open – meaning global.can_pause is false (lines 5 and 12). Because of this, we change the value of global.can_pause at lines 10 and 16 when we open or close the pause menu.

Following the same idea, we set global.can_pause to true when the player chooses the Resume option in the pause menu (line 45).

Now, open up obj_map and add a Draw GUI event. In this event, we will draw in the HUD both the full map and the minimap.

To draw the full map, we just traverse the map line by line and draw each element which has a value different from zero. It's basically a graphic representation of the grid.

CHAPTER 12 METROIDVANIA (PART 2)

Go ahead and add this code to obj_map's Draw GUI event:

```
1   var _cam_w = display_get_gui_width();
2   var _cam_h = display_get_gui_height();
3
4   var _pos_x = ds_grid_value_x(map, 0, 0, map_w-1, map_h-1,
    room_get_name(room));
5   var _pos_y = ds_grid_value_y(map, 0, 0, map_w-1, map_h-1,
    room_get_name(room));
6
7   if open_map
8   {
9       draw_set_alpha(0.5);
10      draw_set_color(c_black);
11      draw_rectangle(0, 0, _cam_w, _cam_h, 0);
12      draw_set_alpha(1);
13      var _cur_x = _cam_w/3;
14      var _cur_y = _cam_h/3;
15      var _box_h = 50;
16      var _box_w = 100;
17      var _box_offset = 30;
18      for(var _i = 0; _i < map_h; _i++)
19      {
20          for(var _j = 0; _j < map_w; _j++)
21          {
22              if map[# _j, _i] != 0
23              {
24                  draw_set_color(c_white);
25                  if map[# _j, _i] == room_get_name(room)
26                  {
27                      draw_set_color(c_yellow);
28                  }
```

```
29                    draw_rectangle(_cur_x, _cur_y, _cur_x +
                          _box_w, _cur_y + _box_h, 0);
30                  }
31
32                  _cur_x += _box_offset + _box_w;
33              }
34              _cur_x = _cam_w/3;
35              _cur_y += _box_offset + _box_h;
36          }
37      }
```

Lines 1-2: We get the width and height of the camera. We need this to properly draw elements on the screen.

Lines 3-4: Calculate the position of the room in which the player's character is in that moment. We search for the X- and Y-coordinates inside the DS Grid map using ds_grid_value_x and ds_grid_value_y. We need this information to correctly draw both the full and Minimaps.

If the map is open (line 7), we draw a semi-transparent black background; and then, from 1/3 of the camera width, we start to draw one by one all the elements in the grid that represent rooms, using rectangles of 100 × 50 pixels (lines 13-36). The rectangles are separated by an offset of 30 pixels.

For each element, we check whether its value is zero or not. If it's zero, we skip it and leave the space blank.

If the value of the element is not zero, we check again whether the value is the name of the current room or not. If it is, we draw a yellow rectangle; if it's not, we draw a white rectangle.

The result is a representation of the grid where the room in which the player is is highlighted in yellow, so that the player knows where they are in that very moment, compared to the vastness of the map (well, in this case there are just two rooms, but you get the point).

CHAPTER 12   METROIDVANIA (PART 2)

The Minimap is something very similar to the full map, aesthetically, but its code is very different. In fact, the Minimap shows only a subsection of the full map. We want it to show only the rooms adjacent to the current room. Also, the Minimap will always be visible during the gameplay (except when the full map is open) in the top-right corner of the screen.

To correctly draw the Minimap, we have to check if the element containing the name of the current room has any elements in the eight directions around it: north, north-east, east, south-east, south, south-west, west, north-west.

For each of these elements, we have to check whether it's a room or not and eventually draw it, if it is. Even if in this case we always draw the current room in the middle, we apply the same coloring rules of the full map: a yellow rectangle for the current room and a white rectangle for all the other rooms.

So, just under the code for the full map, append the following code to draw the Minimap when the full map is not open:

```
1   else // if the full map is not open
2   {
3       var _box_x = _cam_w-100;
4       var _box_y = 80;
5       var _box_w = 40;
6       var _box_h = 20;
7       var _box_offset = 10;
8
9       // draw the current room
10      draw_set_color(c_yellow);
11      draw_rectangle(_box_x, _box_y, _box_x + _box_w, _box_y + _box_h, 0);
12
13      // draw the rooms adjacent to the current room
14      draw_set_color(c_white);
```

```
15
16      var _west_room = _pos_x > 0;
17      var _east_room = _pos_x < (map_w-1);
18      var _south_room = _pos_y < (map_h-1);
19      var _north_room = _pos_y > 0;
20
21      if (_west_room) // draw the west room
22      {
23          if ( map[# _pos_x-1, _pos_y] != 0 )
24          {
25              var _b_x1 = (_box_x) - (_box_offset + _box_w);
26              var _b_x2 = (_box_x) - (_box_offset);
27              var _b_y1 = _box_y;
28              var b_y2 = _box_y + _box_h;
29              draw_rectangle(_b_x1, _b_y1, _b_x2, b_y2, 0);
30          }
31      }
32
33      if (_east_room) // draw the east room
34      {
35          if ( map[# _pos_x+1, _pos_y] != 0 )
36          {
37              var _b_x1 = (_box_x + _box_w) + (_box_offset);
38              var _b_x2 = (_box_x+_box_w) + (_box_offset + _box_w);
39              var _b_y1 = _box_y;
40              var b_y2 = _box_y + _box_h;
41              draw_rectangle(_b_x1, _b_y1, _b_x2, b_y2, 0);
42          }
43      }
44
```

```
45      if (_north_room)
46      {
47          if (map[# _pos_x, _pos_y-1] != 0) // draw the
                                                         north room
48          {
49              var _b_x1 = _box_x;
50              var _b_x2 = _box_x + _box_w;
51              var _b_y1 = (_box_y) - (_box_offset + _box_h);
52              var b_y2 = (_box_y) - (_box_offset);
53              draw_rectangle(_b_x1, _b_y1, _b_x2, b_y2, 0);
54          }
55
56          if (_west_room) // draw the north west room
57          {
58              if (map[# _pos_x-1, _pos_y-1] != 0)
59              {
60                  var _b_x1 = (_box_x) - (_box_offset +
                        _box_w);
61                  var _b_x2 = (_box_x) - (_box_offset);
62                  var _b_y1 = (_box_y) - (_box_offset +
                        _box_h);
63                  var b_y2 = (_box_y) - (_box_offset);
64                  draw_rectangle(_b_x1, _b_y1, _b_x2,
                        b_y2, 0);
65              }
66          }
67
68          if (_east_room) // draw the north east room
69          {
70              if (map[# _pos_x+1, _pos_y-1] != 0)
71              {
```

```
72              var _b_x1 = (_box_x + _box_w) + (_box_
                offset);
73              var _b_x2 = (_box_x+_box_w) + (_box_offset
                + _box_w);
74              var _b_y1 = (_box_y) - (_box_offset +
                _box_h);
75              var _b_y2 = (_box_y) - (_box_offset);
76              draw_rectangle(_b_x1, _b_y1, _b_x2,
                b_y2, 0);
77          }
78      }
79  }
80
81  if (_south_room)
82  {
83      if (map[# _pos_x, _pos_y+1] != 0) // draw the
                                            south room
84      {
85          var _b_x1 = _box_x;
86          var _b_x2 = _box_x + (_box_w);
87          var _b_y1 = (_box_y + _box_h) + (_box_offset);
88          var b_y2 = (_box_y + _box_h) + (_box_offset +
                _box_h);
89          draw_rectangle(_b_x1, _b_y1, _b_x2, b_y2, 0);
90      }
91
92      if (_west_room) // draw the south west room
93      {
94          if (map[# _pos_x-1, _pos_y+1] != 0)
95          {
96              var _b_x1 = (_box_x) - (_box_offset +
                    _box_w);
```

```
97                  var _b_x2 = (_box_x) - (_box_offset);
98                  var _b_y1 = (_box_y + _box_h) + (_box_
                    offset);
99                  var b_y2 = (_box_y + _box_h) + (_box_offset
                    + _box_h);
100                 draw_rectangle(_b_x1, _b_y1, _b_x2,
                    b_y2, 0);
101             }
102         }
103
104         if (_east_room) // draw the south east room
105         {
106             if (map[# _pos_x+1, _pos_y+1] != 0)
107             {
108                 var _b_x1 = (_box_x + _box_w) + (_box_
                    offset);
109                 var _b_x2 = (_box_x+_box_w) + (_box_offset
                    + _box_w);
110                 var _b_y1 = (_box_y + _box_h) + (_box_
                    offset);
111                 var b_y2 = (_box_y + _box_h) + (_box_offset
                    + _box_h);
112                 draw_rectangle(_b_x1, _b_y1, _b_x2,
                    b_y2, 0);
113             }
114         }
115     }
116 }
```

Let's analyze the code above. First, at lines 10–11, we draw the current room; then, we check for every one of the eight directions if there is an element adjacent to the element that contains the current room (lines 16–19).

For each one of the directions, if there is an element, we check if it's a valid element or not (has a non-zero value), and we draw it on the screen in the right position.

The concept to calculate the eight directions inside the grid is pretty straightforward too. An element is at the north of another element if it is one row up, and it is at the south if it's one row below. Similarly, an element is at the east or at the west of another element if it is, respectively, one column ahead or behind the current element.

Basically, for an element at position x,y, we can check the eight directions around it in the grid, like this:

- **North**: One row up, same column (x, y-1)
- **North-East**: One row up, one column ahead (x+1, y-1)
- **East**: Same row, one column ahead (x+1, y)
- **South-East**: One row down, one column ahead (x+1, y+1)
- **South**: One row down, same column (x, y–1)
- **South-West**: One row down, one column behind (x-1, y+1)
- **West**: Same row, one column behind (x-1, y)
- **North-West**: One row up, one column behind (x-1, y-1)

Now, before you save and run the game, make sure that you put the obj_map element in room0. Running the game, you should be able to open and close both the pause and map menus without overlapping them.

The map menu will show the room in which the player's character is at any time.

If you want to create new rooms and make a more complex map, just create the rooms and add them in the DS Grid in the position you like. Don't forget to complete all the rows with zeroed elements.

For example, if you want to add a room just below room1, the map should look like this:

```
1   map[# 0,0] = room_get_name(room0);
2   map[# 1,0] = room_get_name(room1);
3   map[# 0,1] = 0;
4   map[# 1,1] = room_get_name(room2);
```

Ok, now it's the time to save and run the game to enjoy the simple yet effective map we created (Figure 12-5)! This is a very important achievement! You learned about a lot of things: DS Grids, map design, and even concurrency and race condition! But more importantly, you also managed to create something out of the learning! So congratulate yourself, enjoy your new toy, and get ready for the next section, in which we are going to focus on the next big thing: items and inventory!

Figure 12-5. *The full map featuring three rooms as shown in the map screen*

CHAPTER 12 METROIDVANIA (PART 2)

Items and Inventory

A fundamental feature that any metroidvania and action-adventure game has is the possibility to pick up objects and use them. In particular, a very popular thing among those games is the concept of equipping special items like weapons or armors and making our avatar more powerful. But to have this kind of items, we have to implement the possibility to carry them with us. For this reason, it's not very convenient to represent items as object's instances. We need some more light and manageable kind of data: a data structure.

An important thing to note is that items should carry some information with them:

- **ID**: We want to uniquely identify each item in the game, so that we are able to distinguish between two items of the same kind, like two potions, two identical weapons, and so on. Actually, it's not very smart to use the id word, since it's a reserved word of GML. Probably it would be better to use something different, like key.

- **Name**: We want to access a human-readable name for that item. This is what we will show to the player in the inventory.

- **Description**: Of course, we need a description of the item, so that we can tell the player what's that item and how to use it.

- **Type**: We need a piece of data that can tell us what kind of item is this. Is this a cure? Is this a weapon?

- **Value**: This is a jolly field. Depending on the kind of item we are treating, this can be, for example, the amount of HP cured by a potion or the attack power that gives to the player's character.

CHAPTER 12   METROIDVANIA (PART 2)

We can add as many fields we want to our items, but those are pretty much the basics.

To organize all those fields, we could use one of the data structures offered by GameMaker. In particular, the most fitting for this case is a DS Map.

A DS Map is a data structure that lets you store pairs of keys and values. DS Maps are particularly useful to store mixed-type data (strings, numbers, etc.), and since they store data organized with keys, they have the fastest access to data. You just need to provide the key to access a specific value.

GameMaker offers a wide variety of functions to manage DS Maps. Let's see some of the most interesting.

ds_map_create()

This function creates an empty DS Map. It returns the empty DS Map.

For example:

```
1   var my_map = ds_map_create();
```

ds_map_add(id, key, val)

This function adds a key,value pair to the DS Map indicated by the id value. The function fails if the specified key already exists inside the DS Map.

For example:

```
1   ds_map_add(map_id, "name", "Seb");
```

ds_map_replace(id, key, val)

This function is used to add or replace a key,value pair inside a DS Map. Differently from ds_map_add, this one won't fail if the key already exists inside the DS Map, but it will replace the value.

For example:

```
1   ds_map_replace(map_id, "name", "Sebastiano");
```

ds_map_empty(id)

This function checks whether the DS Map is empty or not. It returns a Boolean value.

For example:

```
1   if (ds_map_empty(map_id)) exit;
```

ds_map_find_value(id, key)

This function reads the value associated with a certain key, if it exists. If no such key exists, it will return undefined.

For example:

```
1   var my_name = ds_map_find_value(map_id, "name");
2   if is_undefined(my_name) exit;
```

So that's the idea: we can represent items as a collection of keys and values like in Table 12-1.

Table 12-1. Keys and values

Key	Value
ID (or key)	123456…
Name	"Health Potion"
Description	"This can restore your HP!"
Type	item_type.cure
Value	1

Using this format, it will be pretty easy to carry them with us! In fact, it will suffice to create a list to store all the items carried. Picking up an item means copying it into the list.

So we need an inventory, which, as we said, is basically a list of all the items the character owns. We already saw lists in Chapters 3 and 4. We used them to manage our deck of cards, shuffle it, sort it, pick cards, and compare them. That's not too different from what we need to do right now with items!

CHAPTER 12   METROIDVANIA (PART 2)

Let's create the inventory in obj_player as a DS List. We will use it to manage the items that the player decides to bring with them.

Open up obj_player's Create event and append these lines at the bottom of the code:

```
1    items = ds_list_create();
2    equipped = ds_map_create();
```

At line 1, we define our inventory as a DS List, as we discussed. We will add the items found to that list.

At line 2, we define a variable representing the item that we are currently equipping. The equipped item is an item in our inventory that we want to wear or wield. We cannot equip an item that is not in the inventory, and we can only equip one item at a time. Equipping an item while another item is already equipped will automatically unequip the currently equipped item.

Items, as we said, can be differentiated by their type. In this project, we only have two types of objects: weapons and cures. We will represent them using an enum, so that we can refer to the different types in a human-readable fashion. So head to obj_controller's Create event and add the following lines of code:

```
1    enum ITEM_TYPE {
2        WEAPON,
3        CURE
4    };
```

With this piece of code, we will be able to distinguish between weapons that we can equip whenever we want and cure items that we can use only one time and have the immediate effect of increasing the player's HP.

The inventory will be shown in a dedicated screen, just like the pause menu and the full map.

CHAPTER 12 METROIDVANIA (PART 2)

To create and manage an inventory screen, we need a controller variable which tells us when the inventory is open and a cursor variable that can help us keep track of the position of the cursor while navigating in the inventory.

Let's create those two variables by appending the following lines at the bottom of obj_controller's Create event:

```
1   inv_open = false;
2   inv_index = 0;
```

To manage the opening and closing actions for the inventory, just as we did for both the pause menu and the map screen, we have to add yet another check for inputs at the top of obj_controller's Step event:

```
1   var inv_key = keyboard_check_pressed(ord("I")) or gamepad_button_check_pressed(0, gp_face4);
```

The inventory key is set when the player presses the letter I on the keyboard or the Face 4 button on the gamepad (triangle on PlayStation gamepads or Y on Xbox gamepads).

The first thing to do is to check if the inventory is already open when the inventory key is pressed by the player, and in that case, we close it (lines 4-9 of the following code). If the inventory is not already open, we have to check if the screen is already claimed by another menu (line 12) or if we can open the inventory menu; in that case, we claim the screen by setting global.can_pause to false, we set the controller variable to true, and then we change the game state to paused (lines 13-15).

Let's do this by appending this code at the bottom of obj_controller's Step event:

```
1   if (inv_key)
2   {
3       audio_play_sound(snd_menu, 1, false);
4       if (inv_open)
```

```
5       {
6           global.game_state = STATES.PLAYING;
7           global.can_pause = true;
8           inv_open = false;
9       }
10      else
11      {
12          if (not global.can_pause) exit;
13          global.game_state = STATES.PAUSED;
14          global.can_pause = false;
15          inv_open = true;
16      }
17  }
```

Now, if the inventory is open, we want to show each item that's in the items DS List and give the possibility to the player to navigate that list with a cursor.

Moreover, we want to give the possibility to equip one item when the cursor points to an equippable item (a weapon) and to use it if it's a consumable item (a cure).

To achieve this, append the following code just below the code we just wrote in the previous paragraph, in obj_controller's Step event:

```
1   if (inv_open)
2   {
3       if (instance_exists(obj_player) and ds_exists
            (obj_player.items, ds_type_list))
4       {
5           if ( move != 0 )
6           {
7               audio_play_sound(snd_menu, 1, false);
8               inv_index += move;
9           }
```

CHAPTER 12 METROIDVANIA (PART 2)

```
10
11          if ( inv_index< 0 )
12          {
13              inv_index = ds_list_size(obj_player.items) - 1;
14          }
15
16          if ( inv_index>= ds_list_size(obj_player.items) )
17          {
18              inv_index = 0;
19          }
20
21          if ( enter_pressed and ds_list_size(obj_player.
            items) > 0 )
22          {
23              var _current_item = obj_player.items
                [| inv_index];
24              if (ds_exists(_current_item, ds_type_map))
25              {
26                  var _item_type = ds_map_find_value
                    (_current_item, "type");
27                  switch(_item_type)
28                  {
29                      case ITEM_TYPE.WEAPON:
30                      {
31                          var _cur_equipped = obj_player.
                            equipped;
32
33                          if ( (ds_map_empty(_cur_
                            equipped) or
34                              ds_map_find_value(_cur_equipped,
                                "key") != ds_map_find_value
                                (_current_item, "key") ) )
```

```
35                          {
36                              var key = ds_map_find_value
                                (_current_item, "key");
37                              var name = ds_map_find_value
                                (_current_item, "name");
38                              var type = ds_map_find_value
                                (_current_item, "type");
39                              var value = ds_map_find_value
                                (_current_item, "value");
40                              var desc = ds_map_find_value
                                (_current_item, "desc");
41                              var bullet_type = ds_map_
                                find_value(_current_item,
                                "bullet_type");
42                              ds_map_replace(_cur_equipped,
                                "key", key);
43                              ds_map_replace(_cur_equipped,
                                "name", name);
44                              ds_map_replace(_cur_equipped,
                                "type", type);
45                              ds_map_replace(_cur_equipped,
                                "value", value);
46                              ds_map_replace(_cur_equipped,
                                "desc", desc);
47                              ds_map_replace(_cur_equipped,
                                "bullet_type", bullet_type);
48                              ds_map_replace_map(game_data,
                                "player-equipped", _cur_
                                equipped);
49                          }
```

```
50                              else
51                              {
52                                  ds_map_destroy(obj_player.
                                    equipped);
53                                  obj_player.equipped = ds_map_
                                    create();
54                              }
55                              break;
56                          }
57                          case ITEM_TYPE.CURE:
58                          {
59                              if ( ds_exists(obj_player.
                                items[|inv_index], ds_type_map) )
60                              {
61                                  obj_player.hp += ds_map_
                                    find_value(obj_player.items
                                    [| inv_index], "value");
62                                  ds_list_delete(obj_player.
                                    items, inv_index);
63                              }
64                          }
65                      }
66                  }
67              }
68          }
69  }
```

The code above handles the cursor movement through the items in obj_player's items list using the same idea we used to create the various options in the pause menu. To know where the cursor is located in the list, we compare its value to the index of each object in the DS List (note that the cursor loops between 0 and ds_list_size(obj_player.items) as you can see in lines 5-14).

When the enter key (or Face 1 button on the gamepad) is pressed, the currently selected item is selected to be equipped or unequipped by obj_player, if it's a weapon (lines 20-46), or to be consumed if it's a cure item (lines 47-51).

If the item selected to be equipped is already equipped, we unequip it.

To equip an item, we replace every field of the currently equipped item with the fields of the item we want to equip (26-38).

To unequip an item, we just destroy the equipped DS Map and reinitialize it (lines 42-43).

Let's see now how we can show this information in the inventory menu.

Head to obj_controller's Draw GUI event and append this code at its bottom:

```
// --- DRAW INVENTORY --- //
if (inv_open)
{
    if (instance_exists(obj_player))
    {
        draw_set_alpha(0.5);
        draw_set_color(c_black);
        draw_rectangle(0, 0, _cam_w, _cam_h, 0);
        draw_set_alpha(1);
        
        draw_set_font(fnt_menu_h1);
        draw_set_color(c_white);
        draw_text(200, 100, "ITEMS");
        
        draw_set_font(fnt_menu_h2);
        draw_set_color(c_white);
        var _list_x = 200;
```

```
19          var _list_y = 300;
20          var _text_offset_x = 500;
21          var text_offset_y = 50;
22          draw_set_color(c_silver);
23          draw_text(_list_x, _list_y - text_offset_y-20,
            "Name");
24          draw_text(_list_x + _text_offset_x, _list_y - text_
            offset_y-20, "Description");
25          draw_text(_list_x + _text_offset_x * 3, _list_y -
            text_offset_y-20, "Stat");
26
27          if (ds_exists(obj_player.items, ds_type_list))
28          {
29              for (var _i = 0; _i<ds_list_size(obj_player.
                items); _i++)
30              {
31                  var _cur_item = obj_player.items[|_i];
32                  if (ds_exists(_cur_item, ds_type_map))
33                  {
34                      draw_set_color(c_white);
35                      if (inv_index == _i) // draw cursor
36                      {
37                          draw_rectangle(_list_x - 50,
                            _list_y + (text_offset_y * _i),
                            _list_x - 30, _list_y + (text_
                            offset_y*_i) + 20, 0);
38                      }
39
40                      if (not ds_map_empty(obj_player.
                        equipped))
```

```
41                          {
42                              if (ds_map_find_value(_cur_item,
                                    "key") == ds_map_find_value(obj_
                                    player.equipped, "key"))
43                              {
44                                  draw_set_color(c_yellow);
45                              }
46                          }
47                          var g_name = ds_map_find_value
                                (_cur_item, "name");
48                          var g_desc = ds_map_find_value
                                (_cur_item, "desc");
49                          var g_value = ds_map_find_value
                                (_cur_item, "value");
50                          draw_text(_list_x, _list_y + (text_
                                offset_y * _i), g_name);
51                          draw_text(_list_x + _text_offset_x, _
                                list_y + (text_offset_y * _i), g_desc);
52                          draw_text(_list_x + _text_offset_x *
                                3, _list_y + (text_offset_y * _i),
                                string(g_value));
53                      }
54                  }
55              }
56          }
57  }
```

Just like we did with the other two menus, also for the inventory, we check whether it should be visible or not by relying on the controller variable (line 2); then we check if obj_player exists (so that we can access the inventory) and start drawing the inventory menu.

CHAPTER 12   METROIDVANIA (PART 2)

First, we draw the usual black semi-transparent background (lines 7-9); then we draw the title of the menu (lines 12-14) and the label of each column (lines 17-27) so that we can make the player understand what the information shown means.

Lines 29 to 54 are basically a loop between all the items in obj_player's items DS List. We loop through them one by one; we draw the cursor at the right position, comparing the cursor's index to the item's index in the DS List.

Finally, we check whether the item is equipped by comparing the key values (it's equal to the content of the equipped variable), and if it's the case, we draw its information (name, description, and value) in yellow, or else we draw the information in white.

Ok, now that we have a working inventory and a structure to represent items, we only need to create the actual items to pick up.

Since we want our items to be uniquely identifiable, we need a function to generate a unique key. So, before we start creating items as GML objects, let's create a new script by right-clicking Scripts in the Resources sidebar and call the new script generate_key. Open it up and append this code in it:

```
1   function generate_key()
2   {
3       return room_get_name(room) + object_get_name(object_
        index) + string(x) + string(y);
4   }
```

That's it. This function will generate a unique id by concatenating the name of the room, the name of the instance that called the script, and its coordinates.

This is called a hash function, as we saw earlier, and it's how you identify and access items inside a map data structure.

It's not easy to create good hash functions, but it's fairly easy to create good enough hash functions.

CHAPTER 12   METROIDVANIA (PART 2)

Now that we have our hash function, let's make our first item by creating a new object named obj_item. Assign no sprite to it and just add a Create event with these lines of code in it:

```
1   key = generate_key();
3   data = ds_map_create();
4   ds_map_replace(data, "key", key);
```

Line 1: We create a unique key for the item calling the generate_key function.

Lines 2-3: We create the map that represents the item and add the unique key to it using ds_map_replace.

That's it for the generic item. We will add more detailed information like the name, the type, and other things in the children objects of obj_item.

Anyway, we need to manage one more event for obj_item. We want that when obj_player touches an instance derived from obj_item, it can pick it up by basically copying the data map we just defined in the items DS List.

So let's add a collision event between obj_player and obj_item in obj_item and let's write this code in it:

```
1   ds_list_add(obj_player.items, data);
2   ds_list_mark_as_map(obj_player.items, ds_list_size
    (obj_player.items)-1);
3   instance_destroy();
```

When obj_player collides with obj_item or an instance derived from it, the data DS Map belonging to the obj_item instance is added to obj_player's DS List (line 1). We also need to mark that newly added element as a DS Map, since GML needs to know that this is not a normal base type of data, but a data structure (line 2). Finally, since we don't need anymore the instance, we destroy it (line 3).

CHAPTER 12 METROIDVANIA (PART 2)

All the items we are going to create will act like that. So, as you can see, even if they are very different, the items in a game can be treated all the same in an inventory (unless you need to access specific information that only a type of item has).

Let's create our first item derived from obj_item, starting from this template.

Create a new object called obj_weapon_light. Assign spr_upgrade_light to it and select obj_item as its parent object.

Now add a Create event to obj_weapon_light and insert the following code in it:

```
1   event_inherited();
2
3   ds_map_replace(data, "name", "Common pistol");
4   ds_map_replace(data, "type", ITEM_TYPE.WEAPON);
5   ds_map_replace(data, "value", 2);
6   ds_map_replace(data, "desc", "Average fire power");
7   ds_map_replace(data, "bullet_type", spr_bullet_light);
```

At line 1, we inherit the code from obj_item's Create event, so that we have the key generated.

Then, from lines 3 to 7, we add the various fields to the data DS Map we defined in obj_item.

Since this is a weapon upgrade, we also define a field containing the sprite we want to assign to the bullet (line 7). We will need this information when it will come the time to make Maria shoot with her gun.

Now let's create two more items, just to see our inventory grow up a bit! We will create another weapon upgrade and a cure item.

Let's start by creating a new object called obj_weapon_heavy and set its sprite to spr_upgrade and set obj_item as its parent. Then in obj_weapon_heavy's Create event, insert the following code:

```
1   event_inherited();
2
```

483

CHAPTER 12 METROIDVANIA (PART 2)

```
3    ds_map_replace(data, "name", "Super pistol");
4    ds_map_replace(data, "type", ITEM_TYPE.WEAPON);
5    ds_map_replace(data, "value", 5);
6    ds_map_replace(data, "desc", "Super fire power");
7    ds_map_replace(data, "bullet_type", spr_bullet_heavy);
```

Create another object, call it obj_cure_paracetamol, and select obj_item as its parent object.

This object is a cure, and it will give the player a bonus HP when used from the inventory. For this object, use the sprite spr_cure and add this code to its Create event:

```
1    event_inherited();
2
3    ds_map_replace(data, "name", "Paracetamol");
4    ds_map_replace(data, "type", ITEM_TYPE.CURE);
5    ds_map_replace(data, "value", 1);
6    ds_map_replace(data, "desc", "A common medicine");
```

It's all done! Now just drop an instance for each of those three objects in one of the two rooms and run the game!

You should verify that everything works right. You can see and pick up the objects and see them in your inventory by pressing the inventory key (Figure 12-6). You can even equip them (one at a time) and use the cure to gain a bonus heart! But still, we can't attack or use the equipment yet. Don't worry. We are going to fix this in the next section!

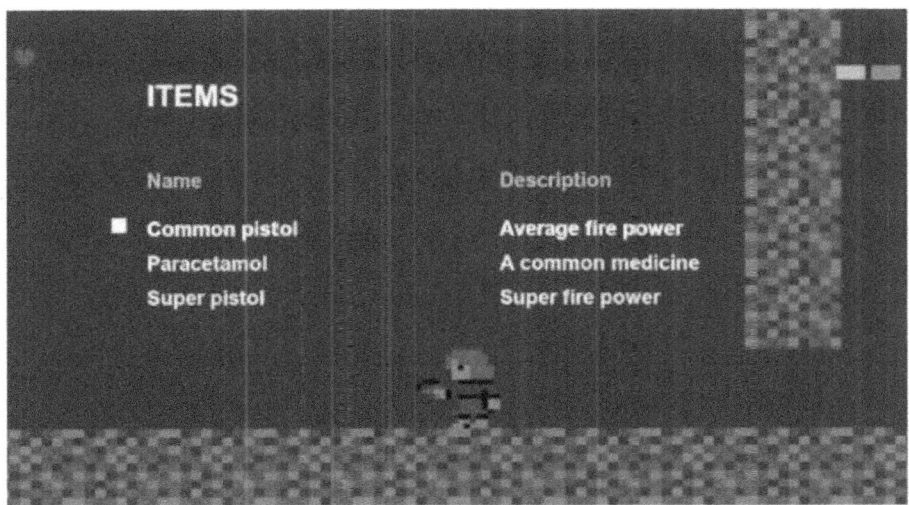

Figure 12-6. *The inventory screen showing all the items carried by the player. The yellow highlighted item is the equipped item*

Creating the Combat System

We have an inventory that we can fill with cool weapon upgrades, but we can't use them. Let's fix this by implementing the possibility to shoot. We want the player's character to be able to shoot only if they equipped an upgrade for the gun. The upgrade will define the fire power of the gun.

The shooting itself will be very similar to the one we implemented in Space Gala. We will check for the user input and then generate a bullet instance that will start travelling at a certain speed in the direction obj_player is facing.

We will set the bullet's sprite and attack power based on the data retrieved in the item equipped (the value and bullet_type fields in the DS_Map that represents the item, as we saw in the previous section).

CHAPTER 12   METROIDVANIA (PART 2)

Let's start from the bullet object. Create a new object and rename it obj_bullet. Add to this new object a Create event, and put the following code in it:

```
1   speed = 30;
2   atk = 0;
3   start_x = x;
4   shoot_range = 200;
```

At line 1, we define the bullet's speed, since we want the bullet to start going forward as soon as it's created.

At line 2, we created the atk variable which serves to the scope of representing the attack power of the bullet. We will update this value when shooting based on the equipped item.

At line 4, we set the maximum range of the bullet. The range of the bullet allows us to make the bullet travel only for a predefined amount of space; then it will be destroyed. We will see it in greater detail in a bit.

Now create obj_bullet's Step event and add the following code in it:

```
1   if (abs(xstart - x) >shoot_range)
2   {
3       instance_destroy(id, false);
4   }
```

Here, we calculate the amount of space covered by the bullet, and if it's greater than the maximum range of the gun (line 1), we destroy the bullet.

It's important to give a range to a weapon, to avoid the possibility that the player can shoot and kill enemies from the other side of the level which would extremely reduce the challenge.

Another solution would have been to destroy the bullet as soon as it reaches the sides of the camera as we did in Space Gala, but in this particular case, the weapon range can be also useful to distinguish the various weapons. In fact, it allows us to think about future improvements where we can define and change the range of a weapon through the equipment.

We want our bullets to be destroyed when they collide with a wall, so let's create a collision event between obj_bullet and obj_event. Add the event to obj_bullet and insert this single line in it:

```
1   instance_destroy();
```

Now create a Destroy event in obj_bullet and add this single line:

```
1   effect_create_layer("Instances", ef_spark, x, y, 0.4,
    c_yellow);
```

Now, when the bullet hits a wall, it gets destroyed in a particle effect.

The bullet object is complete, for now. Let's now dedicate on the actual shooting.

Open up obj_player's Create event and append these lines at its bottom:

```
1   // combat
2   can_attack = true;
3   atk_speed = 0.3;
```

In the code above, we created a couple of variables that we will use to regulate the attack rate. The controller variable can_attack will be switched on and off every 0.3 seconds (the value of atk_speed).

Now, in obj_player's Step event, just under the last input check, add this line to handle the attack key input:

```
1   var attack = keyboard_check(ord("C")) or gamepad_button_
    check(0, gp_face3);
```

To attack, we will use the C key on the keyboard and the Face 3 button on a gamepad (X on an Xbox gamepad or square on a PlayStation gamepad).

CHAPTER 12   METROIDVANIA (PART 2)

Finally, append this code at the bottom of obj_player's Step event:

```
1   // ATTACK
2   if (attack and can_attack and not ds_map_empty(equipped))
3   {
4       var bullet = instance_create_layer(x, y, "Instances",
            obj_bullet);
5       bullet.direction = direction;
6       bullet.sprite_index = ds_map_find_value(equipped,
            "bullet_type");
7       bullet.atk = ds_map_find_value(equipped, "value");
8
9       can_attack = false;
10      alarm[1] = room_speed * atk_speed;
11
12      audio_play_sound(snd_shoot, 1, false);
13  }
```

The first thing we do (line 2) is to check if the player can attack. The player can attack if they are pressing the attack button, the controller variable can_attack is true (meaning that more than 0.3 seconds are passed after the previous bullet was shot), and the player equipped a weapon item.

Then we create a new instance of obj_bullet (line 4), and we assign the right sprite to it according to the value of the bullet_type field in the equipped item's DS Map (line 7).

We then assign the bullet the same direction of the player's character (which we are updating anytime the character turns left or right) and use the value variable of the equipped item to set the bullet's attack power (lines 5 and 6).

Finally, we set can_attack control variable to false (line 9), and we start the alarm (line 10) which will reset can_attack to true, so that we can attack again after atk_speed seconds (which is 0.3).

CHAPTER 12 METROIDVANIA (PART 2)

We also play a sound effect for the shoot at line 12.

The last step is to create an Alarm 1 event for obj_player and insert this one line:

```
1    can_attack = true;
```

Ok, now it's all ready to be tested! Save and run the game and enjoy the shooting and your new shiny items and inventory system (Figure 12-7).

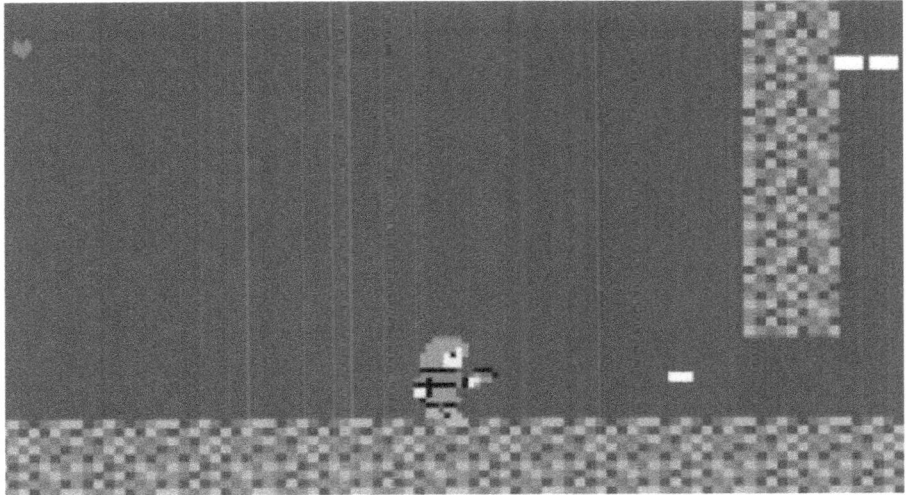

Figure 12-7. *Maria trying her new gun!*

You can now add as many cure and weapon items as you like, and, changing a couple of things, you can also create new kinds of items, for example, armor items giving defense bonuses or items that boost speed or jump height or weapon range extenders as well as new equipment slots. Free your imagination and customize your inventory system as you like!

A combat system is pretty pointless without something to kill. It's now time to add enemies, so that all those bullets don't go wasted!

CHAPTER 12   METROIDVANIA (PART 2)

Old Enemies

As we anticipated in the GDD in Chapter 11, in Isolation, we are going to use the same enemy we created for Cherry Caves 2. Why? Well, because creating more interesting enemies is not really the purpose of this chapter, but still we need them to complete our combat system and make our gun be a bit more effective. There's no shame in using our own creations.

In this section, we will create the obj_octopus_green from Cherry Caves 2. We won't cover obj_octopus_purple, since its implementation is pretty straightforward. After creating obj_octopus_green, I want you to try and add it by yourself, as an exercise.

As you probably remember from Chapter 9, obj_octopus_green moves between two markers or blocks. We have the blocks, but we lack the markers. Let's create them! Create a new object called obj_marker, assign spr_marker to it, and uncheck the Visible property from the Object Editor. That was pretty fast, right?

Let's make our enemy object by creating a new object and calling it obj_enemy. This, as we already saw in Chapter 9, will be the parent object that we will use to manage collisions and other events that should affect any enemy.

Leave this object without a sprite and add a Create event containing these two lines of code:

```
1    hp = 1;
2    atk = 0;
```

We also need a Step event to check whether the HP of the enemy has dropped to 0. In that case, we want the instance to be destroyed. To do that, append this single line to obj_enemy's Step event:

```
1    if (hp <= 0) instance_destroy();
```

That's it! Now we just need to create his child: obj_octopus_green.

Create a new object called obj_octopus_green and assign spr_octopus_green to it. Add obj_enemy as the parent of obj_octopus_green.

Add a Create event with this code:

```
1   hp = 10;
2   spd = 4;
3   dir = 1;
```

In the previous code, we redefine the basic properties of the object by setting the HP, speed, and direction to arbitrary values.

As usual, create the Destroy event and add this single line to it to create a particle effect, and play a sound effect when you kill this monster:

```
1   effect_create_above(ef_firework, x, y, 1, c_purple);
2   audio_play_sound(snd_kill, 1, false);
```

Finally, add a Step event. We will use this event to manage the movement and the logics of this particular enemy. Add this code in obj_octopus_green's Step event:

```
1   event_inherited();
2
3   if ( global.game_state == STATES.PLAYING )
4   {
5       if place_meeting(x, y, obj_block) or place_meeting
            (x,y, obj_marker)
6       {
7           dir *= -1;
8           image_xscale = image_xscale *-1;
9       }
10
11      x += spd * dir;
12  }
```

CHAPTER 12   METROIDVANIA (PART 2)

We already saw in Chapter 9 how this enemy works. It walks back and forth between two instances of obj_block or obj_marker. The code is exactly the same.

An enemy is not such if it doesn't hurt you. We have to handle the collision between obj_player and obj_enemy to make this happen.

To handle the damage from obj_enemy, we need to create a couple of variables in obj_player. In fact, we don't just want to take the damage when we touch an enemy, but we also want the player's character to become invincible for a second, just after being hit, and we also want to push them away from the enemy. We achieve the invincibility by using a switch that tells us to deactivate the collision with the enemies, and we jump away by adding a new controller variable that can trigger the jump when switched to true, just like the bouncy platforms in Cherry Caves 2.

So we must define two variables into obj_player's Create event:

```
1   // damage
2   invincible = false;
3   force_jump = false;
```

We will handle the logic in the Step event, as always. So, in obj_player's Step event, add this code:

```
1   // Flashing when invincible
2   if invincible
3   {
4   visible = not visible;
5   }
```

The idea behind the code we just wrote is to simulate the blinking of the avatar like in Super Mario Bros., by activating and deactivating the visibility of the sprite constantly until invincible gets set again to true. We will write the logic of when activating and deactivating the variable in the collision event with the obj_enemy (which we are going to cover in a bit).

CHAPTER 2 METROIDVANIA (PART 2)

Now head to obj_player's Step event, in the jump-related section. We want to change this part so that the jump code is executed also when the variable force_jump is true. force_jump is deactivated anytime the jump code is executed, so that we trigger only one jump. So modify that section like this:

```
1   if (force_jump or (jumping and  (grounded or wall_jump)))
2   {
3       force_jump = false;
4       grounded = false;
5       vsp = -jspd;
6       if (wall_jump)
7       {
8           dash_recharging = false;
9           effect_create_below(ef_smoke, x, y, 1, c_white);
10          facing_dir *= -1;
11          image_xscale = facing_dir;
12          direction = point_direction(x, y, x +
                facing_dir, y);
13          wj_goal_x = x + 80 * facing_dir;
14          already_walljumping = true;
15          wall_jump = false;
16      }
17      sprite_index = spr_player_jump;
18      audio_play_sound(snd_jump, 1, false);
19  }
```

Now that we have everything set up, we only need to add the logic we talked about when obj_player collides with obj_enemy. So add a new collision event between obj_player and obj_enemy in obj_player, and insert the following code in it:

```
1   if ( not invincible )
2   {
```

493

CHAPTER 12   METROIDVANIA (PART 2)

```
3          audio_play_sound(snd_hit, 1, false);
4          hp--;
5          if hp > 0
6          {
7              force_jump = true;
8              invincible = true;
9              alarm[2] = game_get_speed(gamespeed_fps) *1;
10         }
11         else
12         {
13             audio_play_sound(snd_kill, 1, false);
14             global.game_state = states.gameover;
15             instance_destroy();
16         }
17     }
```

In the code above, we check whether the invincible variable is set or unset (line 1). If it's set, it means that we must ignore the collision with obj_enemy, so we do nothing. If invincible is not set, it means obj_player's instance can be hit; so we play the hit sound (line 3), decrease by one obj_player's HPs (line 4), and check if that value reached zero (line 5). If it did, we play a sound effect to report the death, change the game state to STATES.GAMEOVER, and destroy the instance (lines 13-15); otherwise, if it still has some HP, we force the jump and the invincibility trigger by setting force_jump and invincible both to true, and finally we start a new alarm to stop obj_player to be invincible after 1 second (lines 7-9).

Lastly, we need to create this new Alarm event. Click Add Event ➤ Alarm ➤ Alarm 2 to do it, and add these two lines in it:

```
1   invincible = false;
2   visible = true;
```

CHAPTER 12 METROIDVANIA (PART 2)

Summarizing, when obj_player hits obj_enemy, obj_player loses one HP; it gets bounced away and starts to blink becoming invincible for 1 second. After that second, it stops blinking and can be hit and damaged again.

Everything is in place for what concerns the damage received, but what about the damage done?

Maria's bullets, even if upgraded, don't actually do much. Let's fix this!

Head to obj_bullet and add a new collision event between obj_bullet and obj_enemy. Inside this event, write these two lines of code:

```
1   other.hp -= atk;
2   instance_destroy();
```

At line 1, we access the enemy's HP, and we decrease the value by the attack power of the bullet (which is increased by the equipment), and at line 2, we destroy the bullet, as usual, when it hits something solid.

Ok, now really everything is in place, and we can finally put an instance of obj_octopus in the room and run the game to test it!

You should be able to take hits by the evil octopus by bouncing into it; and, when you equip a weapon upgrade, you should also be able to shoot it down and kill that abomination once and for all (Figure 12-8)!

CHAPTER 12 METROIDVANIA (PART 2)

Figure 12-8. *One step away from death (one HP remaining), Maria manages to shoot down the evil octopus and save her life. I guess the shooting is working!*

Saving Maria

I was born in 1990, when games didn't have a save system. To finish a game, you had to play it all at once from start to finish. Those were hard times, and I managed to finish some games only because I was a kid and had a lot of time in my hands.

To surpass the technological limit of the impossibility to save, many games had a lot of secret warp zones that allowed you to jump straight to a more advanced level, so that you could avoid passing 10 hours straight playing.

Times have changed, and now if your game doesn't offer a save feature, no one is going to play it. So, let's roll our sleeves up and create our save system.

There are many ways to save the state of the game, in GameMaker, but from my experience as a developer, the best way is that which is portable.

GameMaker offers some functions to work with normal text files and a couple of functions to encode and decode data from DS Maps to JSON and from JSON back to DS Maps (namely, json_encode and json_decode).

JSON is one of the most popular standards to store and organize data. The name is an acronym for JavaScript Object Notation and was made popular by the JavaScript programming language for being the de facto standard to serialize JavaScript objects on files as an alternative to XML.

JSON is very convenient since it's organized in a key-value fashion, just like our DS Map data structure; and it's just a simple string, so it can be easily parsed from or written to a text file. The simplicity of JSON is its strength. In fact, it's the most used and supported data-interchange format, which makes it a very portable solution that can be run and easily parsed on any platform and by any application.

How is this interesting for us? Well, having a save file which is easy to read and parse and is a recognized standard by an endless list of languages means that we can, in the future, create some external software to manipulate the save file, like a modding tool or a level editor, or even manipulate it on the Web using JavaScript. The possibilities are endless; and to use a recognized standard to organize our data, it's always a very good software engineering practice that will surely pay in the long run, since the more a standard is popular, the more it is going to be supported in the future. This means less work for us, less bug hunting, less re-engineering. On top of that, working on text files in GameMaker is very easy! Let's quickly see how to do it!

There are many ways to manage (open, read, write, close) text files in GML, depending on the standard we want to use (e.g., there are dedicated functions for INI files, which are text files following a particular syntax, just like JSON). In our case, we want to use the most generic functions to open plain text files. Let's briefly see some of the most important.

file_text_open_read(fname)

This function opens the text file indicated by fname (which is a string) for reading. It returns a unique id of the opened file so that you can use it to read from the file.

For example:

```
1   var file = file_text_open_read(filename);
2   var name = file_text_read_string(file);
3   file_text_close(file);
```

file_text_open_write(fname)

This function, instead, is used to open the file indicated by the string fname for writing. If the file doesn't exist, GameMaker creates it. If the file does exist, it gets overwritten.

The function returns a unique id of the opened file. Let's see a usage example.

For example:

```
1   var file = file_text_open_write(filename);
2   file_text_write_string(file, my_text);
3   file_text_close(file);
```

file_text_open_append(fname)

Similar to file_text_open_write, this one is for writing. The difference is that file_text_open_write overwrites the file if it already exists, while this function starts writing from the bottom, appending the data to the content of the file. If the file doesn't exist, it is created.

The function returns the unique id of the opened file to be used to write on the file.

For example:

```
1  var file = file_text_open_append(filename);
2  file_text_write_string(file, my_text);
3  file_text_close(file);
```

file_text_write_string(file_id, my_string)

This function writes a string into a file indicated by the unique identifier file_id.

For example:

```
1  var file = file_text_open_write(filename);
2  file_text_write_string(file, "Hello, World!");
3  file_text_close(file);
```

file_text_close(file_id)

This function closes an open text file indicated by file_id. It's important to always close the files you open, when you finish using them, or else you risk losing information or creating corrupted files.

Now that we made a little tour around some of the most important functions to manage files in GML, let's get back to our game. Don't forget that if you need more information, you may always go online and check the huge GM documentation on the official website of YoYo Games.

So the idea is to create a DS Map in which we put all the data we need to save (like the status of the inventory, the equipped items, the current room, the player's position, etc.); then, when we want to save the game, we convert the data to JSON and finally write the JSON into a text file. If, instead, we want to load the saved data, we load the content of the save file into a string variable, we convert the JSON string to a DS Map data structure, and we recreate the state of the game based on the content of the saved data.

CHAPTER 12 METROIDVANIA (PART 2)

As you probably guessed, we are going to define that structure in obj_controller. So open it up and head to its Create event and append these two lines:

```
1   game_data = ds_map_create();
2   save_file = "isolation.sav";
```

In the code above, we create the data structure that we will use to store the data we want to save (line 1) and define the filename for our save file (line 2). Note that the extension of the file can be whatever you want. I am using .sav just for convenience since it's a commonly used extension to indicate save files.

To load and save data from the save file, we will use some user-defined functions. It's a common task that we may want to do more than once, depending on the saving policy of the game. Some games save every time you enter in a room, some others when you reach a checkpoint, and so on. So, to support all those possibilities without rewriting a lot of code, we define two functions to do the work.

Let's start by creating the save function. Create a new script by rightclicking Scripts in the Resources sidebar and rename the new script save_game. Inside the newly created script, write the following code:

```
1   function save_game() {
2       ds_map_replace_list(obj_controller.game_data,
            "player-items", obj_player.items);
3       ds_map_replace_map(obj_controller.game_data,
            "player-equipped", obj_player.equipped);
4       ds_map_replace(obj_controller.game_data,
            "player-x", obj_player.x);
5       ds_map_replace(obj_controller.game_data,
            "player-y", obj_player.y);
```

```
6        ds_map_replace(obj_controller.game_data,
         "player-hp", obj_player.hp);
7        ds_map_replace(obj_controller.game_data,
         "player-can_dash', obj_player.can_dash);
8        ds_map_replace(obj_controller.game_data,
         "player-can_wall_jump", obj_player.can_wall_jump);
9
10       ds_map_replace(obj_controller.game_data, "room",
         room_get_name(room));
11
12       var str_save = json_encode(obj_controller.game_data);
13
14       var _file = file_text_open_write(obj_controller.
         save_file);
15       file_text_write_string(_file, str_save);
16       file_text_close(_file);
17   }
```

Line 2: We save obj_player's items list in the game data grid by using ds_map_replace_list. Since it's not a basic type, we need to specify to GameMaker that we are inserting a data structure inside the DS Map obj_controller.game_data. Not doing it may cause GameMaker to corrupt the data and so make the save file unusable.

Line 3: Similar to line 1, here we save the equipped item into the DS Map specifying to GameMaker that we are inserting a DS Map into another DS Map. Also here, not specifying this may cause data corruption.

Lines 4–8: We store important variables related to obj_player, like the position in the map, the HPs and if it can wall jump or dash. Nothing really complex here, we are just inserting variables into a DS Map.

Line 10: Here we save the room name into the DS Map. It's important to not use the id, but always the name of the room, since you don't really have the control on the id, while you have it on the name. So it's safer to rely to an information on which you have control.

Line 12: After we updated the DS Map containing the data to save, we convert it to JSON using json_encode and save the resulting string into a variable str_save.

Lines 14–16: Finally, we open the text file using file_text_open_write which takes as argument a string representing the path and filename of the file we want to open, we write the string into the file using file_text_write_string, and lastly we close the file we just opened via file_text_close.

Now let's take care of the load function. Create a new script and rename it load_game; then write the following code:

```
1    function load_game()
2    {
3        if not file_exists(obj_controller.save_file)
4        {
5            return false;
6        }
7
8        ds_map_destroy(obj_controller.game_data);
9
10       var _file = file_text_open_read(obj_controller.save_file);
11       var _str_data = file_text_read_string(_file);
12       if (undefined != _str_data)
13       {
14           obj_controller.game_data = json_decode(_str_data);
15       }
16       file_text_close(_file);
17
18       obj_player.items = ds_list_create();
19       obj_player.equipped = ds_map_create();
20
```

```
21      obj_player.items = ds_map_find_value(obj_controller.
        game_data, "player-items");
22      obj_player.equipped = ds_map_find_value(obj_controller.
        game_data, "player-equipped");
23      obj_player.x = ds_map_find_value(obj_controller.game_
        data, "player-x");
24      obj_player.y = ds_map_find_value(obj_controller.game_
        data, "player-y");
25      obj_player.hp = ds_map_find_value(obj_controller.game_
        data, "player-hp");
26      obj_player.can_dash = ds_map_find_value(obj_controller.
        game_data, "player-can_dash");
27      obj_player.can_wall_jump = ds_map_find_value(obj_
        controller.game_data, "player-can_wall_jump");
28
29      room_restart();
30      var _rm = ds_map_find_value(obj_controller.game_data,
        "room");
31      room_goto(asset_get_index(_rm));
32
33      return true;
34 }
```

Lines 2–5: We check if the save file actually exists or not. If it doesn't exist, it means we cannot load data, so we just return false.

Line 7: We prepare to load the data by destroying the actual data. It's a good practice to always clean the data structure before reusing them.

Lines 9–12: As we saw earlier, when I presented you some file management functions, here we open up the save file (line 9), we read its content into a string (line 10), and then we decode that string converting it from JSON to DS Map and assign the result of the conversion to obj_controller.game_data (line 10). Finally, we close the file (line 11).

Lines 14–15: Here we initialize both the inventory (obj_player.items) and the equipped item (obj_player.equipped) so that we can use them again to store the loaded data.

Lines 17–23: Here we load all the player-related data from the save file, and we directly inject them into the appropriate obj_player's properties. Note that while loading we don't need to specify to GameMaker that we are dealing with a DS List and a DS Map at lines 17 and 18. We only have to do it when saving.

Lines 25–27: Finally, we restart the room so that all the instances can read from the new version of the game data; and then we fetch the name of the saved room, and we warp to it.

That's it! Our save and load functions are ready! Now let's use them!

We want to add the possibility to load the game or start a new game from the pause menu. So let's open up obj_controller's Create event and modify the options variable so that it looks like this:

```
1    options = [ "RESUME", "LOAD GAME", "NEW GAME", "QUIT" ];
```

Now head to the Step event and head to the section in which we check if the pause menu is open and the enter key is pressed, and change that section like this:

```
1     if ( enter_pressed )
2     {
3         switch( menu_index )
4         {
5             case 0: // resume
6                 menu_open = false;
7                 global.game_state = STATES.PLAYING;
8                 global.can_pause = true;
9                 break;
10            case 1: // load game
11                load_game();
12                break;
```

CHAPTER 12   METROIDVANIA (PART 2)

```
13              case 2: // new game
14                  game_restart();
15                  break;
16              case 3: // quit
17                  game_end();
18                  break;
19          }
20      }
```

When the player presses the Load Game option, the saved game, if present, is loaded, and when they press the New Game option, the game is restarted and reinitialized.

That's great! Now we just need a checkpoint that saves the game for us when activated.

Create a new object named obj_checkpoint and assign spr_checkpoint_inactive to it.

Add to this new object a Create event with this single line in it:

```
1   already_saved = false;
```

We will use this variable, already_save, to switch on and off the saving feature. We need this because we want the checkpoint object to save the game when obj_player collides with it, but we don't want it to continuously save while obj_player is colliding with it. So we use already_saved to regulate when it's possible to save and when it's not.

Add a Step event to obj_checkpoint and write this code in it:

```
1   if place_meeting(x,y, obj_player)
2   {
3       if already_saved exit;
4       sprite_index = spr_checkpoint_active;
5       already_saved = true;
6
```

505

```
7        save_game();
8    }
9    else
10   {
11       sprite_index = spr_checkpoint_inactive;
12       already_saved = false;
13   }
```

At line 1, we check if obj_checkpoint is colliding with obj_player; if it is, we check whether we already saved or not, with the help of the already_saved variable, and if we already saved, we stop executing the code (line 3).

If we haven't saved already, we change the sprite of obj_checkpoint to show the player that we are saving (line 4), then we switch on the already_saved variable (line 5), and finally we save the game (line 7).

If obj_checkpoint is not colliding with the player, its sprite gets set to spr_checkpoint_inactive, and the already_saved variable is switched off so that we can save when we move the avatar upon the checkpoint instance.

Finally, we want that the items picked up won't show up again when we reload the saved game. So, we need to save some information about the single items in the game data and check them when the instances are created in the room. Let's start by creating a key-value pair into the game data when we pick up the object (the collision event between obj_item and obj_player). All we need to do is to add a record with the unique id of the item and a flag that lets us know that the item shouldn't be shown in the room.

So, let's open up obj_item's Step event, and add this line of code just before the instance_destroy function call:

```
1    ds_map_replace(obj_controller.game_data, ds_map_find_value(data, "key"), false);
```

CHAPTER 12 METROIDVANIA (PART 2)

Now, we need to read this value, if it exists, when the instance is created so that we can decide if we want to show the instance or destroy it.

Open up obj_item's Create event and append this code at its bottom:

```
1   var data_item_exists = ds_map_find_value(obj_controller.
    game_data, key);
2   if (not is_undefined(data_item_exists))
3   {
4       if (not data_item_exists) instance_destroy(id, false);
5   }
```

At line 1, we try to load the data about the instance by using the unique key inside the game data. Then we check if the returned value is legit (line 2); and if it is, we check if its value is false; and, in that case, we must destroy the instance at once, so that it won't be available in the room (line 4).

It's that simple! Now drop an instance of obj_checkpoint into one of the rooms and then save and run the game and check that everything works as expected.

You should be able to save the game touching the checkpoint instance and load it via the pause menu keeping all the information on the room, the position of the player, and the items. You should also be able to create a new game via the pause menu (Figure 12-9).

That's great! We have a fully working saving system! Now our game has all the technical features to be a good metroidvania!

507

CHAPTER 12   METROIDVANIA (PART 2)

Figure 12-9. The pause menu now features a Load Game and a New Game option

Conclusion

It was a long run from Chapters 11 to 12. We managed to create a fully featured metroidvania game system. Our game has all the elements that a good metroidvania needs: tight platforming controls, exploration skills like wall jump and dash, a full and a Minimap, an inventory, equipment, consumables, customizable combat system, and a nice saving system based on checkpoints. From there, the possibilities are endless!

The first thing you need to do to improve Isolation is to design some more nice levels, maybe using the tiling technique we saw in Chapter 9! Then you may want to deactivate some skills only to activate them after a certain point in your game. This is easy to accomplish, thanks to obj_player.can_wall_jump and obj_player.can_dash!

Moreover, you can add more types of items to enhance the customization of the player's character! The possibilities are truly endless, now that you have a powerful game system easily customizable!

In the next chapter, we will iterate again on Isolation, by adding one more interesting feature: artificial intelligence!

TEST YOUR KNOWLEDGE!

1. What is a DS Grid? How can it be used to implement a map?
2. What is a race condition?
3. Can you briefly describe how our full and Minimaps work?
4. Which technique can be used to solve a race condition?
5. Why is it a good idea to manage an inventory with data structures?
6. Can you describe the inventory and item system we developed?
7. Create another weapon item.
8. Create another cure item.
9. Add a new *boost* item category and a new dedicated equipment slot.
10. Create a boost item that increments the moving speed when equipped.
11. Add a new *power-up* consumable item category (similar to the cure item type).
12. Create a power-up item which increases the player's attack power for 2 seconds, when consumed.
13. When the player's character gets hit, it becomes invincible for a while. Why is that a good idea? How did we achieve it?

CHAPTER 12 METROIDVANIA (PART 2)

14. Implement a second type of enemy into Isolation: the purple octopus we created in Chapter 9.

15. How can you write data to a text file?

16. How can you read data from a text file?

17. Why is it important to use a recognized standard to export data?

18. Why are we using JSON to save data in this game?

19. How can you convert DS Map data into JSON data?

20. How can you convert JSON data to DS Map data?

21. Can you describe briefly how our saving system works?

22. Add the auto-save feature when you change room.

CHAPTER 13

Extra: Artificial Intelligence

Artificial intelligence (AI) has played a crucial role in the evolution of video games, enhancing their complexity and interactivity. From the early days of gaming, AI has been pivotal in creating engaging and challenging experiences for players. One of the first significant implementations of AI in video games was in Namco's **Pac-Man** (1980). The game featured four ghosts, each programmed with unique behaviors to hunt down the player, creating a dynamic and unpredictable challenge. This AI-driven behavior made Pac-Man an enduring classic.

The revolutionary Pac-man's AI was implemented with a technique called FSM-behavior, which leverages on the concept of finite-states machines (FSM), that we already encountered in Chapter 4, while developing our cards game.

The way that Pac-man was using the FSM concept was by describing the behavior of a single ghost using an FSM. In this representation, a state would represent the behavior that the ghost will show at a certain point in time and the transition between states/behaviors will be based on specific conditions. For example, as you can see in Figure 13-1, a ghost would normally be in roaming state, but then if Pac-man will get closer, they will start chasing him, and if Pac-man eats a pill, they will start running away. The transitions in this case seem to be influenced on Pac-man's proximity and if he had a pill or not.

CHAPTER 13   EXTRA: ARTIFICIAL INTELLIGENCE

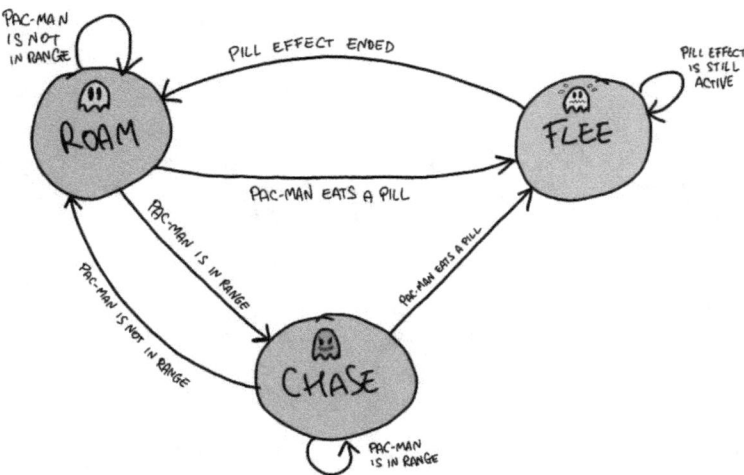

Figure 13-1. The FSM representing the behavior of Pac-man's ghosts

Another landmark in video game AI is Konami's **Metal Gear** series, starting with Metal Gear (1987) and later with Metal Gear Solid (1998). The series introduced stealth gameplay where enemies had varying degrees of awareness and could react to the player's actions. This sophisticated AI created a realistic and immersive experience, requiring players to think strategically and adapt to the enemies' behaviors.

The enemies' awareness in Metal Gear was implemented using another very important technique called Raycasting.

Raycasting is a computational technique used in computer graphics and game development to determine the path of a ray as it interacts with objects in a virtual environment. It involves projecting a ray from a source point, typically the player's viewpoint or an in-game character, and calculating where it intersects with objects or surfaces. This method is commonly used for rendering 3D scenes, detecting collisions, and simulating line-of-sight and field of view.

Raycasting is the foundation on which the more popular raytracing techniques lies.

CHAPTER 13   EXTRA: ARTIFICIAL INTELLIGENCE

Figure 13-2. *A representation of raycasting in action: when the character is not detected by the octopus, it is in patrolling state; but as soon as the octopus detects the character through raycasting, it transitions to a different state*

These early examples laid the groundwork for modern AI in video games, which now includes complex decision-making, learning algorithms, and adaptive behaviors. AI continues to evolve, making games more immersive and engaging, and allowing developers to create richer, more interactive worlds. The advancement of AI in gaming not only enhances gameplay but also pushes the boundaries of what is possible in interactive entertainment.

In this chapter, we are going to move the first steps in the world of Game AI taking inspiration by the two masterpieces we just mentioned: we will implement Raycasting to allow enemies to perceive the presence of the player, and we will implement FSM-behaviors to let them react accordingly.

This new feature will be added to our game Isolation, and being a big change both technically and from a design point of view, it will require us to write an addendum to our GDD, what in the industry is referred to as a Change Request (CR).

CHAPTER 13   EXTRA: ARTIFICIAL INTELLIGENCE

Change Request

A Change Request (CR) in game development is a formal proposal to alter a specific aspect of the game. This could include adding new features, modifying existing mechanics, fixing bugs, or improving performance. Even in small indie game teams, writing a Change Request (CR) document is essential. It ensures clarity and communication by providing a structured way to outline proposed changes, their necessity, and implementation details, reducing misunderstandings and aligning team expectations. A CR document supports structured decision-making by detailing the benefits, risks, and impacts, helping the team make informed choices, which is crucial for small teams with limited resources. It also aids in project management by preventing scope creep, offering a formal process for evaluating and approving changes, thus maintaining the project's scope and timeline. Additionally, a CR document promotes accountability and documentation by recording proposed, approved, and implemented changes, useful for tracking progress and project history. For resource management, it includes an impact analysis to understand resource requirements and risks, enabling better planning and prioritization. Finally, a formal change request process ensures consistency and quality control, as all changes undergo the same level of scrutiny, contributing to the game's overall quality and coherence by aligning each change with the project's goals.

A CR document typically includes several key sections:

1. **Title**: A unique title.

2. **Description**: A detailed explanation of the proposed change, including the current behavior and the desired outcome.

3. **Justification**: Reasons for the change, highlighting benefits and addressing potential risks or issues if the change is not implemented.

4. **Impact Analysis**: Assessment of how the change will affect various aspects of the project, such as gameplay mechanics, performance, and resource requirements.

5. **Implementation Plan**: A step-by-step outline of how the change will be executed, including timeline, tasks, and responsibilities.

6. **Approval Process**: Details on who needs to approve the change and their signatures.

7. **Implementation Schedule**: Proposed start and end dates for the design, development, testing, and deployment phases.

The structured approach of a CR document ensures that all potential changes are thoroughly vetted, discussed, and approved by relevant stakeholders before implementation. This systematic process helps maintain project stability and alignment with the overall development roadmap, ultimately contributing to a more polished and cohesive final product.

The CR we are going to make for this change will lack some information as non-relevant, like the date, priority, start and end date, etc. But nonetheless, let's go ahead and make our first CR!

Isolation: CR – Artificial Intelligence
Change Request Document

Project Name: Isolation

Change Request Title: Implementation of FSM-Based Artificial Intelligence for Enemies

---

CHAPTER 13   EXTRA: ARTIFICIAL INTELLIGENCE

Description of Change

Current Behavior

The current enemy AI in the game is limited to basic behaviors such as patrolling within a defined area. There is no sophisticated state management, and enemy actions are not responsive to player actions.

Proposed Change

Implement finite state machine (FSM)-based artificial intelligence for enemy characters. This AI system will include distinct states such as Patrol and Chase.

The transition between the two states will be communicated visually with a new sprite that will be associated to the Chase state, while the Patrol state will keep the default sprite.

Figure 13-3. *The new octopus sprites for the Chase state are red for rage and literally fuming!*

The enemy will transition between these states based on if they perceive or not the player in the surroundings (Figure 13-4).

The ability of the enemy to perceive the player will be implemented using the raycasting technique.

CHAPTER 13   EXTRA: ARTIFICIAL INTELLIGENCE

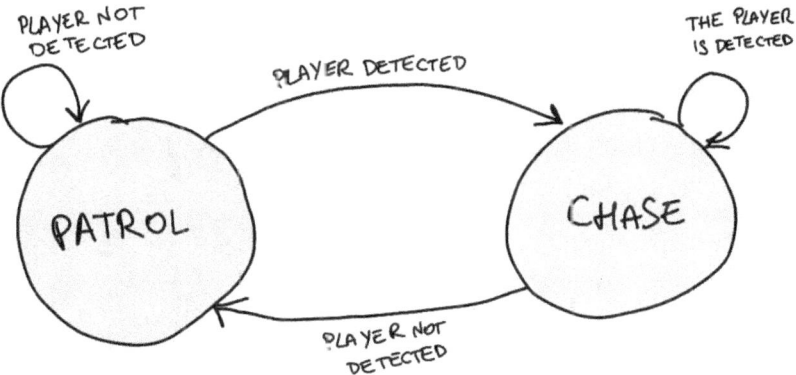

Figure 13-4. The FSM that will define the behavior of our enemies

Justification

Reasons for Change

1. **Enhanced Gameplay:** The current AI lacks complexity, making enemy encounters predictable and less challenging. Implementing FSM AI will create more engaging and varied gameplay experiences.

2. **Player Engagement**: Dynamic enemy behavior will keep players on their toes, increasing engagement and replayability.

3. **Competitive Edge**: Many modern games use advanced AI techniques. Implementing FSM AI will ensure our game meets current industry standards and player expectations.

Impact of Not Implementing

Without this change, the game risks being perceived as outdated or unchallenging, potentially leading to lower player retention and negative reviews.

CHAPTER 13   EXTRA: ARTIFICIAL INTELLIGENCE

Impact Analysis

Areas Affected

- **Game Mechanics**: Introduction of state-based behaviors for enemies
- **Performance**: Potential increase in processing requirements for AI calculations.
- **Testing:** Need for extensive testing to ensure transitions between states are smooth and bug-free.

Implementation Plan

1. **Design Phase**
   - Define states and transitions.
   - Create state diagrams and flowcharts.
2. **Development Phase**
   - Implement FSM framework.
   - Code state-specific behaviors (Idle, Patrol, Chase, Attack).
   - Integrate FSM with existing enemy objects.
3. **Testing Phase**
   - Perform unit tests for each state and transition.
   - Conduct playtesting sessions to observe AI behavior.
   - Debug and optimize based on feedback.
4. **Deployment**
   - Finalize code.
   - Merge changes into the main game build.
   - Conduct final testing and validation.

Raycasting-Based Detection

Now that we have our plan for this big change, let's get started from the raycasting implementation.

To implement raycasting in our game, we need to define a couple of functions to cast the ray and detect obj_player.

So let's create a new script named *raycasting*, and let's add the first function in:

```
1   function check_fov(start_x, start_y, end_x, end_y,
    obj_target, obj_obstacle)
2   {
3       var _ray_length = point_distance(start_x, start_y,
        end_x, end_y);
4       var _ray_direction = point_direction(start_x, start_y,
        end_x, end_y);
5
6       for (var _i = 0; _i < _ray_length; _i += 1)
7       {
8           var _check_x = start_x + lengthdir_x(_i, _ray_direction);
9           var _check_y = start_y + lengthdir_y(_i, _ray_direction);
10
11          if (place_meeting(_check_x, _check_y,
            obj_obstacle))
12          {
13              return false; // Obstacle found, view
                              is blocked
14          }
15
```

CHAPTER 13   EXTRA: ARTIFICIAL INTELLIGENCE

```
16              if (place_meeting(_check_x, _check_y, obj_target))
17              {
18                  return true; // Target found
19              }
20          }
21
22          return false; // Nothing found within the field of view
23      }
```

This function takes as parameters the starting and ending points of the ray we want to cast and then two objects:

- obj_obstacle: which is any object we want to use as an obstacle that will block our ray
- obj_target: the object we want to be able to detect

In the body of the function, we can see how, it checks for collisions with obj_obstacle and obj_target for all the length of the casted ray (lines 6-20) and it returns true if obj_target is found (line 25) and false if either obj_obstacle is found (line 20) or nothing at all is found (line 29).

Now we need a second function that we will call from the enemy instance to detect the presence of obj_player using *check_fov*. We want to look for the player in front and behind the enemy running *check_fov*, but only for a certain distance. This is to simulate the fact that our octopuses are walking sideways (maybe they should have been crabs) and so they keep looking left and right while they walk back and forth, but they have a limited visibility range.

This function will take one single parameter: *fov*, which is the length of our field of view (FoV) that we just defined in the previous paragraph as octopuses' visibility range. Having *fov* as a function parameter, we can easily adjust the field of view case by case, so that we can implement enemies with different perception abilities – like in Konami's Metal Gear games.

CHAPTER 13 EXTRA: ARTIFICIAL INTELLIGENCE

Create a second function in the *raycasting* script:

```
1   function player_seen(fov)
2   {
3       // Field of View check
4       var _enemy_center_x = x;
5       var _enemy_center_y = y - (sprite_height / 2);
        // Adjust height to avoid floor blocks
6
7       // Check in front of the enemy
8       var _fov_end_x_front = _enemy_center_x + lengthdir_x
        (fov, image_xscale * 0);
9       var _fov_end_y_front = _enemy_center_y + lengthdir_y
        (fov, image_xscale * 0);
10      var _sees_player_front = check_fov(_enemy_center_x,
        _enemy_center_y, _fov_end_x_front, _fov_end_y_front,
        obj_player, obj_block);
11
12      // Check behind the enemy
13      var _fov_end_x_back = _enemy_center_x + lengthdir_x
        (fov, image_xscale * 180);
14      var _fov_end_y_back = _enemy_center_y + lengthdir_y
        (fov, image_xscale * 180);
15      var _sees_player_back = check_fov(_enemy_center_x,
        _enemy_center_y, _fov_end_x_back, _fov_end_y_back, obj_
        player, obj_block);
16
17      return (_sees_player_front || _sees_player_back);
18  }
```

Lines 4–5: Here we take the reference position of the enemy, which is the source where our ray will start from.

Lines 8–10: We calculate the end point for the ray, in front of the enemy. The length of the ray is determined by the value of *ray* which is a numeric value passed as an argument representing the field-of-view of the enemy. Then we call *check_fov* to check for collisions on the ray.

Lines 13–15: We do exactly the same things we did at lines 8–10, but casting a ray behind the enemy, to check if the player is behind. Here we do our second call to *check_fov*.

Finally, at **line 17**, we return true if we detected the player in front or behind the enemy; otherwise, we return false.

We want to add this ability to "see" to our enemy *obj_octopus_green*. As a first step, we need to define a field of view value for this object, which we can do in its Create event adding this one line:

```
1   fov = 150;
```

Now that we have the fov value, we can go ahead and modify *obj_octopus_green*'s Step event so that it will look like this:

```
1    event_inherited();
2
3    if (global.game_state == STATES.PLAYING)
4    {
5        if place_meeting(x, y, obj_block) or place_meeting
         (x, y, obj_marker)
6        {
7    dir *= -1;
8    image_xscale *= -1;
9        }
10
11       x += spd * dir;
12
13       if (player_seen(fov))
```

```
14      {
15          // I see the player
16      }
17      else
18      {
19          // I don't see the player
20      }
21  }
```

Lines 1–11: This is the code we already had in this event, since the previous chapter. It just makes the enemy walk back and forth.

Lines 13–20: Here we call *player_seen*, the new function we defined in our *raycasting*script, passing our custom *fov* value as a parameter. This function, as we know, returns *true* if the player is detected in the specified range and *false* if no instance of *obj_player* is detected or if an instance of *obj_block* is detected, instead.

With this code, we have now a perfect place where to put any behaviors we want our octopus to show. But before we can do that, we need to create our states and behaviors!

Octopus, Behave!

In Chapter 4, we introduced finite-state machines as a powerful tool to describe algorithms and flows. We used this concept to organize the flow of the game in its different phases and then we kept using it in our later projects introducing other states for the input management of our menus.

In this chapter we want to use the same principle to define and manage the flow of different behaviors for our enemies, creating a simple AI system.

CHAPTER 13 EXTRA: ARTIFICIAL INTELLIGENCE

The first thing we need is the definition of the behavior states. Since our game and our enemies are pretty simple, we just want two states:

- **Patrol**: The normal behavior for the octopuses in which they will go back and forth
- **Chase**: This is the behavior we want the octopuses to follow when they see the player. They will start moving faster and follow the player. We also want their aesthetic to change to show their new state; for this, we will use the sprites defined in Figure 13-3, which are basically the normal sprites recolored in red.

Then, we also want a way to store what is the current behavior of our little octopuses, so we need a variable for that.

As usual, we are going to define all this in the *Create* event of *obj_controller*. Go ahead and add this definition there:

```
1   enum BEHAVIOURS {
2       PATROL,
3       CHASE
4   };
5   cur_behaviour = BEHAVIOURS.PATROL;
```

So here we defined the two behaviors, and we defaulted our octopus to patrolling.

Now that we have the states in place, we need to define the actions that will be executed when in those states. We will do this in a new script, which will collect those and any other behaviors you would want to create. Let's go ahead and create a new script called *behaviors*.

CHAPTER 13   EXTRA: ARTIFICIAL INTELLIGENCE

Patrol

Our first behavior is going to be Patrol. When patrolling, we want our octopus to just keep walking back and forth without doing anything special and keeping their charming green skin. But wait, isn't this what they are already doing anyway? Yes, it is! And that's why our first behavior will be just a copy paste of the code we already wrote in the previous chapter! Go ahead and add this function to our *behaviors* script:

```
1   /// @desc Function for enemy patrol behavior
2   function patrol()
3   {
4       if place_meeting(x, y, obj_block) or place_meeting(x, y, obj_marker)
5       {
6   dir *= -1;
7   image_xscale *= -1;
8       }
9
10      x += spd * dir;
11
12      return BEHAVIOURS.PATROL;
13  }
```

This is exactly the same code we had in our *obj_octopus_green*'s *Step* event! Nothing changed in the code because when this function will be called from *obj_octopus_green*'s *Step* event, it will be in the scope of that object, and so variables like *dir*, *image_xscale*, *x*, *y*, and *spd*, will be in *obj_octopus_green*'s scope, so related to that specific instance that it's calling the function.

The only difference here is that we are returning BEHAVIOURS.PATROL when we exit the function. This is so that we can communicate to the caller, which one should be the new state. In the case of *obj_octopus_green*, we will assign this value to *cur_behaviour*.

525

CHAPTER 13   EXTRA: ARTIFICIAL INTELLIGENCE

Before we go any further in our behaviors trip, we want to check if what we are doing is actually working. So, let's go ahead and modify *obj_octopus_green*'s *Step* event like this:

```
1   event_inherited();
2
3   if (global.game_state == STATES.PLAYING)
4   {
5       if (player_seen(fov))
6       {
7           // Player detected!
8       }
9       else
10      {
11          // Player not detected
12          cur_behaviour = patrol();
13      }
14  }
```

We removed all the code that was making our octopus move back and forth (because it's now in *patrol()*) and we added a call to *patrol* at **line 12**. Now run the game and you should be able to see that the octopus patrols normally walking back and forth while we are not in range, but as soon as we enter its range, it stops and restarts as soon as we move away. We know that this is happening because the octopus can only be patrolling if they don't see us around, while there is no action associated to when it sees the player, and so it will just stand still.

That's exciting, and I'm sure you can't wait to add the next behavior to the equation!

CHAPTER 13   EXTRA: ARTIFICIAL INTELLIGENCE

Chase

The next behavior we want to implement is *chase*. As defined in our CR document, when chasing, we want the octopus to move faster and start following the player. We also want to make this transition more obvious by switching sprite from green to red, which will also have the side effect of communicating to the player that the octopus is not friendly.

To implement this behavior, we need to

- Change the octopus' direction to face the player.
- Flip the sprite to face the new direction.
- Define the movement of the player based on
  - The new direction
  - Its speed
  - A speed multiplier
- Return BEHAVIOURS.CHASE.

Go ahead and add this new function to *behaviors* script:

```
1  /// @desc Function to chase the player
2  /// @param target
3  function chase(target)
4  {
5      // Calculate direction to the player
6      var player_direction = point_direction(x, y, target.x, target.y);
7
8      // Update dir to face the player
9      dir = sign(cos(degtorad(player_direction)));
       // Convert direction to -1 or 1 based on player position
10
```

```
11      // Apply a speed multiplier
12      var speed_multiplier = 1.5; // Example multiplier
13      x += spd * dir * speed_multiplier;
14
15      // Update image_xscale to face the correct direction
16   image_xscale = dir;
17
18      return BEHAVIOURS.CHASE;
19   }
```

Line 6: We calculate the direction toward the player. We do this using *point_direction* which is a GML function that calculates the angle between two points in space. It takes 4 arguments, which are the x and y coordinates of those two points in space, in our case, the octopus and the player.

Line 9: Here we update the direction of our octopus using the angle we just calculated at line 6. We first convert the angle from degrees to radians, and then we apply the cosine function to understand if the angle we found is facing left or right. We finally get the direction we need, with the *sign* GML function, which takes the cosine of the angle in radians and returns 1 if a value is positive and -1 if it's negative, giving us a ready-to-use direction value for the octopus.

Lines 12–16: Here we define a speed multiplier, and we calculate the movement for our octopus, and we flip its sprite according to the direction we calculated.

Line 18: Finally, we return the value of the current behavior: BEHAVIOUR.CHASE.

This takes care of the movement part, but as we defined in the CR document, we also want to change the sprite of the octopus when it's in the chasing state. We couldn't add this in the *chase* function, because – as we learned – all the graphical changes must be made in a *Draw* event, and we are calling *chase* in the *Step* event.

So, let's create a *Draw* event for *obj_octopus_green* and add the following code to it:

```
1   // Draw the inherited graphics (the pre-defined sprite)
2   event_inherited();
3
4   switch(cur_behaviour)
5   {
6       case BEHAVIOURS.CHASE:
7           draw_sprite_ext(spr_octopus_red, image_index, x, y,
                image_xscale, image_yscale, image_angle, image_
                blend, image_alpha);
8           break;
9       case BEHAVIOURS.PATROL:
10      default:
11          draw_sprite_ext(sprite_index, image_index, x, y,
                image_xscale, image_yscale, image_angle, image_
                blend, image_alpha);
12  }
```

Line 2: We are calling *event_inherited()* to draw the inherited graphics, which includes the pre-defined sprite.

Lines 4–12: We start a switch statement based on the value of *cur_behaviour*. According to its value, we want to draw a different sprite. So if *cur_behaviour* equals to *BEHAVIOURS.CHASE*, we draw the red sprite; while if it equals *BEHAVIOURS.PATROL* or anything else, we draw the green sprite set in sprite_index, as it is the default sprite.

Everything is ready for our last test! Let's save and run and enjoy the result of our hard work!

Running the game, you should be able to see that the octopus walks back and forth normally when we are not in range, but as soon as we get close to it, it changes to the red sprite and starts chasing us moving faster! Then, as soon as we move away from its sight, it gets back to roaming. That's your very first artificial intelligence system! Cheers to that!

Conclusion

It wasn't the longest chapter, but I hope it was fun and that you could see the potential of the FSM-behaviors system, as a simple yet powerful tool to create interesting artificial intelligence and challenging enemies or complex behaviors! With this technique, we created a more dynamic and responsive enemy behavior, significantly improving the gameplay experience.

The potential and power of FSM-based behaviors in game development cannot be overstated. This technique allows for clear and organized AI logic, making it easier to manage and expand enemy behaviors. For small teams working with GameMaker, FSMs provide a scalable solution to create sophisticated AI without overwhelming complexity. The structured approach not only improves the quality of the game but also enhances the efficiency of the development process.

As you continue your journey in game development, I strongly suggest you to expand the existing code to include more states and transitions, or adding support for different types of enemies with unique behaviors. Use this technique and build on it, experiment and have fun, while you create amazing games!

If you're confused about how to design a good game or where to start to make this project more than just a prototype, don't worry! In the next chapter, we will take on this topic analyzing great games and discussing how to create a good and fun video game!

CHAPTER 13 EXTRA: ARTIFICIAL INTELLIGENCE

TEST YOUR KNOWLEDGE!

1. What is a Change Request (CR)? Why is it useful?

2. What information should a CR document include?

3. What is raycasting?

4. How does raycasting work? How can you implement it?

5. What are FSM-behaviors?

6. Why are FSM-behaviors convenient, and what is the advantage of using them?

7. How do you calculate the angle between two points in GameMaker?

8. How do you calculate the direction between two points in GameMaker?

9. Pick a game of your choice, and analyze the behavior of one of the enemies and try to design the FSM that that enemy is following.

10. Expand the code we wrote, so that the octopus goes in an *investigation* state for 5 seconds, after chasing the player and losing sight of them. You decide what the octopus does in this state.

11. Create a camera enemy that looks around for the player, and when it sees them, it goes in an *alert* state, and it alerts all the octopuses that are at a certain distance from it. All the alerted octopuses go in a new state called *hunt*, and they move toward the last position where the player was seen by the camera.

CHAPTER 14

Designing Fun Games

In our journey into game development, we've explored a bit of video game history and genres. We've created some interesting concepts and prototypes, implemented cool features, and studied various game mechanics. We've considered how to do things properly to respect genre standards and meet player expectations, and you've learned some useful game design principles focused on fun and entertainment. But those were genre-specific concepts. So, how can we make all our games fun, regardless of genre? What questions should we ask ourselves? What are the best paths to follow for good game design?

Let's dive into this!

Document Your Design!

The first tool that can help you ask the right questions is the game design document (GDD). I've emphasized the importance of writing a design document for every game we've created for a reason: it forces you to think about what your game should be and which direction you should follow.

A design document keeps your project organized and helps you stay focused on what you've done and what you still need to do. It constantly tracks the progress of your game and serves as a record of your design choices. That's why I strongly recommend using Git or similar versioning software to keep your GDD updated. This way, you can access all previous versions and better understand the direction your game is taking, including what didn't work or could be improved.

CHAPTER 14   DESIGNING FUN GAMES

As you design and describe your ideas in the document, features, potential issues, and gameplay elements start to emerge. This allows you and your team to experiment with them, aiming to find a balance that will (hopefully) converge into the final version of your game.

Experimenting is a crucial content creation mechanism for your games. It involves prototyping new features and letting game testers evaluate them. Feedback from game testing allows you to either commit the changes if the feedback is positive or discard them and start over if the feedback is negative.

Negative feedback indicates that your game isn't delivering a fun experience for some reason. Your job is to understand why. The reasons behind bad feedback can vary. Maybe the player felt frustrated because the level design failed to teach the mechanics or didn't allow enough time to practice skills. Technical problems like bugs, glitches, crashes, or poorly designed hitboxes (collision masks in GameMaker) can also make the experience unfair or inconsistent. Sloppy controls might make the player feel like they can't properly play the game, or a challenge might be too difficult and unforgiving, leading to frustration. The possibilities are endless. Being able to debug your design and understand what is frustrating the player is a crucial skill for good game design, and it distinguishes good design from bad.

Writing a solid game design document and considering feedback from playtesting are great ways to study your game and improve your design. Additionally, how you treat your own game greatly influences how it is perceived by the player.

Respect Your Game

A fun game is a good game, and a good game is one that respects its own nature. The first thing to outline in your Game Design Document (GDD) is the purpose of your game. What's it about? Who is its audience? Every game has a specific purpose and audience, and these should be the main pillars guiding your game design. If you fail to deliver the right experience to your audience or meet the purpose of your game, the whole project can be perceived as a failure.

Take Euro Truck Simulator 2 (SCS Software, 2012) as an example; it's a game about driving trucks across Europe to deliver goods. Players need to respect traffic laws, refuel, rest when tired—essentially, do everything a real truck driver does. Why is it so successful? What's fun about driving trucks all day and following real-life rules? The answer lies in its authenticity. The game is fun because it faithfully simulates the real-life experience of truck driving. It doesn't try to be something else or a parody; it's purely and simply a truck-driving simulator, executed to perfection.

Respecting a game's core idea means giving depth to the gameplay and dignity to the activity of playing. If a game can't be brave enough to stay true to its fundamental concept, it's unlikely to attract and retain players. This is also why some hybrid games with interesting concepts fail—they don't succeed in properly blending multiple elements because they don't give enough respect and depth to each component.

By focusing on the purpose and audience of your game, and respecting its core idea, you can create a compelling and enjoyable experience that resonates with players.

Keep Your Players Immersed

Immersion is the feeling you get when you play and forget it's just a game. You feel the weight of every action, fear the consequences, and every need becomes real. It's one of the most sought-after features in a game. But how can we achieve such a condition in our games?

As we discussed in Chapters 9 and 10, various game mechanics and elements can drive player engagement and immersion, from intuitive controls to fair challenges, and these often depend on the game genre. But are there general rules we can follow to create engagement and immerse the player in the game flow?

Fortunately, the answer is yes. According to the psychological theory of self-determination, engagement can be triggered by satisfying three key psychological needs:

- **Autonomy**: Allowing players to feel they have control over their actions and decisions.
- **Competence**: Ensuring players feel they can succeed and improve their skills.
- **Relatedness**: Creating connections within the game world or with other players.

By focusing on these needs, you can create a more engaging and immersive experience for your players, regardless of the game genre.

Autonomy

Autonomy is the perception of being in control of your own actions. Players need to feel free to act as they want or at least have the illusion that they can decide what to do, how to do it, and in which order. A game where the player must follow a strict path without making any decisions becomes more like a passive pastime, similar to watching a movie or reading a book. While these are enjoyable activities, they do not provide the interactive experience that players seek in games, leading to a decrease in player interest.

A prime example of a game that excels in offering autonomy is **The Elder Scrolls V: Skyrim** (Bethesda, 2011). Known for its immersive experience, Skyrim features a vast fantasy world filled with so much content that even after hundreds of hours, players continue to discover new books, lore, and side quests. The game allows a highly customizable experience starting with detailed character creation, which immerses players right from the start by letting them create an avatar they resonate with. This depth of customization is particularly important in role-playing games, where embodying a character that feels personal enhances immersion.

After character creation and a brief narrative introduction, Skyrim thrusts players into a massive world with only a suggested direction from an NPC, leaving them free to choose their path. This lack of enforced quest order, combined with meaningful in-game actions, gives the world a credible, living feel, even if it's not technically perfect.

Dark Souls is another excellent example of autonomy in gaming. It allows players to choose their playstyle by offering a variety of equipment that can be combined to create different builds. Despite providing some directional guidance, Dark Souls lets players decide their approach and order of challenges, which adds to both the sense of autonomy and replayability, especially in New Game Plus (NG+).

In summary, fostering autonomy in games involves offering freedom of action, extensive customization, and ensuring that player actions have significance within the game world. These elements are crucial for creating an engaging and immersive experience and should be carefully considered to fit your specific game genre and design goals.

Competence

Competence is the player's ability to successfully complete an activity. Every player needs to know how well they are performing and receive continuous feedback to help them improve and optimize their actions for the best outcome with minimal effort.

Different game genres use various feedback systems to communicate performance. For example, many platformer games use a score system, providing granular feedback. Players earn points for positive actions, giving immediate and clear feedback about what is good and what is wrong. The continuous increase in score indicates progression and keeps players focused on the main activity. Players always seek feedback from the game; if it is hard to understand or detect, they get distracted by trying to find it.

Strategy games, like "Victoria 2" (Paradox Interactive, 2010), have more complex feedback systems. Managing an empire involves monitoring expenses and income, building military forces, ensuring regional stability, researching and implementing policies, maintaining public happiness, and managing diplomatic relations. In these games, scores are insufficient. Instead, players need graphs, numbers, and colored maps that provide political, geographical, economic, and social information. These sustained feedbacks show how players perform over time, helping them understand the effectiveness of their actions and how to improve.

In addition to granular (score) and sustained (graphs) feedbacks, there is cumulative feedback. This includes badges, achievements, and leaderboards, which measure overall competence by comparing players with others or showcasing their achievements. A classic example is Gym Badges in "Pokémon" games. Players earn badges by defeating Gym Leaders, each specialized in a discipline or Pokémon type, testing specific game mechanics. Each badge represents a lesson learned and a skill mastered, culminating in victory at the Pokémon League.

By integrating these feedback systems – granular, sustained, and cumulative – games can effectively measure and communicate player competence, enhancing the overall gaming experience.

Relatedness

The last of the three psychological needs, relatedness, is about the player feeling like they are part of a group and that their actions can impact NPCs, other players, and the game world. It's a mix of feeling relevant and bonding with characters or relating to the game world, lore, and story.

Relatedness is a powerful concept that can be leveraged through coherent world design and meaningful stories. A meaningful story adds a narrative overlay to game mechanics and concepts, delivering a message that keeps the player engaged with the game world and its characters. To enhance relatedness, it's important that the player can impact other characters' stories and the world itself. This sense of making a difference makes players feel involved in the story, keeping them glued to the game as they strive for their own happy ending or experiment with different decisions to see alternative outcomes.

"Undertale" (Toby Fox, 2015) is a prime example of a game that excels in this area. Players connect so deeply with the game world and its characters that many have completed the game multiple times to see all three endings. This accomplishment highlights the importance and power of relatedness in fostering engagement and motivation.

In summary, designing a game that allows players to feel a sense of relatedness through impactful choices and meaningful narratives can significantly enhance their engagement and overall experience.

Having Fun Means Learning

All these ideas are worthless without the concept of learning. The secret to a fun game is that it constantly teaches you something, providing evocative stimuli every time you play. Whether it's a new concept or a new level of competence in the game, the key is to keep progression continuous and avoid stagnation. If your game stops stimulating the player, they will lose interest and stop playing.

The trick is to combine the theory of self-determination with the theory of fun through learning. To create a fun and engaging game, design it to satisfy the player's psychological needs (autonomy, competence, and relatedness) while continually teaching them.

CHAPTER 14   DESIGNING FUN GAMES

Autonomy can be combined with learning by allowing players the freedom to experiment with new paths and ideas. A great example is **Minecraft** (Mojang, 2011), which successfully combines freedom of action with continuous learning. Players can constantly experiment by combining tiles and creating whatever they imagine.

Competence measures can help players improve and better understand the game world and rules. This involves practicing and testing knowledge and skills, essentially learning how to optimize actions for the best outcomes.

Relatedness can significantly boost learning. Relationships with NPCs can motivate players to complete tasks that teach them something. NPCs and the game's story can provide a rich narrative and lore, giving players deeper knowledge about the game world, allowing them to master concepts and foster immersion.

Games like **Dark Souls**, **Hollow Knight**, and **DOOM** excel in delivering knowledge through environmental storytelling, a technique that uses the environment to tell a story. For example, the decay in Dark Souls' settings vividly conveys the world's history without direct exposition. Similarly, the isolation in **Super Metroid** and the decadence in **Hollow Knight** immerse players in their respective stories.

In Chapter 9, we discussed creating a first level that introduces players to game mechanics by anticipating how they will face challenges, providing room to practice new skills, and understanding how to navigate the world. Effective level design balances pressure to avoid frustration and boredom, teaching players how to play incrementally.

Creating a good, fun game is challenging, and becoming a good game designer requires making many games. Practice is crucial, but knowing where to focus and what to improve can distinguish between being stuck with bad design decisions and knowing how to fix your game.

Conclusion

It's been a long journey, but you've learned so much that you can now design and develop a full game all by yourself! On top of that, you've created a bunch of game prototypes and demos for your portfolio. From here, you can start new projects or expand on some of the games we made together, adding your own unique touch to the indie video game scene. But to truly make your mark, you need to learn how to publish your game and make it available to everyone. That's what I'll teach you in the next chapter! You'll learn how to publish your game on some of the most popular stores and platforms, making it accessible to the world.

CHAPTER 15

What's Next?

This has been a wonderful journey, hasn't it? You've created a lot of games, studied video game history, learned the rules of good game design, and even picked up some software engineering best practices. You've officially stepped into the world of game development and are ready to become the next Will Wright or John Romero (depending on whether you want to make games about creating or destroying lives). So, how do you bring your games to the people?

In this chapter, we'll explore the most interesting game publishing platforms, analyzing the pros and cons of each. Whether you want to sell or freely distribute your game, we'll cover everything you need to know to officially enter the video game industry and share your creations with the world.

Itch.io

The first game distribution platform I want to introduce to you is Itch.io. Itch.io is an open marketplace specifically designed for independent digital creators, focusing on indie game developers. It's a great option to sell your game, especially if you're just starting out, because there are no requirements for game approval. You design your store page, set your price, and upload your game using their dedicated tool. You can also choose to give your game away for free or use a pay-what-you-want model, allowing players to donate to support your project.

CHAPTER 15   WHAT'S NEXT?

Itch.io lets you decide the revenue split between you (the seller) and the platform. You can even set it to 0% and keep the entire amount paid by your customers if you prefer.

To upload your game, you first need to register it as a new project on Itch.io (Figure 15-1). Log in to your Itch.io account, click the arrow beside your username in the top-right corner of the web page, and select "Upload New Project." This will open a page where you can register your game and create its store page. Here, you can add all the necessary information about your project, including its name, type, monetization settings, and release status.

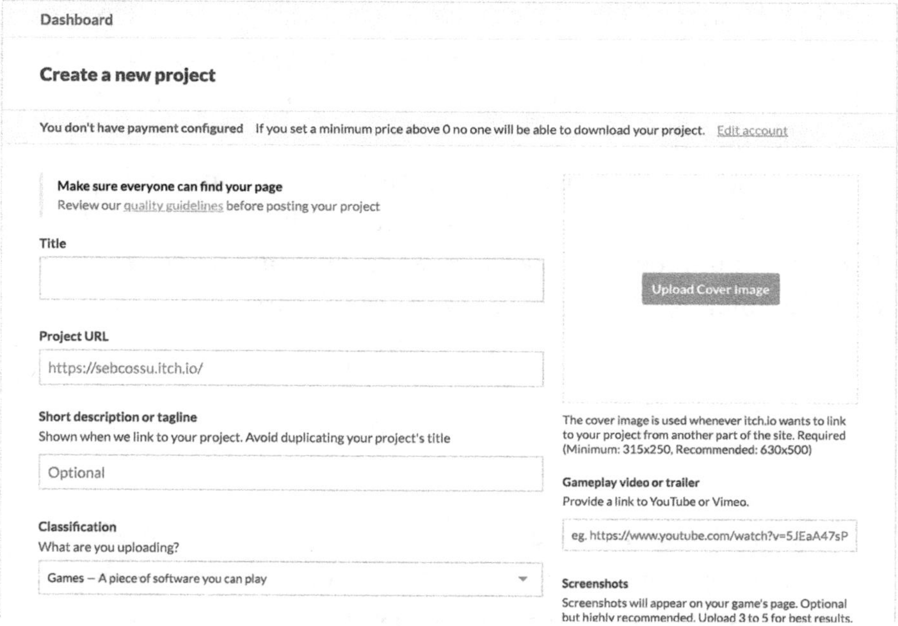

Figure 15-1. At this page, you can register your game on Itch and add a lot of useful details

CHAPTER 15   WHAT'S NEXT?

From this page, you can also upload your game directly from your disk or by linking a Dropbox folder with the option "Choose from Dropbox." Alternatively, as Itch.io suggests in the documentation, you can upload your game using Butler, Itch.io's command-line tool for managing your games.

You can download Butler from Butler's Itch.io page (`https://itchio.itch.io/butler`). If you already have the Itch.io app installed on your PC, you don't need to manually download and install Butler, as it's already included in the app.

To use Butler, you need to add it to the Windows Path so you can run it from the command line. Open the Advanced System Settings window (press the Windows key or open the Start menu and type "View Advanced System Settings"), and click "Environment Variables." Then select the Path variable and click Edit. In the new window, click Add to include the path to the Butler executable. If you installed it with the Itch.io app, you can find the Butler executable in `%appdata%\itch\broth\butler\versions\<itch version>`.

Now that you have Butler set up, you can use it from the terminal (cmd.exe on Windows). The command to upload your game with Butler is:

```
butler push your-game-folder your-username/your-game-name:platform
```

where

- `your-game-folder` is the folder where your game package is stored.
- `your-username` is your Itch.io username.
- `your-game-name` is the name of your game project on Itch.io.

545

CHAPTER 15 WHAT'S NEXT?

- `platform` is the platform compatible with this build of the game (Windows, Linux, Mac, Android). You can specify more than one platform by concatenating them with a dash, like this: win-linux-mac. Itch.io will automatically tag the game with the appropriate platform icon.

An interesting feature of Itch is that it's an HTML5-first platform. This means that you can upload the HTML5 version of your game on Itch, and it will be playable online right from the game's store page (Figure 15-2).

That's all you need to know to start publishing your games on Itch. If you want more information on Itch, there is a very complete documentation covering any topic you may want to deepen at https://itch.io/docs/creators/getting-started.

I strongly suggest you to join Itch since it's very easy to get started with it and it features a huge community of indie developers and indie game lovers which is wonderfully supportive to new projects and developers. Itch may be your best first option if you are an indie developer and this is your first experience.

CHAPTER 15   WHAT'S NEXT?

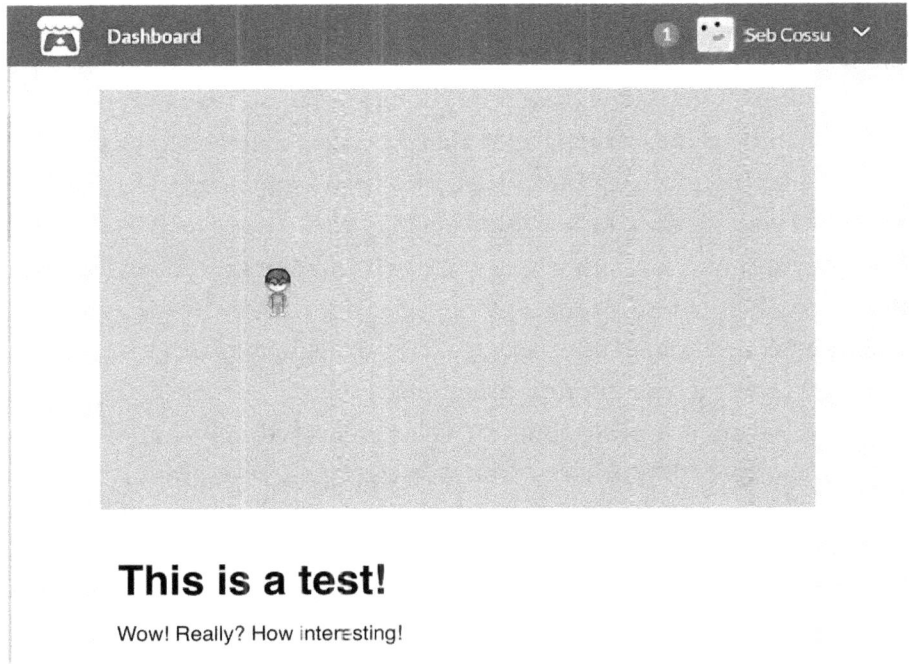

Figure 15-2. You can upload and run HTML5 games on Itch!

GOG

GOG stands for Good Old Games. It's a platform created by CD Projekt Red, the studio behind the award-winning RPG saga The Witcher. Initially, GOG aimed to bring back classic games from the past and distribute them DRM-free. Before GOG, many of these games were unlicensed and often freely downloadable from abandonware websites, which collected old, unlicensed games abandoned by their developers.

Thanks to GOG, you can now buy these classic games and play them without the hassle of using emulators; they are ready to run as soon as you download them from the website or the GOG Galaxy app.

CHAPTER 15   WHAT'S NEXT?

Today, GOG is not just a store for old games; it has become a DRM-free haven with a vast catalog of both old and new titles. It's particularly popular among indie game developers due to the platform's support and interest in indie games, much like Itch.io. However, unlike Itch.io, you don't have full control over publishing your game. You need to submit a request for your game to be accepted at `https://www.gog.com/submit-your-game` and wait for their response, which will provide all the necessary information for the next steps. On that page, you can specify your game's details and your planned release date. You can also indicate if you plan to release DLCs or include microtransactions.

The good and bad thing about GOG is that everything is handled by humans, so expect to wait some time for a response. They are very popular and have minimal automation in their workflow. Nevertheless, GOG is an excellent option, especially because of their strong support for indie game developers.

GOG is a fantastic platform for indie developers who want to reach a broad audience while keeping their games DRM-free.

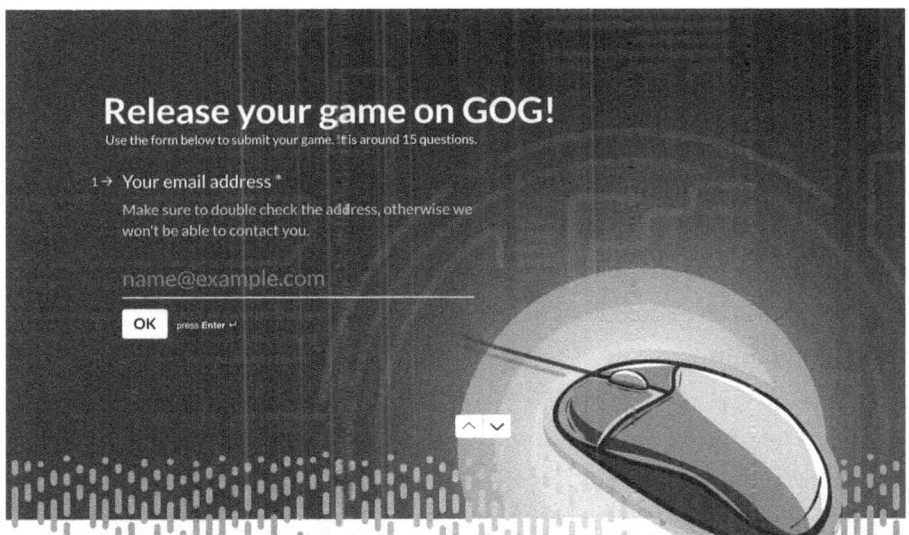

Figure 15-3. To upload your game to GOG, you have to register it on that form and wait for their reply

Humble Store

Humble Games, the publishing arm of Humble Bundle, offers a unique platform for indie game developers to reach a wide audience. Known for its "pay what you want" bundles and charitable contributions, Humble Bundle has carved out a niche in the gaming community. Humble Games extends this reputation by supporting indie developers with both funding and marketing resources, helping them bring their games to market.

To publish your game under Humble Games, you need to submit your project for consideration. The process involves filling out a submission form on their website, detailing your game, its development status, and your vision for its release. Unlike platforms like Itch.io, where you have full control, Humble Games operates more like a traditional publisher, providing a range of services from funding to marketing support, but also expecting a higher degree of collaboration and oversight.

CHAPTER 15   WHAT'S NEXT?

One of the key advantages of working with Humble Games is their extensive reach and established customer base. Your game benefits from their marketing expertise and the goodwill associated with the Humble brand. Additionally, they often include published games in their bundles, providing significant exposure and potential revenue.

However, this partnership approach means that acceptance is not guaranteed, and you will need to go through their evaluation process. This can take some time, but the potential benefits, including funding, marketing support, and increased visibility, make it a worthwhile consideration for many indie developers.

For more detailed information on submitting your game and understanding their requirements, you can visit Humble Games' publishing page (`https://www.humblegames.com/submit-a-game/`).

Steam

Who doesn't know Steam? Valve Corporation's video games store is so popular that it has become synonym with PC gaming. With a massive user base and robust distribution network, Steam offers an unparalleled opportunity for indie games to gain visibility and reach a global audience.

To publish your game on Steam as an indie developer, you must go through the Steam Direct program. This process involves several steps:

1. **Setup and Fee**: You need to pay a $100 fee per game, which is recoupable after your game earns $1,000 in sales.

2. **Digital Paperwork**: Complete digital paperwork, including tax and banking information, to ensure you can receive payments.

CHAPTER 15 WHAT'S NEXT?

3. **Game Submission**: Upload your game build, create a store page, and fill out all necessary information, such as game description, price, and release date.

4. **Review Process**: Steam reviews your submission to ensure it meets their technical requirements and content guidelines.

5. **Release and Marketing**: Once approved, you can release your game on Steam. Steam provides various tools and features to help market your game, such as Steamworks, which offers detailed analytics, community forums, achievements, and trading cards.

One of the significant advantages of publishing on Steam is the platform's extensive suite of developer tools and community features. Steamworks, the backend suite, provides invaluable insights into player behavior, sales data, and community engagement. Additionally, features like Steam Early Access allow developers to release unfinished games to gather feedback and build a community before the official launch.

However, the competitive nature of Steam means that standing out can be challenging. Developers often need to invest time in marketing and community building to ensure their game gets noticed. Using Steam's promotional tools, such as discounts, featured sales, and community events, can help boost visibility.

For more information and to start the submission process, you can visit Steamworks Distribution Program's page (https://partner.steamgames.com/steamdirect).

Anyway, I suggest you to not dive into Steam publishing at your first project. Maybe it's better to use the indie-friendly alternatives, like Itch, GOG, and Humble Games (especially if you need a publisher) first, and then include also Steam, when your business is more stable.

CHAPTER 15   WHAT'S NEXT?

End Game

Being a game developer is no easy quest. You put in countless hours each day to get the work done, and if you don't have a publisher or crowdfunding, you might not see any money until the release. But being a game developer is about being a dreamer who loves their work and dreams of bringing emotions and amusement to the world through their creations.

This path can be incredibly tough, and there will be times when you feel like giving up. Your resolve will be tested constantly, and it's likely you'll face failures early on. Don't let this stop you! When times are hard, always remember why you started, why you want to be a game developer, and what you want to bring to the world. Let this be your motivation to keep going!

Just think about your experience with this book: you began knowing nothing about game development, and now you've created six fully featured games! If you can achieve this, you can do amazing things!

I wish you all the best in your career, and I hope you create incredible games!

Good luck!

Index

A

AI, *see* Artificial intelligence (AI)
Artificial intelligence (AI), 511
    analysis, 518
    behavior states, 524, 525
    chase state, 516
    chasing implementation, 527–530
    CR, 514–515
    current enemies, 516
    development/design phases, 518
    isolation, 513
    justification, 517
    Metal Gear series, 512
    octopus sprites, 516
    Pac-Man, 511
    patrolling function, 525, 526
    raycasting, 512, 513
    testing/deployment, 518
    transition, 516

B

BCPL programming language, 17
Bosses
    boss fights, 235, 236, 241
    Ceaseless Discharge, 236
    definition, 235
    Draygon boss fight, 236
    learning, 237
    motivation, 239, 240
    Space Gala, 240, 241
    Zelda series, 237, 238

C

Card games, 45
    card object
        actions flip, 53
        card working/flipping, 61
        events, 54
        if-then-else, 55, 56
        implementation, 54
        obj_card object, 54, 55
        properties, 52
        sprite_index, 60
        switch, 56–61
    deck (*see also* Decks (DS))
        arrays, 63–65
        data structures, 62
        First-In-First-Out (FIFO), 66
        grids, 70
        Last-In First-Out (LIFO), 65
        lists, 68
        maps, 68, 69
        priority queue, 69, 70
        queue, 66, 67

INDEX

Card games (*cont.*)
    stack, 65, 66
    two-dimensional
      array, 63, 64
    FSMs (*see* Finite-State
      Machines (FSMs))
Cartesian coordinate systems
    (CCSs), 450
CC, *see* Cherry Caves (CC)
CCSs, *see* Cartesian coordinate
    systems (CCSs)
Change Request (CR), 515
  definition, 514
  document, 514
  isolation, 515
  structured approach, 515
Cherry Caves (CC), 246
  assets, 249
  boundaries, 258
  controls, 248
  enemies, 248
  font, 253
  gameplay, 247
  HUD, 282–284
  representation, 247, 248
  scrolling (CC2)
    assets, 307
    coins, 311
    controls, 304
    enemies, 305
    falling platforms, 306, 309
    fonts, 312
    gameplay, 302
    green octopus, 305, 310
    items, 303, 304
    moving platforms, 306, 309
    purple octopus, 305, 310
    skybg, 308
    sound effects, 312
    spr_land, 307
    star, 303
    story/setting, 302
    terrain, 312
    title screen, 311
    trampoline platforms,
      306, 309
  sound effect, 253
  sprites
    spr_ball_green, 252
    spr_ball_purple, 251
    spr_block_brown, 251
    spr_block_red, 250
    spr_cherry, 252
    spr_goal, 252
    spr_ladder, 251
    spr_player_climb, 250
    spr_player_idle, 249
    spr_player_walk, 249
  tasting cherries, 247
Cognitive flow, 375
  collections, 382–385
  controls, 375, 377
  credible/recognizable
    places, 384–388
  Dark Souls 1 (DS1), 378
  fair collision mask, 378–380
  level design, 385–387
  memorable levels, 385

INDEX

metroidvania sub-genre, 379–381
OST (Original Soundtrack), 382
Phantomilians, 382
Super Mario Bros, 381
Super Meat Boy, 377
symmetrical levels, 388
C programming language, 17
CR, *see* Change Request (CR)

D

Decks (DS)
  creation/setup
    dot notation, 77, 78
    obj_controller, 76
  designing decks
    constructor, 71
    game controller, 72
    loop, 73–76
    obj_controller, 73
  loops
    control statements, 73–76
    Do-Until, 74
    for/while, 75
    repeat, 73
    while, 74
  shuffle cards
    creation/setup, 79
    flipping cards, 85
    functions, 79, 82
    GML functions, 81, 82
    mathematical functions, 80
    modulo function, 84
    scripts, 81
    source code, 82–86
    variables, 83
Design document
  immersion
    autonomy, 536, 537
    competence, 537, 538
    features, 535
    key psychological, 536
    relatedness, 538, 539
    learning, 539, 540
    negative feedback, 534
    respects, 534, 535
    video games, 533, 534
DnD, *see* Drag and drop (DnD)
Drag and drop (DnD), 3

E

Event-driven programming, 53

F

Finite-State Machines (FSMs)
  AI (*see* Artificial
        intelligence (AI))
  coding process
    cover_all_cards code, 100
    enumerator, 94, 95
    events/callback
          functions, 101–108
    get_game_speed function, 96
    global variables, 96
    GUI drawing, 111
    noone, 95

555

INDEX

Finite-State Machines (FSMs) (*cont.*)
    obj_controller, 95
    reset_selection script, 99
    source code, 97–100
    time-based
      gameplay, 109–115
    user experience (UX), 101
  features, 92, 93
  inputs/outputs, 87
  insert option, 89
  memory card game, 91
  Pac-man, 511, 512
  states, 90
  transition, 89
  vending machine, 87, 88
Fixed and scrolling shooters, 174, 175
FSMs, *see* Finite-State Machines (FSMs)

G

Game design, 4
Game design document (GDD), 45
  definition, 46
  design document, 533
  development process, 52
  documentation, 46
  genre (*see* Space Gala (GDD))
  graphical elements, 46
  isolation, 391–396
  memory
    casual audience, 50
    game flow, 48
    rules, 47
    target system, 50
    time-based mode, 48–50
    spr_cardback, 50
    sprites, 50
    spr_rain, 51
GameMaker (GM)
  blank game, 19
  cards (*see* Card games)
  definition, 3, 4
  fonts, 30
  menu bar, 18
  objects
    concepts, 26
    definition, 27
    events, 27–29
    game loop, 27
    GML code, 29
    window, 26
  rooms, 31, 32
  sprite, 24–26
  start page, 17, 18
  Steam, 15, 16
  Studio 2 download page, 10
  system requirements, 10
  tile set, 30
  UI (*see* User interface (UI))
  Windows, 11–13
GameMaker Language (GML), 2, 3
  draw event, 40–43
  event creation, 33
  loop control statements, 73
  mouse option, 38, 39
  sprites, 32

INDEX

variables, 34, 36, 38
    binary operators (AND/OR), 35
    Boolean expression, 35
    numbers, 34
    scope, 36
    strings, 34
    unary operator (NOT), 36
    undefined, 34
GDD, *see* Game design document (GDD)
Genres
    definition, 118
    history of, 117–119
    shmup (*see* Shoot 'em up (shmup) game)
    Space Gala, 119
GM, *see* GameMaker (GM)
GML, *see* GameMaker Language (GML)
GOG, *see* Good Old Games (GOG)
Good Old Games (GOG), 547–549
Graphical User Interface (GUI), 110
GUI, *see* Graphical User Interface (GUI)

H

Hello, World
    GM, 17–32
    GML, 32–43
    project result, 42
    test program, 17
Humble Games, 549, 550

I

IDE, *see* Integrated Development Environment (IDE)
Inheritance
    definition, 201
    event process, 202
    hierarchy concept, 201, 202
    obj_enemy, 203
    obj_enemy_red, 205
    obj_player, 204
    representation, 201
    stats, 201
    step event, 203
Integrated Development Environment (IDE), 4
Itch.io app
    Butler page, 545
    distribution platform, 543
    Dropbox folder, 545
    features, 546
    HTML5 games, 543, 547

J, K, L

JavaScript Object Notation (JSON), 497
JSON, *see* JavaScript Object Notation (JSON)

M, N

Mac version, 14, 15
Map screen, 448
    approach serves, 448

INDEX

Map screen (*cont.*)
    DOOM's world map, 448
    genre benefits, 448
    grids/DS grids
        advantages, 450
        ATM programming, 455, 456
        draw GUI event, 460, 461
        elements, 451
        functionality/
          performance, 452
        minimaps, 452, 454
        obj_controller, 457, 459
        source code, 456
        two-dimensional arrays,
          449, 450
    hybrid map, 449
    minimaps, 461–468
Memory card games, 45, 48
    design, 45
    GDD (*see* Game design
        document (GDD))
    logic flow, 49
Metroidvania game
    assets, 396
        bullet_heavy, 402
        checkpoint platform, 401, 402
        cures, 400
        fonts, 403
        ground_brown, 401
        heart, 398
        idle position, 396
        jump animation, 397
        light weapon, 402
        marker, 399
        octopus_green, 400
        sound effect, 403
        spr_player_jump_fall, 397
        upgrades, 400
        walking animation, 397
        wall jump, 398
        warp zones, 399
    combat system
        bullet object, 486, 487
        can_attack control, 488
        implementation, 485
        obj_player step event, 488
        save/run game, 489
    dashing movement
        controls handling section, 425
        game design possibilities,
          429, 430
        Mega Man series, 423
        phases, 424, 426–428
        variables, 425
    enemies, 490–496
    exploration-based game, 439
    features, 447
    game flow
        definition, 430
        draw event, 436–438
        isolation, 431
        obj_controller, 431–436
        step event, 438
    history of, 390, 391
    isolation (GDD), 389, 391
        controls, 392
        enemies, 394
        face buttons, 393

    gameplay, 392
    green octopus, 394
    inventory, 395
    map system, 395
    mechanics/atmosphere, 396
    setting, 392
    skills, 394
    standard equipment, 394
    victory condition, 392
items/inventory
    add/replace function, 470
    ds_map_create(), 470
    empty/value, 471
    event creation, 483, 484
    GameMaker, 470
    hash function, 481
    implementation, 469
    inventory screen, 473–478, 485
    keys and values, 471
    menus, 480
    obj_controller, 473–478
    obj_item, 482, 483
    obj_player, 472
map, 448
Metroid/Castlevania, 390, 391
obj_warp instances, 442–447
platforming base
    controls, 408
    controls handling
        section, 414–416
    gamepad mapping, 409–411
    gravity, 412–414
    jump button, 415
    jumping/falling, 407

    keyboard controls, 409–411
    meaning, 404
    obj_player, 407
    persistent option, 405, 406
    scrolling platformer, 405
    vertical collisions, 414
save files, 496
    append, 498, 500
    close, 499
    JSON, 497
    load function, 502, 503
    manage (open, read, write,
        close) text files, 497
    obj_checkpoint, 505
    obj_item, 507
    pause menu, 504, 507, 508
    reading, 498
    script creation, 500, 501
    string, 499
    writing, 498
wall jump (wall kick), 416–423

O, P, Q

Object-Oriented Programming
    (OOP), 201–206
OOP, *see* Object-Oriented
    Programming (OOP)

R

Random number generator
    (RNG), 82
Raycasting technique, 516

INDEX

Raytracing techniques, 512
    definition, 512
    implementation, 519–523
    obj_octopus_green, 522
    parameters, 520
    raycastingscript function, 521
    representation, 513
RNG, *see* Random number generator (RNG)

S, T

Scrolling platformer
    camera scrolling
        built-in function, 334
        object following, 336
        viewport, 334, 335
    Cherry Caves, 302–306
    different platforms
        controller variable, 348
        falling platforms, 348, 350, 351
        horizontal collision, 353
        jump button, 345, 346
        moving platform, 354
        obj_platform_falling, 349
        obj_platform_moving, 352, 353
        trampoline, 345, 347
    duplicate project, 313
    first level
        Cherry Caves, 371
        concepts, 368
        creation, 366
        jump function, 367
        learning session, 368
        platforming dynamics, 369
        trampoline, 370
    items/power-ups
        beast, 361
        cherries, 363–366
        coins, 361–363
        collision event, 363
    level design/tiles
        blockbusters, 324
        blockers layer, 331–333
        blocks/ladders, 323
        green tile, 330
        grid toolbar, 329
        panel features, 328, 329
        properties view, 327
        room editor panel, 326, 328
        set properties window, 324, 325
    magenta squares, 357–363
    metroidvania game, 405
    obj_ball_red/obj_ball_green, 337–344
    purple octopus, 360
    quality of life (QoL), 313
    title screens
        background layer, 316
        cognitive flow, 314
        controller object, 318–320
        events panel, 320, 321
        logics, 320
        PRESS START text, 323
        properties panel, 317, 318
        title screen, 315

INDEX

Shoot 'em up (shmup) game
  boss fights, 226–231
  cameras/viewports, 186
    boundaries, 192
    obj_bullet_player, 194
    obj_camera, 187–190
    obj_controller, 195–197
    obj_enemy_red, 192
    obj_player, 190, 191
    point_in_rectangle
      function, 193
    properties, 187
    visual explanation, 186
  color-switching
    designing process, 197–200
    enemies, 209
    function, 174
    gameplay mechanics, 225, 226
    obj_controller, 198
    special attack, 219–225
    X-bomb, 224, 225
  definition, 117
  enemies, 209
    blues, 210–212
    closed path, 214
    object/events, 216–219
    obj_enemy_walker_red,
      213, 215
    path layer, 213
    paths, 212–216
    path_start, 215
    spr_enemy_blue, 216
  fixed shooters, 174, 175
  gameplay mechanics, 225, 226
  Ikaruga's polarization system, 173
  inheritance, 201–206
  shooter games, 173
  shooting, 206–209
  Space Gala v.2.0, 175
    aliens, 179
    assets, 180
    audience, 180
    camera/camera view, 186
    color-switching system, 176
    controls, 177
    enemies, 178
    game mode, 179
    gameplay, 175
    games/influences, 180
    menu, 177
    mission level, 176
    pace events, 177
    setting/stroy, 175
    sounds, 183–185
    spr_boss, 183
    spr_bullet_blue, 182, 183
    spr_bullet_red, 182, 183
    spr_enemy_blue, 180
    spr_enemy_red, 180
    spr_enemy_ufo_blue, 182
    spr_enemy_ufo_red, 181
    vertical scrolling level, 179
    X-bomb, 176
Single-screen platformer (SSP), 301
  ball-shaped enemies, 285–288
  benefits, 246
  characteristics, 243
  cherries, 289–291

INDEX

Single-screen platformer (SSP) (*cont.*)
- Cherry Caves, 246–253
- cherry object, 288, 289
- collecting items, 246
- Donkey Kong, 245
- game flow
  - finite-state machine, 272
  - game state system, 272
  - HUD, 282–284
  - obj_controller, 274–282
  - transitions, 273
- game mechanics, 244
- hero games
  - Berry development, 253–257
  - blocks hierarchy, 258
  - boundaries, 257–262
  - climb ladders, 266–272
  - gravity representation, 262–264
  - jump/fall back, 266, 267
  - keyboard_check, 255
  - obj_block, 261
  - physical system, 261
- inspiration, 243
- level design
  - caves designing, 293, 294
  - obj_green_ball, 296
  - reinforces, 295–299
  - single-screen 2D platformers, 292
- Mario Bros, 245
- platformer games, 244

scrolling platformer (*see* Scrolling platformer)
Space Panic, 245
Space Gala (GDD), 119–122
- arithmetic operators (+, *, /),-, 132
- assets, 123
- assignment operator (=), 131
- background image, 128, 129
- built-in function, 162, 163
- bullets, 127
- collision mask button, 125
- controls, 120
- designing rm_level_1, 149, 150
- enemies, 121
- features, 130
- fnt_messages, 129
- fnt_score, 129
- game mode, 122
- games/influences, 122
- HUD event, 159–161
- menu, 121
- menu option, 163–170
  - event crestion, 164
  - obj_controller, 164, 166–168
  - RESUME, RESTART, and QUIT options, 169
- movement, 131–138
- obj_enemy_red, 162
- red alien spaceships, 128
- rm_level_1, 129
- satisfaction/motivation, 120
- shooting, 138–149

built-in variable, 139
bullet object, 138
collision event, 140
destroy event, 148
effect_create_layer function, 141, 142
events section, 142, 144, 145, 147
obj_enemy_red, 145, 146
randomize function, 147
spr_life, 127
spr_player, 123-126
states flow, 151-160
story/setting, 120
target audience, 122
version (v.2.0), 175
SSP, *see* Single-screen platformer (SSP)
Steam
direct program, 550, 551
GameMaker, 15, 16

U

UI, *see* User interface (UI)
User interface (UI), 19
assets browser, 20, 21
build settings, 23
inspector, 21
quick buttons, 23
settings, 22
workspaces, 22

V

Video games
assembly, 2
bosses, 235-241
coding, 5
features, 2
FSMs (*see* Finite-State Machines (FSMs))
game design, 4
GM (*see* GameMaker (GM))
history and genres, 533
instructions, 9
Mac version, 14, 15
map (*see* Map screen)
overview, 6-9
professional/enterprise version, 9
software, 2

W, X, Y, Z

Windows
components, 13
components screen, 12
installation process, 11
license screen, 11
location screen, 13

GPSR Compliance
The European Union's (EU) General Product Safety Regulation (GPSR) is a set of rules that requires consumer products to be safe and our obligations to ensure this.

If you have any concerns about our products, you can contact us on

ProductSafety@springernature.com

In case Publisher is established outside the EU, the EU authorized representative is:

Springer Nature Customer Service Center GmbH
Europaplatz 3
69115 Heidelberg, Germany

www.ingramcontent.com/pod-product-compliance
Lightning Source LLC
LaVergne TN
LVHW022305230126
830359LV00030B/42

9798688808784